THE PARABLES OF CHRIST

James E. Kifer

New Harbor Press
RAPID CITY, SD

Copyright © 2024 by James E. Kifer.

All rights reserved. No part of this publication may be reproduced, distributed or transmitted in any form or by any means, including photocopying, recording, or other electronic or mechanical methods, without the prior written permission of the publisher, except in the case of brief quotations embodied in critical reviews and certain other noncommercial uses permitted by copyright law. For permission requests, write to the publisher, addressed "Attention: Permissions Coordinator," at the address below.

Kifer/New Harbor Press
1601 Mt. Rushmore Rd., Ste 3288
Rapid City, SD 57701
www.NewHarborPress.com

Ordering Information:
Quantity sales. Special discounts are available on quantity purchases by corporations, associations, and others. For details, contact the "Special Sales Department" at the address above.

The Parables of Christ / James E. Kifer. -- 1st ed.
ISBN 978-1-63357-456-4

Contents

PREFACE 1
THE SOWER 11
COUNTING THE COST 27
FINDERS KEEPERS 43
WHAT LIES BENEATH 59
LITTLE THINGS MEAN A LOT 75
A GRAIN OF MUSTARD SEED 89
FISHES IN THE WEEDS 105
LOST AND FOUND 119
THE PRODIGAL SONS 135
MISTAKES IN SELF-ESTEEM: THE PHARISEE
AND THE PUBLICAN 147
FORGIVE AND FORGET (SOMETIMES) 161
THE RICH FOOL 177
THE STEWARDS 189
PARABLE OF THE TALENTS 201
LABOR TROUBLES IN THE VINEYARD 215
THE GOOD SAMARITAN 231
CHRIST, THE PRO-CHOICE SAVIOR 247

PREFACE

What is a parable, a word while certainly not archaic, just as certainly it is not a component of the typical modern person's vocabulary. The standard Sunday School definition, taught to multitudes of children throughout untold numbers of generations, is that a parable is "...an earthly story with a Heavenly meaning." All well and good, and this simple phrase captures the essence of much of the teachings of many parables. Still, many of the parables say nothing of eternity or Heaven, and often find these concepts the interpretative reader must strain himself mentally and spiritually to wedge in such a meaning. Actually as we hope our study demonstrates many could more competently be described with a reversal of the subject words and so described as a Heavenly story with an earthly meaning. This definition should not be discarded, but neither should it fetter our understanding of this wondrous teaching technique.

Each parable possesses a uniqueness of story, an emphatic stress on certain moral principles and a factual scenario of its own. It was the apostle Paul who described himself as "...all things to all people," and the parables have a certain kinship to the moral thrust of his argument.

For over two thousand years, parables have been defined in a plethora of ways, and no one definition has ever seemed to corner the market on accuracy and truth. Here, our text could make a lengthy review of parabolic definitions, but hopefully we shall spare the reader from having to travel that road of tedium. One definition, so popular and not without great amounts of substance and reality, bears a brief moment of contemplation, though. This is the standard, most popular, and most widely accepted of viewing each parable as an allegory. While we should never accept any dictionary entry as Divine Truth one such definition, of allegory, though, is succinct and helpful:

"A story, play, poem, picture, etc.,
in which the meaning or message is represented symbolically."

This is certainly and fairly applicable to many, perhaps at least in part to all the parables, but it, too, at times falls short. Although we postpone its substantive discussion until later, the most famous of the parables, the story of the Good Samaritan, can only be seen as an allegory by running the risk of missing the substance of its meaning. Its setting is strikingly realistic, its characterization of persons, both good and bad, is shakingly realistic, and it not only stands but presents a tower of truth and meaning, none of which require any props of understanding other than the reality of the story's events.

Parables historically, spiritually and in a literary sense traditionally have been deemed to be fictional stories. Perhaps they are but a majority of them can easily be seen as factual even by a non-believer. The situations, persons, motives and actions are drawn so clearly only the totally unimaginative person can fail to see the simplicity but a deep simplicity of their meaning. Almost all fall within the realm of realistic plausibility, so plausible and even likely that the reader is tempted to certify their variability as fact. They are as far from the scripturally condemned "cunningly desired fables" which many of the ancient great minds had conjured as is the east from the west.

So far, the majority of our words have been devoted to the negative argument of which a parable is not. Far more importantly, we must pivot and seek to define the essence of a parable. It is both the earthly and the eternal blessing of humanity, that parables are incontrovertibly associated with the Master Teacher of all, Jesus Christ, but they have been utilized, especially Biblically, by others. As with all His teachings Christ employed an economy of words, so beautifully, brilliantly and precisely that it is impossible for any other teacher, no matter their sincerity and/or ability to speak so much in so few words. Those persons who are familiar with such stories as the Good Samaritan or the Prodigal Son but who have never read them may likely suppose that they are the length of a novel or at least a short story. The Biblically unlearned would be surprised to learn that a number of even the most famous parables have a length of fewer than one hundred words. From childhood and youth throughout a long professional life bedecked and powered by endless words, decades of teaching and the writing of numerous books the author is aware of both how difficult and important it is to employ a brevity of words. In all His Life and Teaching the Master established these standards, and they seem to have attained their zenith in the parables. Parables, though short, seem to be constructed in a manner to be understood at multiple depths and levels. The serious student will continue to detect ever deeper moral lessons, and the views of a disciple at age twenty may be quite blinkered compared to what he or she will see at age seventy. When we speak, write or teach in parables they are not designed to exclude all but one narrow interpretation. As the disciple's knowledge and faith grows so will the burgeoning understanding of the parables follow.

For an answer to any question of importance of the parables the inquirer must start with the recognition, startling as it may seem, that over one-third of the recorded words spoken by Christ were in the text of the parables. The Savior was personally present with us for but three years of actual teaching and ministry, so every moment of His time was of platinum value. He had no hesitation filling that precious, but tightly prescribed time, with parables. His time and attention alone establish their importance, but other reasons for their beautiful essentiality and importance are easily grasped.

Stories, tales, mythologies and the like have always been a highly preferenced way for teachers and cultures to impart truths, teachings and legends. A first, penetrating glance, logically leads to the observer asking just how Christian parables are really any different from Greek and Roman mythologies, both of which have been at the heart of the Western canon and tradition for over two thousand years. Many are engaging, fascinating and have certainly been amenable to artistic expansion and exposé through novels, plays and cinema. Still, though, they often retain an historical, even purposely other worldly quality. Save for our knowledge of their originator and teacher it is well-nigh unbelievable that one man could produce so many stories of fascinating factual interest coupled with towering, eternal moral significance as did Christ with the parables. The Romans and Greeks, intelligent and imaginative as they were, packed their reigning mythologies of tales of powerful, yet flawed, even wicked gods and goddesses, who were at war with others. The stories were often populated with fantastic beings, crippled deities, entities that were half-human, half-beast, and even then, the heroes and heroines succumbed to evil desires.

The parables of Jesus spoke of the misfortunes of life, the duties and obligations to all, even strangers and the necessity and Divine pleasure which God experiences when we show kindness, and mercy to our neighbors. At great length and with frequency they speak of the most intimate relationships between brothers and sisters, fathers, mothers and children and even husbands and wives. Not a word of them is dated. Our mind's eyes see their characters perhaps dressed in ancient clothing and speaking another language, but the characters and plots are immediately and seamlessly capable of being transferred to the modern gaze's easy understanding. About them is no such quality as cultural datedness, for they are timeless.

The parables were designed for the humble, simple Galileans among Jesus lived, but they retain a freshness and force which should be easily (though often not) highly intelligent and credential modern information technology expert. As with any lessons of any sort, of any subject and at any time, the parables make certain prerequisites for their understanding.

The understanding of a parable requires a serious, certainly a curious and open-minded student who will attempt with serious mindedness to understand the parable's increasingly more profound meanings. These stories which we call parables have been interpreted, analyzed, reinterpreted and reanalyzed since that pure beautiful voice of Jesus first spoke to them, and many of these have had repetitive interpretations so monotonous that they cling to them like barnacles of an old sailing ship. Actually, with most, but not all, of the traditional interpretations hopefully this work will be evidence that we have no quarrel. All parables, though, plead and cry out for lifetime interpretation and bid the disciple to see that the breadth and depth of their meanings are never exhausted. We hope to honor the long-accrued wisdom of most of the traditional interpretations while simultaneously dividing our attention to even more expansive construction. Only each individual reader is the proper judge of whether we succeed.

So what exactly is the modus operandi of our study. Perhaps if we limit ourselves to only two words they would be "depth" and "complexity." The maximum depth of Christ's teachings is beyond our reach, but nevertheless while examining it our attention is to eschew complexity. The end result of the study of any subject may be largely determined by the attitude which the student brings into the study. For example, many of the Pharisees and scribes, among the most committed of Christ's detractors, failed in their understanding of the Savior's not because of a lack of knowledge and understanding but rather due to the "carnal" attitudes which were a toxin to their minds. The disciples, often lower on the social and educational scales understood because their hearts were hungry for spiritual substance. Today, any student should ever remember not to complicate the lessons of the parable. The oft repeated words of Jesus should ever be a guide, and one of the most cited is that He is the Light of the World. Darkness, despair and despondency will never be found in a true understanding of a parable, but rather their opposites of light, optimism, hope and promise. They are meant as a lamp unto our feet.

Again, the so-called "traditional" interpretations of parables are generally true and rarely miss the mark. Still, tradition should never be a barrier to a deeper, even a more poignant understanding of these magnificent narratives given to us by Christ. What, then, should be our attitudinal approach when we approach them? Because we live two thousand years distance from their first oral publication by the Master Himself, we are advantaged in so many ways. To us has been granted not just the parables themselves, these direct words of Christ always remaining the best evidence, but now supplemented by some twenty centuries of study by sincere men and women, both scholarly and simple, who have reaped a warehouse from an ever-replenishable harvest of lessons. Still, and at the decided risk of the error of repetition, as readers and hearers today we should always seek depth but not complexity. Never to be forgotten is the primary composition of the receptive element of the Savior's audience which first heard them. Standing there in Galilee by a large lake or at the Temple in Jerusalem who were these early "church-goers" (a phrase not to be taken with complete literalism). Most were "ordinary" Jewish people, usually literate, productive and serious minded. To greater or lesser degrees they were familiar with the dense history of their own nationality and its Law of Moses, a law of basic morality. Doubtless some were of somewhat higher social and economic standing, but all obviously interested in the teachings of the unusual Rabbi from Nazareth. Just as undoubtedly, too, they must have shared another trait. They knew something about, the tools and strains of making a living, the joys and at times heart-breaking realities of family relationships and the basic certainty that this life could terminate without a moment's notice. In short, they were very similar to those persons in any era and place who are receptive to the teachings of Christ. It is from people such as these that Jesus has always drawn the bulk of his flock. While worldly, as to some extent are we all, the light of spirituality burned within the. To this day, it is from this group that Christ draws the majority of His disciples. This number is the fertile ground for the reception of the parables.

    Never did the Son of God seek to mystify anyone by His teachings. He came so that the disciple might have a greater, clearer, not a murkier understanding. Christ called for a follower to have the innocent gaze and heart of a child coupled with the understanding of the mature and sagacious servant. More startlingly He told His apostles to strive to be as "... wise as serpents and harmless as doves." As we get older it generally requires more to "excite" a person and to evoke strong enthusiasm for any subject. We venture that to the spiritually minded disciple this matter may be at least partially assuaged by the richness of the parables and by their ultimately demonstrating the love that God has for each of them.

Parables are short beautiful literary expositions that are meant to be practical. When it comes to actual interpretation when it is all said and done it is a matter of the individual reader's conscience, needs, proclivities and just that natural tendency which we human beings of each seeing a story or situation just a bit differently. Since this is a Preface, the author will permit himself a bit of self-expression and self-indulgence on this issue. Although it will become obvious that many of the parables are so layered and rich with a multitude of lessons this should never become an impediment to our seeing the one or two main lessons which mark any parable and upon which we should concentrate. One example of many is in the famous parable of the Prodigal Son which serves as an endlessly producing well of rich moral lessons about youthful recklessness, sibling rivalry and jealousy and false friendship, all good lessons but all in the shadow of its greatest teaching about the Divine love and forgiveness which is God's.

The subject matter of the stories is the deepest reservoir of lessons ever presented by one man and all over a short span of time and recorded in a single book, the New Testament. In just a few dozen short stories Christ covered with Divine breadth and wisdom such evergreen topics as the use and abuse of wealth, the proper and improper employment of time and resources, and attitudes to the poor, which will often seem to us as somewhat disturbing and disconcerting, the importance of true justice certainly based upon foundations of law and eternal standards of right and wrong but bolstered and tempered by compassion and mercy. In so many parables forgiveness will be seen as paramount and one of the defining qualities of God, but its generous reception will be enjoyed only by those who themselves are willing to forgive. Just this brief partial summary of the messages of the parables should dispel any argument that they are not relevant to modern times.

Two of the greatest writers in the canon of Western literature are the nineteenth century Russian novelists Leo Tolstoy and Fyodor Dostoevsky, literary geniuses of the first magnitude, the magnum opus of Tolstoy <u>War and Peace</u> and that of Tolstoy <u>The Brothers Karamazov</u> and <u>Crime and Punishment</u>. All three, as well as the authors' other works are dense and lengthy, and especially with Tolstoy very, very lengthy, <u>War and Peace</u> extending to some 1,200 pages. To the serious reader and moralist they repay the reading, though. They are multi-layered with large casts of characters, realistically drawn and portrayed and who readily engage our interest. The moral philosophies, especially those of Dostoevsky, are guided in the main by Christian ethics and principles and generally align with an "orthodox" (a loaded word religiously) view of Christianity. Still, with a total upwards of a few thousand pages they pale in comparison to the short parabolic stories of Jesus Christ.

This present work adds to the endless reservoir of words which an army of teachers and scribes have put forth in efforts to explain and expand the stories. It is really not my intention to do either, but rather to mine their depths so that the present bounty of understanding may be enhanced, and additional nuggets of wisdom mined. Neither myself nor any other is the teacher because The Teacher has long ago spoken. May we join those disciples and even the apostles of ancient times and sit at the feet of Jesus.

CHAPTER ONE

THE SOWER
Matthew 13:1-8 and 18-23

Agricultural production is the unheralded wonder of the advanced, modern world. For thousands upon thousands of years farming techniques varied but little, and all were based upon the simplicity of planting a seed, watering, cultivating and harvesting, all of which remain the superstructure of producing the first true physical essential for mankind. Since this chapter, least of all this book, has no pretense in this direction let it suffice to aver that the last century and especially the last two or three decades have wrought changes in farming production, most of which have gone unnoticed by a world oblivious to what is provided for it.

Let us take for our physical template the farmlands of the American Midwest and the Great Plains states which abut them on their western fringes. Already rich in nutrients the soils have been over time carefully prepared to supply a super-abundance of nutrition to their crops. The fields are plowed and tilled with modern machinery, and the best of them are a bucolic version of an artist's easel, awaiting the touch of a master's brush to produce a cornucopia. Transversing these immaculately groomed and well-prepared fields will be the most modern mechanized vehicles and machines that modern technology has produced. These mechanisms, though, are but little constrained by traditional ways in sowing the seeds (shall we say, of grain) which hopefully will yield harvests of a magnitude undreamt of in the past. The seeds are not merely strewn upon the ground but are individually dropped in holes of a depth which has been measured, computerized, digitalized and every other version of "ized" which the modern mind can imagine and articulate. Such methods and others beyond the ken and ability of the author to delineate, have given the farmers and their beneficiaries, in effect the entire world, material blessings both unimagined by past generations and unappreciated by the present. It is neither your father's nor your grandfather's farm, and certainly it is not the farm of the New Testament time of two thousand years ago. No one more simply but eloquently described the methods of first century Judea than Jesus when He began a parable thus:

> "Behold a sower went forth to sow;
> And when he sowed, some seed fell by the way side,
> and the fowls came and devoured them up."

In the twenty-first century a relatively small proportion of the population is engaged in farming, but the numbers of gardeners remains great. It is a fact, a truth and a hardship that a percentage of effort will be thwarted with an immediacy that disappoints and disheartens. All the planning, all the efforts, the hopes, and to a farmer his vital source of living itself, suffer an immediate blow when the seed vanishes, succumbing to the ravenous appetites of birds, squirrels, or whatever creatures that may be lurking. It can be so dismaying that the novice may be tempted to quit, to throw in the towel and go upon his or her way. Yet all human endeavor is met with abundant failure, and much of the failure may come early and with an immediacy that saps the spirit, even squelching the will to go forward. From religion, those matters of eternal concern, to personal hopes and ambitions the dreams, plans and desires crushed so early as to be practically stillborn, are legion. We are fortunate in a blessing for the text to offer Christ our detailed explanation for the beginning of this parable:

> "When any one heareth the word of the kingdom,
> and understandeth it not,
> then cometh the wicked one, and catcheth away
> that which was sown in his heart.
> This is he which received seed by the way side."

Numbers rarely have great Biblical significance, especially in the New Testament, but a safe, but sad, averral is that this initial description in the parable is the majority of mankind. The seed, the truth, right, the opening lights to the path of life, simply bounce away from any reception in the hearer's heart and mind. He or she immediately becomes easy prey to Satan, and that is the last we hear of them. The seed of truth to them is as the 'pearls cast before swine" referenced by Christ. The sad, immutable truth and known better by Christ than any man who ever lived is that the mass of people who have ever lived are unmoved by the Great Story of Christ and would have slumbered through His Sermon on the Mount. He, above all, knows this.

In this great parable of Jesus the sower walked upon a variety of terrain, and his seeds were spread upon them all. Ancient Judea, especially in certain places, offered a topography found in much of the world, and Jesus utilized this as He continued His parable:

> "Some (seed) fell upon stony places, where they
> had not much earth:
> and forthwith they sprang up because they had
> no deepness of earth."

Topsoil. Dirt, but the giver of life. Where present on the earth it is usually at a maximum depth of five to ten inches. It is a substance of organic matter and minerals capable of holding water and air which encourages biological language. In plainer terms, it is dirt which sustains life. In its absence life collapses. What farmer or gardener would not wish the crop sown in topsoil? It beckons, it promises reward and ultimately it honors the sower with life and success. Yet, its use may be precarious, because in the Savior's words it is shallow and difficult for a root system to develop. In the plainest of terms the seed starts well, becomes stunted or even strangled by weeds, blocked by rocks and starved of nutrients. Already, by the time of Christ the Bible was replete with examples. Lot, the nephew of the great patriarch Abraham, was a "righteous" man, but a man who decided to move his family to that city whose name is still synonymous with evil, Sodom. Although Lot was counted righteous even into New Testament days his character and reputation was forever soiled and tainted by its being choked by the evil which surrounded him. From a righteous man he fell to the level of a father who offered his own two daughters to a Sodomite mob who sought pleasure from, of all beings, two angels who had visited Lot. Not many days thereafter we find a "righteous" but drunken Lot engaging in incestuous sex with his own daughters. Again, though, it is Christ who best describes the meaning and character of Lot and others, well intertwined but too easily dissuaded, for the Master explained:

> "But he that received the seed into stony places,
> the same is he that heareth the word,
> and anon with joy received it.
> Yet hath he not root in himself,
> but endureth for a while,
> he when tribulation ariseth because of the word,
> by and by he is offended."

The world from the Church's inception is filled with churches which are continually welcoming new members to the fold. Sometimes, perhaps may we say, "oftentimes" these new converts, new Christians, are abuzz with enthusiasm, veritably crackling and sparkling with joy, which in astonishingly short periods of time begins to fade and eventually to a vanishing point where they are never seen again. Ultimately, only God is the judge of any person's character, but to us mere mortals so many of these persons fit the precision of Christ's definition of having no root in them.

Let us not stray too far from the metaphorical scenario of Christ's great parable of the sower. Stones and rough ground often are not even necessary to choke the discipleship of certain novice Christians. Their own root systems, for perhaps a multitude of reasons, are too shallow to survive almost any dilatory condition. Doubtless the world over landscapers and gardeners are familiar with many varieties of weeds which bloom early in the spring. Some initially bear flowers and have a superficial resemblance to the more desired flowers and greenery, In the part of our nation from which this is being written, the landscaping or gardening enthusiast is familiar with at least two such weeds by the names of chickweed and henbit. The latter is particularly interesting, for very early in the growing season it can cover an entire lawn with greenery and its purple flowers. Its staying power, though, is enjoined by the first few days of really warm sun or even by a simple mowing. It has no staying power, and no efficient lawns keeper would be bothered by attempting to extract it. It has little root system and may be easily knocked or brushed aside. Sadly, yet truly, the same has always been applicable to many disciples. Satan likely does not even bother with them, inasmuch as the problems and vicissitudes of life easily topple them on the way to the eradication of their souls.

Even on a small farm or perhaps even a garden Christ knew that a variety of souls are present. In an almost terse manner he also described:

> "And some fell among thorns,
> and the thorns sprung up, and choked them."

Choking, strangulation, or whatever term may be employed is obviously one of the most horrible deaths, a demise wherein the victim literally has the life squeezed from him or her. No one needs to receive a detailed lecture on the difficulties of having "the wind knocked out of you." Surviving heart attack victims commonly proclaim that one of its worst aspects is the panic of not being able to breathe. Certainly it is aptly symbolic for life's and the world's working on every human spirit, both good and bad. For the good the image of Martha, one of three siblings especially close to Jesus and whose moral virtue is unchallenged. Observing her in a frenzy of worry she was cautioned by Jesus Himself as to the damage which life's thorns could exact when He calmed her with the ever so gentle admonition:

> "Martha, Martha, thou art careful and troubled about many things..."

Martha, as strong a disciple as the New Testament recounts, doubtless regained her composure, and she certainly remained one of Christ's truest disciples. Still, Jesus above all, knew the spiritual lethality of cares. In His explanation of this segment of the parable He explained that:

> "He also that received seed among the thorns is
> he that heareth the word;
> and the care of this world, and the deceitfulness of riches,
> choke the word, and he becometh unfruitful."

In so many almost numberless ways "the care of this world" is universal and burdens the good and the bad. Both the productive citizen and the pernicious thief are daily concerned about having enough to eat, sufficient clothing and a dwelling to protect them from the elements. The worries are ubiquitous, and among those qualities which may be described as from the cradle to the grave just the worry about having an adequacy of life's sustenance is at the top. The Biblical examples of this are so legion as to really require no citation, and daily life and struggle keep them ever before both the saint and sinner. The man or woman who has joyfully received the Truth has done so sincerely and with an open heart. The demons of Hell itself, though, are almost omnipresent to literally blind that disciple by shoving daggers of supposed "greater" worries into his heart. No matter the religious enthusiasm and dedication of the disciple is basic worry about business, the tenuousness or loss of a job and the dwindling and evaporation of bank accounts will allow the afflicted no time or room for spiritual matters. Satan is choking him to his spiritual death.

All of this is so true that even a sincere observer might say "yes, but any normal person knows that life can be tough, rigorous and harsh," so what is so special about Jesus's observance of this fact. A fair enough inquiry, and one which invites a cogent response. Certainly, Christ makes this parabolic observation about the cares of the world, but it is a statement where He shows its harshness may be softened by a trust in Him. Later His great apostle Peter, a man who himself knew something about worry and care wrote:

> "Casting all your care upon Him, for He careth for you."

Even more to the point and to answer the universal worries of humanity Christ taught to His disciples and assured us that:

> "...your Father knoweth what things ye have need of, before you ask Him."

Still, though, these benefits promised by the Master are conditional, but as a contingency in the best and purest meaning of the term. The "catch" is discipleship, and in this great parable the cares of the world, ubiquitous and universal, often overwhelm the promises of Christ and His apostles. Though the cares of this world, so numerous that they are resistant to inventory, are manifold, great and deadly, their "thorniness" is really secondary to the other danger to which Christ cautioned His hearers, the "deceitfulness of riches."

Wealth, money, filthy lucre, riches or whatever name by which materiality is known, is an evergreen theme of both of the Testaments. Never once does money have to scripturally bear the title of "evil," but rather it is always proceeded by terminology such as its love, its deceitfulness, its false promise, etc., but put together it has never ceased to be a danger to any man or woman who has ever lived. Riches have changed form, quantity, quality and proportion throughout the ages, but they have been present since the dawn of creation. So often political movements, especially those of a revolutionary character, literature, ancient, medieval or modern, cinema, and what we might consider the folk-wisdom of the populace, traditionally aligns and synchronizes riches with wickedness in contrast to the ennobled honest poor. Not so the Bible, as a few strikingly prominent examples will on this point suffice.

The progenitor of all Semitic peoples, Abraham, was one of the wealthiest men of his time, so wealthy that he and his nephew could not dwell together due to the friction caused by their abundance. Ever suffering Job, the epitome of patience, was a rich man who lost the bulk of his wealth but whose undying faith in God was blessed by his wealth being far greater at the end of his days than at the beginning. Two of the Church's greatest evangelists, Barnabas and the apostle Paul, were men of great means, Barnabus explicitly and Paul by implication. Wealth and money are themselves neutral, but Christ's explanation of His Parable of the Sower explicitly names their real danger, their "deceitfulness." They most certainly can provide pleasure, comfort and even power, and their possession and enjoyment is an allure. Their temptation, though, is to a life that appears to be so comfortable that it may even be bereft of problems and difficulties. Its possession may fill the possessor with a spoken, or maybe even unspoken, belief that he or she has attained superiority over the common herd. Their deceitfulness, though, lies in many places.

Riches may allow, especially in modern advanced societies, a certain deceptive isolation from the common lot of the mass of humanity. This means better food, more comfortable dwellings, a greater variety of entertainment and amusement, better and safer schools for their children, ad infinitum. None of these are opprobrious evils and in fact individually and in the proper perspective, a positive good. In the aggregate, though, the spiritually shallow may see them as triumphant competition over Christ that wrap their tendrils around the Truth and in the words of the Savior, "choke the word."

At this point the sadness and even tragedy of this parable is palpable. Wherever the Sower has scattered his seeds he has met failure face to face, sometimes immediately and sometimes with a modicum of delay. In any activity this usually means discouragement, depression, despondency and even despair. But... the sowing has not been concluded. Christ, as He almost always did, ended His story with a triumphal flourish of hope and encouragement:

> "But other seed fell into good ground, and brought forth fruit,
> some an hundredfold, some sixtyfold, some thirtyfold."

Sowing the seed, evangelizing, teaching, even to those most committed at times seems the definition of futility, of hopelessness, of wasted effort and a pit of despair for those conscientiously and sincerely engaged. So, too, it must have been in the time of Christ and His generational successors. The apostles. Yet, among all the seeds sown, all devoured, all trampled, all that never even germinated, it was to be found those kernels or grain which fell in good soil, in the right places, and grew. But where, when and how was it done then and just as importantly how is it done now? Does Christ's great parable have any value, any practicality, in the savagely secular modern era?

It is not pessimism nor defeatism to recognize and admit that most teaching of the Word falls on the ground most described in Jesus's parable, that is the ground that provides no or only temporary nutrition. If numbers of seeds maturing into beautiful plants is solely the measuring stick that Christ Himself and His apostles were failures. Jesus recognized that "... many are called but few are chosen." Christianity in this life remains a minority religion, and such it has ever been. God knows bitter disappointment. His Son, Christ, the Founder of the faith knows disappointment. God is inured to the sower's numerical failures, and each Testament is in its own fashion a testimony to a certain failure. Still, the Divine Plan, which most definitely includes sowing the seed, was commenced before the "... foundation of the world."

For our study purposes and our parabolic metaphor let us commence with the ancient calling of a man named Abraham (nee Abram) from fabled Ur of the Chaldees, from whose descendants God promised to make a great nation. That nation was Israel, later Judah or if you prefer, Judea, from whom the King of Kings would come. Almost all the remainder of the Old Testament, spread over a couple thousand years, is the detailed history and narrative of the Jewish people, unfortunately in the main a story of indifference to God, betrayal, rebellion and even abject hostility. God, save for a remnant, a veritable remnant of the Sower's seed, abandoned this people before the Savior ever arrived on Earth. His Word, His Law, the seed of Truth was not defective, but His chosen people's rejection of it followed the precise pattern set forth in the Parable of the Sower. Finally, with the sending of the Savior, God's only Son, Jesus, an opportunity for the Jews to come back and demonstrate that they were good soil was in the offing.

Even after the Death, Burial and Resurrection there was an abundance of signs that the Jewish nation was finally ready to prove itself productive as good soil upon which the seed of truth had fallen. On Pentecost, the day of the Church's founding, over three thousand, each a Jew, followed Christ in obedience, and suddenly the Church had a great start. In the Biblical phraseology the "word (i.e. the seed) grew and multiplied" and through the obedient efforts of the apostles and others, the Church spread beyond Jerusalem, even into predominantly Gentile areas. Still, for years every single Christian was a Jew who had accepted Christ. It took but relatively little time to reverse the accuracy of the prior statement. By the conclusion of the first century and the chronicled period of the New Testament the Church was becoming increasingly Gentile. With a relatively few generations and continuing to our present time the Church became almost exclusively Gentile, with but few adherents of Jewish background and ethnicity. Sadly, this historical truth, of monumental importance in the history of the prior two millennia shows no indication of changing. So harsh ultimately was the Jewish reaction to Christianity that the one-time "Hebrew of the Hebrews," the apostle Paul turned to the Gentiles. The Jewish people, for all their talents, accomplishments and astounding resilience have remained, in the main, poor soil ever since and show no signs of change.

So where is the good soil and where are the potential Christians? Again, it was Paul, not easily discouraged who saw potential good soil in one of the strangest of places, the person of King Herod Agrippa II. Later in life Paul, a prisoner in chains, was ceremoniously brought before this monarch so that the King could see and hear him before Paul was transported to

Rome to answer charges before the Emperor himself. Paul, perhaps history's most effective moral advocate of any cause, not Christianity alone, spoke before a royal assembly that included the Roman governor Festus, Agrippa and assorted power brokers and dignitaries.

Drama is so frequently found in contrast. After the customary pomp and circumstance there sat on the throne the latest in a long line of Herods, which had begun with Herod the Great, who in his ghoulish quest to kill the infant Jesus had slaughtered untold numbers of male babies, his son Herod Antipas, a coward to the core, and the murderer of John the Baptist and maybe the worst of them all, King Herod Agrippa I, stupefied by the splendor of his own power and himself the murderer of the apostle James. Now, his son Herod Agrippa II sat in power, and presumably the last place in the world one would look for spiritually fertile soil. Or so all must have though, except for the shackled prisoner before Agrippa, the aging but still brilliant and fearless Paul. The great apostle immediately seized control of the forum and was met with the mockery of Governor Festus who exclaimed loudly:

> "Paul, thou art beside thyself; much learning doth make thee mad."

Paul, save for one occasion on a trip to Damascus, was never at a loss for words, respectfully brushed aside Festus's taunt with his assurance that he spoke "... the words of truth and soberness." Then the great evangelistic apostle turned to what he deemed potentially good soil and flatly declared to King Agrippa that "... I know that thou believest." Poor, poor King Herod Agrippa II was emotionally, spiritually and publicly cornered by a truth which he knew to be just that, the truth, but could only respond sadly, even mournfully, thus:

"Then Agrippa said unto Paul,

Almost thou persuadest me to be a Christian."

With that, with his wife Bernice, arose and walked out of the forum. In the end, Herod Agrippa II was soil into which the seed of truth could only have a superficial effect.

So, after all, where did the apostles and the other early great evangelists, men such as Stephen, Barnabas and Philip find the good soil? After all the early Church grew by leaps and bounds.

In the early days of the Church Philip was directed by God to go south from Jerusalem to the desert locale of Gaza (a place definitely known at the time of the present writing) and find a man from Ethiopia, a eunuch, and the queen's treasurer. He was returning from Jerusalem where he had gone to worship. Thus, it is almost certain that this man, scripturally anonymous, was either a proselyte Jew (a Gentile who followed Judaism) or an ethnic Jew who lived in Ethiopia. As he was traveling in his chariot Philip joined him and noticed that the eunuch was reading from the Old Law in the book of the prophet Isaiah. The Ethiopian, possessing the foundational factors of any good student, confessed to Philip that he did not fully understand the text and that he needed the assistance of a teacher. Philip (not called "the Evangelist" for nothing recognized the opportunity and expounded to him that the ancient prophet spoke of a Messiah to come, that in the person of Jesus Christ He had come and provided Salvation to all who followed Him. The queen's treasurer, doubting not the substance and veracity of the message and the messenger, eagerly obeyed, was baptized by Philip, and "... he went on his way rejoicing."

Philip, the sower of Truth, had found the good soil in the desert of Gaza. Here, it was an important man of high positions, but unlike most such men, the treasurer did not neglect spirituality. Undoubtedly, he returned to Ethiopia and continued to serve Christ and worship God. Still, the reader is entitled to ask whether the man really made any impact beyond himself. We cannot state anything with precise certainty, but we may engage in intelligent speculation.

Ethiopia is a large sub-Saharan African land, and is one of the world's most ancient nations. In the 1700's and 1800's when the white European nations began to engage in colonialism, (both for good and bad) Ethiopia was one of only two African nations not subjected to Western rule. The Europeans eventually sent hosts of missionaries to Africa, and there they found most of the people and their tribes engaged in various branches of paganism of the most primitive variety. The one exception was Ethiopia, where the westerners formed an existing "Coptic" Church and masses of the population with Christian beliefs. Maybe the queen's treasurer had discovered additional good soil.

CHAPTER TWO

COUNTING THE COST
Luke 14: 28-33

In the 1800's the great but reclusive American poet Emily Dickinson entitled one of her many lyric poems "To Learn the Transport by the Pain." She wrote beautifully but enigmatically, and this title and opening line has been translated often to become a question of "is the transport worth the pain?" Whatever our brief essay may be it is not a text on paraphrasing and analyzing poetry, a common method of teaching two or three generations past. In plain colloquial Ms. Dickinson seems to pose the query of whether the effort is worth the expenditure. As famous as she became and brilliant writer she was, this New England poet was neither the first nor the last to pose this question. For instance, in World War II America of the 1940's where rationing of so much was necessary and even legally mandated, automobiles and their parts ceased to be manufactured for civilian purposes. Necessarily adjunct to this was the rationing of gasoline, all of which gave rise to the querical and common catchphrase, "Is this trip really necessary?" Again, was the expected gain from time and travel worth the expenditure of precious and finite time and resources? As striking as this phraseology, both poetic and prosaic, may be, it is less memorable than the lesson featured by the Savior in a short parable of two millennia past. Unsurprisingly, Christ summarized a question which each individual should ask of himself before commencing any new endeavor, and He did so in a thematic phrase of only three words, when we are told to always "count the costs." How plentiful and often colorfully may this concept be expressed.

So much of life is choice free. As long as a person remains living and animate, he or she will wake, customarily sometime in the morning, but even the most indolent must wake at some hour. All must eat and depending upon an abundance of circumstances he or she may have little choice as to diet. Our heritage, generally our locale, generally (but not exclusively) our looks have been assigned to us. Much, but not all, the world's long evil of slavery, has been eradicated. Yet, the person who remains in bonds has no choice in the selection of his day's activities. These factors all have a substantial, often overwhelming, vote in our election of activities. Still, even the bedraggled prisoner in a maximum-security prison, retains certain choices of which he cannot be deprived. All men and women retain choices as to their attitudes, their characters, their thoughts and the ranking of life's important to trivial matters in their thinking. To a large extent a person is who he or she chooses to be. As a principle this may stand, but it would require a moral smugness, even an arrogance, to aver that every person has carté blanche to choose his or her life. What Christ appears to proffer as truth by His parable is that a person's attitude and heart is the prime determinant of which he or she will be. The Master is very careful and deliberate in expressing caution, maybe even warning, that each of us should "count the costs" of what our lives and endeavors will bring us. Realistically, He will demonstrate in a short parable but with two vivid examples the potential pitfalls of the failure to so do.

Freedom to choose is a wonderful asset, but by its very nature and essence, it is the freedom to make superlative choices but also many mistakes. The ultimately important decision made by anyone, regardless of their awareness, is whether to become a disciple of Christ. In His personal dealings with many disciples and would be disciples He often cautioned them to "... look before you leap." Hasty, unpondered spiritual decisions are condemned. Perhaps even more opprobrious to Christ was and is the moral drift, which is to be encountered in so many lives, that person who never plans but only reacts to all the moral and immoral forces which surround him. The purposeless life is a life of dual worthlessness, of no value to its possessor and certainly of no value to God. These are persons, their numbers being legion, who are shuttlecocks in the moral winds, and go wherever the drift of life takes them. As the apostle Paul remarked they are the ones who "... are carried about with every wind of doctrine, by the sleight of men." They meander from day to day as if life had no overriding purpose, and they may easily become fodder for any sort of doctrine, or belief, or perhaps worst of all, nothing at all. Their lives, whatever the length, become as are cynical philosopher of a few centuries ago observed "short, nasty and brutish."

Christ, though, with the wisdom and knowledge of only the Divine, knew that many people have and seek purpose in life even though the purpose may be different from the Truth. Let us approach this parable with a bit of modern accounting and business terminology, terms of which Christ demonstrated with which He would be comfortable. The method and examples which He employed, if compressed, could easily fit into the rubric of "is your life cost effective: or even more to the point "is your discipleship cost effective?" Just as many businesses and business decisions result in disappointment and perhaps even abject failure so do the moral decisions in lives. In any of life's endless endeavors certain questions always abound and recur. The thinking person should always inquire of himself whether he or she really wants the prize for which so much time, effort and resources are sacrificed. Again in Emily Dickinson's words "... is the transport worth the pain.?" Sometimes we may acquire the prize, the goal or the object for which we strive and then wonder with a strange sense of apathy and melancholy whether all that effort was really worth the prize. But we always have a choice as to where our resources and time are committed. The immortally famous British Prime Minister Winston Churchill is historically renown for much, but his famous words and deeds in the early days of World War II have never been eclipsed. In the early days of the war in 1940, when Britian's future was not merely bleak but black Churchill offered to his nation that he had brought with him only the promise of "... blood, toil, tears and sweat." He knew the costs of victory and survival were not just political but personal to every man, woman and child. Both the British and Churchill succeeded, but two thousand years earlier an even greater mind, a more magnificent man and eloquent speaker and teacher understood it better.

The Laughable Mockery

Due to His brevity of expression we quote the factual scene from the first of the parable's lessons:

> "For which of you, intending to build a tower,
> sitteth not down first, and counteth the cost,
> whether he have sufficient to finish it.
> Lest haply, after he had laid the foundation,

and is not able to finish it,
all that behold it begin to mock him.
Saying, This man began to build, and was not able to finish."

Construction, public, commercial or residential is a haphazard and sporadic world. So many, many projects that are conceived, designed and partially financed in the boom times of prosperity are gradually, but more often, suddenly confronted with changes in conditions and economic downturns. The money supply is slowed to a trickle before it soon stops altogether. Houses, office buildings, high rise apartments and various commercial enterprises stand silently in mockery to those who began them but could not finish. The city's residents pass by these skeletal structures, and relieved that they are not bearing the financial ruin or the taunting, join in the jocularity and mock the victims of the poor and short-sighted planning. Such was not native to ancient Judea nor modern America alone. It is endemic to the human race.

In the early 2000's Chinese officials and bureaucrats determined to construct a model city in the remote area of Inner Mongolia, a berg that ultimately bore the name of Kambasha, a place of stunning but bleak post-apocalyptic style architecture designed to comfortably accommodate over one million residents. The officially atheistic Chinese government was going to use it as a representative shining jewel in the crown of Chinese communist culture. Most of the buildings were completed, but today it is all but a ghost town, perhaps the largest and most expensive in history. The population of Kambasha is less than ten percent of its proposed one million. Few either wanted it as a residence or could even afford to move there. Its main purpose now seems to be sustenance for various cinematic and television documentaries, YouTube videos, and an abundance of internet information, from which this brief recounting is taken. A perfect example of what Christ foretold in that its originators counted not the costs (not merely financial) but now which stands as a mockery to their short-sighted hubris. The story of Kambasha could not have been told a mere twenty-five years ago because it had yet to occur. Another, more famous one, though, has echoed through thousands of years of history and is still found in the depths of Biblical antiquity.

When the earth was still young, and populations were not as scattered as they are today, Genesis records that:

> "The whole earth was of one language, and of one speech."

Again, and how often both before and after, is Satan's Edenic promise to humanity accepted with glee by mankind in its striving "... to be as gods." In the enticingly curious language of the story "... the Lord came down to see the city and the tower, which the children of men builded." God saw that man's plans were to build a tower that would extend into heaven and that:

"... let us make us a name,

lest be scattered abroad upon the face of the earth."

In these early mechanically primitive times, primitive both in physical capability and spiritual understanding man counted no costs other than the expenditure of men and money, which seemed to be of little concern to the originators of this idea. This failure cost them dearly and altered the course of mankind for that entire tenure of his stay here on earth. Knowing His fallen creation the scripture well expressed His concerns:

"And the Lord said,

> Behold the people is one, and they begin to do:
> and now nothing will be restrained from them,
> which they have imagined to do."

So, early one morning all the managers, supervisors and workers began to assemble to continue this massive construction project, an endeavor that seemed to be proceeding smoothly and well. And then... gibberish. Where the day before a laborer could easily and quickly receive authoritative direction from his boss, now the sounds that came were pure blather, meaningless and indecipherable. Differentiation in language was born, and easy communication between the earth's peoples ceased, a state in which it yet remains. Whether these were the ancestral tongues of the European, Semitic or Asiatic varieties which reign today is unknown, but humanity had been thwarted in an effort which was itself unworthy to be undertaken. Mankind became scattered, language became a barrier which could not be easily hurdled, and its differentiations have contributed to massive misunderstandings and in many cases have provided excuses for war. The men who had stated this tower had failed to count the cost. So was the tale of the Tower of Babel.

Cities and towers have an importance, but such is fleeting. The souls of men and women are priceless and eternal, and it is for them Jesus really directs this parable. Any Christian, especially a thoughtful mature disciple, recognizes much of the real import of His teaching. So many Christians begin a good race, but quickly they tire, become discouraged and/or disinterested. Often the construction of their character has been commenced by their parents, who have raised them, well or poorly, in their faith and maybe the faith of their ancestors. The building of character has begun with a decent, perhaps even a strong, solid foundation. With age and desired maturity the young man or woman often shuns or ceases altogether the construction of Christian character. Christ and His Church become an ever-fading memory, and maybe even subjects of mockery. Sometimes, the thorns and thistles which plagued the sower of Chapter One choke out any Christian fervor or even quiet discipleship, and the building of character ceases. He or she had started on a path of discipleship, maybe even a blind path and the troubles which mount have ceased all construction, too often for a lifetime. He failed to court the spiritual cost, and when the price of discipleship became too dear discipleship itself ceased.

Let's Go to War

Try as we might the entirety of the four gospel accounts of Christ contain not a single statement wherein the Savior expressed an opinion an any of the day's political issues. His concern was the soul of His creation, not temporal (i.e. "temporary") human government. He was, though, keenly and perfectly aware of history and mankind's proclivities for certain actions, including war. Succinctly, as the second part of this parable He expressed:

> "What King, going to make war against another king, sitteth not down first,
> and considereth whether he is able with ten thousand
> to meet him that cometh against him with twenty thousand?
> Or else, while the other is a great way off,
> he sendeth an embassage,
> and desireth conditions of peace?"

Some eighteen hundred years following Christ's words Emperor Napoleon Bonaparte of France was at the top of his game and the dominant figure in all Europe. France, with this Corsican (nee Italian) soldier as its dictator effectively controlled almost all of Europe. With minor exceptions Napoleon either by direct rule or servile alliances Napoleon controlled all Europe with but two exceptions. By the year 1811 it was evident that his most intractable enemy, Great Britian would never voluntarily submit to him. The other was the great bear of the East, the monstrously huge Russian Empire, at times an ally, at other moments an enemy, but always a worry. Ever restless and driven by a hubris that "enough is never enough" by 1812 had assembled by alliances, conscription and promises essentially all of Europe and invaded the great Empire of Tsar Alexander I. Napoleon commanded an army estimated at 500,000 men, a figure then by stupendous enormity and began to roll into Russia to bring the Tsar and his empire to heel. Battle upon battle was fought, and as usual Napoleon, his Grand Army and their allies would emerge triumphant. The greatest of all was fought at Borodino, on the western outskirts of Moscow. Naturally, another French victory, and according to Napoleon's plans the enemy would now surrender. Napoleon, by now as experienced a general who ever commanded an army, was counting upon the Russian surrender. The invasion had cost him enormous causalities, but it mattered little to him. Only one action counted, the anticipated Russian surrender. It never, ever happened. Napoleon with his still enormous army was stuck in Moscow with the legendary, even mythically severe Russian winter beginning to bite. The French Emperor had no choice but to leave Russia, and so with is army he did in history's most legendary retreat. Tis retreat, the centerpiece of many films, books and most famously Leo Tolstoy's <u>War and Peace</u> reduced his army to a mere 20,000 men who limped and hobbled westward across the Russian borders. That translates to a casualty rate of 96%. Amazingly Napoleon held to power for a few months and still flashed much of his military brilliance, but he was brought to bay at Waterloo in 1815 and exiled on a barren rock in the Atlantic for the final six years of his life. When the Son of God spoke His parable so long before in ancient Judea doubtless, He knew of this acclaimed king/general who failed to "count the costs." So was the story of one of history's greatest conquerors, but not so great that he could escape the pure simple truth of the teaching of the Son of God. Our aim, though, is not a historical survey, no matter how interesting nor is Christ's teaching primarily a cautionary flag to the would-be hero. It is something greater, each eternal soul of a presumptive disciple, usually one of marked enthusiasm.

The New Testament is among other things a book of Christian conversions. Unsurprisingly, when a man or woman decides on the path of Christ often the text will employ the words of joy, joyful, rejoicing or some variation to describe their experience. So it should be, for the words are aptly illustrative. The thrill, the exuberance and the rush of joy is wonderful but also almost always temporary. No daily endeavor and certainly no lifelong journey can be propelled fully or even primarily by joy. The Christian experience should include a super abundance of joy, but it cannot serve as the daily diet. The costs of the faithful, virtuous, devoted Christian life. We sadly must ponder the realization that some of the early Christians who had their moments of joy also suffered death at the hands of persecutors. The most famous of Christ's disciples were His apostles. Ultimately, they were thirteen in number, and it is believed all save John died violent persecutorial deaths. Surely, none were surprised, though. In that claustrophobic upper room the night before Good Friday, Jesus had told them that they would be "hated of all men for my name's sake." He added, starkly, that many that killed them would believe that they were performing God's service. He did not use His parabolic phrase, but they were being told to count the costs. To the glory of God and the blessings to disciples forever all these men did. But so many do not, and neither did they at the time of Christ.

This work's intent is to illustrate the words of Christ, but we must assert a central truth known to all sentient contemporary observers. Numbers wise and world spanning, the Church is in the throes of suffering a huge hemorrhage of Christians. We may offer endless political, social, cultural, etc., reasons for these losses, and most, if not all, would contain much truth. Many, likely most of the early Christians adhered faithfully to God throughout the blackest days of persecution. Likely many if most still do. Still, the cost of faithful service is rarely a violent death, and Christians have fallen away due to discovering their religion's costs.

We should never minimize anything as lackluster or bland sounding as the "cares of the world." Christ Himself spoke without hesitation about the endless cares and worries of everyday life. Many are in isolation quite trivial, but their constant accretion begins to weigh heavily on the spirit and the joys of life. They are "costs" of living, and more than a few Christians have fallen away due to the endless tedium and vicissitudes of life, from which no one, even the disciple, is spared. In contemporary, yes even in popular culture, perhaps this danger to the spirit is well illuminated by a bit of dialogue from a very successful motion picture of several decades past. A man, struggling to regain his self-worth and pride after years of crippling alcoholism remarks that "… Anyone can face a crisis. It's that day to day living that gets me down." The costs which they can exact on the soul and the human spirit are enormous, and no one knew this more than Christ. He dealt with people living day-to-day and saw what life, its worries and temptations could exact even upon His followers. He knew that the real "costs" of living are always high, but He was and is willing to pay the invoice.

Many of the costs of becoming a Christian are capable of much more specific description, delineations which the scriptures are not loathe to provide. A running theme, the waters of which show no signs of abatement well into the twenty-first century, is that of family. Christ, by his own Word, splits families, mother against daughter, father against son, and in the worst of cases husband and wife. These are costs which the prospective disciple should reckon, for they may later exact payment in a destruction of the family ties and the discouragement and falling away of the disciple. The Christian whose faith is weakening so many facets of life starts to become explicable to him/her in a manner different than the fervor of new faith. Worries become harbingers of defeat and doom, illness and debilities become precursors of death, temptations now return to what they once were, invitations to sin, and the costs of discipleship begin to be borne by discarding discipleship itself. In the words of the Master Himself the sliding Christian is in fear of the enemy and "... he sendeth an embassage, and desireth conditions of peace." Our disciple, usually with a profound unwariness, often seeks accommodation or compromise with the enemy, perhaps seeking some respite from what Christ is costing him, yet maintaining some veneer of Christianity. It is a delusion, though, since the only real enemy, the only real adversary, who Christ Himself identified as Satan has ever desired and ultimately offered but one type of peace, unconditional surrender to him.

No Discount Given to God

Although the query strictly is outside the bounds of Christ's parable it naturally befalls the Christian to inquire of whether Christ and His Father counted the costs of their actions. For but a moment let us return to the beginning, "The" beginning to attempt to answer this. God created it all, and the Genesis story tells in intricate and beautiful detail the story of Creation, its time, phases and splendors, with God's crowning creation humanity itself. He pronounced it "Good" and rested from His Divine self-appointed tasks, with man's only purpose to live in splendor and perfection and glorify the Father. But then come the great calamity, the Fall of Man, where God's highest creation was defrauded and deliberately chose a path of destruction and desolation. By his own foolishness and choosing Man revealed himself to be flawed, imperfect and missing the mark of God's expectations. All the progeny which would ensue, the entirety of the race of Adam, his descendants, would likewise be imperfect. Satan had, in his own warped brilliance, claimed a victory in Eden. In actuality the Prince of this World (as described by Christ) had turned the key that opened the door behind which lay his own destruction. He would find that from time before time, before the "foundation of the world" its Creator had always been willing to pay the costs to redeem His own Creation. Not just the costs of labor, terrestrial expenditures or even any heavenly commodity, save one, His own Son.

Among the most cognizable of Satan's victories in Eden was his introduction of death into the world, the fate of every animate being that has ever lived. To obliterate Hell's victory would require the most precious commodity in the Universe, the blood of His own Son. Before the foundation of the world, though, each had known this cost and were willing to bear its expenditure. God so loved his Creation and its pinnacle of humanity that He would not suffer Satan to destroy it. To redeem it (that is, "us") He was willing to bear the most onerous of costs.

With the Fall, death reigned, and it still reigns in the world and with most of humanity. Still, a remnant, to borrow an Old Testament term, survives and always will. It is a remnant that has rejected death and gladly accepts God's great expenditure, Jesus Christ, no matter the cost. Christ, the only human through whose veins flowed entirely innocent blood, willingly left Heaven, lived among us and suffered the horrors of death in its most vile form so that His disciples could no longer be weighed with its fear.

A modern term is "buyer's remorse," basically being a term to cover the regret that a person later experiences for paying too high a price or for even making the purchase in the first place. Did God ever have "buyer's remorse" or second thoughts about His creation and redemption of mankind. Most assuredly, for early in the world's Antediluvian days He saw that:

> "... the wickedness of man was great in the earth,
> and that every imagination of the thoughts of his
> heart was only evil continually."

God, rarely a silent, inactive observer was so stirred by grief that:

> "... it repented the Lord that He had made man
> on the earth,
> and grieved Him in His Heart."

Thus, the Great Flood, but God relented in any thought of total destruction, and He was still willing to pay the greatest costs, the ignoble and hideous death of His son. On that dark afternoon thousands of years hance, on that hill outside Jerusalem, how the Almighty must have regretted that He ever fashioned humanity. For the sake of those who love Him and follow Him, and His Son how literally and eternally grateful are they for Christ's statement, perhaps the most famous sentence ever spoken:

> "For God so loved the world, that He gave His only begotten Son,
> that whosoever believeth in Him should not perish,
> but have everlasting life."
> The cost of the believers' redemption had been weighed by Good, and Christ tipped the scales in our favor.

CHAPTER THREE

FINDERS KEEPERS
Matthew 13:44 - 46

Whenever we hear that the odds of something, anything, happening, are 10,000 to one, our attention is almost reflexively taken. Although not in the multi-billions to one to which we moderns have become accustomed by "DNA" recurring type odds, this is still a formidable figure. Although the reference sources will vary "10,000 to one" is roughly the figure given for the occurrence of the coveted pearl in an oyster. No wonder it was Christ Himself who gave us a phrase still extant in one of His shortest parables. The Redeemer likened the Kingdom of Heaven to a merchant (probably what we would call a broker) who was seeking valuable pearls. Finally, he found one pearl, a "pearl of great price" that he took all his worldly possessions, sold them, and purchased that one invaluable pearl. Certainly, in Christ's parable the man's profession required that he know pearls, their types and values. It remains, though, that the great multitudinous majority of the population, including this author, know little or nothing of pearls. A brief discourse into pearls in necessary for a more complete understanding of this parable.

The earlier quoted odds of 10,000 to one, when viewed in the light of value, are actually too generous. They are far more daunting. Pearls originally found in oysters or other similar sea creatures, such as mollusks, begin as an irritation when a small foreign particle, usually a grain of sand, becomes trapped in the oyster. To protect itself the oyster secretes two chemicals, aragonite and conchiolin, which together coat the sand with a hard covering known as nacre, or traditionally "mother of pearl." The cycle is sometimes repeated so often that the sand has become round, large and shiny and resembles the pearl so well known. Overall the odds of an ouster producing a pearl of commercial value are so great that by the time one is found, treated, processed and made ready for sale the value of this little hard sphere has become enormous. Like almost all tangible and even intangible objects pearls may be divided into categories, of which our essay will concern itself with only three.

Into what does all this underwater chemical activity translate and how does it have any parabolic, must less spiritual meaning? Other than the mechanics and marketing, little has changed with pearls since the first century. Of their three basic categories the first is the most easily recognized and understood. Massive quantities of jewelry, artificial to the core, are manufactured and sold the world over. The general category has many names, but perhaps the most famous is "costume" jewelry. Nothing is inherently wrong or wicked about costume jewelry, and it may be all the buyer can afford. Measured in the metrics of value, though, it is junk. The glass, plastic, silicon or whatever spheres sold as pearls are faux pearls, of no lasting value, and most often tried, worn for a bit and then discarded. They have neither innate nor lasting value, and almost always their buyers know (or should know) that fact.

The second category of pearl is laden with great value. They are cultivated commercially and known as "cultured" pearls provide great beauty. Highly prized by the women who wear them they carry both monetary value and beauty. A description of pearl cultivation is beyond the scope and competence of this essay, yet we can recognize that they start in the oyster or shellfish as all pearls do, are removed and then cultivated with the same chemicals that, well, make a pearl a pearl. Their value and beauty is prized, with a rich sheen and luster, and undoubtedly only a real expert can discern a cultured from a natural pearl. Still, in the term's strictest definition they retain a certain manmade artificiality.

Finally, at the pinnacle of "pearldom" rests the natural pearl, created purely by God and His natural forces, emerging fully, perfectly and beautifully formed from the oyster. They are indeed rare, and their value markedly higher than even the best of the cultured pearls. Scarce they remain, but to those who seek them they are coveted beyond words.

Maybe all this on pearls is interesting, but maybe not. More importantly, though, what importance does it maintain in the teachings of Christ? The Master most assuredly is deeply committed to the material well-being of His disciples, but it is absurd to believe that this short two-verse parable is solely about a merchant's good business fortune. As with all the parables an examination of their symbolism, if any, is in order.

As with the costume pearls so common in the marketplace most of what we hear is junk. Not necessarily ordinary and typical daily business and family conversation but the increasingly raucous cacophony of modern communication. Entertainment, news reporting, media, both traditional and its new "social" form are often little more than the emptying of sewage and sludge into society, the body politic and its members. Pearls, real pearls, occasionally may make it through the filtration system, but in the main it is junk. Sadly, even pathetically, much of religion is costumed in finery but in reality, is junk. Continually changing with every breeze of air and current fashion, this "faith," even in its extremely attenuated Christian form is worthless.

The descriptive arrows shot at junk jewelry are not to be aimed at cultured pearls. A cultured pearl may be exquisitely beautiful, of astounding value and rightfully desired by its admirers. The word "cultured" is a happily appropriate term for the metaphorical pearls of our civilization. The seeker for truth, value and substance has a plentiful and deep reservoir of moral and intellectual stature to satisfy the soul, the heart and the most demanding of minds. From antiquity the student may sample the philosophical wares of such as Socrates, Plato and Aristotle, men who were not acquainted with the God of the Bible but who nonetheless possess stores of wisdom. From the ancient scriptures, in this case the Old Testament, the scholar may draw from a seemingly endless roster of intellectual and moral giants such as Abraham, Moses, Elijah, David, Isaiah and Jeremiah. The passing of antiquity and the early Middle Ages brought to the fore such intellectual and spiritual giants as Thomas Aquinas, Martin Luther, John Calvin and William Tyndale, the first the great propagator of Roman Catholic doctrine and the latter three giants of the Reformation and the translation of the Holy Bible. Latter centuries brought more secular fare in the lives and works of literary numeracies such as Nathaniel Hawthorne, Leo Tolstoy and C. S. Lewis. All these men and an endless roster of men and women made Western civilization with insight, wisdom and greatness of spirit. Their lives and works are cultured pearls, of great worth, at time ultimately instructional and inspirational, but never infallible.

Exalting but human, just as the cultured pearl is beautiful, but imperfect and so it will ever be.

So, where is the genuine, authentic pearl of Christ's parable? Where is that pearl of great price that the merchant sold all that he possessed. The real pearl, the natural flawless jewel can be no one or nothing else than Christ Himself, "the way, the truth and the life." It is the same man who stood before Governor Pontius Pilate, moments before the Roman official condemned Him to death, but did not recognize that his prisoner was Truth itself. This pearl, the real pearl of great price, is even more valuable, beautiful and lustrous at the end than at the beginning. He is the real pearl who pleads for all to cast their "... care upon Him, for He careth for you." Is this the same pearl, the same redeeming Messiah who promised His disciples that He would never leave nor forsake them, and that "... I am with you always, even to the end of the world." Is it any wonder that the merchant gave everything for the real pearl?

The Land Speculator
Matthew 13:44

It is the shortest of parables, but one verse, and it both permits and invites a full requotation:

> "Agan, the Kingdom of Heaven is like unto a treasure hid in a field:
> the which when a man hath found,
> he hideth, and for joy thereof goeth and selleth all that he hath,
> and buyeth that field."

That is all, nothing more, so what possible moral lesson(s) may be extracted from the purchase of a tract of land. Historically, many have called this land speculation, and not necessarily as a term of approval. Without consulting a dictionary let us point that land speculation is the simple act of purchasing land in the expectation or at least hope that its value will increase, and a profit be made from its resale. It was obviously known in ancient times and now in the twenty-first century it remains as prominent and even popular as ever. Many men and women in all types of societies, but particularly those of the West, have grown prosperous or even wealthy beyond conception by effective land speculation. It is an easily understandable and explainable path to the riches of kings. Likewise, it may be a gilded path of promise to bankruptcy and financial distribution. Our speculator may grow fabulously wealthy, but his life of financial promise may collapse in material catastrophe.

Is this the person Christ hails and exalts as a great disciple, a land speculator? First, we find no Christian prohibition against any person making a profit, or even a livelihood, from the land. It is the backdrop for too many Biblical stories to suggest that it carries some intrinsic evil. In Christ's short single verse parable it is missing the mark to focus on either "land" or "speculation" as being the primary importance, for neither is such. The golden word of the little, short story is "treasure," for this is where lies the value.

Almost all men and women seek treasure, some tangible reward that makes life sweet, that lessens woes and problems or maybe even allows him/her to luxuriate rather than endlessly toil. A common treasure of very era of human history is gold (and to a lesser extent silver), a precious metal which is central to Biblical history and a key component of scriptural text and metaphor, and so it remains in the modern age. We, and so many generations before us, venerate this precious metal by such terms as gold standard, the Golden Age, gold medal and even in mockery with phrases such as "all that glitters is not gold." Neither is all treasure found buried in the land. The promise of riches has so often turned to bitterness and despair when the found gold in the land is merely a trifle or iron pyrite, historically mocked as "Fools Gold." Land may yield, and has for well over a century, national and personal treasure, by the production of oil and gas, but many promising prospects have proven dry or of limited reserves.

Pure materialism does not satisfy all men and women. The wiser person is seeking sustenance, a morality to guide him, a purpose for living and a promise of something more and better to come. Christ proclaims, and certainly not by this parable alone, that this particular "land speculator" has found that treasure when he unearths the Truth, the Word, which the apostle John proclaimed was and always will be God. Most people are in their initial actions somewhat akin to the land speculator of this parable. They seek something very valuable in life and hope and maybe even work for their acquisition to grow in value and somehow enrich them. Be it land, treasure, pearls, jewels or minerals they seek an accretion to their value. Much of humanity, how much is mainly speculative, seeks other treasures not just in materiality but also in concepts, ideas, modes and systems of philosophy and living. The scriptures are replete with recognition and at times detailed discussion of such philosophies as Epicuresism, Stoicism, Gnosticism ad infinitum. It gives not short shrift to them, but the Bible, in spite of its historical reputation, can be quite cynical and even bitter about many things. In some sense that concept reached its zenith (or perhaps nadir) in Ecclesiastes when its life weary author proclaimed "Vanity of vanities. All is vanity."

The investor seeks appreciating assets, but the trust is, whatever the economic system, most assets of this world depreciate.

All in the long run will be destroyed and vanish. So many philosophies and especially religions have an initial aura of fascination, logic, depth and maybe even a bit of glamour. Yet the historical graveyard of exhausted and dead moral systems and laws is a large one. No one worships the Roman and Greek gods and goddesses, so numerous and intellectually acceptable in classical times, and they remain of interest for historical and cultural purposes only. Stoicism is now a common word for a personality trait, not a religion. None, except for the learning of interested students, had any lasting value. Only the man of the parable found a treasure of any lasting value, and it was even more, that of everlasting value. He or she is the person who knew that something of spectacularly consequential value was discovered in that field, and it was a treasure which will never cease appreciation. As wonderful as this treasure may be what the disciple has seen and read about so far is incomplete, for what the apostle John promised is that in Heaven "we shall see Him as He is." That is no speculation – it is worth all we have or may be gained in this world.

New Wine in Old Bottles
Luke 5:37, 38

This subsection begins with an awkwardly mixed metaphor if ever one was "coined." Wine is a two-sided coin, but it has always been one of history's most ubiquitous currencies. Very early humanity discovered that exposure of certain juices (for our discussion, that of the grape) permits fermentation to that point where alcohol is produced, and ordinary grape juice assumes what are the main desirable qualities. Its moderate consumption relaxes a man or woman, and the Old Testament lauds without condemnation its use as a source of conviviality and merriment among friends. Flip the coin and immoderate usage leads quickly to drunkenness and all manner of troubles, for which it is without Biblical exception condemned. Christ Himself drank wine as recorded on numerous occasions, but more to our present purposes He employed its imagery as a teaching mechanism. With words of great enigma to the modern observer He began a short but informative parable:

"No man putteth new wine into old bottles."

On its first reading, this is puzzling. What could possibly go askew by pouring a new wine into an older bottle? A brief detour into ancient history and customs is required to properly make sense of both the parable and its meaning. Wine was ubiquitous in ancient Judea, but it was not the commercially fermented and processed wine commercially sold today. Basically, it was grape juice, the storied scriptural "fruit of the vine" that was taken and exposed to the air, whereof came the yeast, the fermenting agent, which would settle upon the juice. After the fermentation began, and it was generally a rapid process, the newly made wine would be put into "bottles," but not bottles of the sleek glass variety. A bottle was essentially a bag or satchel from animal skins, usually sheep or goats, but to the initial primary Jewish audience of Christ, goatskins. Like all things a wineskin had a limited lifespan. The constant daily filling and refilling of the "bottle" would of necessity weaken it, its seams pressured to the breaking point and blemishes of weakness appear. "New wine" was not fully fermented, and this fungible liquid was still expanding to the point where the old wineskin would burst. Any person of any cognitive sense knew that new wine had to be placed in new, stronger containers. Of course the Savior knew this, and the second phrase of His parable reads:

> "... else the new wine will burst the bottles, and be spilled,
> and the bottles shall perish."

An interesting story perhaps, perhaps not, to we modern denizens of the twenty-first century, may express some mild interest before moving back into our world of processed products pre-packaged in well-designed containers. Still, though, how can such a mundane example contain a spiritual meaning so great as to be utilized by the Messiah.

This small parable goes to the very depths of the heart of the opposition, fierce, violent, unreasoning, vitriolic, animus, which many of the Jewish people, especially their leaders, had with this new Rabbi from Nazareth.

This is neither the time nor the forum for a lengthy exposition on the history of the Jewish people in Bible times. Let our discussion proceed from a recognition that the Jews had an ancient history of which by the first century they were proud, even inordinately and offensively so. They lived by the Law of Moses, given on Sinai by God Himself, and almost the entirety of the post-Torah Old Testament is a story of this people's continual rise and fall, from devotion to the God to outright rejection, abandonment and paganism. Now, though in the 20's A.D. Jesus was speaking to a people that had for over two hundred years generally been adherents of the Law and were attempting to follow the Mosaical moral code and worship Him alone. Yet the Jewish spirit of service and obedience had grown old by the time of Christ, not old in years, but old in attitudes. It was the Jewish spiritual hierarchy, the priesthood and the brain trust which claimed full, absolute authority over all religious issues and questions. These were the sects of the Sadducees and Pharisees who with the scribes had cornered the market on all interpretations of the Law. They claimed to worship the God of Moses and to strictly follow the Law, but in reality, the Law's interpretation had been throttled, choked and encrusted by generations of their own private interpretations. As always, the matter was expressed most succinctly when speaking of the Pharisees and scribes He stated:

> "But in vain they do worship Me,
> teaching for doctrines the commandments of men."

Jesus showed that the religious establishment, a force that may vary in form and intent, but which is always extant, was an empty vessel, whose very structure was blemished, torn and stretched to the breaking point by the time of the advent of the Savior. This establishment controlled Jewish religious life and thought, and it does not belabor the point to say that many, if not most of them, but especially the small coterie of leadership, were the sworn enemies of the Son of God. Were these the men to whom Jesus's new message was to be entrusted as the foundation of His building? This new gospel would be wasted, this elixir, or more topically this wine, would be wasted if placed in the care of the Jewish establishment. They were the very essence, if not the epitome, of "old bottles." In actuality these men formed the criminal conspiracy to falsely accuse Jesus of Nazareth of imaginary crimes, the same persons that the Savior had plainly called "scribes, Pharisees...hypocrites." He had derided them because they had played for Him, and then found that He would not dance to their tune. If ever a religious establishment was played out with their tiresome beliefs and their message corrupted and even poisoned by their own character, it was the Jewish religious leaders at the time of Christ. They were the epitome of old bottles who were already bursting with their lies, half-truths, hypocrisy and self-deception.

Jesus, though, came with a new doctrine and He Himself was of the new wine, but where were the containers for this golden commodity? Christ knew that He was the new wine and so beautifully expressed:

> "A new commandment I give unto you,
> That ye love one another; as I have loved you,
> that ye also love one another.
>
> By this shall all men know that ye are my disciples,
> if ye have lone one for another."

It was not new, and Jesus was so aware. The idea of Love was always central to God's plans, but it had been buried in the bog and the bric-a-brac of religious minutiae, which had become the container of Jewish religion. This same old religious establishment was to be entrusted with the new wine of Christianity, so where would Christ turn for the new bottles?

The original twelve apostles were a collection of men who were probably known for one thing only at the time of their selection by Christ, the "honor" shared with most men and women of being unknown. They were all Jews, apparently in their entirety despised Galileans. The most famous of the group, Peter and John, were soon identified with mockery and condescension by the priests of the Sanhedrin as "ignorant and unlearned men." In trade and occupation they continued a precedent established by God when His Son was born on earth. Save for His parents, the first persons to see the infant Savior were lowly and humble shepherds. Of the apostolic dozen the scriptures plainly reveal that at least four and probably seven or more were Galilean fishermen, a blue-collar working-class designation if ever there was one. One apostle, Matthew, was a despised publican. It is likely the other four were of similar credentials. Nobody, but nobody, absolutely no one who ever lived, would have selected these twelve men to be the initiators, the very foundation, of the most important enterprise the world would ever know. No one but Jesus Christ. They were His strong new bottles, young sincere dedicated tough and pious men with plenty of potential and room to grow and hold the new wine of Truth, Christianity. Save for the infamous traitor Judas Iscariot, they failed Him not. Christ must have seen these beloved men as the embodiment of the new wine and the purest example of His disciples when one day He looked upon a crowd of followers and spoke:

> "I thank Thee, O Father, Lord of heaven and earth,
> because Thou hast hid these things from the wise and prudent,
> and has revealed them unto babes."

When commissioning them they were hard working, toughened physically, knowledgeable in the Truth, but still He admonished them to be as "... wise as serpents, and harmless as doves." Jesus with apparent joy and relief went to the poor in spirit, the humble for His messengers of good news, not to the tired, old, cynical, often corrupt hierarchical Jewish religious establishment for His new vessels. Perhaps there lies an enduring message for us all.

Still, Jesus had a total of only thirteen apostles, so how does this short parable have any particular applicability to us, the great majority of the remainder of His disciples? A continual scriptural theme is the conversion of the old to the new, not necessarily in personal ages, human conditions or other temporal matters. Rather it is the change from the old spirit to the new when one encounters the Savior, believes Him, accepts Him and obeys Him.

For all this, though, it was not the Jewish religion, nor wine or any other commodity that the Son of God came to make new. It is the human soul that exists beyond any animate property or even the Church itself. So often did the Savior teach and explain that He came to make new souls of the old men and women of the world. It befell Jesus's most personally beloved disciple, the apostle John, to decades later author the beautiful but enigmatic proclamation:

> "I write no new commandment unto you;
> but an old commandment which ye had heard from the beginning.
> The old commandment is the word which ye have heard from the beginning.
>
> Again a new commandment I write unto you,
> which thing is true in Him,
> and in you because the darkness is past,
> and the new light shines."

But what is this enigmatic commandment, a veritable paradox that is both old and new simultaneously. It is very old and the answer to the ancient question raised by Cain in these old dark days of "Am I my brother's keeper?" Christ's answer then is the same as it was in the olden days of Cain, the same as when Jesus trod the shores of Galilee and the same forever:

"He that loveth his brother abideth in the light."

Neither man nor woman can accept and obey Christ and truly please God unless the old person of sin is destroyed to become the new person of Light. This is the true new wine in new bottles. Any essay on newness in Christ could easily become an extravaganza in biblical quotations because, being a central theme, their numbers are legion. We content ourselves with this one final but illuminating observation from Paul:

> "Therefore, if any man be in Christ, he is a new creature:
> old things are passed away; behold, all things are become new."

So, this quiescently puzzling parable of new wine in old bottles becomes simplified by the simple, willing heart of a disciple who realizes that the new bottle is the sincere, willing disciple and the new wine is the simple Truth and person of Christ. The "old man of sin" is transformed into the new person of faith for a Christ spoke in the Bible's penultimate chapter:

> "Behold, I make all things new."

CHAPTER FOUR

WHAT LIES BENEATH

In 1948 a lady named Ann Omley composed a short, simple song which has been sung by little Sunday School boys and girls throughout the globe. This elementary time likely has been sung by tens of millions of small children, sung and rarely forgotten. Its music is on the level of a simple ditty and its words and phraseology remarkably repetitive, but rarely irritating. The song is "The Wise Man Built His House Upon a Rock," words taken verbatim from a parable which Jesus spoke towards the end of His Sermon on the Mount. The song, which is little more than a religious nursery rhyme, but its lyrics abide with the singer and the hearer a very long time indeed, but sadly its message less so.

This parable of the wise man is certainly similar to many, if not most, of Christ's parables. The Master illustrates His lessons with not just one, but two men, the wise and the foolish, and as in so much of His teaching His points are made, and the messages delivered by way of contrast. One acts wisely and survives, even prospers, while the other is destroyed by the same calamity. Wherein lies the real difference between the two men?

Of all the many parables of Christ this one may claim a rightful place as the most "natural" of His stories. Jesus of Nazareth was born to a young couple and His father Joseph made his living as a carpenter. Until He was thirty years old Jesus Himself pursued the carpenter's trade. For two thousand years this young Nazarene carpenter has been pictured and imaged in a variety of media building tables, chairs and other small items of furniture, and accurately too, for this was probably a large portion of His trade. Rarely have we imagined His building houses, dwelling places, etc., but this, too, must have been a large measure of His trade. In the plainest of language here we see the duality of Jesus as He taught. He was the Son of God who could extract the spirituality from any transitory reality, but He was likewise the son of Man, the carpenter who could and did build houses. More than His contemporaries and more than any person who ever lived He knew that what lies beneath the shell of the house ultimately determines its fate.

Here in the twenty-first century with this earth and every portion of it covered in houses all people have, or at least should have knowledge, of this basic fact that any structure must have a strong and proper foundation. This is a truism to any homeowner and all legitimate building contractors, but amazingly it is still blithely disregarded, and not just by the ignorant or in primitive cultures. Periodically, especially in spring, the news may feature tragic stories from California of mudslides which wreak havoc on dwellings, often ornate and shockingly expensive (as all of California seems to be), of multi-millionaire professionals, businesspeople and the occasional Hollywood celebrity who stands with tears streaming down their faces, witnessing the collapse of houses built too near the coast or upon too steep a hill or mountainside. At the other end of economic spectrum are mobile homes and mobile home parks. These words are written from central Oklahoma, the tornado alley of the world, and it has become a subject of grim jocularity that tornadoes seek out mobile home parks because so many seem to be destroyed by tornadoes. No, common to popular mythology, cyclonic winds do not seek mobile homes; however, because they contain little or no foundation they are easily smashed and blown away. Ours is not to condemn, and anyone, rich or poor, who suddenly is homeless merits the sympathy of all who claim any decency.

Still, this is a parable, and its deepest meaning is not to be found in a symposium on foundational materials, but rather in the spiritual lessons at the parable's core. At the time Jesus of Nazareth walked the lands of Galilee and Judea He knew the nature of the foundations that lay beneath the feet of every man and woman. The Savior knew those with whom He lived and taught, that most of his fellow Jews possessed a fealty to their religion, their nation's history and heritage, and in doing so Christ knew that not all, but most had built their faith, religion and spiritual loyalty upon a weak and sandy foundation.

Neither an inter-testamental history nor a full analysis of the gospels is necessary for an understanding of the foundations of the Jewish religion at the time of Christ in the first century. The old days of pagan idolatry were blessedly gone, and the Jews of the first century worshipped the one true God without an admixture of pagan idols. All religious factions, of which both fame and infamy have attached themselves, in some manner pledged their loyalty to God and their fealty to the Law of Moses, which God had given Moses on Sinai circa 1200 BC. This was a foundation, and properly understood, a true foundation. The currently extant Jewish state, though, had its foundation laid in the 160's BC with the Maccabean Revolt against the Seleucid Dynasty. After heroism, savagery and bloodshed the

Jews threw off foreign rule, essentially reestablished independence and became a type of theocracy under the Hasmonean Dynasty. For decades the nation of Judah was effectively, if not always de jure, independent, and the head of state was the Jewish high priest, the man who held the clerical office which God originally entrusted to Aaron, the brother of Moses. Jewish history, being what it was and yet remains, this period of stability and relative peace had but a short lifespan. The Jewish people and especially their religious leaders, remained of essentially the same disposition as they possessed since the ancient days of the twelve sons of Jacob. Their society was riddled and honeycombed with factions and sects, many of a strange mixture of the political and the spiritual. It was in this period that the two most noteworthy sects of New Testament renown came into the spotlight. These were the Pharisees and the Sadducees, two groups so bitterly opposed to each other that they literally engaged in bloody civil war.

The year 63 BC marked a watershed for Jewish history, for world history and civilization and most importantly the Divine Plans of God. The legions of that great western power, Rome, arrived in Judah and as part of their great eastern conquests under the great general Gnaeus Maximus Pompey, the Jews for the foreseeable future lost their independence. Yet the priesthood and that amorphously shaped body known as the "religious establishment" survived and in fact saw little of their power diminished. The high priest was still the de facto head of the Jewish state, but now he answered to the real power, the appointed governor, who naturally took his orders from Rome. Religiously the Romans proved to be mild rulers and generally kept hands off their subjects' religion so long as they paid their taxes and did nothing to breach the peace.

Sectarianism and factionalism survived and were even nourished by the Roman conquest. The Sadducees held the priesthood, and their bitter foes the Pharisees in conjunction with the scribes proudly, but adamantly and with an authoritarianism claimed to represent the populace, i.e. the common people. By the time Christ came the religious caldron, although always aboil, simmered at a level of mutual, if unconceded, consensus, between the rival factions. Religion and truth itself, and thus the foundations of life was based upon the Law of Moses. Yet, to paraphrase an American Supreme Court justice of generations past, who spoke of the constitution and judges, the Law was what the established religious elite said it was. This was the foundation for their thinking, force-fed to the Jewish people, and the Law's interpreters brooked no opposition. Their religious house had been carefully constructed on a decades, perhaps even centuries, and its most representative symbol was the Great Temple, itself in the center of the capital, Jerusalem. To the enthusiast, some perhaps would say, the fanatic, Jew, the Temple served as the physical representation of all their beliefs, even life itself. It was the foundation, the super-structure, the ornamentation and the pinnacle of Judaism itself. Nothing, except for the keepers of the Law, could exceed the glories of the Temple. It was all so impressive, the learned and educated men of faith and religion, circulating through the city and countryside, in their specially designed clerical robes and religious garb, directing the business and lives of the lesser "laity," who "knew" so much less than did this self-appointed clerisy. If not, the love they held the respect and esteem of many and the fear of all Jews for this magnificent religious edifice which they had constructed by the first century A.D. Still, though, it was the near perfect illustration of what delineated in this parable. A great house indeed, but the Jewish religious establishment had built upon a foundation of sand.

Even if the student and/or the reader accepts the basic premises of what has been stated he is entitled to the question of "Yes, but can you or anyone else do any better?"

In this parable of the buildings on rock and sand there is nothing mysterious or obtuse about the author's language, especially in the context of His life and all His other teachings. Our essay has spoken at some length about the derivation and background of those groups who were so much at enmity with Christ, but what of the background of Jesus Himself? This may seem to be a peculiar inquiry since we are talking of the Son of God and the Founder of the Christian religion, yet for this moment let us review his life's story as Jesus of Nazareth, Son of Man. Even judging Him solely as a man and momentarily laying aside His Divinity this son of Mary and Joseph has an impressive pedigree upon which to build a life and legacy. The gospel writers Matthew and Luke meticulously and thoroughly trace His lineage back to Creation itself, accounting for over forty generations, each ancestor being specifically named. Among the luminaries in His heritage is King David himself, the most legendary of leaders and perhaps the most "glamorous" figure of the Old Testament. Painstakingly the writers leads us to His earthly parents, Mary and Joseph, each from the house of David, prestigious in itself. As a child, a youth and even as a grown man the most valuable asset of Jesus's growth as a man was the admirable character of His mother and father. From His parents He learned and enhanced His own qualities of obedience and self-sacrifice. He had neither notice nor notoriety outside His own family or the precincts in which He lived. Yet he worked hard, and by work it is meant manual labor, simply because it was a necessity for survival in a first century Galilean village. Though He as yet lacked notoriety the son of the carpenter was not short on respect for "... Jesus grew in wisdom and stature, and in favor with God and man." It is impossible, and perhaps rightfully so, for even the most devoted Christian to separate the Son of God from the Son of Man. Still, unequivocally let it be posited with certainty that Jesus, the Son of Mary and Joseph, walked in and eventually away from Galilee with a foundation of granite beneath His stride.

May we not find comfort and assurance in the warmth of the realization that although Jesus left His boyhood home of Nazareth, He above all others knew that His parents, childhood and youth all had lain a solid foundation for the remaining three years of His life. These were the years in which He was preparing and would, in fact, lay the foundation of permanence for a building that would never pass away. Jesus, the son of Joseph, and among so many other attributes still a builder and a carpenter, was walking with some of His apostles in a day in which the lengthening of earth's shadows was falling upon His time and ministry on earth. He and at least that "inner circle" of His apostles were walking in that famed city of Caesarea Philippi, a locale known for idolatry and where pagan images were carved into the rock formations for all to see and worship. As they walked in the fetid atmosphere of idolatry Christ turned to His disciples and simply asked "Whom do men say that I the Son of man am." They responded with an assortment of characters, as some related that many claimed that you are John the Baptist, Elijah, Isaiah or one of the other prophets returned to life. As would an investigator or lawyer seeking the real answer to the inquiry, that for which He was searching He now simply asked "But who do you say I am?" Simon, still known two millennia hence for quickness of response is consistent, but this time he more than does honor not only to Christ but to himself when as he gazes upon all the sone idols which surround them he responds:

> "And Simon Peter answered and said,
> Thou art the Christ, the Son of the living God."

The Son of Mary and Joseph and also the Son of God responded with a statement that literally will last throughout eternity:

> "For I say unto you that thou art Peter,
> and upon this rock I will build My Church;
> and the gates of hell shall not prevail against it."

This was, is and ever shall be the foundation like no other, the firm foundation that is not moved, does not suffer damage, and which lifetime is never shortened. The Roman Catholic teaching is that the apostle Peter is the rock upon which Jesus built His church. As great and admirable as he was Peter never claimed preeminence among the apostles. The rock, the firm, immovable, everlasting foundation is that Jesus is the Savior and the Son of God. It is unchangeable and immutable, and is the very foundation for all.

While the Church is not the foundation it is the structure which rests upon the firm foundation of the Divinity and redemptive power of Christ. This brief excursion into the parables is not the appropriate place for a two thousand year or even a Biblical history of the Church. Let it be noted, even celebrated, that as Jesus ended His Sermon on the Mount with this parable the continued existence of the Church is living proof of the accuracy and efficacy of Christ's promise. In spite of everything, all persecutions, any apostasies, any fools or charlatans in positions of leadership the Church is alive and is always a living, breathing, pulsating entity.

Fate of the Two Houses

Like all the parables this one of the two houses is capable of multiple construction, and in the matter of our current mode of study lends itself to an infinite number of examples. For the moment we have chosen but two, the Jewish religious establishment, emblemized by the Great Temple in Jerusalem and the Church which Christ Himself established. But Christ's parable does not end with the identification of the subject matter, but rather with its fate, which our essay must elucidate. From a misdirected sense of fairness it is tempting to assert that the two had different trajectories, and their "end" results somewhat differing. Such would be inaccurate, wildly, ludicrously, extravagantly inaccurate, for their fates track to the nth degree what Christ prophesied in His parable. Let us first peer more deeply and thoroughly into the house with the foundation of sand, the Jewish religious establishment.

By the time of the occurrence of the events and the giving of the parables, circa 30 AD, the Jewish house was quite impressive. With the historically presumed burdens of Roman occupation and ultimate direction the religion and its leaders was in apparently fine condition. Although we have no historical description of the Temple at this time, likely it was in good condition, ornate as ever and a spectacle of beauty, piety and religiosity. As both the scriptures and secular sources reflect a not inconsiderable number of "religions" Jews practically worshipped the Temple itself. As far as earthly representations of the Divine go, the Jewish Temple was first rate and in a term of ubiquity and bureaucracy, which both worked and worshipped in the magnificent edifice, was well organized and replete with educated, well and impressively dressed, and self-important men fulfilling important places.

It was not on that terrible Good Friday of Christ's crucifixion that the magnificent, elegant Temple began its fall. At the moment of Christ's death as recorded by Matthew:

> "Behold, the veil of the temple was rent in twain
> from the top to the bottom;
> and the earth did quake, and the rocks rent:
> And the graves were opened;
> and many bodies of the saints which slept arose."

The death knell for Judaism as the chosen religion for God's formerly chosen people had sounded. The Temple itself stood for another forty years, and this façade of religion now served a false purpose for the old, fulfilled religion of God, the same God who made the Temple holy and who was now destroying the building. Most definitely it still stood, but its foundations had been cracked and would serve it no more. Caiaphas, the virulently vindictive high priest who had organized the conspiracy against Christ remained in office until circa 40 AD, when the Romans unceremoniously discarded him, never again to grace the pages of the New Testament. Still, the Temple as an edifice stood, but the foundations beneath it and all of an out-moded (and as practiced by the Jews) often false Judaism were now rapidly crumbling and disintegrating.

From 63 BC forward the Roman province of Judea was never at peace, be it religious, spiritual or political. Always seething with hatred for the Romans, an often-justified hatred, many of the Jews were continually aflame with even greater hatred for each other. They were factionalized, and though they had momentarily united in their hatred for Jesus Christ the animus which the Pharisees, Sadducees and others held for each other never really subsided. Armed conflict was ever a part of the rivalry that was Jewish sectarianism, a conflict which too often broke out into civil war. Yet, these professional sectarians could still unite in the face of a common enemy, and this was always therein present with the colossus of Rome. By 66 A.D. Judea was in open rebellion against Rome, and the First Jewish-Roman War commenced. By 70 A.D. the immensely more powerful Romans, their army under the command of the future emperor Titus besieged the capital of Jerusalem and eventually broke through the city's defenses. The atrocities and carnage which ensued are forever written in blood red ink. The Romans literally razed the city to the ground, killing or capturing its defenders and exacting a death toll of tens of thousands of Jewish men, women and children. Thousands were publicly crucified. It remained, though, that the Temple, the very essence and symbol of the Jewish nation and religion stood, but momentarily. The Roman legionnaries broke through even the Temple's defenses, and the squalid carnage invites a lengthy quotation from the Jewish historian Flavius Josephus:

> "As the legions charged in neither persuasion
> nor threat could check their impetuosity:
> passion was in command.
> Crowded together around the entrances many
> were trampled
> by their friends, many fell among the still hot
> and smoking ruins of the colonnades
> and died as miserably as the defeated.
> As they neared the Sanctuary they pretended
> not even to hear Caesar's commands

and urged the men in front to throw in more firebrands.
The partisans were no longer in a position to help;
everywhere was slaughter and flight.
Most of the victims were peaceful citizens, weak and unarmed,
butchered wherever they were caught.
Round the Altar the heaps of corpses grew higher and higher,
while down the Sanctuary steps poured a river of blood
and the bodies of those killed at the top slithered to the bottom."

Our text will impose upon the reader's patient indulgence for one more quotation, though not as lengthy as the foregoing. As He dragged the cross along the Via Dolorosa some four decades before the suffering Christ spoke of this day to the many women He saw were in distress:

"Daughters of Jerusalem, weep not for Me,
but weep for yourselves, and for your children.

For behold the days are coming, in the which they will say,
Blessed are the barren, and the wombs that never bare,
and the paps which never gave suck.

Then shall they begin to say to the mountains,
Fall on us; and to the hills, cover us.

> For if they do those things in a green tree,
> what shall be done to the dry?"

It was over. The Temple burned to the ground and the Jewish people began to be scattered to the four winds. The Law of Moses and the nation of Israel, both ordained by God, were very good things, but by the time of Christ they were expropriated by what Jesus called simply "sinful men." They had built a religion not based on worship and reverence to God and service to men and women but upon self-regard, self-promotion, intellectual insularity and smugness and just plain hypocrisy. Their house was the house of the foolish man, built upon a foundation of sand. When it fell, great was the fall of it.

The wise man's house, though, was built upon a rock, and stands yet today. It is a house like no other, and its construction methods and materials of construction are unique for so many reasons. This house was singular from the outset inasmuch as its founder, foundation and the house itself are one and that one is Jesus Christ, His Church itself being the house. Morally, physically, emotionally, ad infinitum it has weathered storms and terrors more odious and even more grotesque than that inflicted by the Romans upon the first century Jews. With all that, though, the great chronicle of its founding, beginning, growth and early history, is neither shy nor remiss in recording and laying bare its early troubles. The church of the scriptures, what later Christians often describe as the "first century Church" has an unhidden record of internal strife, racial, religious and ethnic fissures, petty jealousies, self-seeking and self-glorification by some of its membership, occasional sloth, moments of gross immorality and every other weakness and sin endemic to humanity. Still it prospered, it grew and spread beyond Jerusalem into all Judea, Samaria and Galilee and into the larger Gentile world beyond the borders of tiny Judea. So extravagantly successful were the early evangelistic efforts of Christ's apostles that one of the Church's foes in the great Macedonian city of Thessalonica remarked of them that "... these that have turned the world upside down are come hither also,"

Building any structure is never easy. The apostles had Jesus Christ as the very cornerstone of their foundation, but they themselves suffered agonies, hardships and the pains of not just death, but horrible, macabre deaths. Yet the house, this new Temple of God, this Church of Christ Himself stood firm upon the Rock. The centuries that followed, though, record growth, some acceptance, more persecution and even worst of all, apostasy. The exceeding centuries demonstrated that men, sometimes evil, sometimes sincere, could twist the truth and distort the Church into an unrecognizable structure. Reformation, restoration and various forms of both ensued. The most hideous grotesquerie, at least outwardly, erupted in the forms of "religions" was in the late Middle Ages and early modern periods. Religious belief, but not true Christianity, was spread at the point of a sword or the barrel of a gun, with intense hatreds raging on all sides of any issue or dichotomy of beliefs. Still, in spite of the follies and evil of men and the heart's desire the Church survives.

Back in its day the Great Temple in Jerusalem and its legions of servants and assorted acolytes was beautiful and imposing. The priesthood with its chief pinnacle being the high priest, the most notorious being the regnant figure of the scriptures, Caiaphas. The "professionally" religious class of Judaism was accorded place, sanctimony and servility. They had their day, or as Christ said before His trial and crucifixion, their hour. It was all a flimsy house of cards, a sham built upon sand. When the real political power had enough of it, they destroyed it all, the temple, the priesthood and every bit of regalia and bric-a-brac built upon a displaced house of sand. Many winds blew upon this power structure and the rains came tumbling down, and in 70 A.D. it collapsed, until as in the Savior's words in the Temple not one stone remained standing upon another. The majority of the Jews were dispersed, the priesthood with its finery, pomposity and ultimate rule by terror died, the Great Sanhedrin ceased to function, and Judea as a separate Jewish entity ceased, as the Romans swept away its granular remnants. The winds and the rains had their way.

The Church lives still, a living, pulsating entity and ultimately its true populace known by God alone. All the persecutions, the hatreds, the blows and even its self-inflicted wounds ultimately have recoiled from this beautiful bride, as so described by its founder Christ. The winds and the rains will doubtless continue to inflict damage, but this bride of Christ will ultimately defeat the gates of hell itself. Its members await the return of the King.

CHAPTER FIVE

LITTLE THINGS MEAN A LOT
Showtime – The Great Banquet
Luke 14:7-14

Whether fervent believer or sardonic skeptic the four gospels are filled with social occasions, be they simple meals, family or otherwise, gatherings of a few friends or formal banquets the pages of these four short accounts are not remiss in providing a full, even deep, account of the social life of Christ and His apostles. Jesus Himself drew attention to this reality when He upbraided the scribes and Pharisees for their hypocrisy and implacable demands on this subject. My cousin and forerunner, John the Baptist, lived a solitary life, withdrawn from much of the day's social life, and you condemned him, spoke the Master. Now I, Jesus, come "eating and drinking" and you condemn me as a "glutton and a winebibber." So what is correct, and how can you be pleased? The question was ripe for a parabolic answer, and as ever, the Savior was not found wanting for words.

He chose the story of a host who committed his time, money, and energy to providing a great festive meal for an apparent and veritable multitude of persons from what we now describe in our neutralized and astringent bureaucratese as being from many "socio-economic" classes. In plainer and more descriptive terms he invited the rich and poor, the famous and the unnoticed, the powerful and the powerless, all to the same place for the same socialization, the same bill of fare and at the same time. In that almost sacred term of modernity the guest list was "diverse."

True diversity is one the most difficult of all conditions to attain and maintain, as the introduction to the parable reflects in His opening sentence, as Christ remarked to the core of His audience that "...those which were bidden... chose out the chief rooms." To some honor, respect and even a special salutation is never enough. An historically famous American baseball great long has had attributed to him, quite possibly incorrectly, that "... I have to be first in everything, all the time." This had become an animating spirit and ethos of many of the prominent, reigning Jewish religious leaders at the time of Christ, and it extended even to events that were designed (or at least should have been) as respites from the drives and chaos of life, even moments of mirth and conviviality. Yet not to a certain type of person, and it is an absurd conceit to believe that the characteristic is limited to certain Jewish prelates of twenty centuries past. In comparative terms, but still within the context of Christ's parable, these are the persons who must be at the chief table at any gathering, those who crave, even demand special recognition that they are just a "cut above" the common herd. In that timeless language of adolescence, which any teen, boy or girl, of any place or time, will immediately grasp they set forth a predicate of behavior that all recognize and treat them as being "cool." That word would have meant nothing to an audience of Christ's day, but its meaning would have been packed with an understandable potency.

Dinner parties, banquets, social events of all sorts have always worn a patina of happiness, fellowship and just a general good time. So it is with many and so it is with many of the attendees, but leave it to Christ to see and discern the underside, the emotional traumas and the hurt they may bring for some. Nothing is more embarrassing, more degrading, more humiliating and often just maddening than to be told that your presence at a certain place is not welcome. Social events are a prime, if not the prime, milieu for such emotions, as Christ so poignantly recognized:

> "When thou art bidden of any man to a wedding,
> sit not down in the highest level;
> lest a more honorable man than thou be bidden
> of him.
>
> And he that bade thee and him come and say to
> thee,
> Give this man place,
> and thou begin with shame to take the lower
> room."

Suddenly, with but a sentence and in a moment that invigorating brace of having "made it" is replaced by the hot sting of embarrassed humiliation. At a social soiree this is the very spotlight anyone seeks to avoid, and that is the glaring light of public recognition that one is not as good and important as he thinks himself to be. For this guest, unless he be an obnoxious boor of the highest degree any decent person will possess at the least a modicum of sympathy. Likely the very pith of this sympathy is the realization that the humiliated person could easily be, and likely has been, oneself at times.

In this moment of pathos (and let it be treated with a seriousness it deserves), we are reminded of the author of this parable. Never did the Savior describe a situation, a pitiable state of a man or woman, or the wretchedness of a life and soul without offering a solution, or at the minimum the means of making a bad situation better. Of course, the ideal solution to any problem is its complete evidence, although life seems to be abundant with unavoidable difficulties for both the good and the bad. Christ's admonition is remarkably wise and prescient:

> "When thou are bidden,
> go and sit down in the lowest room;
> that when he that bade thee cometh, he may say unto thee,
> Friend, go up higher:
> then shalt thou have worship in the presence of them that sat at meat with thee."

The thrill, the honor and maybe even satisfaction of being so unexpectedly honored would warm the heart of the recipient and challenge the vocabulary of any writer. It is a portion, a large portion, of both the heart and the spine of any true believing Christian.

Certainly life is more than a succession and endless chain of social events. A fair, likely even a majority percentage of the world's population has passed their earthly sojourn without an invitation to a large, particularly a formal, social gathering. All of us, though, answer a daily summons, an invitation as to speak, of any day's particular demands, hurdles and opportunities. In the aggregate, this constitutes much of human life itself. Christ's proscription of a rigid "social" caste structure on its face is a point well made. As with all His parables they shine as stand-alone stories without further and deeper construction and interpretation. Any social gathering the atmosphere and prevalent attitude of which makes its invitees and attendees uncomfortable and embarrassed is an abject failure. One which subjects an invited guest to public humiliation is an abomination, be it family, friends, employment and yes, church itself.

This short parable, as a number do, establishes a contrast of two attitudes, two codes of conduct, and two diametrically opposed results. Many words correctly and properly come to the fore of our thinking. That wonderful tool of expression, the English language of the King James Version, provides two words that are known by all, grasped by almost all but truly and properly practiced by too few, exalt and humble. Let us consider the exact wording of the Master Himself:

> "For whosoever exalted himself shall be abased;
> and he that exalted himself shall be humbled."

None of this, though, is any new or special theme which Christ introduced by this parable alone. The clash and dichotomy of humility and self-exaltation is one of the Bible's primary themes, especially that of the gospels and the remainder of the New Testament. The birth, life and death of the Christian religion's Founder, Jesus Christ, is the purest and most thoroughly inclusive example of this assertion. Humility was a desired and accessed goal. Born to humble parents in an almost singularly humble manner, raised without fanfare or notoriety in an obscure village in an obscure province He was generally unnoticed except for one trait, His character. He had come from the exalted right hand of the Father in Heaven to willingly, even gladly and happily live the life of an ordinary man. Jesus found His glory in obedience and service to His Father, and as seemingly contradictory as it may seem, His greatest exaltation in being lifted on the humiliating, degrading and grotesque cross to die for the sins of all humanity. He proclaimed in stark distinction to all false god or pretended Savior that "... the Son of man came not to be ministered unto, but to minister, and to give His life a ransom for many." Likely the most poignant moment of His Spirit of humble service was seen when in the famed upper room just hours before His crucifixion He got on His knees and washed the feet of His apostles. The King of the Universe, in the midst of His most severe earthly test, was humbling Himself to serve those He loved.

Christ humbled Himself, of course, but in the ultimate act of humble service and, to the world, debasement, He reached the pinnacle of exaltation for His short time on earth. With the Son of God so intermeshed in His thinking and Spirit were the concepts of pain, abasement, service and humility that in Gethsemane He could pray to God "... O Father, glorify me with thine own self with the glory which I had with Thee before the world began." Only Christ, who sometime before had made the enigmatic proclamation to His apostles that:

> "I, if I be lifted up from the earth, will draw all men to me."

Only later did they and now we comprehend that only Jesus could conflate crucifixion with exaltation and glory.

The disciple must recognize that his task is more than to be an impressed witness of Christ's glorious humility, but must himself be part and parcel of it. The persons in the parable who purposely made themselves inconspicuous by their humility and willing acceptance of a humble place were those who were praised, honored and exalted by the master of the feast. Likely they will not have adoring puff pieces about their virtues and public charitable work publicized in the local media. The shelves, mantels and walls of their homes maybe at best sparsely filled with awards of merit, certificates of service, and plaudits from their contemporaries. But the parable stands strongly and dare it be said proudly for the proposition that they engender rejoicing in Heaven merely by their pure, simple spirit of humility. Perhaps this spirit was wisely captured in a Psalm from a man who rendered God magnificent service but who almost destroyed himself with self-will, Israel's mightiest king, David, who said:

> "I had rather be a doorkeeper in the house of God
> than to dwell in the tents of wickedness."

As wise as King David could be James, the earthly brother of Jesus, enunciated the thought with a greater, more beautiful and more comforting solace when he wrote:

> "God resisteth the proud, but giveth grace to the humble."

The words themselves perhaps are unspoken but here in Christ's beautiful parable is implicit the qualities of self-denial, self-abnegation, and above all, gratitude. The humble man or woman who willingly takes the inconspicuous place, the lower, less prestigious table is simply first and foremost happy to have been invited to the banquet. He sees the host as the most important personage and is certainly willing to do his bidding and act according to the host's preferences and pleasures. The great host notices this character and quickly willingly exalts his humble guest to the position of favor and blessing. The host is the fully realized exemplar behind Christ's beautiful proclamation:

> "For whosoever exalted himself shall be abased;
> and he that humbleth himself shall be exalted."

One of the most dangerous entrapments of success, acclaim and both public and private renown is that the warm, inner glow of success spreads from the heart to the head and encourages the successful, even famous, man or woman begins to be both ensnared and propelled by the feeling that the good times will forever roll forward, even with exhilarating and increasing speed and thrills. The wise man or woman knows that they are "but for a season" and that the great rewards await in the next life; however, the virtuous disciple is not unrewarded in our terrestrial sphere. Christ's personal benediction to His apostles and other closest disciples, all humble men and women, before taking leave of them was that wherever they (also we) went he would never leave nor forsake them. Ultimately for humble service at the banquet in the words of the Master Himself "great is (their) reward in heaven."

But what of the self-exalting, who during the time of Christ's ministry were often scribes and Pharisees, those that wanted the applause and hosannas in the marketplace, the Temple and the synagogues, and who loved and lived for the public adulation in the marketplaces of life. Very tersely, and more than once, Jesus remarked that here on earth "they have their reward." He never spoke of their Heavenly reward.

The Lamplighter
Luke 11:33

The Good Shepherd was such a master of words at times His English-speaking disciples need to be reminded that He was not speaking in English. His ability was so comprehensive that He sometimes could express a parabolic tale no just in one paragraph but in one sentence, as He does here:

> "No man, when he have lighted a candle,
> putteth it in a secret place, neither under a bushel, but on a candlestick,
> that they which come in may see the light."

Beautiful thought indeed and expressed in beautiful words, but this statement, as all words spoken by the Savior are not meant to be viewed in isolation and must therefore be placed in the context of everything which Jesus spoke. Herein, at first rendering a problem is seen lurking by the juxtaposition of this parable with that of the banquet invitees just discussed.

This chapter's initial section focused upon Christ's teachings about the dangers of self-regard and generally selfish behavior in projecting oneself as overly important. Here, though, it is followed by a parable, however brief, which seemingly extols the desire and necessity of garnering and gathering personal attention as a desirable Christian virtue. Has the Son of God, however unintentionally, contradicted Himself? This is a legitimate question for a disciple and a potential, if not apparent, snag for a detractor of Christianity who is looking for such matters. Is it possible for a Christian or any person to be inconspicuous, modest and unassuming and simultaneously making certain that he lets his "let shine before men?" Unsurprisingly to the reader the answer is a resounding yes. The genesis for this positivity begins, in point of fact, in the Book of Genesis and is consistently and beautifully developed all the way through the scriptures.

The duality of the metaphorical and the real is nowhere found in purer form than if God's use of the word "light." The Genesis account of the beginning and of creation bestows on us an awareness of its importance when the first words God is ever recorded uttering are "God said, let there be light, and there was light." The sun and the moon were thereby revealed, and scientifically plain evidence demonstrates that this is the source of this world's light. Our sun, though brilliant and bright, and the diffuser of light itself is not its creator, and of course, neither is that lesser light, the moon. Every object that appears on this earth is a diffuser o light, but none, save one, has ever been its creator or its origin. It is seemingly an anomaly when Christ promises that our "light" should shine before men, for from whence does this supposed light arise.

We should register no surprise when we realize that the third verse of one of the beginning four books of the New Testament, the Gospel of John, echoes the third verse of the commencement of the Old Testament, where now the apostle John writes:

> "All things were made by Him;
> and without Him not anything made that was made.
> In Him was life, and the life was the light of men."

Jesus Christ is so many, many things, most pertinently here the Alpha and the Omega, the Beginning and the End. He is the spiritual and celestial compendium of all good things, in which the element of Light is always included. So many times did Christ not just associate Himself with Light, but He proclaimed Himself to be Light, as when He proclaimed:

> "I am the Light of the world,
> He that followeth me shall not walk in darkness,
> but shall have the light of life."

The Savior's continual usage of the word and metaphor Light is so scripturally common and plentiful that it resists incessant and continuous quotation.

Light is not only good, but itself is goodness and truth, and it emanates from the Son of God Himself. Should any man or woman profess allegiance or claim discipleship to Him that person must radiate light himself/herself. We now remind ourselves of our short parable, to which we have committed this brief discussion, for "... no man, when he have lighted a candle putteth it is a secret place." Fair enough, and let not our parable be made obtuse or woven into a network of confusion. But ... everything we are taught to be as a Christian, literally a "little" Christ, His disciple, emphasizes modest, self-effacement and humility in the world. Now, though, the Master plainly teaches to let "your" light shine before others. This parable to some sincere believers may become what quizzical and it proffers a question or two worth studying. Such may be expressed in as many ways and words as there are Christians, but in essence it comes to this – "How can I, as a humble and modest Christian, remain so when I am expressly ordained to allow all men and women to notice my light."

The answer to the preceding paragraph's question lies in a true understanding of the meaning, origin, and efficacy of the word "light" itself. No man or woman who ever lived, past, present or future, be they the most beautifully drawn saint or reflecting nothing but the darkness of sin can himself generate and produce light. We are not merely physiologically advanced fireflies, and the source of light which we may possess comes not from internal generation. We may, in fact, become the "Light of the World," but only because we reflect the only true source of Light, who dwells in His disciples through His Holy Spirit. A merely mortal human being generates nothing of himself, no independent faith, no good works, no sanctity of any sort. All, everything good comes from God, including, actually especially, the good that resides within a Christian. It was the great apostle Paul who most beautifully cogently exulted "... it is not I but Christ who lives in me." Also, it was again the apostle Paul who proclaimed that all good things come from God. What the Creator wishes the world to see in each Christian is the humble, ministering Spirit of His son, the Spirit of Christ. It is that Spirit of modesty, gentleness, kindness, patience, humility and a thousand other qualities. The Christian who possesses such is the Christian indeed, and he or she really does not have to worry about a performance of a tally or quota of "good works." With this ministering Spirit, this humility of character, this true Light of Christ will be seen by others in the good works, the good lives, which these Christians live. The last thing a Christian disciple of this mettle possesses is a candle placed under a basket. He or she is the true possessor of the only light, the Light of the World, which is Christ.

For exemplary consideration our essay offers a well-known Biblical figure, who is known for many things, but rarely is the pure goodness of His character included in their inventory. This is John the Baptist, the cousin of Jesus of Nazareth, the last and greatest of the prophets, and the immediate forerunner of Christ Himself. This man has been solidified in history as a wild man, raving against the sins, injustice and hypocrisy of the established religious order of the day. His forthright public contention that Herod Antipas was an adulterer, and a murderer was hardly the denunciation made by a nervous shrinking violet. Maybe more than any follower who ever lived this prophet John understood certain things about his cousin. Once, when John's own disciples noted that Jesus seemed to be gaining in recognition and disciples while John's ministry had reached its high-water mark John, not with regret or self-pity, but with an understanding spirit of satisfaction remarked that:

"He must increase, but I must decrease."

The true Light, the Spirit of Christ, never shone brighter at the moment of that statement. So it may be with all Christians.

CHAPTER SIX

A GRAIN OF MUSTARD SEED
Matthew 13:31, 32

Large, loud noises, objects and especially people have no trouble garnering our attention. Even in the natural world our gaze is often riveted upon not just the largest, but even the gargantuan. Children learn (or at least once they did) the names, locations and pertinent associated facts such as the world's highest mountain, its deepest ocean, the longest river, the hottest and coldest locales, ad infinitum. The large and predominant is somehow deeply embedded in man's nature, and modernistic or perhaps even futuristic attempts to displace it likely are futile. Certain peripheral facts, though, are subject to increasing inconspicuousness as in the modern world the great bulk of its population has been displaced from rural and agricultural days. This, though, was not the reality of the first century world of the Bible.

Mustard is an herb, a spice, a cooking ingredient and a condiment and remains popular in at least modern Western culture. Most of its consumers, though, have little or no idea as to its origin, planting, cultivation or growth process. The mustard seed is tiny, insignificant in size and a lone seed placed on almost any background likely will be overlooked and unseen. When planted, though, the seed germinates within just a few days, and a healthy plant grows to several feet even as it spreads out its branches. In ancient Palestine, in a differing climate from America, and within different varieties of a wide range of mustard types, the mature mustard plant could grow much larger, as the heart of Christ's parable testifies:

> "The kingdom of heaven is like to a grain of mustard seed,
> which a man took and sowed in his field.
>
> Which indeed is the least of all seeds:
> but when it is grown, it is the greatest among herbs,
> and becometh a tree, so that the birds of the air come
> and lodge in the branches thereof."

That is quite a feat for a tree which started as an object no larger than the period at the end of this sentence. Enough, now, of horticulture and herbology, legitimate and important subjects to be certain, but the Son of God came not primarily as a biologist, and our responsibility, like that of the first disciples who listened to the parable's initial pronouncement, is to discern its practical and spiritual meanings.

As with most of the parables of Jesus the words are vehicles to take us to the truth, sometimes in a straight line, but perhaps in a circuitous route or more than one thoroughfare. Most often for two millennia scholars and just ordinary studious disciples have interpreted the "seed" as a metaphor for the Word of God, the teachings of Christ, and such is certainly true and really impervious to any cogent argument. In close companionship with the Word, though, this essay is meant to suggest that the mustard seed is a fine very adaptable and applicable "seed" which is inextricably linked with its early germination and propagation. This would be the first Christian disciples and especially the original twelve apostles (discounting the traitor Judas). Of course it is also inclusive of the forever honored names of such as Mary, Joseph, Elizabeth, Mary of Magdalene, and Martha and her siblings Mary and Lazarus. All were disciples of the Master, and all had many things in common along with that discipleship. Not only were they all Jews, but each was a Galilean, as with Jesus of Nazareth. All appear to be faithful Jews even before the advent of Christ, and each seems to be a good "solid" moral man or woman. Parabolically, though, and to our point as the world reckoned and still measures each was "insignificant," a "small" person in a world where emperors, kings, rabbis, priests bestrode the walkways of power and fame. An even harsher rendering reflects the unavoidable truth that their lives (to the world) were the existences of "nobodies." Yes, they were mustard seeds, small, unnoticed, unnamed, but as the scriptures, history and life itself would demonstrate, the epitome, the polar opposite of "insignificant." A quick and summary review of that now historically famed dozen, the original twelve apostles is appropriate.

Undoubtedly, the first four apostles who come to mind are two sets of brothers, James and John, and Simon Peter and Andrew, all four of whom had more in common than sibling relationship. Each was from the town of Capernaum, a fishing community on the edge of the Sea of Galilee, a freshwater lake of moderately substantial size in Galilee itself. They are specifically and scripturally called by Jesus Himself while they were actually fishing to become "fishers of men." Two others, Nathanael and Thomas, are identified as going fishing with the others in those days after the Resurrection and before the Ascension of Christ. Matthew is specifically and prominently identified as a publican, a tax collector, and that is, in point of truth, a type of significance. He was significantly despised by other Jews because of his occupation. The other five, James, the son of Alpheus, Philip, Thaddeus, Simon and Matthias have little written of them in the New Testament. Their occupations are unknown, and their earthly claim to fame is simply having been an apostle.

Since at least one-half (and likely more) of the apostles were fishermen a brief plunge into that topic is requisite. Socially, it had zero, perhaps even negative, standing. Fishers were physically hard, tough men who daily traversed the waters of the Sea of Galilee, casting out heavy nets in hopes of a profitable haul of fish, particularly tilapia, a food fish still common and popular today. The work was backbreaking, tiring in the extreme, imposing in its weather from cold, rain and the heat of the sun. As is any activity on water it was hazardous, fraught with danger and the jaws of a watery death constantly below and surrounding the fisherman. It was also dirty, smelly, literally "fishy," and as anyone who has ever shared the experience the lingering odor of fish is hardly one of nature's perfume fragrances. We should remind ourselves of the drawbacks of antiquity where daily showers and bath, deodorizes, lotions and the like were not a part of life, which must have been especially exasperating to the Jews, an historically clean and hygienic culture. Their work was hard, tedious, disappointing (known by anyone who has ever been fishing) and their social status was zero. The non-fishermen among the apostles doubtless held occupations as non-prestigious as fishing. The only apostle likely to have risen above insignificance with a bit of fame was Matthew. His fame took the form of being significantly hated by his fellow Jews.

The other early close disciples were in the same boat as the apostles when it came to significance, for they had none. Yes, we know them now, but in the early part of the first century Mary, Joseph, Elizabeth, and Mary Magdalene had no social standing. The three siblings so close to Christ, Martha, Mary and Lazarus lived prosperous lives, but no indicia of fame and certainly not of power marks their lives. In totality the apostles and early disciples parabolically were truly mustard seeds, small, easily looked past, of no value and importance to the world. But not so with Christ.

No man or woman deserved celebrity, honor and notice simply because of their earthly stature, and the apparent long shadows which their lives cast. Neither does any person deserve special accolades for being small and insignificant, or in Christ's terms a "mustard seed." The real significance is discovered in the second portion of this short parable. Its brevity and succinctness permits its brief re-quotation:

> "(The seed) becometh a tree,
> and the birds of the air come and lodge in the branches thereof."

Botanically this world is full of all types of trees, from the breathtakingly majestic California redwoods to the miniature but elegant Japanese Bonsai. The one great tree of Christ's parable is His Church, where His disciples gather, not for salvation (for only the person and blood of Jesus saves), but they gather and coalesce under that tree because they are saved. It is the tree planted by the Son of God, and in it, despite our errors, mistakes, shortsightedness and all the sins and frailties to which humanity is prone, it is indestructible and gives so much, including shelter. Christ is the Alpha and Omega, and it is the Savior who is the object of His own parable. Yet it was the apostles and other early Christian disciples, those tiny mustard seeds, who nurtured and grew that Church from its worldly insignificant, practically invisible beginning. So what exactly did they do?

Less than a generation after its founding the Church's detractors and persecutors in the Gentile metropolis of Thessalonica lamented and agonized "...they have turned the world upside down." The influence of these dozen men so limited in their youth to likely just family and a few friends had spread from Galilee, to Judea, to Jerusalem to Samaria, to the continent of Europe, encompassing Greece and eventually Rome itself. Small churches sprung up and grew, not only among the Jews but soon within the larger and more extensive world of the Gentiles. These insignificant blue-collar working men simply dressed and even more simply spoken had truly revolutionized a world that even in the twenty-first century was irrevocably altered. A few non-descript nobodies had taken their Master's commission and done more to revolutionize the world's attitudes and thinking that the still celebrated (and usually with substantial reason) great philosophers such as Socrates, Plato and Aristotle.

Greece and Rome, the lauded classical civilizations, were and yet remain important, and they are requisite to the construction of that often-derided article known as Western civilization. Those twelve inconspicuous Galilean apostles along with the later apostle "born out of due season" are the men who showed Christ and salvation to the world. Along the way and unknowingly they supplied the true foundation of Western culture, which is the true foundation of the eternal spirit, Christ and His Church. The concepts of individual freedom, law, harmony among nations and people, and the ultimate worth of each human soul and life which was spread by these men remains foundational. Of course the history of the past two millennia is wracked with terrors, hypocrisies, wars and cruelties, but the saving Christian ideals disseminated by the apostles are as true and powerful as ever.

These apostolic seeds, so innocuous, so annoying and so deplorable to the world occasionally and with increasing frequency came to the notice of those who planted themselves squarely athwart the paths of Light. Early in the Church's history the apostles Peter and John were dragged to the forum of the Great Sanhedrin led by the leader of the conspiracy against Christ, the high priest Caiaphas. Immediately the same men who had condemned the Son of God recognized these two apostles as "ignorant and unlearned" men. Caiaphas and his father-in-law Annas, a once powerful high priest, released them but only after a beating and pummeling which had no deleterious effect upon them.

The establishment and spread of the Church and the founding of Western civilization seemingly makes all other accomplishments somewhat pedestrian. Perhaps, but another feat of these early Christian men and women is worthy of remark. It is their names. Names, personal names, any intelligent reader is entitled to note and to seriously question the importance of something so personal yet ultimately so apparently trivia. Perhaps, but now our essay will indulge the patience of its reader with a listing of the names of what were ultimately thirteen apostles. Peter, James the Greater, John, Andrew, Philip, Matthew,

Thomas, Nathaniel, James the Less, Thaddeus, Simon, Matthias, and Paul. For good measure let us know again the names of the gospel's earliest disciples, Mary, Joseph, Elizabeth, Joanna and Martha. All these names, at least these English versions of them have at least one characteristic they share. For two thousand years they have remained au courant, and even in these vastly different times of the twenty-first century none have gone out of style, and many remain as popular as ever. For a moment let us be reminded of another category of nomenclatures, those that set their face, might and power against Christ and these "miniscule" followers of His, these veritable mustard seeds. We recall the names of Caiaphas, Annas, Herod and Pilate, and it would be a rare person who could recall any child bearing these names. These tiny mustard seeds of the Savior's parable grew into beautiful, verdant trees that still protect, comfort and assure. The Son of God planted seeds that never died.

A Grain of Yeast
Matthew 13:33; Luke 13:20, 21

The Bible, deepest and most profound of all books, still does not speak in terms of the presumed complexities of science but rather in the timeless terms immediately recognized in both antiquity and the modern. Jesus reached the zenith of this approach, and it is easily noticed when we perceive that daily He spoke and taught in understandable and timeless terms. Continually, He referenced the plainest and simplest of these, and nowhere more in evidence when He spoke of two of life's most basic elements, bread and water. It is to the former that we devote this brief examination.

Bread is a simple, multi-faceted wonder, that has been existent since the commencement of time. Its form, flavor, complexity and taste are practically limitless but let us look upon the basic bread of a typical first century Jew. Its basic inventory of ingredients were indeed sparse with its primary substances being water and flour, likely wheat or maybe even barley. The baker combined the two, kneaded what became dough, and waited for her concoction to "rise" before baking it. Yet, from where did the element of "rise" itself arise, from magic, spirits, demons, etc? Of course not, for it came from yeast, or as the older English translations express "leaven." The yeast came from several sources; itself being a fungus which would appear on the leaves of certain plants, or perhaps a modicum of the substance being found in the flour itself or sometimes just exposure to the open air. Proper usage would prompt the flattened dough to arise and be baked into the loaves and pastries so prized by modern consumers and connoisseurs, but risen none the less. (The appetizing breads so prized in modern Western culture did not become common until the development and perfection of a type of yeast by the Hungarian Jew turned American, Charles Fleischmann, in the late nineteenth century.)

Leaven changes everything, and the alteration is thorough and within exception. Christ, as was His way, expressed such in this short, almost terse, parable:

> "The Kingdom of heaven is like unto leaven,
> which a woman took,
> and hid in three measures of meal,
> till the whole was leavened."

The construers and interpreters of this parable have long debated the exact quantity of "three measures," from anywhere ranging from three to sixty pounds of dough. Actually, this seems to have an essential irrelevancy since the true measuring is obtained by grasping the simple fact that just a few grains of yeast, a fine, granular, even powdery substance can change a mass much greater than itself.

Christ is this simplest of parables expressed a universal truth that spans a kaleidoscopic spectrum of topics and issues. Just as leaven makes an unformed mass of bread and water appetizing and edible just a trace of certain poisons may instantly slay a large, strong man. A few well-spoken words in a flood of oratory may change a man or woman's heart, character and trajectory of life. The examples of these and many more are close to endless, but we focus no one, that which is really the subject and soul of Christ's one sentence parable. The Son of God Himself is the leaven, the subject of His own parable. He was born into a poor and obscure provincial Galilean family at a time when geographically, culturally and spiritually the two poles of the wide world He inhabited were Rome and Jerusalem. Rome, the mightiest military and cultural power on earth bestrode the world as an unchallengeable colossus, and the Jewish religious hierarchical establishment centered in Jerusalem retained a spiritual chokehold on its own people. Jesus of Nazareth, but one man, was the Son of God, the leaven who forever changed it all.

Christ was and is the Leaven of Truth, and this one life forever altered the great heretofore unshaped structure of life and existence itself. Yet the small conceptual context of His parable cannot express the full extent and magnitude of its author. He is the leaven in the loaf, but Christ is the Bread itself, for He had proclaimed that:

> "I am the Bread of Life:
> he that cometh to Me, shall never hunger;
> and he that believeth on me shall never thirst."

God, who created man, knew that His creation was ever hungry, and especially after his Edenic fall he was in the straits of desperate starvation. His pinnacle of creation had fallen, broken, and in need of reconciliation, a reconciliation achievable only through His Son, the bread of life. Mankind needs nothing less, and just as certainly he needs nothing more. In the fictionalized but dramatically spellbinding words of the currently popular television drama, "The Chosen," Jesus spoke to a certain desperate man that "... you only need Me." All men and women are starving, most are spiritually emaciated, and only the leavened Bread of Truth accords true sustenance.

A standard and prolifically common interpretation of this parable has always been that Christians, no matter how few, are the leaven in the unformed, spiritually inchoate vastness of society that nonetheless, even with their dearth of numbers, may alter and change that society and its culture for the better. With this generally enunciated proposition our brief essay offers no argument. Still, it appears that the more powerful and cogent position is that Christ Himself is the leaven in His own parable. It is consistent with its teaching and in no way is it meant to trivialize when the claim is presented that a little teaching of Christ goes a long, long way.

The history of Christianity is the last few generations cannot be fully and accurately related without a recognition of the missionary and evangelistic efforts of countless men and women in (at least to Western civilization) the far reaches of the world. In major part this has been the realization of Christ's Great Commission to life and has overlaid much of the world with Truth and Christian morality. Sometimes, and by many persons, in many places and in many fashions the zeal may have malformed itself into a passion of ordering the details of person's lives in a manner at least faintly reminiscent of the scribes and Pharisees with whom Jesus contended. Christians have sought often to be more than planters and servers of the seed and the leaven but also to straitjacket the new Christians in manners best left to Christ. The Savior is the leaven that expands a person's heart and character, and as the apostle Paul, history's greatest evangelist once remarked, we may water the seed, but it is Christ "who giveth the increase." It was this same Paul who boasted that he and his companions "preached Christ and Christ crucified."

The disciple's charge remains the same as it was in the first century, to preach, teach and disseminate the leaven of Christ. At the risk of being misunderstood the assertion is made that our teaching should be more Christ and less Church. Such is not in any way meant to be heretical. The Church is so important that Christ gave His life for its establishment. It is His Body, a beautiful and glorious "Bride of Christ," but the Church has saved nary a soul. The Savior is Christ. He is the leaven that changes the lump of unformed dough, any person, place or institution. The Christian is the conduit for the Truth, and to employ archaic terminology within the structure of the parable Christians are the "baker's helpers," for the leaven effects the real change. The Christian offers companionship, fellowship, friendship and love, but the sustenance of life itself remains the Savior.

Endless Persistence
Luke 18:2-8

The Lord's followers, from Genesis to the present, have sometimes wondered if He hears and responds to their prayers, plea and petitions. Not God's enemies, His scorners and mockers, but His disciples. Moreover, the Almighty has never for a moment lost sight of this reality, and through James, the actual earthly brother of Jesus, He assured us that:

"The effectual fervent prayer of a righteous man availeth much."

Yes, but how long must the Christian pray, must she be in spiritual agony and suffer the slings and arrows of this world before Divine relief is granted. Jesus knew the concerns of His disciples and so presented them with a parable of some density, which quite honestly, can seem somewhat obtuse. A widow came before a judge or magistrate with a cause of action and pleaded for justice and restitution from an adversary who had grievously wronged her. Unsurprisingly the judge who had jurisdiction was a deplorable man, "… one who feared not God not regarded man," a stratus the ubiquity of which has not diminished with the passage of two millennia. For so long her pleadings to "avenge me of mine adversary" continually fell upon his deaf, judicial ears until finally he admitted to himself that although he had no regard for either God or man, he would hear her case because she "wearied" him. She received her desire, although it required her importuning a bad man and an indifferent judge for a lengthy time. So Christ adds the wording which makes to parable have meaning:

> "And shall not God avenge His own elect,
> which cry day and night unto Him,
> though He bear long with thee?"

Often legal and judicial proceedings move at a glacial pace before any resolution. Lifewise, God's answers to prayers are not immediate and certainly not immediately conclusive. The terrestrial civil matters proceed at the pace of the courts, while God's answers come in His time. Yet, they will come, for they have always come, whether to Moses, Elijah, the apostles any and all of His children and to His own Son. The pace of courts, judges and the legal system can be maddingly slow, while that of the Lord of the Universe slow to unfold. But always the answers come, and the author makes this averral upon a foundation of decades as both a practicing lawyer and a practicing Christian.

Christ concluded His thoughtful parable with both a statement of promised relief and a question:

> "I tell you that He will avenge them speedily;
> Nevertheless, when the Son of man cometh,
> shall He find faith in the world?"

A large segment of the Christian's faith is the bedrock belief that the disciple is blessed by God above all other men and women. So he or she is, but often the Christian bears the burdens of persecution that the world inflicts, yet does not itself suffer. In the parable both God and the magistrate are cast in the roles of judges, but quickly the likenesses and similarities between the two begin to dissolve. The magistrate hears the widower's case only to "get it over with" and halt her ceaseless pleading. God offers Divinely judicial relief "speedily," but the speed is synchronized to His determination of time, patience and justice. He cares about the wronged litigants, for He and He alone can and will avenge them. The magistrate is a truly exemplary figure of worldly authoritarianism not authority. He grants judgment only because it solves his problem of the nagging widow and benefits him. This parable, often swept aside in study, has been a conundrum to many serious scholars. At a minimum the Christian, though, may rejoice in an understanding that whatever the world gives it comes from a bitter, begrudging heart. What the Savior and the Father give is from wise, prudent love.

CHAPTER SEVEN

FISHES IN THE WEEDS

One of the blessings of living in pre-modern times was the luxury, doubtless unappreciated at the time, of living in a world in which its residents were spared the agony of a constant bombardment of statistics, from which we moderns, alas, suffer in the twenty-first century. Statistics there are aplenty which measure every activity of the human, the beasts of the field, the creatures of the deep, nature and its elements ad infinitum. Ceaseless numbers, formulae and predictions, usually of chaos and doom, are generated in daily life by statisticians and their "algorithms," the latest catch word (ugly though it may be) that has been invented to measure and describe human behavior. We are blessed, though, with contemporary observers of the ancient world who spoke not in mathematical formulae, physics or algebraic equations, but rather in simple terms based upon life's observations. It is unsurprising that the master of this was the Master of all things heaven and earth, Jesus of Nazareth.

The Savior well knew the world which He helped create, this same sphere of life and living in which He dwelled for but one generation. Never did He lure His audience with dry, desiccated numbers and statistics, but He knew them to the nth degree. Living in tiny Galilee in the Roman province of Judea Christ could easily surmise that a solid majority of His fellow Galileans and Jews made their living through one of two occupations, farming and fishing. His inner coterie of twelve apostles bears eloquent witness, inasmuch as a likely majority of this dozen were fishermen by trade. Further, He could always look around Him and see verdantly productive fields of crops which were planted and tended by farmers, and innumerable villages and small cities that were developed around the fishing and farming trades. It is little wonder that the Master Teacher generated copious usage and examples from two occupations which the majority of His listeners thoroughly grasped. These trades were not just their livelihoods, but also the tableaux of which was painted their understanding of life itself. As bright a realization of Christ's teaching method as may be found is located in one of the gospel's great parabolic chapters, Matthew 13, where Christ places almost back-to-back the scenarios of water and soil to teach similar (but not quite identical) lessons, in two parables commonly described as the parables of the net and the tares.

Parable of the Net
Matthew 13:47-50

Is fishing work or recreation? Modern society with its plentitudes of production and leisure time most decidedly will opt for the view that fishing or angling, can be one of life's greatest pleasures, even though like almost everything else, it is not for everybody. Many individuals, men and women alike, plan weekends and vacations around fishing trips to lakes, rivers, streams and mountain locations. Whether they have a taste for fish or just revel in an outing in nature, sometimes in a peaceful bucolic setting, a magnificent lake or in a clear, clean, beautiful mountain stream their thoughts, yearnings, time and money are devoted to the pleasure, relaxation and recreation of fishing. Kept within its boundaries delimited by life's obligations and responsibilities fishing is a wonderful recreation which only the most churlish would begrudge their fellow men and women.

The solitudes or if one prefers the convivial fellowship of friends and family is both a real but at times idealized view of fishing. The world in which we live is two-thirds water, and this water, salt or fresh, is the home to an abundance and volume of fish greater than the standard terminology at our disposal to express. This is a good thing, for the stark truth is that the world's appetite for fish, whether from preferences of taste or of necessity, is ravenous. These fish and in these essential numbers are not caught by elegant fly-fishing rods or the bob of a cork on the surface of a quiet pond, but rather they are ensnared in volume. They are caught, harvested and processed industrially by men on ships and boats all over the globe's watery surface. From the frigid and turbulent waters of the North Sea, the fishing grounds off the coast of Newfoundland, New England and the icy waters of the Pacific that lap the coasts of Alaska to the tropical and sub-tropical heat and storms of the South Pacific and South Atlantic commercial fishing for sustenance and profit is dangerous. Everything done on the water is dangerous, for death always lies outside the immediate confines of the boat or ship. So it was and is in the little freshwater lake in northern Palestine, perhaps the most famous body of water in the world, the Sea of Galilee. Here, two thousand years ago Jesus called His first apostles, a group of fishermen who had just experienced a very bad, depressing night of arduous labor in which they had caught no fish. Anyone who has ever baited a hook or cast a lure into the water and been rewarded with nothing more than a wet hook or a damp lure understands this emotion. But these men were not baiting hooks nor were they casting lines, but rather they were dropping fishing nets as deep into the water as possible hour upon hour, cast upon ever increasingly fatiguing cast, and all with no results. This was more than the disappointment of not having fish for dinner on the morrow. Too many sessions such as this meant occupational and financial ruin, ultimately financial hardship and penury for themselves, their wives and their children. No catch of fish meant no living, no food, and ultimately and most terrifying, no money to pay the oppressive tax burden exacted by the Romans, who had shown little sympathy to the problems of the Jewish working man.

Early one morning two fishing boats, vessels that were emotionally flying the flag of failure, had come to the shore of Galilee, but only after a long backbreakingly weary night of fishing failure. The fishermen, those named being two sets of brothers, Simon (Peter) and Andrew and James and John with Zebedee, the father of the latter pair, were ashore tending their nets. A rugged looking young man but one with a kind and welcoming countenance spoke directly too Simon with a pregnant promise of success:

> "Launch out into the deep, and let down your nets for a draught."

Disappointed, disconsolate and dead tired they answered with a negative rejoinder that they had been fishing all night without success but "...nevertheless at thy word I will let down the net. The haul of fish was so enormous that each boat began sinking, and it required the full complements of each vessel to harvest the fish. These men after the abyss of abject failure had netted the greatest catch of their lives. As great as was their catch, though, it was the man on the shore the director of this operation who netted the greater, for in one incident Jesus of Nazareth had enticed and enlisted four great foundational parts to His work, the apostles Peter, Andrew, James and John. With this miraculous catch of fish foundational building blocks of His Church were being lain.

A night of rigorously hard toil led to a morning of despair and gloom for the fishermen, the soon to be "Fishers of Men," and Christ's cadre of followers had been historically strengthened and buttressed. At the risk of being accused of assuming a supercilious air about a great and a sacred moment we pose the question, "but what about the fish." In defense of the posing of this question we offer Christ Himself who likely had this moment in mind when he offered our subject parable of the net:

> "And again the kingdom of heaven is like unto a net,
> that was cast into the sea,
> and gathered fish of every kind.
>
> Which, when it was full, they drew to shore, and sat down,
> and gathered the good into vessels, but cast the bad away."

The Sea of Galilee, that illustrious and gloriously famed body of water has a modern-day surface area of a little over one thousand square miles, certainly a good-sized lake but tiny compared to many others and especially to the Earth's oceans. This lake has been modern reckoning (i.e. credit to Wikipedia) a total of twenty-seven types of fish, but only ten of which are edible and of any value to humanity. The good fish are mainly types of tilapia, still common and popular, and the bad valueless. Very interesting (or perhaps your proclivities lead to very boring) but of what value is this in a lesson on parabolic understanding. As usual, it is Christ Himself who provided the answer. The Master provided the answer when He explained His parable's meaning and lesson:

> "So shall it be at the end of the world;
> the angels shall come forth, and sever the wicked from among the just.
>
> And shall cast them into the furnace of fire:
> there shall be waiting and gnashing of teeth."

The harshness of this explanation and foretelling clashes with the sensitivities of modern ears which have become accustomed to the imagined softness and omni-forgiveness of the Prince of Peace. These terms are not utilized in mockery of the Savior, but instead are meant to illustrate that there exists a punishment for evil, a subject on which Jesus Christ spoke more than any other Biblical character. Yet, just who are these "bad fish" that will be cast into a lake of fire (or more precisely hell)? A proper response to this question appears to be the very heart of Christ's parable.

The cornerstone of the foundation of judging humans, or fish as Jesus has so deftly illustrated, is that in the end it is beyond the reach and ken of humanity. Judgment belongs to Christ because this authority was given Him by His Father. By His life, His teachings, and His grace we know His will, but justice, eternal judgment, belongs to God alone. This is the superstructure of meaning to be given one of the most popularly quoted Bible verses that we "judge not, lest we be judged."

Parables are rarely fashioned by Christ to be received by His followers in the most literal sense, but neither should we ever stray too far in our interpretation from the original template of words which Jesus has provided us. With this in the forefront of our thoughts let us examine the words and their intended meanings as so provided by the Master. Those of us who are extant Christians are the fishers, the casters of the nets meant to draw in more fish. The net is the Word of Christ for it remains the only means by which the hearts and minds of listeners can be attracted, taken, and held in the boat, metaphorically the Church. The Word or Truth is a substance of absolute purity, for it is interchangeable in meaning with Christ Himself. Its beauty, though, is that it may be presented and offered to the would be adherent in some fashions. The net of the Word, the Truth, may be cast by direct evangelism of which the apostles and a few other Biblical worthies such as Stephen, Barnabas, and Apollos were exemplary masters. It may be cast by private one-to-one teaching, or in a small classroom or any other sites in which the disciple intersects with the world. Maybe most commonly, most effectively and most overlooked is that the nets are cast by simple Christian example and above all, by prayer. Still, though, as vitally and important as these points of evangelism we sense that the parable's foremost purpose is found elsewhere. This is where and when the fish are reeled or hoisted into the boat. Some are good fish, tasty, vital and nutritious, and unfortunately some which become entangled in the net are "trash," fish, of no value to anyone.

The simple, unvarnished truth of Christ's parable is that so often we cannot tell the good from the bad. The individual Christian, no matter his/her age, maturity and experience can still be hoodwinked. Even a multiplicity of mature Christians may have a variance, an important gauge of measurement, about other Christians. Our wisdom is limited, finite, and even the most Solomonic of our number may be prone to mistake-ridden judgments. Only the Master, the Son of God, has the wisdom, the perfection of judgment which allows Him and only He to make astute, absolute judgments about individual Christians. His disciples charge is to catch the fish, the would-be disciple, but in the end, as with all Matters, Jesus will make everything right and sort out and dispose of the bad fish.

Nothing in this parable nor this construction of it is meant to be detrimental to the keeping of harmony and unity within the Church. The scriptures are later quite specific on how certain "disorderly" conduct is to be handled. Christ's parable of the fish, though, is spot on the mark when it implants the directive that His disciples, we Christians, ancient or modern, are to be as He charged His apostles "fishers of men." We fish, evangelize, teach, fellowship and love, but ultimately it is God alone who judges and only with a lachrymose outpouring of bitter tears casts out the bad fish. This section concludes with an old homily, but trite as some may be many have a certain dynamism of truth. Man proposes, but it is God who disposes.

Parable of the Tares
Matthew 13:24-30, 36-42

The houses, mansions and for the royalty, palaces, of Europe for centuries have been noted for the beauty, at times stunning with overwhelming splendor, of their gardens, paths, walkways and lawns. Paintings and in the modern era photography have often captured the green verdancy of lawns that have an almost sensual splendor to them. To many persons these earthly patches of beauty are the apotheosis of earthly perfection, and reflective of charm and gracious, even elegant living. They are also reflective of long, intense labor and expense, labor rarely performed by royalty or the aristocracy but rather by humble employees. Still, they are beautiful and much admired. For all their fame and magnificence they actually represent a golden age of a certain style of living, an age long since faded.

While the age of aristocracy may be historically relegated to the past the golden age of the "lawn" shone through in post-World War II America and shows few signs of having abated. Lawn and garden care and suburban and exurban life have for decades become two sides of the same prosperous coin. Men and women, mainly, though not exclusively middle and upper middle class, spend hours compelled by some combination of pride, love of nature, adoration of aesthetic beauty and the prestige of recognition to create an immaculately trimmed, lusciously green patch of earth where they can spend many hours of pleasure, neighborhood and familial conviviality or just the simple satisfaction of imbibing the fruits of labor for a job well and beautifully done. Certainly, nature, the owner's health, financial difficulties or assorted problems must have their accounting as the lawn's enemies, but the diligent landscaper and homeowner is ever conscious of perhaps the plainest, simplest but most powerful enemy of his lawn, the simple and humble weed.

The types, species, shapes and sizes of weeds which torment American gardeners and landscapers are legion in their number. Such green irritations as crabgrass, Johnson grass, spurge, henbit, clover and chickweed may overwhelm the serious tiller of the soil with their ubiquity. Each year vast sums of money are expended on herbicides and other chemicals and likely the amount of labor which landscapers devote to eradication of the humble but tenacious weeds would be enough to construct a small city. Still they persist and still weeds remain in lawns, frustrating the landowner and tainting the beauty of the landscape. For all this, though, in actuality it is the extent of the lawn weed's detriment and damage. Nature, though, ever persistent still produces another type of weed that is far more devastating to humanity. This is the weed that imposes and implants itself in good crops, choking the life from them and diminishing and even eliminating the nutrients necessary for survival. In the New Testament it is called the "tare," and it is the persistent, oft hidden, deadly foe of true productivity. Christ introduced them into the scriptural text and reminded His audience, perhaps a majority of whom were farmers, of the lethality of this simple plant, as He spoke:

> "But while men slept, (the farmer's) enemy came and sowed tares among the good seed in his field."

It is a rare climate and land which is untouched by the growing grain, especially that of wheat, which is here mentioned. Even the most secluded and benighted denizens of the urban centers generally can recognize a stalk of wheat with its life growing seeds. But what is the tare of which the Master warns? The tare was and remains a weed which bears a remarkable resemblance to wheat. While most picture wheat as a beautiful golden grain wafting in the breeze it is that only in its maturity. For most of its life the stem of wheat is green, as is the tare, or "darnel," the plant it is believed to reference. In structure and color it is almost identical to the wheat, yet the proof of difference lies in the end production. It has a seed pod, but its grains are worthless, while the wheat gives us the "staff of life" itself.

We implore the reader's patient forgiveness with the infantism of our expression – wheat is good, but tares are bad. The instinct of the farmer, even the most sagacious and experienced is to remove the tares immediately. That same sagacity and experience, though, informs him that to do so roughly and too quickly will also destroy quantities, perhaps in large volume, of the wheat. The farmer will come to regret quick, hasty action, however well-intentioned it may be, that destroys a portion of his valuable crop. Christ's example of the farmer is, in fact, truly exemplary, for when his servants implore him to destroy the tares he wisely responds:

> "Nay, lest while ye gather up the tares,
> ye root up also the wheat with them."

He tenderly reminds his servants that he alone is master of the harvest and that the harvest of the crop comes at the end:

> "Let both grow together until the harvest:
> and in the time of harvest I will say to the reapers,
> Gather ye together first the tares,
> and bind them in bundles to burn them;
> but gather the wheat into by barn."

The essentiality of one of the main lessons here taught in this parable has not been neglected in the development of the English language, which contains many sayings and truisms such as "all that glitters is not gold" or "you can't judge a book by its cover." Christ had no reticence in explaining the meaning of this parable and its cast of characters when He plainly explained that:

> "The field is the world;
> the good seed are the children of the kingdom,
> but the tares are the children of the wicked one."

Be patient, He consoles and instructs His apostles and all Christians everywhere for all time, for I, the Son of God, shall render justice in the end, in My time, when I will make all things right. With sad regret and some bitterness the sincere Christian must lament that the past two-thousand-year history of Christianity often has revealed an opposite story.

This chapter may only in an abbreviated, even truncated form, explain how Christ's admonition has been ignored throughout most of the history of Christendom. False doctrine, untruths about Christ and His Church are identified in the New Testament and firmly, at times sternly, taught against by Christ and His apostles. Yet so is the spirit of sectarianism and division which has plagued Christianity for its two-millennium existence. Perhaps unsurprisingly since the apostles were among the very first disciples, they are the first to be corrected for showing the sectarian spirit. Early in the Savior's ministry, John, the specially beloved apostle came to Jesus and informed Him triumphantly:

> "Master, we saw one casting out devils in Thy name:
> and we forbad him, because he followeth not with us."

Thus, the sectarian spirit had not yet been totally extinguished among the dearest of the apostles, and Jesus responded:

> "Forbid him not: for he that is not against us is for us."

Theologians, scholars and good, sincere Christians yet debate the fullness of this statement's meaning. Within our parabolic context may we not safely assert that where John saw a tare, Jesus saw wheat.

The unfortunate history of what was once called Christendom is a narrative in part of divisions and schisms and of various types of tares which did, in fact, greatly damage and even contaminate the Body of Christ. We have neither the space nor the inclination to go into the various and fierce, even to the point of violence and grotesquerie of the upheavals of the 1400's, 1500's, and 1600's, the era of the Enlightenment, the Protestant Reformation, the Catholic Counter-Reformation and the religious wars, most notably the Thirty Years War of the 1600's. Here, men, and not a few women, literally took up arms to butcher and bloodily uproot and remove the perceived heretics, the tares as each person saw it, which plagued the "true" Church, again as each saw it. The tare removal became so cruel and obscenely violent that centuries later many of these events are utilized to disgrace and disparage Christ and His Church.

With His parables of the net and the tares Jesus was in the full glow of His Divine wisdom and splendor. Each parable is a commission to the devoted, faithful Christian and the Church to teach, live and exemplify the message and life of the Church's founder and Rock, Christ himself. They are heralds to cast the net, sow the seed, to be "... instant in season and out of season" and to make His Church the beautiful Bride of Christ that the Master Himself founded, rules and loves. As certain as the east is removed from the west, most assuredly Christians and the Church are charged with teaching and living the Truth. Completely they are also given the duty of revealing and disclosing lies, corrupt meanings and that Biblical ubiquity of "false doctrine." That charge, though, is not inclusive of tossing the fisherman's catch back into the waters or of violently rooting up tares, and more dangerously perceived tares, so that much of the good wheat may be damaged or destroyed.

Admittedly, at times the Christian and the Church must walk a fine line. Christians and the Church's leadership are given no license to ignore trouble or false teachings within the Body of Christ in any form. The New Testament is replete with warnings and admonitions regarding "wolves in sheep's clothing" and the pernicious effects of teaching that may be melodious to the ear but proves to be chaotic and destructive in practice. The great counterpoint, though, is that in the words of Christ in His great Sermon on the Mount, a phrase perhaps quoted more than any other in the Bible is that we are to "Judgment, that ye be not judged," and even with more impact that "we condemn not, and ye shall not be condemned."

The two great parables of the net and the tares teach so many valuable lessons, not least of which is the omniscience and omnipotence of Christ and the Father and the finite limits of even the best of men and women in judging others. We leave them with assurance, though. The strong net of Christ never loses a fish, and the harvest of wheat will be great. The penultimate chapter of the Bible comforts with the words which an old human renders "... no tears in heaven." As there are no tears, neither will we find tares.

CHAPTER EIGHT

LOST AND FOUND

The Christian believes that the story of life in this world and in the eternity of the next is that we have a Savior who has paid the price of sin with His own blood, redeemed us and reconciled us to God. It is the bedrock foundation of faith, and the words Savior and save are ubiquitous in the scriptures, especially in the New Testament. An old maxim of many languages and in various wordings pronounces the fact that "... he who says A must say B." Truly, this is more than a cleverly worded snappy statement. Jesus Christ assumed the role of our Savior, but to save from what? We gladly steel ourselves against any accusations of triteness to state simply to save us from being lost. No reference books nor concordances have been consulted but a familiarity with the Bible suggests that its text and stories speak as much about being lost as they reflect about being saved.

The story of being lost is an early theme which begins where else but in the beginning in the opening volume of Genesis. With the Fall mankind was lost, Adam and Eve driven into strange hostile territory east of Eden and now were living and laboring under an extremely harsh and novel set of conditions for which their Edenic lives had given them no inkling and no preparation. Now, humanity had to find its way in a new realm without the Divine protection of the old. Soon, their first son Cain would discover what it meant to be lost in a hostile world. After committing the world's first murder by the slaying of his brother Abel he was condemned to roam the earth, shiftless, rootless, the original pioneer of homelessness and lost to anything good.

So it continued through Genesis and on through the multi-thousand-year period covered by the Old Testament. In the words of the Savior, except for a tiny nation, a heritage of Abraham, all men and women were lost and in darkness without the illumination of true Light. They, and we, were lost. Yet, what really does it mean to be lost?

Before we enter the realm of Biblical theology let us ponder the previous paragraph's question in the exemplary arenas which all men and women have lived and almost instinctively understand. One of the greatest examples of being lost is an event in which all of humanity has participated and yet no one retains any cognitive memory. The first nine months of life after conception the baby spends in the safest environment which he/she will ever experience, the mother's womb. Emerging into the world is a traumatic and terrifying experience, as anyone who has ever seen a newborn's shock and protest will recognize. The infant is lost, the warm, safe, security of the womb never replaced and so it never shall in this world. But a concerned mother and father, attending nurses and other caregivers begin to alleviate that terror of being lost. But it always returns and always in childhood does this terrifying fear of abandonment and loss, even though temporary, plague the child. Even with growth and maturity that lurking terror of being lost clings to the child. All have experienced the trauma of the realization when we as children have turned and seen, even but for a moment, no parent, no older sibling, no one, to protect us. Almost all children are found, most within a few moments, but it is unlikely the remembrance of a trembling terror ever departs.

Not with the human infant alone is the terror of being lost and along to be seen. To keep our discussion within reasonable limits the worlds of the two domestic animals closest to humans must have their reckoning. These, of course, are the cats and dogs which begin as kittens and puppies. Along with the human infant the newborn puppy or kitten is the very picture and essence of innocence. Just as certainly they are the epitome of the weak and helpless. Continually they cling to their mother (and she to them) for nourishment, comfort, warmth, shelter and love. After they have mastered that first segment of life, they become bolder, more playful and in their minds more capable. They tumble, tussle and chew upon their toys and upon each other sometimes with a yelp or a meow, of assumed courage and bravado. Should their mother be absent, even briefly and momentarily, their emotions coalesce into but one, the fear of abandonment, of being lost.

This brief introduction to loss has so far been decidedly one sided, for it has aimed to introduce the subject from the viewpoint of the lost. It would wreak of short-sightedness and half-coverage were it to be left there. We have related that the scriptures are abundant with lessons on the lost and in particular the parables on which we now gaze. For every story of a lost animal, a lost son or a lost daughter a corresponding story of a grieving and suffering parent, ultimately God Himself, is offered. If the puppy or kitten feels the horror of being alone suddenly overcome his/her little emotions and previously secure world, so much greater may be the mother dog or cat's desperate search for her lost baby.

From time immemorial children have become separated from their parents, and even the gospels record the frenzy of Mary and Joseph when they believed their twelve-year-old son, Jesus, was lost. (the author has a distinct memory from over twenty years past when he witnessed the terror-stricken demeanor of a young mother, herself a highly accomplished physician who could not find her little toddler daughter in, of all places, church. The terror vanished and the joy was unconfined when the little girl soon appeared unharmed, to her parents). The illustrative memory yet lingers.

Unlike certain other fears, being lost is worse than even the fear and dread of being lost. The joy of reunion, of returning to the proper place and proper persons or perhaps even being there for the first time is a joy better experienced than described, except in the Bible. Some of the most moving and emotionally wrenching of Christ's parables cover the finding and return of the lost. They also demonstrate that in the spiritual no animal, no parent, no person of any sort or goodness suffers more from a lost child than does the Heavenly Father. Neither does anyone do more "to seek and save the lost." This chapter's short journey begins with the tale of a woman who has suddenly found herself to be somewhat poorer than she assumed.

A Parable of Diminished and Replenished Wealth
Luke 15:2-10

In almost every locale and at any time gold has been more valuable than silver, often overwhelmingly so. Still, silver as a precious metal retains a high value, so high that the customary title for this parable, the "lost coin" has been replaced with the current heading emphasizing value and wealth. Especially in modern life a single coin of any denomination has so little value that it is too weak a reed to support an argument based upon wealth. In Christ's short parable a woman has lost one of her ten silver coins, or more dramatically expressed 10% of her wealth. An impoverished person would likely give great notice to suddenly being bereft of 10% of her assets, but so it works much the same at the other end of the scale. Men such as Elon Musk, Bill Gates and Jeff Bezos boast of assets measured in the tens of billions of dollars, but it is likely a certainty that each would notice if 10% of those assets vanished in a moments time.

We would be remiss if we fail to know how often in all His teachings and especially in the parables did the Master utilize material matters to illustrate lessons. Unlike so many religions and their teachers it was Christ who exclaimed that while "... man does not live by bread alone" he must have bread. With the parables Jesus found His perfect vehicle to illustrate that while money and materiality are important, they remain secondary but still instructive to lessons of the spirit.

The lady in the words of Christ seems to be prompted to a type of diligent frenzy to find the missing valuable coin, as He poses the rhetorical question:

> "(I)f she lose one piece doth (she) not light a candle,
> and sweep the house,
> and seek diligently till she find it?"

In other words all her other work, responsibilities and desires instantaneously become secondary as she redoubles her efforts to find the valuable that is missing.

The simple truth is that money and material tangibles are important, actually quite important assets in life. Most men and women live whether consciously or unaware of their own thoughts with a fear of not having enough money. The Sermon on the Mount is full of references to human emotions of this ilk, and Christ was never bashful about utilizing these frets, fears and worries as substance for His teaching, especially by the parables. Here, it is only ten percent of the lady's money that has escaped her control. That one tenth is noticeable by any woman, regardless of her financial status. To a lady with limited, even finite resources it is cause for grave concern. The sincere reader, though, may still offer the question which goes somewhat as follows, "... yes, but do not nine coins yet remain?" Substitute the words "child" and "children" for "coin" and "coins" before the answer is given. In its larger, parabolic sense the lady who has lost the coin is Christ. While He remains joyous of the ninety percent who remain the one that is gone merits and receives the main portion of His attention.

The woman called for help from her neighbors, freely admitting her griefs and worries, and intensely begins the search for the lost coin. She illuminates her home by candlelight and diligently sweeps the floors. Surely Christ's story also will bear the weight of that classic phrase that "... she left no stone unturned." At last, the worries instantly turn to joy, the perspiration of worry on her brow ceases, and she rejoices when the coin is found, and her fortunes are again secure. Jesus was and is the Master of all things in heaven and earth, and He remains the Master of Words, as He then spoke:

> "Likewise, I say unto you,
> there is joy in the presence of angels of God
> over one sinner that repenteth."

The world and life, especially the modern world of speed, frenzy and technological marvels and not a few curses cares little for the sole woman or man and her/his "petty" financial problems. Even less does this world even notice or acknowledge her emotional and spiritual problems. Those of this one lady, or one man and even, perhaps especially, those of a child remain in the fore of Christ's thinking.

The joys of both Father and Son in the ninety percent that are safely within the Master's hand is not to be discounted. God, though, retains that comfort as a faithful parent daily revels in the continual comfort of the child who loves him and never falls or departs. The Father and the Savior have no diminution of joy in the knowledge that their family remains safely cloistered one within their loving grasp. Their joy becomes complete when the lost is found and rejoins those which were never lost.

The parable demonstrates the incredible arch, extent and reach of God's love. The Creator of the Universe is not content with but ninety percent, but as the woman of the parable, He seeks the joy of having the totality of that which belongs to Him.

<u>Appropriate Dress Required</u>
Matthew 22:2-14

Almost all cultures and societies require appropriate dress for appropriate occasions. Even in this the twenty-first century, in which many entire segments of culture have trashed the idea of proper dress a basic structure of respect for many, perhaps even most, segments of society may be noted. From the relative triviality of sports and games to the more serious sectors of life such as law enforcement and the military, not only is propriety but also uniformity of dress may be required. The chief of police and his ranking associates, the highest-ranking officers in the military and even the executives in large and small corporations retain the right to demand certain appropriate dress. For good or ill (and likely a combination of both) standards have fallen and are quite noticeable, especially in the venue of social occasions, such as weddings. While some weddings remain quite formal the modern traits, often exaggerated, of casualness and informality, are very much on display. Depending upon the level of society, the desires of the bride and usually her mother guests dress in any number of fashions, from the formality of business suits, tuxedos, lavish and beautiful dresses to clothing that is little more than is customary for a walk or a trip to the park. Yet, ultimately the guests do not determine the dress code or the style of fashion, as this remains the prerogative of the hostess (usually) or the host. It was no different in the time of Christ.

Jesus told the parable of a king who was planning to host a wedding for his son, a prince of the realm. The father dispatched his servants to invite and welcome his close associates to the magnificent wedding and reception that was in the making. The invited guests "made light of it," treating the whole affair as some type of joke while a "remnant" of his friends, for reasons best known to themselves, "...made light of it" and murdered his servants.

Disgusted, hurt and angered the king still wanted his son honored at the wedding feast and so now instructed his servants anew, but only after venting his rage and wrath upon the first invited guests. He "... destroyed those murders and burned their city," but still he desperately desired that his son be honored, even though the first invitees were unworthy. New directives were given the king's servants:

> "Go ye therefore into the highways
> and as many as ye shall find,
> bid them to the marriage."

So they did, and the royal servants gathered many "...both good and bad," and the wedding proceeded, and the reception and meal were a great success. The original guest list had effectively self-destructed, but the king and his son, the bridegroom had so many new friends and loyalties.

All on the guest list, whether the original group or the new invitees were free agents, all given the voluntary choice of whether to come. The first group rejected the offer, while many on the second accepted. Still, the terms and conditions of attendance were possessed by the King and his son, and they alone retained the decision of who was a "welcome" guest. In ancient Judean weddings and feasts, some which could go for days, dress was important. A guest was welcome only if he or she wore an appropriate "wedding garment," ultimately solely within the determination of the host.

Now, the bride and groom were married, conviviality, merriment and friendship reigned, and the King grandly and proudly strolled among his guests on this glorious day. Suddenly the great monarch was startled and temporarily ceased his rounds:

> "When the king came in to see the guests,
> he saw there a man which had not on a wedding garment."

Apparently and good heartedly believing that some misunderstanding or miscommunication could readily explain the guest's effrontery, kindly the king spoke:

> "And saith unto him,
> Friend, how commest thou in hither not having a wedding garment?
> And he was speechless."

In modern parlance this man was an interloper, a wedding crasher or a party crasher. He simply had no place at the wedding reception, but the question that demands answer is "why" or perhaps ore tersely, "why not?" Throughout it all the man had either forgotten or ignored, and probably some combination of the two with a strong dash of apathy thrown in the mixture, that it was the king's house, the king's son, and the king's prerogative to determine the conditions of attendance. To enter and avail himself of food, drink, friendship and hospitality but possessed of only an insulting manner of dress was the height of disrespect and effectively a taunt to the king. In Christ's own words the unwanted interloper paid dearly:

> "Then said the king to the servants,
> Bind him hand and foot, and take him away,
> and cast him into outer darkness;
> there shall be weeping and gnashing of teeth."

With deep reverence towards Christ's words still may we not remark that the man paid a stiff penalty for violation of the dress code? Actually, Christ's wording provides an excellent transitional phrase from the bare facts of the parable to its greater spiritual meaning.

From the moment of the Fall of Man to now humanity has in general believed that it has the right to dictate the terms of the relationship between itself and God. Succumbing to the serpent's temptation to "be as gods" man has generally substituted his judgment for the Divine. The grand story related in the scriptures and in this particular parable is the story of God's generosity and love in redeeming and reconciling men and women back to the Almighty. Here, unfortunately though, in the greatest of all stories, God's record is mostly failure, and this parable succinctly tells the story of man's belief that he has "found" himself while actually going deeper into an abyss of darkness.

The wedding's original invited guests spurned the king, just as the Old Testament is a narrative of the Chosen, the Jews, wholesale rejection of God. The remnant of which Jesus speaks, that group which in his story killed his servants, is the parabolic representation of the remaining Jews who still rejected, maltreated and persecuted God's prophets in the latter days before Christ. Certainly, the son is Christ Himself, rejected by the Chosen Jewish people and now offering Himself and salvation to the entire world, which now includes the Gentiles. In various and sundry ways God sought faith and obedience for which He now offers salvation through His Grace to any and all who are summoned. Yet, it must be on His terms, although mankind has always shown the proclivity to accept God on the terms dictated by man. The uninvited and unwanted guest is any man or woman who seeks an alliance and approval of God, but only on his own human terms. The king, the owner of the house, the father of the groom bids, welcomes and pleads for all to come to His house, but the entrance must be on God's terms. This speechless guest was not properly dressed, and in spiritual terms we are instructed that the sinner's wedding garment is Christ Himself, who he must put on in obedience. Without the Savior this guest, as all such others, has not found himself at the wedding banquet, but rather he has lost his soul.

The Lost Sheep
Luke 15:4-7

With apologies to all sheep and shepherds everywhere and for all time let it be announced that sheep, for whatever their attraction, are not intelligent animals. Actually, guided by the

Holy Scriptures and thousands of years of history it has become obvious that they are, with apologies, quite "dumb." Still, they have always held the securest of strongholds within the heart of God. In a book compassed over several thousand years, the Holy Bible, a compendium of among other matters a volume bursting with stories and lessons about animals, the humble sheep is supreme. Not only the sheep, but both testaments are built around stories of shepherds, their humble keepers and guardians. Abel, a faithful shepherd, was the first murder victim, and God called Abram, a man of wealth and great flocks, from Ur of the Chaldees. The two most written about characters of the Old Testament, Moses and David, each had substantial backgrounds as shepherds. The story of sheep and shepherds attains its pinnacle in the New Testament when the Son of God, Jesus, with no hesitation boldly proclaims Himself as both the Good Shepherd and the Lamb of God.

What is it about sheep that makes them so beloved to God and so exemplary in countless stories? Like all His creation of animals they are not only innocent but perhaps more to the point, they look innocent. At least in English, the phrase "innocent as a lamb" long ago passed into our vernacular. A sheep may do bad things, inconvenience or even hazard the life of its shepherd, but it does no evil, lacking the knowledge of good and evil. Moreover, sheep are not the most intelligent of creatures, and they demand constant attention from their shepherds, even the loyal associate of the shepherd, the sheep dog. Continually they stray and wander away or perhaps get lost in the same thickets and brush that has entangled them so many times before. To "ride herd" (yes, a cattle country expression) upon sheep requires endless perseverance, a diligent, hard-working master and a shepherd who places the health, safety and security of the sheep above all, even his own. Perfectly worded, beautifully expressed and enunciated is Christ's proclamation:

> "I am the good shepherd:
> the good shepherd giveth his life for the sheep."

Sheep, especially lambs, possessed of touchingly pristinely faces, constantly and dare we say, stupidly, always straying and getting lost. A sheep may stray from the herd and time and again follow the wrong path, and a good shepherd will notice immediately that his flock is diminished by the absence of that one sheep. It was this same Good Shepherd who told the short, simple story of a successful shepherd, a man who had a flock of one hundred sheep but who noticed that one of the flock was gone. The shepherd loved his sheep, but he was even more than their protector and benefactor. He was a businessman whose substance depended upon his flock, but now he was confronted with a dilemma. Should he leave the ninety-nine sheep, safe and secure, to seek the one who had foolishly strayed, or should he, in modern terminology, "write off" the one lamb, leaving it to the elements and predatory wolves? To the Good shepherd the answer was obvious. He would temporarily leave the main body of the flock, doubtless only after their safety and well-being was secured "... and go after that which is lost until he find it."

So the shepherd acted. He found his lost sheep and doubly secured it for the return journey back to the flock, as "...he layeth it on his shoulder rejoicing." The smiles, not just of joy, but of glee and jubilation, shone on the shepherd's face when he came home and announced to his friends and neighbors:

> "Rejoice with me; for I have found my sheep which was lost."

All this time, emotion, worry and ultimately joy was expended for but one little sheep, a creature who should not have strayed or been lost in the first place.

A common, to the point of overuse, trope in literature and drama, especially the modern and post-modern variety is to have a sober, faux-intellectual character express that "man is insignificant, and his existence meaningless when compared with the vastness of the universe." Wrong to the nth degree. The Creator of the Universe gave His Son for His creation and His disciples, the sheep that so often stray but remain intensely loved. When a single, lowly, humble sheep, an animal to whom all but its shepherd will say is of no account or maybe even just worthless is the passionate love of its shepherd. The parable, interesting though it might be, has but a limited value until it is the Good Shepherd Himself who pronounces its true meaning:

> "I say unto you,
> that likewise joy shall be in heaven over one sinner that repenteth,
> more than over ninety and nine just persons, which need no repentance."

The lesson is not that the safe, secure sheep are of less value, joy and love to the shepherd, but rather the joy which they bring him is constant and continual. But the flock, the family, is not whole without the lost sheep. It is only Christ who is possessed of the Divine gifts of allegorical understanding and expression who can reveal the rejoicing in Heaven over the lowliest (as if there were such a one) lamb, the sinner who rejoins the safety and nurture of the Shepherd's flock and fold. He is to be taken at His literal word when He, the King of Heaven, exclaims that the angels themselves rejoice when the lost and hurt lamb returns to the fold. Why the lamb was lost is not mentioned. Neither where nor how he was lost is given a word of explanation. The centrality of the parable is rejoicing is the radical change in the lamb's condition, from the dark, grasping, enclosing thickets of the world to the broad, sunlit uplands of salvation and Heaven. It is due entirely to the Good Shepherd, a man who had such confidence in His flock of ninety-nine that ne was confident that for a moment He could count on their faith and fidelity and devote Himself to finding and redeeming that one lost sheep.

These three parables of Christ are remarkably pure and inspiring stories of just that, purity and inspiration and of course, the joys of redemption and reconciliation. Among all others matters, the Master, Jesus of Nazareth, was the greatest author of stories and the most heart-stopping dramatist the world has ever seen, though He Himself wrote not a single word. His enunciation of these three parables is the perfect backdrop to His telling of another story of redemption, recollection and many other things, a parable and short story acclaimed by many as the greatest story ever told.

CHAPTER NINE

THE PRODIGAL SONS
Luke 15:11-32

This chapter originally appeared as Chapter 12, "Gains and Losses" in the work, <u>Bible Parents</u> (New Harbor Press, copyright 2018) by the same author.

The story has been told and retold, examined and re-examined so many times and in so many ways for two thousand years that even the strongest disciple may question whether anything is to be gained by revisiting its narrative. Even though it has often been called the single greatest piece of literature ever crafted is there any moral lesson or treasure yet to be mined from its rich seams? Actually, the succinct answer to this question is yes. As the apostle Paul once recorded this story's depths and riches are fathomless, for in a brief scenario and the employment of a few hauntingly moving sentences Christ paints a picture of family life and relationships that spans time, generations, races and cultures and draws characters with whom all can identify. It has been called by many titles but most frequently is it known as the Parable of the Prodigal Son.

A very wealthy father evidently possessed much land and controlled a fair amount of wealth, most notably in the persons of his two sons, the younger of which had reached the end of his patience, often a patience of very short duration with young men. The younger son, though, possessed two qualities that often are discovered in great abundance in young men, the desire to be independent and "on his own" and the burning desire to be free of any restraints, especially those of his father, to whom he now goes with a demand, a demand met by his father. The youth wants his inheritance now, and his father offers no resistance. Without compulsion of any sort the father divides the inheritance between both his sons. If he acted in accordance with Jewish law and custom the elder brother received twice the share of the younger. Nonetheless to the young man he had received enough so off he went free at last.

He went far from home and with money in his pockets it was everything he dreamed it would be. Farms offered only limited carnal delights, and besides he found himself with fellow sophisticates, witty, clever men and girls who knew how to have a good time, so he became the life and the banker of all events. Events – they have a manner of intervening unexpectedly, and so they did. He ran out of funds, likely sooner than later, and a famine ravaged the land. As Christ explained the youth's days of "riotous living" had passed and he was now bereft of so many things. His friends were gone, having vanished simultaneously with his money, homeless, hungry and most of all now totally lacking in pride or self—esteem. He, a Jew, born and bred, now took the lowliest most disreputable job that could be imagined. He became a feeder of swine, but even the pigs were better off than he for "...he would fain have filled his belly with the husks that the swine did not eat." It is so tempting to offer that the youth could not descend lower, but this is incorrect inasmuch as humans have an almost innate ability to sink deeper into a moral abyss. He did not, though, and Christ records that terse but meaningful phrase "He came to himself." Now, sitting in a filthy sty with the stench of swine assaulting his nostrils and his clothes stained by their effluvium "home" took on a different hue. It was now not the place of rules and restrictions, of arising in the morning to go to work and being surrounded by dull people, but rather it was the Edenic paradise where even the hired servants had enough bread "...and to spare." He now found true repentance when he examined his life and its options.

He is intelligent enough to know that one course only is left to him, and that is to return home; however, he knows that the return will not be as glorious as his departure, so he memorizes an introductory speech to deliver to his father:

> "and I will say unto him,
> Father, I have sinned against heaven, and before thee,
> And am no more worthy to be called they son:
> make me as one of they hired servants."

His journey home begins but travels not the entire route home. A long way from home his father espies him, runs to him, and in a moment of pathos collapses on the young man, kissing him and experiencing joy in its most unadulterated state this side of heaven. The son recites his spiel, but the father replies not with servitude but with honor and esteem. He is draped in a robe of fine fabric, the family signet ring placed on his finger and shoes on his feet. In the phrase that resounds yet today he directs the killing of the "fatted calf," and a party with music and dancing. For his son, once lost and dead is now found and alive. The father had been in an abyss of his own, a pit of worry and grief over the state of his young son, and the unending worry, pain, self-persecution and self-doubt over his own character. What kind of father was I to allow this to occur he must have inquired of himself incessantly. In the twinkle of an eye all this now vanishes in view of the joyous homecoming. This is the time for celebration as no father could treat this an as ordinary day. Any father or mother in even the most remotely similar situation recognizes and more importantly feels the inexpressible elation of the father. Such is not exclusive to parents, for it is close to the same exhilaration felt when any who are meant to be together, then apart are reunited. Further, as intense as these emotions are in the parent-child relationship, neither fatherhood nor motherhood is a requisite to the experiencing of such intense happiness. What a parable and what a story the Master has told. If this was the end of our narrative a great moral story it would remain to this day, and the Parable of the Prodigal Son would be taught as exemplary of the love and patience of God. We would marvel at the unsearchable depths of God's love and the grace He extends to the penitent believer, no matter the nature and course of his previous life and deeds.

But the Savior did not here end the story, and in point of fact has only told the half of it. To be a younger brother one must have an older sibling, and in this story, it is an older brother who now makes his delayed entrance. Commendably he has been working in the field, and as he returns to his home, he begins to hear the merriment and glee of festivities coming from the house. He stops short of the house and inquires of one of the family servants "what these things mean." The servant, undoubtedly over all that has transpired is glad to inform the elder brother that his younger brother has returned with the father proclaiming a celebration not only because of the return but also because he is now home "safe and sound."

The Bible is not a book of melodrama, nor does it contain even a hint of self-dramatics. The scenes given to us speak for themselves, but we are permitted some leeway in commentary on the action and the dialogue. To say that the elder brother was underwhelmed by this rapid recitation of events and the quickly changed atmosphere of the home is an understatement of colossal proportions. Instead of being happy that his younger brother has come home Christ succinctly states that "he was angry and would not go in."

As is most often the case the father makes the next move, comes outside to see his son and literally begs him to enter and join the party. Effectively, though, the father has now given his elder son a stage upon which to air his grievances, obviously long held and perhaps even in some eerie way cherished by him. He opens with an introduction that is simultaneously self-serving and one of the most outrageous falsehoods to ever be uttered:

> "Lo, these many years do I serve thee,
> neither transgressed I at any time thy commandment."

On its face this is as patently absurd a statement as an individual anywhere and at any time could make. No mortal person could ever rightfully claim to never having done wrong in any relationship, especially one as long, emotional and intimate as father and son. Yet this son is not deterred from such an outrage. Even his wording reveals his special insight into his standing with his father, for he employs the word "commandment." Maybe a small child will see the parent-child relationship as command-obey, but a grown man such as the elder son should have put aside this thinking long ago. The text reflects that he is rendering service to a loving, gentle father, not a harsh authoritarian master. It reveals that the older son, while performing dutiful service and work, has always viewed his relationship with his father bathed in a harsh, legalistic glare. He simply does not or will not understand the goodness of his father.

Returning to his assertion or having "never" transgressed, this signifies a moral egoism and hubris that may be even more common than is thought but still is rarely expressed so starkly. This son has created for himself a moral stage on which he is the only player of consequence, and has a childish resentment when others are honored or even considered.

He continues to tear down his façade as the self-designated good son with a statement dripping in self-pity:

> "...Thou never gavest me a kid, that I might make merry with my friends."

Before we proceed with further comment may we not raise a query as to what sort of "friends" a man such as this would possess? In the event self-pity and sorrow is a locale all persons visit from time to time, and it does not necessarily disclose or reveal fatal human weakness. What this remark discloses, though, is a spirit of false self-awareness and in the plainest of terms, a short memory. For however long the prodigality of the younger son was maintained for that same period the elder son retained a place of honor, position and esteem in the house of the father. While the younger brother writhed in the mud and filth of the pig sty the elder brother ate not with the servants but at the table of his father. His memory is somewhat selective as well, and for this we are reminded of Christ's construction of the narrative. When the younger son requested his inheritance, Jesus said, the father divided unto "them" the two brothers the estate. As noted by Jewish law and custom the elder brother had already been bestowed with twice the amount afforded to the younger. The elder's grief and petulance almost demands that we see this as an outburst of "What have you done for me lately?'

The elder son is still not finished with his father. As a viper sinks its fangs into its victim the son has venom to release when he again calls his father to task for celebrating the younger's return.

> "But as soon as this they son was come,
> which hath devoured thy living with harlots,
> thou hast killed for him the fatted calf."

Even the hired servant referred to the younger son as "your brother" but the elder son could only spit two words which became an epithet, "your son" not his brother. When these two words are read echoes of many millennia past resound as again, we hear Cain's response to God regarding the whereabouts of younger brother Abel, "...Am I my brother's keeper?' Fathers and mothers note such as this and in a brief two-word phrase he has given plain insight as to what he really thinks of his father's younger son, and by implication the father himself. In unbrotherly fashion he assumes the very worst of his brother in that "...he has devoured thy living with harlots." Possibly, maybe even probably, this was true, but he had no evidence of such as assertion. His younger brother had been away in a far country, and as for himself, he had even refused to go into the house and see him. True brotherly feeling does not assume the worst of a brother.

Christ's most famous parable reaches its conclusion, and we are left with a bittersweet taste. The father, ever gentle, ever loving, ever optimistic assures his son that he has not been shortchanged in fatherly love and affection, for "...thou art ever with me, and all that I have is thine." He defends his loving and even majestic greeting of his younger son by assuring the elder that the "dead" son was lost and "...now is alive" and "found."

Does there exist such an object as an accounting ledger for parents? Does a father keep a record of gains and losses among his children? Assuming that such a thing does exist, it is time to take the measure of this family. It will not and cannot serve as a final accounting for Christ left the remainder of the family's story untold. Yet at this juncture the status of the father and two sons begs for analysis and examination.

The younger son, invariably presented as the antagonist of the narrative, always has first claim on our disgust, anger and ultimately sympathy and happiness. He is, after all, the Prodigal Son. The natural first reaction to him, though, is one of revulsion and repugnance. The mature mind instantly grasps the foolishness and ingratitude of "demanding" an inheritance which he has not earned. Something else, though, do many minds in their maturity grasp as well, and that is some degree of identification with his arrogant demands. It is so natural for young men to wish to strike out on their own, establish their name and their independence. This is natural as breathing, but unfortunately the young, and especially young men, are great purveyors of ingratitude. This attitude seems to reach a type of pinnacle with the younger son. So off he goes, but the inheritance is not utilized for education or training, to buy a farm or a business, but is rather entirely consumed by the devouring hedonistic appetites of the son and his newfound friends. When the crash comes so come other traits. The reality of life's harshness, the realization of his own stupidity and sin and the recognition that only the Father can provide what he needs. He has been beaten down by life's frequent tremors and by his own folly but has begun to attain the one quality that is indispensable in God's eyes, humility. His pride led to his fall, and on his return home he arrives self-chastised and more than ready to mount the lowest rung on the ladder. He has abased himself, but in the words of Christ those that humble themselves will later be exalted. Satisfied to be a servant he comes home to sit at the table of the King, his own father.

In return to the Father could not have been made unless the Father was with the son in the beginning. Those portentous words of "He came to himself" reveal more than just a recognition of the trouble he had made for himself. To come to yourself implies that there exists some foundation, some moral structure that is always and ever present, regardless of the outward circumstances. That moral superstructure was provided by his father and in a very real way it was his father. Even at the nadir of degradation he knew that his father alone could be relied upon, and even here the younger son far underestimated the love and the strengths of that father. He was resigned to being a servant, but he had finally realized that in his father's house was an abundant supply of what the world did not provide "... and to spare." No doubt the young man's continued life was not an ever upward never interrupted arc into sunlit uplands, but for now he was home "...safe and sound." The father had gained a son.

For all the attention given the younger son these past two thousand years (and rightfully so) it is the older brother who provides a great breadth, depth and span of interest. Except when he relates an obvious falsehood, he should be given the benefit of the doubt and his word taken as face value. As a son and a man, he evidently was a hard and faithful worker, and in fact his appearance in Jesus's parable finds him apparently coming home from work. Of course, we must discard his representation that he had never violated his father's commandments, for no person legitimately may aver such a proposition. He possessed an abiding respect for laws, rules and family proprieties and was likely very dependable in almost all things. Still, these were not the only qualities which he could call his own. A self-satisfaction and self-assurance of his own "flawless" life deeply marred his character. He effectively usurped the position of his own father when he declared to him that his own sterling and longstanding high moral character merited a special reward. His sense of moral self-assurance allowed him to condemn his younger brother's supposed (but unproven and even lacking evidence) dalliance with harlotry, while in the same moment ignoring his own haughtiness in judging his brother.

Unfortunately, the elder's bitterness towards his younger brother has historically clouded and even hidden a greater character disgrace that he owned, an even greater bitterness towards his father. Serious parents notice serious remarks, and the older son's acerbic flippancy in referring to "your son" rather than "my brother" undoubtedly had the sting of a scorpion to the father. We require no depth of this family's history to realize that he is consigning the real blame for the younger brother to the father. It is "your" son, and you bear the onus of his failure. It is so tempting to create a balance sheet for the father and state that on the day he gained one son he lost another. This may be so, but it is perhaps more likely that the elder son was not lost on this day but was already lost in his own self-satisfaction, self-sufficiency and bitterness.

To a father, though, the elder son's greatest sin occurred not in rejecting his younger brother but rather what he did to his father. On this joyous, festive, emotional day, maybe the greatest of his father's life, the older son casts a heavy blanket of darkness over every laugh, every note of music, every glad heart by his morose hateful attitude. The father's joy in the younger is now mortgaged to regret and worry for the elder. Perhaps Christ was thinking of the elder brother when He remarked of the scribes and Pharisees:

> "(T)hey honoreth me with their lips, but their heart is far from me."

In the historical record of the telling of this parable one character only has received the title billing, the younger son, always known as the lost son or more commonly, the prodigal son. Yet it is the father and alone the father that emerges as the central figure, the one truly indispensable person in the story. Throughout the ages and in all stories, fact, fiction, metaphorical, allegory, etc. it is almost impossible to find a character as consistent as is the father. With a singularity of attitude which rises to all demands and situations we see that his main attribute is the spirit of giving.

At the outset when the impatient young son demands an inheritance that is unearned the father gives it to him without acrimony or chastisement. When the prodigal returns from his self-generated and imposed period of moral and physical exile the father overwhelms him by giving up an undreamt-of outpouring of love and forgiveness. He gives the young man a day of festivity where all join in the celebration of his unexpected return. While standing face-to-face with an older son, enraged and embittered, he gives understanding and consolation. The last act of giving perhaps is the most notable of all, for as he gives patience and tolerance, he receives insolence and vitriol.

From the beginning to end the father is concerned most of all with reconciliation, a reconstruction of relationships as they were originally meant to be. He has found reconciliation with the younger son and his joyous attitude sparkles and glitters to all. The elder refuses reconciliation with his younger brother and reveals that he and his father were never really of the same heart and mind.

For all, though, the story still ends with hope. In the wake of receiving his older son's tirade he assures him that all he possesses belongs to him as well. The father gives and forgives, with home and hearth ever open and beckoning. What a father he was and remains forever, and yet we have only revealing, but slight glimpses into His true character. What awaits is eternity where His beloved apostle, John, promises "...we shall see Him as He is."

CHAPTER TEN

MISTAKES IN SELF-ESTEEM: THE PHARISEE AND THE PUBLICAN
Luke 18:10-14

Certainly it is easy to be unsure when attempting to determine whether a story told by Jesus was "merely" a parable or instead a true story in the guise of a parable. One of the strongest candidates for the category of truth in the drapery of a parable is a story of a Pharisee and a publican who each came to the temple to pray to God, but in actuality each sought something different from the Father. This Chapter, while acknowledging freely that the story is described as a parable views the events and characters described by Christ as reality, due in no small part to the inconsistencies with character and the sharp contrasts between the men that invariably are more starkly drawn in real life than in fiction. Either way, though, it is a marvelous moral lesson which clearly illustrates many character traits and flaws, and also that unending but truthful proposition that matters, situations and persons are not always what they seem to be, and especially men and women are frequently suffering from moral self-delusion and false conceptions of their true character.

A pure exemplar of self-regarding, self-anointing, and dare it to be said, early first century Judean self-righteousness arrived at the Temple of Jerusalem to pray. If the story and the moral lessons were not so serious it would almost be comical to note the Pharisee's beaming pride in his accomplishments, that type of smugness and moral self-satisfaction that generations of school children have metastasized in that inglorious term of "teacher's pet." As the man proudly stands in the Temple he addresses God on an almost man-to-man comradely basis with:

> "God, I thank you that I am not as other men are, extortioners, unjust, adulterers or even as this publican."

The Pharisee with one introductory sentence seems to be preparing the Creator with a special treat, the visitation of a highly developed moral specimen such as himself. Still, he has an addendum to add to his prayer, which is actually more of a moral self-proclamation than a petition to God:

> "I fast twice in the week, I give tithes of all I possess."

This man was a marvel of morality and outward morality, and we have no grounds or reason to read into Jesus's parable any cynical underpinnings to his character. In the matters to which he directed prayerfully God's attention he was a paragon of righteousness, the very model of a sincere, observant Jew. Unfortunately, the Pharisee's prayer discloses one obvious, even glaring fault which may be summarized in that common, but often inaptly and overused phrase of "moral self-righteousness." His moral pride in an outwardly sterling character, no doubt born of much inner moral sincerity, bursts through all bonds of self-restraint when he plainly boasts of moral superiority with the repellent phrase of "... I am not as other men are." Even then he could not make this the term and point for his moral pride for he helpfully calls the Divine attention to the odious publican, a man, a Jew, who likewise has arrived at the temple to pray, yet with different words which themselves reveal a far different self-attitude.

Yes, the other prayerful petitioner of Christ's parable was a publican, and in the moral universe of Judea at this time practically the polar opposite of a Pharisee. In the public mind, the publicans were residents of the same moral swamp as were the prostitutes. They openly worked for the conquering Romans and were, in fact, the tax collectors for these invaders from the west. The publicans were the key components of a tax and revenue machinery which harshly ground down the longsuffering Jews. They collected exorbitant sums, sometimes brutally, often with threats and extortion, and the majority, though not the absolute entirety, of publicans well earned their loathsome reputations. And this publican, the subject of Christ's parable, had absorbed and knew all these facts in their most intimate detail:

> "And the publican, standing afar off,
> would not lift so much as his eyes unto heaven,
> but smote upon his breast,
> saying, God be merciful to me, a sinner."

With even greater assuredness it is averred with certainty that the publican was speaking the truth to God. All are sinners, and we all most desperately and definitely need the love of God. The publican, whatever his sins, here is admirable, for he acknowledged them and with an evident true spirit of humility, sadly lacking in the Pharisee.

The moral lessons Christians have drawn from this parable of contrast typically have been good and have been correct. The Pharisee, in public, reputation was a man gilded with coats of public esteem and admiration for being a member of the moral elite, the sect of the Pharisees, who with an overweening self-pride held themselves to be the moral pinnacle of society and in reality, possessed of a goodness exceeded only by a God who was far away. He may and likely was an overtly, publicly, good man and in many ways a moral example to many. Yet he was overcome by too much self-esteem, self-assurance, self-pride, and generally too much self, which diminished his standing before the Savior. The publican, though, of an offensive and loathsome reputation among his contemporaries, may have actually been the better man, especially in the realm of pride and humility. He knew he was in dire need of God, salvation and forgiveness, while the Pharisee seemed to feel that all he lacked was a Divine pat on the head from God.

Christ's moral pronouncement in His parable's is the following:

> "I tell you that this man (the publican) went down to his house
> justified rather than the other:
> for every one that exalteth himself shall be abased,
> and he that humbleth himself shall be exalted."

No speaker or writer has ever or will ever improve on the words of the great Master Himself, yet we are not enjoined but in reality are encouraged to delve as deeply as possible into the meaning. So we shall attempt.

A common frailty and weakness of mankind in his inexorable desire to compare himself and his worth, and it is as true for the ephemera such as any athletic field as it is for the vitally important, the essential moral character of an individual. Comparing the attributes and accomplishments of baseball and football players may be fun, even fascinating, but moral comparison has a spiritually lethal potentiality. In that occasionally wordy language at which he was adept the apostle Paul remarked:

> "For we dare not make ourselves of the number,
> or compare ourselves with some that commend themselves:
> but they measuring themselves by themselves,
> and comparing themselves with themselves,
> are not wise."

One aspect of the comparison carousel never to be ignored is that simple reality that each of us, most certainly including Christians can find someone worse than we are. This leads to the logical conclusion that save for only one of earth's inhabitants (who dwelled here two millennia past) we can also find someone better. Moral comparisons which include ourselves are futile. They may result in false pride, haughtiness, smugness, dangerous self-satisfaction, and at the spectrum's other end, depression, despair and despondency.

One of the keys to a fuller, if never complete, understanding of Christ's parable requires a more thorough examination of the characters of the two men who are its protagonists. A justifiable question is in the nature of how we can possibly discern much about two men from the Biblical offering of only two sentences to describe and delineate them. Fair enough. The scriptures, though, remain an eternal wonder in surpassing any man, woman, or their speech and writings by revealing so much with a sparseness of words. Let us examine this Pharisee and let us do so without neither a spark nor trace of either irony or sarcasm.

By descriptive definition the Pharisee was a spiritually minded man of seriousness, or else he would never have been a Pharisee, that strictest of all Jewish sects as described by their most famous member, the apostle Paul. No historical excursion into the depths of Jewish antiquity is required to understand that the Pharisees were proud to be Jews, members of the Divinely Chosen, and for generations they were well known to an enthusiastic adherence to the Law as they saw it. As a reader of the New Testament knows their devotion to the Law gradually evolved into a devotion to their own customs and traditions and the interpretations of the Law, which they had rigorously lain upon it. With all their faults, they were men of serious thoughts religiously, and in a world of flippancy towards the Divine and the permanent things this is always meritorious of admiration. Christ's parabolic Pharisee was a serious minded religiously observant man, all to his credit.

His prayer reveals that in an abundance of ways he was a Jew and a Pharisee not just in name only but also in observance, weekly, daily, even hourly observance. His own brief synopsis and summary of his life and activities is itself so informative. As a good Jew he was at the temple praying. Contrary to a partial, incomplete and therefore usually incorrect understanding of the man he made no great stir or outward show of his prayer. It is Christ Himself who tells us that although the man was in a public place his prayer was private to God, for he "... prayed thus with himself." It is axiomatic that a person who prays recognizes a Power greater than himself to which he willingly submits. In the context of the Savior's lesson it is easy to contemplatively accept that this Pharisee was a consistent petitioner to the Father.

So often it is expressed that so much of morality is expressed in the negative, and with this no sentient religious observer should have any quarrel. We think of the foundational Ten Commandments from the Old Testament, and the first three words that spring to mind are "Thou shalt not," which adequately express so much of God's morality. The Pharisee, a proudly observant Jew, was well versed in this, and he reported to his Father that he was not an adulterer, and an extortioner and not an unjust man. No matter the moral state of any society these are attributes for which any well-meaning man or woman strives. Likely, this man was better than the average Pharisee, for he did not have the stain of extortion on his character. This was a sin often noted in many ways and in many examples by Christ, and the Master was never hesitant in linking the name Pharisee with extortion. Financial sharp dealing, oppressiveness, monetary greed and materialism all find adequate room under this umbrella of extortion. Our Pharisee was a better man, though, and rose above such moral oppression and degradation. All in all he was a man of sincerely exemplary moral character.

The same cannot be said for the other prayerful attendee at the Temple that day, the publican. His job title was to the average Jew encrusted with so much filth, putrid reputation and general odiousness that a publican was seen only as barely human. But exactly what was a publican?

To answer the preceding question we first find that the publican of the New Testament was not an endemic Jewish institution. When the Romans arrived in 63 B.C and made Judea a part of their empire they also established a tax system, a three-tiered monstrosity that was marvelously efficient in raising vast revenue by extortion, oppression and other necessary means. The top tier was in Rome itself, while beneath the Empire's capitol were numerous mid-level tax agents to whom the third level, the publicans, reported and siphoned the funds which had been wrung from the production of the native subjects. Each publican was given a quota of money to raise, essentially by hook or crook, and few Roman officials would be eager to question his methods so long as the revenue stream flowed unimpeded to Rome. Anything the publican collected above his minimum quota was his to keep. It was a system seemingly crafted for racketeering, extortion and oppression. Yet, as with so much in life it is not easy to put birds of a feather altogether in the same flock. The gospels themselves provide at least two examples of men, though they were publicans, in a good light. Zaccheus, the little man who climbed a sycamore tree to just catch a glimpse of the Savior, ruefully and with a heart full of repentance expressed sorrow and regret for any of his past chicanery and fraud. Then there was Matthew, one of the original twelve apostles, and author of the New Testament's first book. Still, all in all, as a class they likely deserved their scurvy ridden reputation, and likely from his posture and attitude did this present publican who had come to pray at the Temple.

This publican did not attempt to sway God with his eloquence, praise of the Divine, or any sort of obsequious pleading. All we know is that he was so humbled and ashamed and would not even raise his head. Instead, he engaged in a mild self-flagellation, beating his chest and offered but a seven-word prayer to God:

"God be merciful to me a sinner."

On its surface he had very little to lay in offering to the Heavenly Throne. He believed, probably with some justification, that he was no shining exemplar as a keeper of either the spirit or the letter of the law. Effectively he had only himself to offer God, an admittedly shameful, sinful identity that to his fellow Jews and to the Pharisee standing next to him, was opprobrious. An old hymn was formerly sung in many, many churches, a hymn, like much of the old now has a certain scarcity, that contained the admonition:

"Bring Christ your broken life, so marred by sin;
He will create anew, make whole again."

The publican lived long before this hymn, to later be inscribed in the yet unborn English language, had even been written. Still he understood its message, which plainly and succinctly is "I need Christ, for I am a sinner."

The contrasts between these two first century Jewish men are not colored in pale pastels, but are painted boldly. They were different men, very diligent men. Christ, as did He with everything painted their pictures perfectly, and He makes further study and contemplation. Neither man had cornered the market on either virtue or sin, and just with a few words the Master invites further contemplation of their contrasts. From what we see honesty compels a certain reason to our reaction, and thus it is that of the two men most likely we would rather have the Pharisee as a next-door neighbor or even a business associate. He was a man of such discipline that he could fast not one, but two days, per week as an offering to God. He was diligent, attentive to detail, morally upright, likely the kind of man who was a friendly sort to have living next to you, a man who kept not only his house and lawn in order but his personal life as well. As for the publican his associates were likely over-represented by other publicans and characters of that ilk, not the kind of visitors and associates ordinarily welcome as guests in respectable homes. No matter the level of the publican's propriety neighbor's eyebrows may have been raised at some of his visitors coming and going.

Now, for Christ's closing pronouncement to His parable, a summation maybe surprising to many but doubtless not to those who are truly spiritually minded:

> "I tell you, this man (the publican) went down
> to his house
> justified rather than the other (the Pharisee):
> for every one that exalteth himself shall be abased;
> and he that humbleth himself shall be exalted."

The Pharisee, for all his shining moral patina, morality and good works (and the are commendable) whether he knew or not, was expressing to God that he really needed only the Divine seal of approval, a spiritual gold certificate acknowledging that he was somebody special, far above other men, especially the loathsome publican. By whatever means and for whatever reasons he had persuaded himself that his sins needed no forgiveness and his ceaseless good works only praise. The Pharisee's personal theology was constructed as a fortress around his own valuable character, a character into which nothing now penetrated. He was a man now satisfied with his station in life, his reputation, his morality and the many good works of his life. His character and life were so complete that legitimately we may pose a question as to whether there remained within him any room for all.

None of this is to disparage the good of the man, and he is more than faintly mindful of the "rich young ruler," a man who came to Christ with a sterling moral life but was so full o himself that he asked Jesus "...what lack I yet?" Although for reasons not here necessarily pertinent that young man was different, this Pharisee can really receive nothing from God. He has no appetite for the spirit of Christ because he is sated with himself.

For a purchase to occur, be it land, a house, an automobile, or personal chattels of any sort, the prospective buyer must feel, must sense within himself, a need for the product. Without having such he must experience a knowledge of diminution, a feeling or belief, that without the item his life is diminished and is not all it might be. The man or woman who is in need of something knows within themselves that without the proffered product, without his or her attaining it life is not what it could be, and in many cases what it should be. In the spiritual vein the scriptures contain no clearer or greater illustration of this dichotomy of self-knowledge than Christ's parable of the Pharisee and the publican.

The Pharisee, doubtless a moral paragon in many public ways had conducted an inventory of his character, had weighed himself in the balances and found himself "not wanting." He had passed his own muster and moral inspection with flying colors and now awaited and needed only Divine approval and a moral gold star of merit.

When we say that anyone is the polar opposite of another person it is a mark of triteness of expression. Humans are far too complex, individualistic and varied to have a scientifically opposite extant. Still, in a few markings the populace of the first century would have so described the Pharisee and the publican. The Pharisee could walk and appear anywhere and receive the plaudits of men. He was a Pharisee, by definition and reputation and not without reason to be learned, scholarly, a moral exemplar, a good man, diligent in prayer, sacrifice and service. Many sincerely and morally striving Jews may have pointed to him and encouraged their sons "to be like this man." The publican on the other hand was not to be found in respectable company, his friend's and companions being other money grubbing and parasitic publicans preying upon their own people. If he was, in actuality, an honest, reputable publican he was a member of a very small minority group. He would be forced to find his fellowship in his fortune, his riches and his position, but certainly not in fellowship with other Jews. He was a member of a prosperous, yet feared and despised group. What is most telling, though, is that he knew it, and through that was who he was, a man of prosperity but a figure so covered in shame that he could not raise his eyes upward to Heaven.

The two protagonists of Christ's parable were strikingly different men, but they each possessed one condition best and most succinctly described by a great French thinker, a mathematician and philosopher, Blaise Pascal, who wrote:

> "There is a God-shaped vacuum in the heart of every person
> which cannot be filled by any created thing,
> but only by God, the Creator, made known through Jesus Christ."

The Pharisee, by no measure a diabolical man, had attempted to fill that God shaped vacancy with a consciousness of his own self-worth and that deadliest of all sins, pride. He attempted, perhaps unwittingly, but his reliance was upon himself and his own, not the Savior's righteousness. The publican knew that he had hollowed out his heart in the service of Mammon, but he wanted to atone and repent. As Jesus said only one went to his house justified, the one who understood:

"God resisteth the proud, but giveth grace to the humble."

CHAPTER ELEVEN

FORGIVE AND FORGET (SOMETIMES)
Matthew 18:23-34

The King's councilor, Polonius, in William Shakespear's immortal drama "Hamlet" spoke the famous aphorism:

> "Neither a borrower nor lender be;
> For loan oft loses both itself and friend,
> And borrowing dulls the edge of husbandry."

This is good, sound advice for any age, and its actual practice would insulate a person from the rigors, tensions, hardships and heartaches of much of financial affairs and even daily life. But, really, is it practical? Practical or not, the Holy Bible recognizes the inevitability of debtors and creditors. Almost from the onset of its great story the reader finds money, time, goods and whatever else being loaned, borrowed, and unfortunately at the very heart of many of the problems of its dramatic cast. The scriptures are, among other things, an endless compilation of debtors and creditors, the difficulties, stresses, heartaches and at times the outright crimes committed in the avoidance of lawful debt or the harsh brutality of collection. No speaker or teacher in either Testament spoke more of debt and credit than did Jesus Christ Himself. The Master acknowledged debts of all kinds, spiritual, moral, eternal, etc., but his basic mode of illustration was debt understood just as easily by a first century Jew as by a twenty-first century American, money. The teachings of Jesus are eternal, but money and monetary value are given life only in this temporal world. Still, the Master knew how important the "lucre" of the scriptures would always be and so remain. First century Judea possessed a primitive yet generally prosperous economy, but it was seemingly much more distant than a mere stone's throw from modern capitalism. Still, though, similarities are to be discovered between ancient and modern, and the superstructure of this parable so illustrates. Debt is bad, perhaps unavoidable, but it is not for nothing that modern accounting parlance universally refers to debt as a "liability." It is upon this factual foundation that Jesus told a story.

A great king, though titled such he seems to be more an emperor than a king, boasted great lands and possessions and the fealty of many servants. His debtors were not beggars in the streets but were themselves never of great substance financially. One of these was a man who had accumulated a debt of ten thousand talents to the king. A "talent" was a unit of measurement primarily, if not exclusively, for precious metals, namely gold and silver. To this date scholarly opinions differ, but a common one is that a "talent" was a weight of approximately seventy-five pounds. Accepting such as generally true, the debt which this servant owed his king was approximately 750,000 pounds silver or gold. By whatever scale of weights and measures and ancient to modern monetary conversion we might employ, Christ has made His point. The servant owed the king a debt so preposterously great that it was impossible that this one servant could ever repay it. Even for a king 750,000 pounds of silver or gold is so staggeringly enormous that it is not easily written off the royal accounting ledgers. The King's ability and chances of collecting such a debt from his recalcitrant servant may be expressed most clearly in one word only, and that word is "impossible." The debtor, who had foolishly accrued a debt of gargantuan proportions may have possessed the desire to repay it, but he lacked the other requisites, such as time and ability. The king, rightfully angered as any creditor would be, was enraged by the injustice that his royal person was about to suffer and so determined:

> "But forasmuch as he had not to pay
> his lord commanded him to be sold,
> and his wife, and children, and all that he had,
> and payment to be made."

The royal wrath was to be unbound and forever would his servant be enslaved, he and all he loved, to be degraded and humiliated, and forever. This sum could never be repaid, in whole or in part.

At this juncture the king's choices were but two, in that he could either write off the debt or write off the debtor. In more spiritually palatable terms, the monarch could forgive the debt or forgive the debtor. The words of Christ as recorded by Matthew most eloquently give voice to the king:

> "The servant therefore fell down, and worshipped him,
> saying, Lord, have patience with me, and I will pay thee all.

Then the lord of that servant was moved with compassion,
and loosed him and forgave him the debt."

The king's desire for vengeance, for retributive justice, melted in light of and was subordinate to the pitiable condition of his servant and the man's horror. The king did not attempt a compromise, a deal, a negotiation, a partial forgiveness, or any such thing. He forgave not part, but all, and set no new conditions upon the servant. Truly, this man was royalty and well deserving of his title, praise and homage. The servant's workload was not increased, no more tribute money was to be exacted from him, for he was forgiven, totally, purely and simply for his past debts. No "working out" scheme was to burden him, and as the king knew and certainly the servant must have known, the man was absolutely incapable of paying such a debt. The only positive and productive action could and did issue from the king.

Happily, even gloriously, the servant was free of a debt so great that it blotted out the light from his life. A great, marvelous story, and standing on its own the parable in this abbreviated form certainly would withstand the tests of time and study. The story, though, is now only half-told. Our servant had very real troubles with money. As a debtor he had incurred obligations of astronomical size, so huge that he was fortunate to owe them to a king/creditor defined by astonishing amounts of mercy and forgiveness. It was in the man's other part as himself a creditor, where his actions relieved a character, not just flawed but in a free fall of moral plummet.

We humans have an ever-present temptation to succumb to the belief that two schemes of justice should ever be extant, one for ourselves and one for others. The king's forgiven servant was not to be presented with this temptation as Jesus continued with His narrative:

> "But the same servant went out and found one of his fellow servants,
> which owed him a hundred pence:
> and he laid hands on him and took him by the throat,
> Pay me that thou owest."

One hundred pence, yes, but what is a pence? It was, of course, a coin in current use, a fraction of the Roman denarius, and depending upon the source consulted, may have had a value of sixteen cents. Thus, this man's fellow employee owed him a grand total of sixteen dollars, perhaps the value of a nice lunch to which untold numbers of friends and fellows treat each other every day. Our king's servant possessed a strong, durable memory which had entered that debt in bright red in his heart and mental account ledgers. Most persons, especially those whose livelihood is dependent upon the collection of money owed them, are familiar with the frustration, even anger, which an elusive or "forgetful" debtor can engender by not paying. Our forgiven servant resorts to physical violence, and the threat of more, savagely more, violence is definitely suggested. He, at least for the moment availed in Western countries within the last two or three centuries:

> "And his fellow servant fell down at his feet, and besought him,
> saying, Have patience with me and I will pay thee all.

> And he would not:
> but went and cast him into prison, till he should pay the debt."

What a dichotomy of result is found within the person of one man, the king's forgiven servant. For himself he was granted freedom from the absolutely crushing and destructive burden equal to the national debts of many nations combined. From this same forgiven servant emanated barbaric retribution for the delayed payment of a trifling sum. Unfortunately the king's servant would find neither solace nor silence from his fellow servants:

> "So when his fellow servants saw what was done, they were very sorry and came and told their lord all that was done."

The king was now incensed at the shockingly insolent, heartless and unforgiving behavior of his servant and called him for a reckoning:

> "O thou wicked servant,
> I forgave thee all that debt because thou desiredest me:
>
> Shouldst not thou also have had compassion on thy fellow servant,
> even as I had pity on thee?"

The king's wrath was great, and he was not soon or easily assuaged and "...he delivered him to the tormentors, till he should pay all that was due him."

A splendid, shocking story this is, but the Master of Creation and of words added a coda to His parable:

> "So likewise shall my heavenly Father do also unto you,
> if you from your hearts forgive not every one his brother their trespasses."

As with all the Master's words His parable is superb, sporting an intense density of words, thoughts and lessons and even greater than it first appears.

This essay suggests a meaning, though by no means does this exhaust the story's inventory of value. The king's servant is in a totally, absolutely, hopeless condition for he has allowed himself, by design, misfortune or a combination of both, to place himself in servitude and imprisonment for the remainder of his days. He has no choices, no options, or there is literally and absolutely nothing that "he" can do about his own indebtedness to the King. Figuratively and symbolically this servant is every man and woman who has lived since the Fall, which is another manner of saying everyone. Any help, aid, assistance, or dare he hope, salvation, must come from without himself. It must come from the creditor, the king. It must come from God, and it does as He forgave him the debt. It was the King, it is God who does it all, offers, extends and sacrifices everything, even to the ultimate pinnacle of His Son, to save any servant. The servant did nothing, just as none of us can do a single good work, offer a single prayer or offer a spotless life to receive salvation. In its entirety it comes from the Father, for this is the grace of God.

To this day and to the end of the terrestrial world it is difficult for some and impossible for many to believe that the God who created the universe is so loving and giving. This number includes not just the heathen, the evil and the darkness of the world but believing Christians as well. Maybe even especially believing Christians. Forgiveness and salvation from the king's wrath comes from the king, or God alone. It is harder than most people, including many sincere Christians to fully realize that they are saved by grace, and not of works, because many Christians have a background that places a strong emphasis on good works, hard work and what is now called meritocracy.

The king's servant and later the man to whom one hundred pence was owed are one and the same person. This man by his own existence, life and conduct had placed himself into a position from which it was literally to extricate himself. So often did the Master illustrate and advance His Word and His teachings by material examples yet these examples were actually the mere conduits of greater spiritual, even eternal lessons. The man had been forgiven of all his debt, not 10% now with the remainder to be paid on some sort of spiritual payment plan. Rather he had received absolute, total forgiveness of a debt which he could neither bear nor pay. Now, by the king's grace all had been forgiven, the debt wiped off the account books forever and no claim for its payment would ever again be made. Hopefully, the reader will pardon the insertion of a phrase which any competent lawyer will understand, but the King's claim had been "dismissed with prejudice." By the monarchial grace the servant would never again be compelled to account for it. But...

What of this servant's future? Once in the King's embrace of forgiveness and grace would the servant so remain? In the parlance of theology for the past one-half millennium, commencing with Martin Luther and the Reformation was the servant forever in grace, certain never to fall, and in the terse catchall phrase "once saved, always saved" or "once forgiven, always forgiven?" In the parable the King is informed of the harshness of his servant's attitude and conduct and responds thus:

> "O thou wicked servant,
> I forgive thee all debt, because thou desiredst me.
>
> Should not thou also have had compassion on thy fellow servant,
> even as I had pity on thee?"

The king's servant was freed from the binding, crushing load of debt, and he was living in the euphoria of grace, beautiful, luxuriant grace, longed for and wonderful to experience. Recklessly, he threw it all away, and in words that are rejected by many sincere believers he "fell from grace." Impossible say many, yet here it is, and for this the servant would no longer luxuriate in the ether and emancipation of grace but would suffer being:

> "... delivered to the tormentors, till he had paid all that was due unto him."

Let us now step back from the dark, theological thickets into which our discussion has begun to transverse and rather look upon the great simple lesson of the parable, the words with which Christ brings it to a close:

> "So likewise shall my heavenly Father do unto you,
> if ye from your hearts forgive not every one his brother their trespasses."

Forgiveness was, is and forever will be a huge, even dominating matter with God. Never was the subject of forgiveness and grace more starkly, yet beautifully, illustrated than by this parable of Jesus; however, it is hardly a singular or a new topic with the Savior. When once asked by His disciples about prayer He responded with the so-called Lord's Prayer, a short petition which includes His admonition and standard of "forgive us our trespasses <u>as</u> we forgive those who trespass against us." To the Christian Christ's admonition is beautiful, but should we retain malice in our hearts to a brother or sister the prayerful petitioner is condemning himself with his own words.

The gentle Master taught and yet teaches that forgiveness and grace are exquisitely beautiful and impossible of true human description. They are obtained by turning to Him, obeying Him and walking in His Steps. The entire New Testament is, among so many matters, a compendium on the wonders of forgiveness and grace and an almost inexhaustible reservoir o stories of men and women who receive it. Once given it is not easily lost, and no man nor devil can capture our spirit and strip it of grace. Yet the Christian, man or woman, young or old, may toss it away by spurning Christ's forgiveness in his failure to offer it to others.

One of our culture's oldest of old sayings is the simple "To err is human, to forgive Divine." Christ, by this parable and really His entire life called us to truly have His Spirit, which is no better or more beautifully expressed than by forgiving others.

Great is the Sin; Greater is the Forgiveness
Luke 7:41-50

Not every Pharisee was a bad man. From the New Testament accounts, though, the plurality of them seemed to slip into villainous roles with ease. The scriptures, though, provide several examples, many highlighted by Christ who seemed to be sincere, although like everyone flawed, seekers of truth. One such was a Pharisee with the common name of Simon who invited Jesus into his home for a meal and conversation. Christ gladly accepted and while He, Simon and others were dining and engaged in discussion:

> "And behold, a woman in the city which was a sinner,
> when she knew that Jesus sat at meat in the Pharisee's house,
> brought an alabaster box of ointment.
>
> And stood at His feet behind Him weeping,
> and began to wash His feet with tears,
> and did wipe them with the hairs of her head,
> and kissed his feet and anointed them with the ointment."

Although the narrative of the great historian Luke does not further describe her appearance likely the lady who was a sinner was so marked by her dress. Bejeweled with ornate gems and bedecked in colorful finery her physical appearance would have proclaimed the likelihood of what she was, a woman of the street, or a prostitute. As such she was living in the nether regions of society, and the house of a man such as Simon ordinarily would be foreign, even alien, to her. Yet, here she was, and for one reason only, that being the presence of this miracle working rabbi from Galilee.

Simon was disgusted and appalled, but he was a man of breeding, of propitious behavior and remained silent yet:

> "(H)e spake within himself, saying,
> This man, if he were a prophet,
> would have known who and what manner of woman
> this is that seeketh Him, for he is a sinner."

Simon was both right and wrong, right is assuming that Jesus would have known that she was a sinner, but wrong in ever thinking of Him just as a prophet. He was the Son of God. Simon, to his edification and education, was short sighted in keeping his thoughts to himself and thinking their secrecy was secure, for Christ knew them. He knew the background of the woman, that she was drowning in evil, and He was just as aware of the proud spiritual stance of His host Simon, for now He utilizes this (and let us be plain) extremely awkward situation for a combination of a moral object lesson and parable.

Demonstrating yet anew that this world has seen only one true Teacher, Christ with His customary minimum of words responds with a simple questioning two sentence parable which forces Simon to the only possible conclusion:

> "There was a certain creditor which had two debtors:
> the one owed him five hundred pence, and the other fifty.
>
> And when they nothing to pay, he frankly forgave them both.
> Tell me, therefore, which of them will love him the most?"

Beautifully presented, simply but majestically worded, the Master has presented the parable's meaning in the form of an inquiry, a rhetorical question which can intelligently be answered only one way. Simon rose to the demands of the moment when he responded, perhaps though with a bit of blasé nonchalance:

"I suppose that he, to whom he forgave most."

Christ replied with approval, but then He brought His story to a direct personal plane. The three principals, Christ, the woman and Simon knew one fact, which was the woman was a great sinner, a fact she did nothing to conceal. Her life contrasted poorly with the outward appearance and respectability, terms not to be mocked, of Simon. More importantly her behavior at this meal was starkly different than that of Simon, its host. Simon, a man wise enough to invite Christ into his home had committed a raft of social faux pas, as Jesus now brought to Simon's attention. At this time and in Judea it was common to wash the feet of any social guest, "... but I entered into thine house, and thou gavest me no water for my feet." What a contrast with the repentant lady who "...has washed my feet with tears, and wipest them with the hairs of he head." Moreover, Christ continued, the personal love, intimacy and humility of the woman has been astounding as "... this woman since I came in has not ceased to kiss my feet," added to the ointment with which she had anointed His feet. The Savior seemed to highlight the woman's conduct not so much in a spirit to shame Simon but rather to mark the genuineness of the woman's sincerity.

Simon's faults do not seem to be cruelty, excessive materialism or selfishness. Obviously, he was neither a stupid nor a foolish man for it was he who invited Christ into his home, an act of a certain moral stature and courage in view of the virulent and eventually lethal opposition which many, if not most, of his fellow Pharisees maintained against the Savior. Simon's failing was that he wished to meet and deal with the Son of God as an equal. Jesus, the most humble person who ever lived, was not Simon's equal, for He has never had such a peer. Certainly Simon wished to know more of this unique man who he had hoped was a prophet and doubtless was genuinely eager to discuss with Him religious, spiritual and moral matters. All this is admirable, and in fact wonderful and with a certainty is pleasing to both the Father and Son. Simon, though, was not yet aware of the primary reason any person should invite Christ into his home, life, heart or however it is to be phrased. The first reason any man or woman needs the Savior is that the awareness of his or her own sins is the engine that drives the real believer to Christ. Simon's awareness of sins was his knowledge of not his, but the woman's sins.

This poor woman, who knew very well who she was and just as importantly she was keenly aware that others, including her shocked host Simon, knew her character, still was bold enough to approach the Son of God at a social gathering to which she had not been invited. From her heart came an outpouring of regret, sorrow and apparent repentance from which her life had become. From her eyes came tears, from her hands service to the Savior and from her heart courage and a proffered expression of repentance and a desire for forgiveness, a combination of which Christ is never resistant and is ever open. His final statement to her was plain but lyrical:

> "And He said unto her, Thy sins are forgiven.
> Thy faith have saved thee, go in peace."

Christ's dealings with Simon are left open ended, as there are no parting words, no benediction, no forgiveness. Still, hope remains for Simon. He was a man with seemingly good intentions, as He hosted, however inadequately, Jesus as a guest and seemed to be eager to learn more. The Savior certainly did not scrimp in the lessons which He demonstrated to His host. From our text, though, remains a stark contrast between the penitent woman and Simon. Simon approached Jesus as an equal, but the woman came to Him as a supplicant desperate for forgiveness. Simon came with an attitude, albeit correctable of moral superiority and self-righteousness. No better pain can be found to illustrate and amplify Christ's statement:

> "For every one that exalteth himself shall be abased,
> and he that humbleth himself shall be exalted."

We are not immune from a certain optimism that projects a future in which Simon acknowledged and understood his sinful failing and turned more to humble service to God. As for the tearful lady our feelings are different. Spurred by her genuine humility and regret for her past sins she spiritually and literally bowed her knee to Christ and departed forgiven and saved.

CHAPTER TWELVE

THE RICH FOOL
Luke 12:16-21

Rich men (and for this particular chapter the masculine only shall generally be employed) are seldom thought to be fools. Throughout the ages in the canons of most cultures they are often depicted in many ways, commonly as a villain, the "bad guy" shockingly avaricious, cruel, unfeeling towards all others, contemptuous of those with less, self-absorbed, grasping, ad nauseum, but seldom are they shown as foolish, especially in regard to that substance which makes them rich, material wealth, or money. Let us consider but one from the great reservoir of available fictional classics, the now almost mythical Ebenezer Scrooge from the pages of Charles Dickens's <u>A Christmas Carol</u>, a figure now so steeped in our cultural inheritance that he seems as much a part of Christmas as Santa Claus. So common and engrained into our culture is this character that we have no hesitancy in revealing the plot's denounement. After late night epiphanies from his own past and future Scrooge is overcome by remorse and sorrow for the greed and shortsightedness that defined his life, repents of his past and understands that riches alone cannot produce contentment.

May the story be told until the end of time, but alas, if not of singular uniqueness, it is after all fiction and not generally descriptive of the human experiences. Dickens's great character in that trite, overused but sadly under appreciated "learn the error of his ways." Scrooge was not just an unhappy man, but a bitterly hate filled human who saw no good, experienced no good and derived no pleasure from anyone or anything. Only when he began to open his heart and mind to matters other than the mere accumulation of material wealth did he approach contentment. He found it others, in their fellowship, and, dare we say it, in God.

Two millennia before Dickens and his fictional Scrooge lived another man who spoke in both fact and in fiction and so often in His parables in a manner that hardly distinguished one from another. Naturally that man is Jesus of Nazareth, who spoke so often in parables that fully one-third of His recorded words are transmitted by means of this literary device. One of His short and simplest parables, a story that in part but only in part, a template for Scrooge, His parable of the man who wished to build bigger barns to contains his burgeoning wealth.

Christ's parabolic protagonist was a man for whom worldly success was second nature. He was a farmer, but perhaps on a scale so vast that later generations would have deemed him a planter or perhaps a gentlemen farmer. So successful was he, an enviable state for any man or woman, that his latest crop put him over the top. He had an abundance, an embarrassment of riches so great, that he was faced with a perplexity of what to do with it all. Apparently, the market for his grain was already saturated with product, and he had exhausted the capacity of his own storage facilities. He pondered this problem, a dilemma that most would find an enviable quandary as he had to admit to himself:

"What shall I do, because I have no room where to bestow my fruits?"

A plethora of plenty undoubtedly led to some acute, intense mental concentration until the lights came aglow:

"This will I do.
I will pull down my barns and build greater;
and there will I bestow all my fruits and my goods."

Farmers, ranchers, independent artisans, various independent professional and so many others will read this story and wistfully think of the euphoria of success and triumph the man is experiencing. Making a living at any occupation, trade or profession is itself hard enough, the brightness and exhilaration of hoped for success even less common, but the unexpected cornucopia of abundance beyond comprehension is a rarity indeed. Now it has fallen squarely under our man's control. Christ did not even offer a hint of criticism towards the man's success and efforts. With a small-town background and growing up in the artisan's trade of carpentry Jesus knew how hard it was to make money, much less achieve success beyond one's dreams. The Savior simply relates it as reality, as fact, probably because this is not the lesson, not the mora point of the parable. Its moral substance for the great farmer and for all who follow is in his reaction to success:

"I will say to my soul,
Soul, thou hast much goods laid up for many years;
take thine ease, eat, drink, and be merry."

By examining the man's response Christ calls upon us to examine not only his character, but ours as well. "East, drink and be merry" are not curse words, and all three are Divine gifts for the good and happiness of humanity. All three are meant to be enjoyed, and for certain Jesus Himself, as the Son of Man, is often shown pleasantly enjoying all in a spirit of fellowship and conviviality. While Christianity is certainly antithetical to a spirit of hedonism, neither does it require its adherents to endure existence in the "sack cloth and ashes" of the Bible. In actuality, the faith established by the Messiah is the only one of the world's religions that understands that while man does not live by bread alone, still he must have bread. Perhaps the Savior's most succinct and comforting proclamation on this subject comes from His Sermon on the Mount when He proclaimed that "... your Heavenly Father knows that you have need of these things." "Need" of these things, yes, but need to what end and what purpose. Our parable's protagonist now saw need in terms of luxury, plenty, comforts, delicacy and refinement, or much more than simply the daily bread for which we are told to pray. Life's pinnacle had been attained unexpectedly and perhaps at a more youthful age than he had ever dreamed. Now all that lay before him in his imagination, a field much less fertile than those of his lands, was rest, relaxation, fun and endless pleasure which beckoned him for a stay of endless years. Again, never do the scriptures and neither does the Law, the prophets nor Christianity ever condemn a single one of the treats of life of which he would now indulge. From beginning to end, though, the Word and the Deity condemn wastefulness, lives lacking in purpose and at the heart of the matter, lives devoted solely to self and self-centered gain and activity. The materialistic man, he who lives by bread alone is anathema to God.

At this juncture in the story we feel an obligation to the reader to define at least one word, a word of frequency in our discussion of the parable and one without which the parable can bee, at best, only partially understood. Let us now define as best we may the word 'materialism." Sometimes a definition is best procured by the commencement of explanation of what it does not mean. Materialism is not the mere possession of goods, or perhaps in reverse the abundance of possessions. The Bible itself is replete with all types, every strata on the economic scale. The names of such as Abraham, Job, Elisha in the Old and such as Christ's close friends Lazarus, Mary and Martha, and the apostles Matthew and Paul, Barnabas, almost ad infinitum were persons of means, material wealth and none are ever condemned (or celebrated) for the material aspect of their lives. When they and their lives come to find their economic status is a far second to their characters and accomplishments. Money, materiality and the aggregation of money and wealth are often demonstrated and even proverbialized as problems, but nary a single time is their possession itself condemned.

Wealth is always a subject of human interest, and likely ever shall it be. Yet in the still and placid times of contemplation rarely d men and women, at least without bias and prejudice determine how it was and is acquired. Names such as John D. Rockefeller, Andrew Carnegie and Cornelius Vanderbilt were once in the front rank of our studies of the fabulously wealthy, but their luster has begun to tarnish and recede to be replaced by the more modern appellations of Bill Gates, Steve Jobs, Jeff Bezos and Elon Musk, whose fortunes and possessions make the earlier generations of such as Rockefeller and Carnegie paltry by comparison. How did they acquire it, maintain it and even expand it? The cynic, the striving political radical and the unthinking moralist will condemn them all as crooks, thieves and low criminals with high wealth. None of these persons, though, while most do not possess the reputations of St. Francis are not known primarily, or perhaps, at all, for crookedness. So, now they face a phalanx of finger pointing as "rich boys" who inherited great wealth and are living from the labors of past generations. Actually, all these persons, be they the modern examples or the Biblical characters were born into modest, or at a minimum "non-wealthy" families. Most men and women, then and now, acquire what they possess by intelligent thinking, diligence and hard work. All these are without exception universally celebrated in the Biblical canon of morals as virtues. Be it the time of the patriarchs of Genesis, the Mosaical Law or the Christian Age hard work and the fruits of labor are celebrated as virtues. Sloth, jealousy, flippancy, thievery and covetousness are universally condemned as vices.

We return now to our examination of the wealthy man of Christ's parable. The preceding paragraphs are in no manner crafted to minimize the dangers inherent in material wealth. Certainly Christ, our Savior, was constantly warning of the pitfalls they could bring a person. In fact our parabolic protagonist seemingly is guilty of crass materialism, but just as likely the dilatory effects of this sin are surpassed by others, most certainly described simply but deeply and thoroughly by Christ.

It was this same Christ, this Jesus of Nazareth, who knew His Creation and had so beautifully described it more than once as its supreme work, mankind itself, possessing a dichotomy of being, the carnal, or worldly and material and the everlasting, the soul and spirit. The wealthy farmer had slipped into that strata of existence where so many dwell, that of seeing everything in material terms and ignoring the spiritual, the part that lasts forever. He was a good farmer and a fortunate farmer who was given the blessing of an abundant grain harvest much greater than he had expected. It was his to be sure, but now let us confront, as perhaps he never did, his available choices.

First of all he apparently gave no consideration to anyone else but himself. Already an obviously wealthy man the fruits of his labors belonged to him, and he intended them to stay that way. Being a Jew he was obliged to think of others, as even before the Advent of Christ benevolence to others, the less favored and fortunate, was woven into the fabric of the faith. Instead, the barns he had already bursting with product he could imagine nothing better than building bigger barns for yet more plenty. The poor, the aged widow, perhaps even his own employees would have to go begging for he intended to hoard in the purest way, for himself. Still if the existing storage barns were full what could he do with his additional, excess grain? His life and effects, and undoubtedly, he had worked very hard and had been successful, a success which was wondrously peaking at the most opportune time, had come to one sharp, shining point. East, drink and be merry, and let the morrow take care of itself. In even in this supposition, especially in this supposition, he was building upon a false premise. For the rich man was bereft of all tomorrows. In the penultimate statement of the parable Christ expressed:

> "But God said unto him,
> Thou fool, this might thy soul shall be required
> of thee:
> then whose shall those things be which thou hast
> provided?"

In a long list of ways this man was a foresighted planner of the future and a diligent worker of the day. Christ's words contain nary a trifle of a hint that the man had acquired his property by dishonest means. In point of fact, his diligence, preparation (to a point) and tireless hard work were and remain admirable qualities.

To employ an old bromide, one of the oldest and most tired clichés, "...you can't take it with you." Our farmer, though, apparently had little or no time to enjoy it even when he had it because his fate was to shuffle off this mortal coil at the moment he was finally ready to relax and luxuriate in materiality. Whose shall his things, his great riches, now be? Certainly not his, but perhaps his wife, children or even the state would swoop in and take possession. Just as he was his possession would soon be but a memory.

The man who built bigger barns is not an aberration, not an outlier and actually his numbers may be greater now than at any time in history. Until very recently and still only in modern prosperous nations with advanced economics is the idea of retirement and rest from labors even a possibility. Handled properly, judiciously and yes spiritually, it may be a wonderful blessing from God. What man or woman, even the hardest worker, the most diligent, does not become weary of work and its worries. Retirement from a life of hard labor is a blessing from the Father. The perversion of the usefulness of this time into nothing but sloth, indolence, leisure and hedonism is an affront to the God who bestows it. This, of course, is the parable of Christ, and His every word is pure wisdom, jewels of insight and practical application, and so it is with this parable as He closed with this wisdom:

"So is he (foolish) that layeth up treasure for himself, and is not rich toward God."

This exquisitely crafted parable is a primer for storytelling, and its finely honed words and meaning beyond any man's capability. Not a breath, not a word, nor a hint is to be discovered of any concern for someone other than himself. Our man had made it and to him beckoned, in that modern vernacular, a "...lifestyle of the rich and famous." But what if he had lived and had paved before him a road of life's pleasures and luxuries? Would that have guaranteed or even offered to him the pleasure, the endless pleasure, he sought from such a life?

This narrative to this juncture has pointedly avoided referring to any of the man's activities as being what the morality of the Bible designates as "sin." Such is purposeful because Christ Himself never so describes the man's activities as being wrong per se. Eating, drinking, merriment and ease are not of themselves sinful, and if a person wants to imagine Heaven itself having a share of such it would be hard to refute him. All these are good and desirable, and not a one is omitted from the gospel accounts of the life of Christ, a man who came "eating and drinking." When these activities (or perhaps better described as "inactivities") morph into full time pursuits and become the entire reason and purpose for a person's life is when they become sinful and destructive. While life is not meant to be all work, labor and drudgery neither is it designed to be a carnival of endless luxury and pleasures. In reality it is strange that a man who had spent so much of his life in work, accumulation of wealth and constructive endeavors could delude himself in believing that he could find endless pleasure in nothing but luxury and indolence.

Vacation, rest, recreation and the like are positive goods, but they too are subject to the scriptural admonition of "...let your moderation be known to all men." Nothing but rest, idleness, pleasure, recreation is character destroying, and as many persons, especially retirees who have worked without respite their entire lives find it to be more than they want to bear.

Whatever we may assert and opine about the farmer's errors with materialism, free time, idleness and general moral myopia his true downfall lay, as Christ has always noted, in a single statement that he "...was not rich towards God." A man or woman may bungle many aspects of their lives, and in point of fact so do we all, but the lack of a heart towards God dwarfs almost all. Before we finally examine his relationship with God, though, let us open a bit wider the portal of view into his feelings about other men and women.

From the silence of Christ in this parable the man apparently lived on an emotional and material island surrounded by a sea of self-centeredness which isolated him from any and all. Perhaps, maybe even likely, he gleefully looked forward to endless revelry and convivial parties and Bacchanalia with his fellows, but maybe not, for Jesus is silent on the issue. No wife, son or daughter, no kin of any sort appears on the horizon of his thinking, and his imagination, likely one that was festooned in vivid colors, painted an endless tableau of self, be it self-enjoyment, self-indulgence or in a very pure sense, self-centeredness. He seemed to be on speaking terms only with what he deemed to be his "soul," maybe little more than some apparition which rose to no more elevated stature than a drinking companion. Neither was he benevolent in his thinking of the poor. Most certainly most serious minded, even, perhaps especially persons of good will, have become a bit hardened in hearing about the poor. In these times of media omnipresence, be it verbal, print, internet, telephone, etc., we have become overwhelmed with calls for charity to the needy. Some are legitimate, but even just a normally observant person recognizes that giving to "the poor," either by forced taxation or voluntary contribution can become a gigantic con game. From the days of the Old Testament to the present hucksters and various wolfish politicians have achieved office and great power by being faux champions of the poor and the oppressed. So it was, is and ever will be, but none of this grants license to ignore the genuinely poor and suffering. The man of the parable most certainly was a Jew, raised in the Law and the traditions of helping others. His windfall of wealth and benevolence to the poor never crossed paths in his thinking. He was a man who undoubtedly had a long acquaintance with hard work, but now his thinking had been distilled into luxury, ease, indolence and self.

When his problems, his character and his life was distilled into the very quintessence of his problem, though, all these matters and attitudes, important as they are. His real problem was found in Christ's closure of His parable. The man was lacking because "...he layeth up treasure for himself and was not rich towards God."

Eventually, it all comes to an end, for as the scriptures proclaim that "... it is appointed unto man once to die and then the judgment." The Bible is replete with assurances that we know not the date of our death, and the calendar had already reached its final page when our rich farmer began to salivate over the prospective enjoyment of his wealth. Then, is a moment, in the twinkling of an eye he was gone, and so was the comfort of his luxurious life. Surely Christ, who loved all, did not teach this story merely to scare an audience, and really, He likely meant no fright al all. He did, though, show that great wealth, if not always a mirage, is chimerical and capable of vanishing in the blink of an eye. This great malefactor of wealth and its sudden increase was not burdened primarily by riches but by ever developing attitudes by which he had reduced his life to a simple equation of self-equals wealth and riches, which equals pleasure. His accumulation took a few years, perhaps if not likely the better part of his working life, but the demise of himself and his wealth arrived in an instant.

Our civilization and literary canon offers to us many examples, some in the form of great, even classical caliber, of the cold comfort which wealth and materialism provides. Only Christ could craft a parable where the wealthy protagonist is given no time to enjoy the comforts of his wealth. The extravagance of his newly and fabulously increased wealth would be a passage to that type of lifestyle that the majority of men and women covet, but few realize. The dream of the man did not escape him, it did not fade or ebb away, but came in that thunderclap of surprise for which he did not reckon, death. That cavalcade of luxury and merriment which was about to pass from fantasy to reality in his life made an abrupt turn and it ended in a special oblivion of disappointment and death.

The rich farmer is not a man to be hated and certainly not envied. Rather he is a man so similar to an endless multitude of men and women, who in their strivings for wealth and pleasure either forget or perhaps never even acknowledge God. It was all so sad and truly tragic, for the man's life well illustrates what he doubtless learned too late that his "… life is even a vapor that appeareth for a little time, and then vanisheth away." His life was meant to be an endless party, but it came to be neither a party nor endless.

CHAPTER THIRTEEN

THE STEWARDS

These parables, three of which have been selected, are a gold mine of information, lessons and morals, but first they are the progenitors of so many basic questions. What is a steward? Of what is he a steward? A steward for whom? Ultimately, what is the purpose of his stewardship? Hopefully, our modus operandi will be successfully demonstrated and the questions, if not always precisely answered at least will be well discussed in each of the reviews of the three parables. For now, though, we offer some cursory answers to the questions just posed in this paragraph.

As to the exact definition of a steward many excellent dictionaries could be offered, but our preference is for the scriptures in general and the parables in particular to supply the most workable definition. By this directive it is found that the steward is a person who has been placed in charge of something, somebody or some situation and who is answerable to his superior. Whether we employ the more ancient terminology of lord or master or the more modern of employer or even boss he is the person to whom the steward ultimately is answerable.

A steward takes care of many and various things, from lands, houses, businesses, and money, especially the latter, to more intangible items such as children, younger persons, pets and ultimately his or her own spirit and soul. Depending upon his master the steward may be under the restraints of a tight leash or may have such great latitude for his conduct that he is close to being an independent, or, hopefully, not to whittle the verbiage to too fine a point, a semi-independent contractor. Not just our studied parables but the entirety of the New Testament seems to demonstrate that our Superior and Master, Jesus Christ, has consistently granted the greatest of latitudes to His servants.

What is the purpose of stewardship? Here in the twenty-first century the idea of stewardship is just as redolent as it was in Biblical days. When we entrust our property, our possessions, our money, to another, our reasonable hope and expectation is that it be returned to us in as good or preferably better condition than it was when it was so entrusted. Consider the simple, the mundane, operation of taking your automobile to a dealership or car maintenance facility, for either repair work or normal maintenance. As the customer you rightfully expect the vehicle to be returned in as good, or most preferably, better state than it was when it was first entrusted to the steward for repair. We inhabitants of modern society grasp this common occurrence readily. Should the opposite occur (as, alas, it sometimes does) and your property which has been entrusted to a temporary steward is in worse condition than before as a customer, as a "temporary" master, may be angered and in severe cases even enraged. On the other hand if the vehicle has been properly repaired and is now running well as a customer, even though we have paid and maybe even paid dearly for it we are satisfied, perhaps even happy.

Christ, the Master, was master of all, including all stories, narratives and especially His parables. Stewardship was a favorite and a familiar trope with the Savior, and we find the first of our three stories discussing both the wisdom and folly of stewardship.

A Fifty-Fifty Proposition
Matthew 25:1-13

It is an unusual, even a rare, culture in which marriage and amazingly even more so the precursors to the union, the weddings, are not major events, be they religious, sociological or cultural. Or modern era, with some common, but yet some peculiar conceptions, seems to be in the process of discouraging and even dropping much of this. Nonetheless, at the time and place Jesus lived, first century Judea, weddings and wedding parties were a large and integral portion of Jewish social life. This is repeatedly confirmed by the four gospels, and Christ Himself was a willing, even enthusiastic attendee and participant. An elaborate, though parabolic, event is described by Jesus and recorded by the apostle Matthew.

A very large wedding was in the offing, with ten virgins or more contextually ten young bridal attendants to be involved in a magnificent nuptial event. While the structure and moral teachings of this story should be readily understood the facts and characters may seem a bit awkwardly placed to a modern readership. Notwithstanding with just a bit of background information they are quite understandable. The ten virgins, or at least nine of them, are not to be understood as brides but rather bridal attendants, or now colloquially expressed as young women who "stand up" for the bride at her wedding.

The time for the wedding was coming fast, but none were aware of its exact moment of scheduling. Obviously, it could not commence until the bridegroom arrived, and to many of the maidens he was well past time, he was late and likely they began to inquire, at least within themselves if he was coming at all.

At the time and place in which Christ spoke the words of this parable the typica Jewish wedding was both more festive and more formally elaborate than are similar weddings today. The announcement of the coming wedding party was generally noted by a procession of torch bearers or in Christ's story ten virgins bearing lamps. Here, though, at least for some, the proceedings begin to go askew. Only five of the lamp bearers, the "maidens" were worthy of their positions and the entrustment of responsibility, for only five of them had prepared their lamps, or lights. These were the five "who took oil in their vessels" as opposed to the equal sized group that took no oil for their lamps, the light from which was soon extinguished.

Finally, but with a dramatic unexpectation and the shock of surprise the bridegroom came for his bride, but with a shock thus expressed:

> "And at midnight there was a cry made,
> Behold the bridegroom cometh:
> go ye out to meet him."

Who, no matter what his standing or majesty, arrives at midnight? Well, apparently for one, the bridegroom. It was time for these maidens to fulfill their tasks, not really to be expressed in the word "duty" but rather in the nomenclature of "honor." To them was bestowed and vouchsafed the great honor of meeting the bridegroom and serving as beautiful heralds and ornaments to a great wedding. Yet only half were ready, and the other five, like school students panicking at an examination and begging opportunities to cheat, implored the five who were ready to give them some of their oil. The five with the foresight, though, were forced to respond:

> "But the wise answered, saying,
> Not so: lest there be not enough for us
> and you but go ye rather that sell and buy for yourselves."

As the lazy, the unprepared, the lethargic inevitably do the five foolish origins, in a pinch, hoped to benefit from the diligence, work and foresight of the faithful. But this time it fails to work.

An American poet once wrote a very famous verse, still quoted today, that "Of all sad words of tongue and pen the saddest are these, it might have been." The author, John Greenleaf Whittier, revealed great wisdom with such an observation still remembered today, but we offer a simpler, even more direct two-word couplet as the saddest of all phrases, "too late." Too late learning, too late living, too late repenting, and too late following the true path. "Too late" is the precursor to panic, hurried, even desperate activity, that rarely, if ever turns out well. Such is so demonstrated here as the Savior continued with His narrative:

> "And while (the unprepared virgins) went to buy,
> the bridegroom came,
> and they that were ready went in with him to the marriage,
> and the door was shut."

The wedding, the wedding party, the ceremony, the host, the guests and the five wise virgins now comprised a closed, exclusive community, and those outside the assembly room were literally barred from entering. Badly, with an appeal of agonizing emotion they begged entry with the plaintive "Lord, Lord open to us," only to be met with the chillingly frozen rejoinder of "I know you not."

So, is this a parable about five young women who were dilatory in preparation and irresponsible in preparing for a wedding? Of course not. The literal consequences of their actions, which are by no means unusual in life at any time and place, might be some hurt feelings, ruffled feathers and maybe an ounce or two of unrequited anger among friends. With persons of good will and good heart such hurt feelings are capable of being assuaged, sometimes with surprising ease and dispatch. Like all Christ's parables it is emblematic of a deeper story and meaning, one that goes far beyond the mundane. Only Jesus had the ability and the mastery of words and language to unlock the meaning, and so He does in but one sentence:

> "Watch therefore,
> for we know neither the day nor the hour
> wherein the Son of man cometh."

Christ's statement should be a foundation to the thinking of all who ever lived. For those who deny He ever lived in the first instance of necessity a denial that he could come again follows. Their foolishness in ignoring the statement from the Son of God Himself that only the Father knows the time of Christ's Second Coming. Their foolishness then in trying to affix a date otherwise is obvious. It is to two other groups that are represented by the five wise virgins and the five foolish virgins that we draw our most salient lessons.

The wise virgins are the faithful Christians who ever walk the path of Light, who are conscious of God and His Son and who seek to worship and serve them. They are not required to live on a sort of moral pin cushion but rather God and eternity are not afterthoughts in their life and moral calculations. To the prepared "virgin" the bridegroom's coming is the opening of heaven's gate to wonder and rapturous joy and certainly not a bedevilment of thoughts of Christ coming as a type of spiritual class monitor to inflict dreaded punishment. In point of fact, He is the opposite, the strong figure, ultimately impervious to the wounds of celestial warfare who has come at last for His true bride, His own Church, founded and ceaselessly loved by Him. His supplicants, His ladies in waiting, cumulatively His bride, the Church of Christ Himself, awaits the eternal marriage designed by Him before the foundations of the world. The joy which awaits both bride and groom is one of unimaginable but eternal, not for a term of years, but eternal rapture.

Yet sadly and ominously this door to a heavenly Edenic existence is closed and secured against the foolish virgins. Yet, how can this be? Surely this indescribably wonderful man who healed the sick, raised the dead and still gives hope to all, the Prince of Peace Himself, cannot be so cruel as to close and bolt the door to Heaven? In the end does He transform Himself into a God of vengeance? No transformation is made, but so many, the lost, and in the parabolic context the foolish virgins, now see Him for what He has always been, a God, not of vengeance, but of justice. The wise, the faithful, diligent Christians, the wise maidens, are saved not through their wisdom but rather because their wisdom leads them to the source of salvation, the Justice of Christ, for which they have lived, acknowledged and prepared. The foolish virgins are lost, not because of some special evil which tarnishes their characters, but rather due to their shunning Him and ignoring the agency of His Salvation. They are not said to be especially evil or sinful, but rather they serve as prime examples of who many that claim to be followers of Christ actually are. Until the last moment they possessed faith, but it was that ever so common yet today or at any time, the "faith without works." Their faith in the bridegroom's coming was a mere acknowledgment of His existence, as it had moved them to do nothing in preparation for His coming. Their lives effectively went unchanged by their belief. The door to eternal peace had been closed to them because "...I know you not." "Too late – the true saddest words of tongue and pen."

The Fig Tree
Luke 21:29-36 and Matthew 21:18-22

The fig tree was ubiquitous in ancient Judea and in fact most of the Mediterranean world that it has, with the olive, become a horticultural symbol of this vast and historic region. From the earliest chapters of Genesis its stories spread throughout both testaments, and it is irrevocably associated with Christ Himself and many of His parables. The tree, generally ranging in size from twenty to thirty feet tall, remains popular in the world for the sweet fruit it produces. So many products, dishes, desserts, etc., are its product as well as being appealing to so many for its inherent tastiness that it easily claims a niche as one of the world's great fruits.

Jesus and His apostles practiced a walking ministry, trodding the rough roads of not only Judea but also Galilee and Samaria for three years. The road and the landscape that bordered it became the Master's classroom, and in such locales, He taught far more often than in formal settings on a spring day, that time when trees and flowers begin to foretell their short seasons of radiance and glory by blooming and blossoming, He began a parable:

> "Behold the fig tree, and all the trees;
>
> When they shoot forth,
> ye see and know of your own selves that summer
> is now nigh at hand.
>
> So likewise ye, when ye see these things come
> to pass,
> know ye that the Kingdom of God is at hand."

Christ was all things to all people in His expectant Kingdom. He was its herald, its prophet, its raison d'tre and was its King, so He certainly knew of what he spoke. For millennia He and His Kingdom had been endlessly prophesied, and now its appearance was in the immediate offing. Here we should note that Jesus prophesied, taught and lived with an amazing consistency. By the first century AD the world had already viewed and experienced many great kingdoms and empires, the Persian, Babylonian, Macedonian, Egyptian, Roman ad infinitum, but Jesus likened His Kingdom's coming to the looming and fruition of a humble fig tree. Aggressive, forthright, loud generals and armies with the inevitable slaughter of thousands so often blazed the trail of these great kingdoms and empires. His apostles, disciples, enemies and all men and women were then given the pronouncement of Christ's special blessing when He told them simply:

"Verily I say unto you,
This generation shall not pass away till all be fulfilled."

The Messiah now was not speaking in riddles or enigmatic terms as he pronounced without their understanding, that the Church was about to be founded and established in a matter of months, if not weeks.

No disciplined, yet savage, military force would thunder in to establish His Kingdom, but it would be done not by an act of earthly shame, but heavenly glory. For thousands of years, God had prepared the soil and Christ came with the seed, the Word, which would establish the only lasting Kingdom, the Church. It was now time for rich verdant growth and harvest, but would the fig tree bear fruit?

The Watchful Servant
Luke 12:35-40

The Church and Christianity are so many things that it is close to impossible to truly define them in a single word or even a phrase. Christ and later His apostles continuously were likening the Church to something, some other object which would be known by the heavens of the teaching. Jesus Himself began many lessons with the words "... the Kingdom of Heaven is likened unto..." so we do not feel especially self-conscious in likening it to still another object, the prototypes of which Christ often utilized in His teaching.

We inhabitants and residents of the twenty-first century are certainly familiar with business enterprises and corporate conglomerates larger than could have been drawn from the wildest dreams (or perhaps nightmares) of the business titans and tycoons of just a generation or two past. For example today when we think of vast, even gargantuan, at least in the Western world we think of the technological giants and riches that are centered in the aptly named Silicon Valley of northern California. Wealth, information, policies and at times seemingly even the direction of the human race seemed to be determined by but a handful of persons dwelling there. As powerful and potent as they are, though, and likely often to their chagrin, they have presumably "faithful" servants to whom they entrust large portions of their decision making and supervisory capacities. Some seem to have gained notoriously short fuses to their tempers and maintain a willingness to demote or discharge managers and executives which displease them. But really – noting new in any of this, inasmuch as the head man, the chief executive, the boss, has always kept his attention and interests on his own enterprises, often founded personally by himself.

Christ spoke to His apostles a parable which beautifully encapsulates these matters. In the Master's parable He describes the setting where the "lights are burning," and upon the Lord's knock on the door it opens to him immediately, for they are prepared and elated to see him. Effectively, he is the boss who has come to review his employees, their attitudes and their productivity. These are the servants, the employees, so approved by him, that he arranges for them a celebration, a banquet "... and made them to set down to meat and will come forth and serve them." Yes, the top man comes to serve his workforce.

Christ continued with His parable and spoke of the Lord's coming in the second watch or perhaps even the third and find the house deserving of blessing because the goodman and his servants were still watchful. The praise the rewards the future for these servants are defined by their limitless character, but what of the bad manager, the neglectful, indolent, employee? What is his fate? Here, the Master beautifully transitioned the meaning of the parable from the temporal to the spiritual, as He commented that if the goodman had known "... he would have watched, and not have suffered his house to be broken into." Spiritually, though, the watchman comes at the terminal point of this life, in that dread word of wrath. The scriptures ring with the ominous sound of those words "... it is appointed to man once to die, and then the judgment." But when? As for the judgment, the Second Coming of Christ even He admitted He knew not the hour, as that knowledge was known by His Father only. Unless we remain alive, though, the hour of the watchman's coming, is the moment of death, the knowledge of which is vouchsafed to no man or woman.

Recently, the author heard a young woman remark that she was not religious "at this time in her life," the unspoken expectancy, of course, being that she would turn to religion at the Biblically "more convenient time." How foolish, and as Ecclesiastes proclaimed this life is all vanity anyway. The faithful, though, is never denied that reward of eternal life, and it is only the faithful who remains ever watching.

CHAPTER FOURTEEN

PARABLE OF THE TALENTS
Matthew 25:14-30

So, what exactly is a talent? As customarily employed in the ancient world of the Bible it was a measure of weight, primarily for the precious minerals of gold and silver. Various sources offer various modern calculations, but it is reasonably precise to say that a talent was approximately seventy-five pounds in weight. A talent of silver, then, would be a commodity of enviously high value, but a talent of gold would confer upon its owner recognition as a quite wealthy individual. Talents were most often the measurements of major commercial transactions or the currency of exchange between nations, the ordinary person being denied access to talents of silver and gold.

Ancient languages are interesting, and the student soon finds that the scriptures were written primarily in two tongues, the Old Testament in Hebrew, and the New in Aramaic, an ancient dialect of Greek commonly used by many persons, including Jews, in daily life. Although Hebrew remains extant, Aramaic is essentially an historical curiosity. An early translation of the

New Testament was into a dialect called "Koine" Greek, a lingua franca of the common people and of commerce. Ultimately, of course, after centuries of struggles, heroism and even martyrdom the scriptures began to be translated into modern European languages. In the fifteenth and sixteenth centuries men such as John Wycliffe and William Tyndale translated the Bible into English, Tyndale's translation becoming the basis for the most famous literary work of history, the King James Version of the Holy Bible. Very interesting (or perhaps the bored reader would say otherwise), but what does all this have to do with the Parable of Talents, a full, lengthy narrative in which Christ described three men who were entrusted by their employer with "talents," and from the text these are the original meaning of measures of wealth. Yet, with the passage of the centuries and the development of the English language "talent" has come to have a far different and even deeper meaning than a commercial and financial measure. A modern, common and practical definition of "talent" is rendered thus in <u>The Concise Oxford Dictionary of Current English</u>:

> "A special aptitude or faculty (a talent for music,
> has real talent)

> Or

> High mental ability."

As we delve into Christ's great Parable of the Talents its original meaning of wealth can serve our studies well. Yet happily we English speakers are blessed with a modern definition of "talent" which serves the meaning and depths of Christ's teachings beautifully. Without any intention to negate but rather to elucidate the meaning of Christ's great parable it is the modern reading of "talent" which we will most often employ.

A very wealthy man, a highly successful farmer and a commercial entrepreneur of enviable success had decided to absent himself from his business enterprises for a time, and thus called together his most valued and trusted servants, three in number. Without doubt he must have considered himself fortunate, for he counted not one, but three subordinates who were reliable and worthy of great trust. Having one man or woman to whom your business and fortune may be entrusted in your absence us a blessing, but having three is a true windfall.

The man was no wide-eyed innocent naif, for he knew that even among his servants their characters and abilities were not uniform. What an ideal leader he was proving to be, and he did not succumb to the fallacy that all men and women are equal in their capabilities, and yes, their talents. Thus, his plan of management in his absence was to entrust them with whatever the traffic would bear, but this master was wise in his reading of that element. His management plan, in absentia, was nicely summarized by Christ:

> "And unto one he gave five talents, to another two, to another one;
> to every man according to his several ability;
> and straightway took his journey."

This was the very model of a smoothly functioning enterprise. Its owner was attentive but certainly not suffocating in his attitude and key people subordinate to him. In modern parlance they were not "micro-managed," which should be more of a foundational principle of understanding and work in the modern Church more often that it is.

In many societies, among whom we should include the New Testament audience of Christ and the modern American scene, many, if not most people, say that they want maximum freedom at work, to be left to do as they dee best and to rise or fall on their own efforts and merits. The cry is often "I want to be my own boss." Well expressed, well considered, well meant and for most a total misperception of themselves. The cynic will offer that the majority, whether they know it or not, desires to be led, to be directed, to even be herded and ordered in the direction of their presumed masters. The Christian is tempted to respond with a vehement "Not so," but perhaps this is one time that the skeptic is correct and the sincere Christian wrong. From the dawn of Creation to the present it is not most, but rather, all of humanity that needs direction. Centuries before Jesus of Nazareth trod the shores of Galilee it was one of God's greatest prophets Jeremiah, who remarked:

"It is not within man to direct his own steps."

On the far side of this human and moral dilemma are history's dictators, rogues and tyrants who view their fellow beings as so many insignificant and expendable creatures to be spent in pursuit of their own goals, almost always selfish, self-aggrandizing and destructive. In their steps have followed, and yet walk, untold numbers of petty tyrants, bureaucrats and functionaries both civil and religious, who are afflicted with the same spirit of dictatorial control. The lord of Christ's parable, though, is the polar opposite. He engaged in no tedious instruction of detail explaining what and where he wanted done. From the factual context the lord seemed to know his servants extraordinarily well, and thus appointed to each of them different responsibilities, to the first, five talents, to the second, two talents, and to the third only one talent. He was directed by his knowledge "... according (to each man's ability) and straightening took his leave."

Whether he was away on business, visiting friends and/or relatives or just on an extended vacation, he was gone. The lord, this ancient CEO was out of the picture for an indeterminate time, and for this time his three servants, or rather managers, were answerable primarily, if not exclusively, to themselves. Oh, the bliss, the euphoria, the Nirvana, yes, the Heaven, of being answerable to no one! These three men, though, were not children, were not even descendants, and their characters were not changed in their lord's absence, but rather they were revealed. The five-talent man was unusually blessed, and examples of this figure, whether male or female, are not necessarily super abundant. Whether by birth, heredity, genetics, inborn ability, or environmental circumstances he is the one who "has it all." We offer an example from the realm and world of the essentially trivial and insignificant, though undeniably interesting, world of athletics in general, and baseball in particular. At least at one time it was said that major league baseball teams were looking for prospects with five particular attributes, the abilities to run, field, throw, hit and hit with power. To discover a prospect who could do exceptionally well in all five was indeed a rarity, and we need to think of names such as Wilie Mays and Mickey Mantle. Their "five talents" even when young and untried attracted attention. Each went on to develop those talents over long careers and today each is in the pantheon of baseball legends.

The five talents of this man of the parable are unknown to us, but a human skill set of that level is itself a source for admiration. Even in the Bible "five talent" persons are not plenteous, and, in fact, can be easily overlooked. Obviously and ultimately only the Almighty knows the exact amount of talents which have been allotted to any and all persons. The New Testament likely contains the stories of several of the five talent men, figures such as Stephen, Apollos, Barnabas, and Paul, but perhaps the most interesting and informative examples were the original twelve apostles. No one would have surveyed a blue-collar coterie of young Galilean fishermen, a despised tax collector and who knows what else as five-talent men. Nobody but one, Christ Himself, who saw the abundance of character and talent which each man possessed, and which would spring forth countless other hidden, but ultimately discernible, talents. At a minimum (and yes, there is not much more) the apostles' lives are an eternal light that demonstrates that more talent than anyone contemplates often resides in the most ordinary and overlooked persons.

The five-talent man of the parable certainly did not disappoint, for he saw this moment as a wonderful confluence of sufficient time, opportunity, unfettered action and his own increasing abilities to create even more. He doubled his five talents to ten, and as for the Master's reaction we defer our narrative for a moment. His second servant was a somewhat less endowed with gifts, possessing only two. The five-talent man certainly and rightfully carries with him the luster of a marvelously gifted man, and he is so entitled. His performance, though, faithful and brilliant as it was, is no more outstanding than the two-talent man. Each doubted his production, the first from five to ten and the second from two to four. Again, as to what they were Christ us silent, but their fidelity and work are equally exemplary.

So many stories, from the Biblical scriptures throughout the classical fairy tales of literature and legend are told in threes. On one end of the scale we note The Three Bears, The Three

Little Pigs, etc., to the more serious and sacred such as the three wise men (though the number three is not employed in the Bible), the three days and nights Jonah was in the belly of the whale and ultimately the three days of Christ in the tomb. Thus our parable is lacking, and in fact its full meaning is grievously wounded, if we do not consider the third man, the lord's servant who possessed only one talent. May our narrative be permitted a bit of digression on a discussion of the man entrusted with only one talent.

An old adage, wise or not, and expresses in various ways is that a man or woman can be whatever he or she wants to be. Perhaps so, but in the full blossoming of that meaning it seems that God has rarely ordained such, inasmuch as any and all talents ultimately find their origin in Him. Likely, a better an maybe even a more incentivized and inspirational form of such a truism is that any person can be more than he imagines Many years ago the United States Army successfully utilized a recruiting slogan of "be all that you can be," and it was met with noteworthy success Apparently many very young men and women understood, either rationally or instinctively, that there was more to him/her than people imagined and thus voluntarily accepted the rigors of hard military training. Few, if any, became a modern General Grant, Lee, Eisenhower or MacArthur, but many became more disciplined and more mature. Many were the equivalent of the one talent, the third of the trio of agents who this master employed and entrusted.

It is likely that most of the world's population is and has always been in their origin and creation one talent persons, for which absolutely no one should be morose or self-conscious in comparison to others. That one talent may be more important and consequential than any combination of two or five talents. Thankfully many, if most of us, have been blessed with good, selfless mothers, the idyllic women who put themselves far behind in any pecking order and always trying to ensure that their children receive the best. Another mother may be multi-talented, a pianist, a great singer, able to engage in intellectual repartee at the highest circle, but have no real desire or aptitude of self-sacrifice for her children. This lady, though, while not malicious or even harsh, may have no aptitude for children, even her own. She possesses three enviable abilities, i.e. talents, each of which may be a positive good, yet she has zero aptitude for mothering the child or children she may have brought into the world, where here she is overshadowed by the quiet, inconspicuous one-talent mother who has given her life for her children. Which lady would any of us choose for a mother? One-talent this is not definitionally subordinate to the two talent or five talent abundance which some enjoy.

So we return to the text of our parable, though, and find that the one talent servant is a man, not a woman, and of course his talent is money. The salient difference between the two more generously blessed servants and himself, though, is not in the enumeration of their talents but rather the attitudes of their hearts.

The Accounting
Matthew 25-19-30

The lord and master was gone for a long, indeterminate period, and soon his servants came for a "reckoning," or in more modern form, an accounting. Unsurprisingly, they came to him in order of their presumed importance. Likely, the five-talent man approached his master with no fear or trepidation, for he was no longer a five-talent man, as he was able to explain:

> "And so he that had received five talents came
> and brought other five talent,

saying, Lord, thou deliveredst unto me five talents: behold, I have gained beside them five talents more."

This man was a marvel and comes to be so appreciated by his master, or for our essay's purposes, his employer. He is the very definition of a self-starter, a self-motivated individual, a man who could thrive on his own, and likely even best on his own. He knew what the master desired, even without specific instructions, and was only to happy to oblige, not just for his employer's sake but also his own. He had ten talents for his lord, whether expressly monetarily or in terms of ability a vast treasure, and the lord was eager to give him even more as he anointed his servant with those beautiful words every Christian lives to hear:

"The lord said unto him,
Well done, thou good and faithful servant:
thou hast been faithful over a few things,
I will make thee ruler over many things:
enter thou into the joy of thy lord."

It is easy to conceive and imagine the servant's euphoric bliss, but after we overlook the "joy of the Lord," who, if anything, is even happier than the servant.

Seemingly, from the parable it is difficult to find anything exceptional or remarkable about either of the two servants, yet there was an abundance of such. They were self-starters, self-motivated, and understood that to work at anything or to work or anyone means to produce and serve. They looked for ways to be productive, to further the estate o their master and to be adjudged worthy of that lord's confidence. It has become an often-shop-worn cliché, but each man possessed the "heart of a servant" and found an ever-burgeoning joy in so serving. Money and material goods and wealth are easily weighed, counted and assayed, and the increase in one's monetary "talents" is capable of specific calculation. Not so the talents of which our essay has discussed. These are the talents, the slow accretion of character that forms both the precious metal and the steel spine of any man or woman who is truly growing in Christ. Of the talents that really counted, the five talent and the two talent men really were unaware of the magnificent growth of their characters, as it was left to their master to praise them. By any measure, ancient, medieval or modern, these men are the servants, the employees, that anyone desires. Throughout this lengthy parable their loyalty and steadfastness is complete and unwavering, they are the definition of dependability, and they honor their employer with their loyalty and, no doubt, their friendship. The ceiling for their service is so high that none is even hinted, and ultimately their servitude has one, and one, natural forum, Heaven itself.

We now return with hesitation to the servant who could not even maintain propriety over the one talent with which he had been entrusted. As with the other two productive servants this man's day of accounting came. In one area of service he was a match for is two more productive cohorts, and that was in the sphere of words. As an aside (though it is central to the structure of the parable) the truly slothful and unproductive can be disingenuous with words and explanations, and in a time-honored expression they "... can talk a good game." So it was with this man, and his words and their elocution did not fail him when he stood before his master:

"Lord, I know that thou art a hard man,

reaping where thou hast not sown,
and gathering where thou has not strained.

And I was afraid,
and went and hid thy talent in the earth;
lo, there thou hast that is thine."

He did nothing, or at least nothing positive. Rather than increasing his talents his own choices doomed the usefulness of the one talent that he had been given. It is easy and the historical frequency of interpretation indicates that overwhelmingly the interpreters, the preachers and the teachers of this parable have shined a harsh light and focused its glare on the actions of the one talent servant, which are certainly worthy of harsh criticism. Yet, it is the attitude that dwells in the man's heart which has condemned him. As the scriptures consistently, even unwaveringly proclaim it is the heart and its attitudes that serves as the birthplace and nursery of sin, even before sin is borne into the shadowed light of its day.

Much of what this unperforming servant says to his master's face is not only incorrect or mistaken but really just a cacophony of lies. When he begs off and with a piteous reasoning states that he knows that his master "...is a hard man, reaping where (he) has not sown," effectively he is accusing him of being a thief. Such allegations of dark immoral behavior are often most easily and thoughtlessly made by those persons themselves who are so guilty. To emphasize the intensity of a metaphor it is suggested that the servants view of his master as a "hard" man stands as a giant granite obelisk a correct view of the master, the man who in the parabolic structure obviously is the Father. This assumedly hard man has left his servant alone, granted him an abundance of time, allowed him to work at his own pace and really in the pursuits that the servant chooses, so long as they serve the master. In return his servant, piteously lazy and cynical, excuses his own conduct with a litany of lies, from the master's alleged harshness to his outright thievery. As to the one talent with which he was entrusted the servant wasted it by burying it in the ground where it serves no purpose. He has made a string of presumptions about his master, just as multitudes never cease to make non-fact-based assumptions about God, almost all of which lack factual and evidentiary based knowledge. From the onset of Creation much of humanity has divided itself into two camps of approach to God, the one viewing God as the original Universalist, all forgiving, all overlooking and a Deity who has somehow indebted Himself into owing mankind its salvation. The other traditionally has seen God as a harsh, violent Deity whose all-seeing Eye is watching Him human creation and tallying the sins and punishments of each man and woman daily. The one-talent servant amazingly has seemed to have successfully placed himself in both camps.

Neither view of the master, of God, is correct. Every parable, Biblical story or allegory that portrays God reflects Him as the Divine personification of the loving father, endlessly tolerant, patient, gentle but expecting of obedience. The first two servants were rewarded with an abundance which reached beyond their expectations, while the third had taken (or in actuality did so himself) the talent he believed was his. The lines of demarcation between the two faithful servants and the one of recalcitrance are two in number. The first is attitude, for the productive two had the appropriate attitude towards their master, an attitude whose light contrasted brightly with the dark cavern of the third's heart. Secondly, and oh how so often is this the essential element of any scriptural story, is the attitude of obedience. The faithful two obeyed their employer, while the one talent man buried what little he had, assuming that his talents would prove ultimately lacking in value. While the latter is condemned to punishment the first two are rewarded with even greater treasure.

As we draw to a conclusion our view of this great and famous parable, we realize that its thorough study requires a bit more detailed examination of the definition of "talent," something which was both gained and lost. Since Christ first gave His disciples this parable two thousand years ago it has enjoyed copious study, endless essays (such as this) teachings and sermons, likely almost all conceived and delivered in good faith. Unfortunately, though, as with much scripture the passing of the centuries has frozen into place interpretations that have become standardized, rote and often quite stringent, with a rigidity that would have been worthy of the Pharisees. The most common, at least in recent times, has reduced "talents" to "additional Christians," always the most worthy of endeavors. Still, it is a gross injustice to reduce "talent" to the ability to evangelize, for this is a talent God has reserved for but a few persons. It was the church's greatest evangelist, the apostle Paul, who remarked that:

> "... He gave some apostles,
> and some prophets;
> and some evangelists;
> and some pastors and teachers."

No sane Christian would ever maintain that all Christians have it within their abilities to become apostles (there were only thirteen of them) or prophets, and likewise not all Christians are suited to become pastors or teachers. Yet, and with both sincerity and reason, the same spirit in which this reply is offered, many have asserted, based upon this parable, that all Christians are either active or dormant great evangelists. Christ rather seems to teach that to the abundance we are given, be it spiritual, emotional and at time even material, will be added more talent, more ability, more blessing, more success, based upon our service to Him. No Christian can appropriately deny that evangelistic ability may be one of the talents provided by God, but to reduce the parable's meaning to such is close to ludicrous.

Sadly, it is often overlooked that the two blessed servants great evangelistic talents were simply in their obedience. By this itself they were evangelizing, just as the slothful servant silenced his influence by burying it. The unfaithful servant extinguished his light, and he was receiving no more. The faithful men, as do all faithful, let "their light shine before men." This was the great parable when spoken by Christ, and so it yet remains.

CHAPTER FIFTEEN

LABOR TROUBLES IN THE VINEYARD

The business owner, farmer, artisan or professional who is without labor problems is a fortunate person indeed. Try as he might he will not always be perceived as fair, equitable and just by his employees even when he has striven with strain and fervor to be as accommodating as possible. The relationship is by nature two sided and those that can maintain a happy equilibrium for an extended time are worthy of commendation and admiration.

One of God's great blessings to His Creation and often overlooked is the understanding of the two-party dichotomy into which so many human, and Divine, relationships sort themselves. Left to His Son, Christ, was the amazing ability to note these, describe them, and make them so plain in actual and even parabolic form. Jesus as always was exceptionally sensitive and attentive to the examples which would strike familiar sounds to the ears of his listeners, and one of His most favored venues was the vineyard, so well known to his audience. He knew that since men and women spent so much of their lives working and striving to make a living, it was a subject that naturally commanded and yet today still does the attention of many persons.

The stories of work, of the conflicts and the harmonies between labor and management have faded not at all, and the universality of their appeal is an attraction to the serious and attentive listener for all time. In short but detailed parables He proved that He knew the structure and the tensions of the workplace, which were representative of those of life as a whole. The friction between employer and employee, the generosity and pettiness which are ever temptations, and the loyalty and betrayal that mankind to which mankind is ever prone are all present in the vineyards of the Master. Two stories, each with great pathos, are starkly illustrative of humanity's work life, and the more important eternal relationship between God and man. The first is an easily understandable story of workers who feel that their master has given them the proverbial short end of the stick.

Parable of the Hired Laborers
Matthew 20:1-16

A modern penny has little value as a medium of exchange with economic growth, a money supply of staggering proportions and harsh, cruel, driving inflation in the United States a penny is a small round copper piece with an engraved image of President Abraham Lincoln. On its own it is difficult to think o anything which it can purchase. Christ, though, began a parable of fascinating instruction with the story of a great householder who began his day by an early morning hiring of a number of workers to whom he promised a day's wages of one penny in exchange for one day's work. Was the man serious? To this question the answer is a resounding "yes," for a penny was the English word for "denarius," a unit of money in ancient Roman days was accepted as the prototypical "fair days pay for a fair day's work." Whatever its measure the vineyard owner had no difficulty in procuring workers for the day. Still the owner had great amounts of work to be done, and at 9:00 a.m. he went back to the marketplace where he found a number of potential workers standing idle. These men, as does any man or woman who actively seeks necessary work, apparently had developed a ravenous desire for employment for Jesus recorded this exchange"

> "(He) said unto them;
> Go ye also into the vineyard,
> and whatsoever is right I will give you,
> And they went their way."

Like all vineyard owners, executives, project managers, etc., this household discovered in stages that sometimes it is difficult to accurately estimate the time required for a particular project and the amount and extent of labor which it demands. Then, not once, not twice, but three time more he returned to the town marketplace to find workers, as the day lengthened to noon, 3:00 p.m., and 5:00 p.m. To these final three groups he made the same offer as he had to those at 9:00 a.m., i.e. he would pay them whatever was right. The vineyard owner, the busiest man of all, finally came to the end of the day and the time to "settle up" with all his workers. To his steward he entrusted this task to his steward with the directive to "call the laborers, and give them their hire, beginning from the last unto he first." To the obvious shock and dismay, doubtless infused with anger, each man whether he worked as many as twelve or as few as one hour, received the identical wage of one penny. So, by strict mathematical and accounting principles the shorter a man's period of work the greater his hourly wage. Demonstrating that as always, the emotional structure of human beings never really changes, and that each man and woman has an awareness of self-justice, whether inborn or developed by life Jesus said:

"But when the first came,

> they supposed that they should have received more;
> and they likewise received every man a penny.
> And when they received it they murmured against the goodman of the house,
>
> Saying, These last hath wrought but one hour
> and thou hast made them equal to us,
> which have borne the burden and heat of the day."

Shone under the harsh, truly unforgiving light of modern management-labor relations and a type of innate equity that many persons possess the householder's actions appear to be unwise, unnecessary and likely to many unfair. They have a type of tendentious unfairness, it is true, but unfair to whom?

The householder did not sign a labor contract, engage in collective bargaining or even make an agreement with an amorphous labor force. Five times he made offers to potential laborers, and five times he obtained employees. It is humanity's proclivity to demand equality, including equality of outcomes for all, a human passion which shows no sign of diminution well into the twenty-first century. That ardency, though, evaporates when equity or equality of outcomes seemingly punishes their work and behavior. Here, though, no man was defrauded. The only persons with whom the householder made a precise agreement was the men in the first group to whom he promised each a day's wage, which was forthcoming. The latter groups, rewarded with a full day's wages, would have had no reason for complaint in any event.

Even two thousand years ago some of the self-assured wronged laborers felt an injustice. With all honesty, no wise employer, especially a believing Christian, would structure his/her pay scale in this manner, and for a day's, week's, or a year's work its principals would need adjustment. It is explainable and the householder's actions definitely defensible. The importance of its workplace application, though, is de minimis, compared to the spiritual, literally eternal lesson of the story. The Savior began His parable with the introductory phrase of "For the kingdom of heaven is like unto a man..." It is not a story of a group of workers picking grapes from vines but a preview of Christ's thinking and determinations for eternal life. Now, our essay will so view and discuss from this vantage point.

In our present parable the householder, the vineyard owner, the master, is certainly a representation spiritually of God Himself. So often, and to this day, the term God the Father and God the Son are employed both in combination and as exact substitutes one for another, and most often correctly. For our purposes we shall continue this mode of expression.

Maybe the first thing about the householder that is worthy of notice, and strikingly so, is that he is an employer who is always hiring. Whatever the time, place and most often the circumstances is deeply and dreadedly known by all those who seek work, a new job, gainful employment, etc. As a prospective employee a person may be willing and eager to supply his labor and skills, but it is to no avail if the prospective employer is in a period of not hiring, which as we know almost instinctively seems to be the natural order of things. Wonderfully and wondrously, though, this master is even seeking new persons for the endless jobs he has to offer. Early in the morning he came to the center of the labor market, and five times hence in the same day he returned. An often downplayed, overlooked aspect of the story is the householder's almost desperate desire for employees. His promised consideration to them is "... whatever is right." His ceaseless trips to the marketplace to find not more money, more property or whatever but more souls is reflective of God's ever standing love and grace which He offers to any and all. His sole commitment is to do "right" by them, not to do the minimum of a contractual obligation or to fulfill a financial duty impossible by law or even by custom and tradition but to do only what is right. Evidently his workers trusted him for when they signed on, they were promised only what was right, with the almost irrefutable inference that the employer alone would determine the meaning of "right."

His employees trusted him and with good reason, for at the end of the day all were paid the wages of a full day's work even if they had worked as little as an hour. Yet at least some of the original group, those employed in the early morning and had worked the entirety of a long day, were (as it must be conceded) naturally disgruntled because their employer had not effectively renegotiated their labor contract. The master's demeanor and response to them is conciliatory, reasonable and even tender as he tries to explain to one of them:

> "Friend, I do thee no wrong:
> didst thou not agree with me for a penny"

He then sets forth a basic principle with consideration and conciliation but most of all with truth:

> "Is it not lawful for me to do what I will with mine own?
> Is thy evil because I am good?"

The master was laboring under no conceivable obligation or commitment to offer work and reward to those who would come to him, and even more certainly god has never incurred an obligation to save any man or woman and receive them into Heaven. Just as work and payment was the employer's to give so likewise the ultimate gift of Heaven and eternal life remains God's to dispose.

As for the vineyard workers they showed themselves worthy servants, but their labors were not equal to their compensation. Even more to the point the working, a church's program of work, "good" works, benevolence ad infinitum can never equal what God allots in return, the gift of salvation. This is the foundation for controversies and intense spiritual debates that have raged from the birth of the Church to these present days of Christendom. From Roman Catholicism to all manner of Protestantism and every aspect of truth and falsehood lying within and without, humanity has had trouble really accepting that men and women do not earn or merit salvation and Heaven. It is an impossibility. As Paul wrote such resounding clarity:

> "For by grace are ye saved through faith;
> and that not of yourselves: it is the gift of God.
>
> Not of works, lest any men should boast,"

All the workers received the same wage, whether his workday began at 6:00 a.m. or 5:00 p.m. Their answer was the heeding of the vineyard owner's call just as the Christian disciple's response should be the heeding and obedience to the call. All received the same reward, and it is almost compelling to posit that all obedient disciples receive the same reward.

We who write, read and function are by definition animate, functioning living beings, and we await the revelations of the afterlife. In the plainest of language none of us have yet to experience the other side of life, the eternal, and it behooves even the most studious tread lightly in a realm which he has yet to experience. It remains Biblically and in actuality the world of which Shakespeare described as "the undiscovered country." Christ never talked to His audience from a mental and spiritual platform so elevated that they and we are incapable to understanding the meaning of His words. When He spoke on any subject, though, without fail He unearthed covered, even obtuse meanings that no other teacher had ever seen. Christ elevated the simple, the mundane, an everyday subject such as the wage and salary scale for a group of putatively non-descript vineyard workers two thousand years ago to a realm of meaning and understanding far beyond the contemplative imaginings of any person.

The payment of one day's wages and the ruffled feathers of a few dissatisfied workers is hardly the substance alone of a parable for all eternity. Jesus was not many things but rather the sum and substance of all matter, the Alpha and the Omega. In His eternal repertoire is the ability to build and climax a story so that the student is left with its real meaning as the last lesson ringing in his ears and settling into his heart. In the penultimate proposition of His narrative the Householder addresses his early arriving workers, those who feel victimized thus:

"Take that thine is, and go thy way:

> I will give unto this last, even as unto thee.
>
> Is it not lawful for me to do what I will with mine own?
> Is thine eye evil because I am good?"

This employee kept his bargain with all his employees, to the first group being remitted his contractual obligation and to all the succeeding groups "whatever is right." No man was defrauded, and in its larger context none had any work or reward save for the voluntary actions of the vineyard owner. No man was cheated, and every man was rewarded. To the Kingdom of Heaven, its earthly manifestation being the Church came all sorts of persons at every conceivable moment and juncture in their differing lives. It is at God's throne of giving, of grace, where true equality is finally found. Some Christians have a deep, intimate knowledge of Christ because they were born to devout Christian parents who so raised them. Others come at various points in their lives, and this example extends even to the apostles, the first twelve being present at the beginning of Christ's ministry with Paul, the great persecutor coming later. Still today many souls pass from darkness to light and life much later in life, either in life's later stages or at the door of eternity itself. The "time served" seems to be of little reckoning to Christ as He ends tis parable of great depth and meaning with the words"

> "So the last shall be first, and the first last:
> for many be called, but few chosen."

<u>Rebellion in the Vineyard</u>
Matthew 21:33-44

Only the Savior could provide a history of the world in but twelve short verses and do so in the form of a parable. Christ never tired of teaching and speaking about vineyards, especially since He was surrounded by them, and his listeners were well familiar with them. Only He had the ability to condense so much information and time into so few words, all of which should have grasped by His original listening audience and by the modern reader, as well as all humanity in between those two points on the spiritual spectrum. He commenced His next vineyard parable with the story of a vineyard owner; i.e. householder, who planted a vineyard and with evident great care, efficiency and thoroughness cultivated the vines, constructed the outbuildings and in general ran a model operation which resulted in an efficiently producing vineyard. The householder was not personally present that instead was away and, in his absence, He entrusted the vineyard to the husbandmen, or vineyard workers.

This vineyard keeper was a rare combination of talents and character. As the parable will demonstrate in the strictest professional sense of the concept, he had an outstanding talent for the running and the management of a vineyard. In the moral sense there appeared and remained something askew with his character. In the true vineyard owner's absence the husbandman's talents and proclivities toward self-aggrandizement, self-dealing, and the usurpation and exertion of pure power had grown enormously. With the time of ripening of the fruit and its harvesting, the true owner of the vineyard and the master of all its men dispatched "...his servants to the husbandmen, that they might receive the fruits of it." A terroristic shock and a disaster awaited them, for as Jesus explained:

"And the husbandmen took his servants,
and beat one, and killed another, and stoned another."

A new power had arisen in the vineyard to displace the true owner. Still, much to that new man he remained in the order of things an employee, a servant.

By his own twisted reckoning the husbandman surely thought that he had done well. The vineyard of the rightful owner had been expropriated to this man's sole usage and he had drained the vineyard of its fruit and produce into his own vessels. Moreover, he had established himself as a man with whom one should not trifle. He did not turn away the servant of the legitimate owner but rather just murdered him. The rightful owner of the vineyard would think twice about any further action. The owner both thought and acted, and in one cuttingly terse sentence Christ explained the next chapter in the drama:

> "Again, he sent other servants more than the first
> and they did unto them likewise."

How frustrated must have been the husbandmen, for the first round of murders did not in the least deter the vineyard's legitimate owner.

At this juncture in the story it is appropriate to comment on an apparently shared quality of the husbandman and the owner. Each was persistent and tenacious, most doggedly so, but their the comparative metaphor begins to dissolve. Always and forever their remains a hard and vast distinction between persistence and tenacity in the cause of good and that of evil. The husbandman had proven by now that he would oppose, persecute and destroy anyone who came in representation of the legitimate owner. The owner's tenacity was evidenced by a continued patience with this embezzler, interloper and murderer of a man who had taken what the owner founded and established and corrupted and perverted it to his own selfish ends.

Still, the patient forbearance and yes, the love, which the owner had for the husbandman and his minions, these corrupt miscreants, had not yet been exhausted. With a resolution which can only be called Divine the owner reached for the true solution:

> "But last of all he sent unto them his son, saying,
> They will reverence my son."

His optimism and good faith does the owner credit to an extraordinary degree, but the futility continued apace:

> "But when the husbandmen saw the son,
> they said among themselves,
> This is the heir;
> come, let us kill him, and let us seize on his inheritance."

The owner, the poor, suffering owner but a man endowed with a goodness of character and an almost limitless patience, had suffered dreadfully and for some stretch of time. The obvious question at this point is in the nature of what or who does he have remaining to send. The husbandman had made good on his final promise and threat for "... they caught (the owner's son) and cast him out of the vineyard and slew him." This portion of the parable and its denouncement is reflected in a brief question and answer with Christ and His audience:

> "When the lord therefore of the vineyard cometh,
> what will he do unto the husbandman?"

The owner has been preternaturally patient throughout all sorts of pain and losses and has responded with an ever-increasing determination to reap fruits from his vineyard. Despite the unspeakably wrong and terrible crimes and murders committed against him, the attempted degradation and destruction of his authority and just outright hatred directed to him his patience with the miserable malefactor has never snapped. We should now be reminded of a famous line from an English writer, some sixteen hundred years hence when John Dryden remarked to "beware the fury of a patient man." The rapt audience of Christ, a group surrounding him, responded in the later spirit of Dryden when they answered the Messiah:

> "He will miserably destroy those wicked men
> and will let out his vineyard unto other husbandmen,
> which shall bless him the fruits in their seasons."

Very interesting we might say, but the modern observer is within his/her rights in inquiring what does it mean historically and what does it mean today.

Interesting, full of malevolence, tragedy and pathos it certainly was, but what is the lasting meaning of the parable? No one has ever approached the Master in His ability to fashion and relate fascinating narratives, but now two millennia later does it retain a residue of meaning? Of course, and more than just a residue for with this story Jesus told the sad story of God's Chosen, the Jewish people, their special blessings and their wholesale, even violent rejection of those same Divine gifts.

From Ur of the Chaldees was drawn a great man, Abraham, nee Abram, and through His plentiful descendants the entire world would receive incalculable blessings. Eventually, one of those descendants, Moses, was called by God to emancipate his people from Egyptian slavery and to establish a great and truly special nation, Israel, which would be God's Chosen. The story of Moses, the Ten Commandments, the Law of Moses and the nation is widely familiar to all disciples. So should be the reality that Moses and a few others were true, loyal, faithful servants of God and were always prey to rebellion, revolution, insurrection and even murder from their fellow "vineyard workers," the Jews. Nonetheless, though God's patience was taken well beyond any human breaking point, His vineyard, the Kingdom of Israel and its Mosaical Law stood. They wandered in the wilderness, at times the mass of them returned to paganism, but still the vineyard remained as did its owner, the Almighty.

Moses died, as did his own great successor Joshua, and eventually this earthly land of Israel became a kingdom, united for the period of but three monarchies before it divided into the northern apostate land of Israel, and the southern land of Judah. God sent plentiful workers for centuries into His vineyard, prophets by the historically famous names of Elijah, Elisha, Jeremiah, Isaiah, Ezekiel and countless others who faced rejection and often death by the husbandmen of the vineyard. Still, the vineyard's owner, parabolically representative of God Himself self-demonstrated Divine patience and remained steadfast in His loyalty to a people who in the man had rejected and deserted Him. Those in the vineyard showed their appreciation by "whoring after false gods" and "killing and stoning the prophets."

Still, the vineyard owner, in spite of insults, injuries, deaths, rebellions ad nauseum, loved His vineyard and its workers. The owner's faith in his workers is touching, for now he sent to them his only son with a touching self-assurance that "They will reverence him." How sad, how tragically, pathetically and eternally sad in that the Jewish people rejected the owner's son, who of course is the foreshadowing prototype of Christ, spat upon Him and killed Him. No, this is not the old canard that "the Jews killed Christ." It may have been a Jewish organized conspiracy, but the sins of all men and women required the atoning expiation of the Son of God Himself. Of course, the early Church and one or two generations hence was at first exclusively Jewish until "exclusively Jewish" gave way almost to "exclusively Gentile." After the Church's foundation and the growth of understanding of the apostles the truth began to spread to the Gentiles. Still, these wants and Christ Himself remained beckoning to the Jewish workers to return to the vineyard. In the main, they never returned, and bitterness has remained and seemingly has even intensified in recent days between Jews and certain fanatical Gentiles. It remains one of not just history's, but eternity's great tragedies, for God called neither Jews nor Gentiles to His vineyard, His home. He calls only Christians.

CHAPTER SIXTEEN

THE GOOD SAMARITAN

Many years after the end of Christ's personal earthly ministry Paul said of himself (not Jesus) that he had become all things to all people. This was not braggadocio for the great apostle by his life, preachings and teachings to all people, whether Jew or Gentile, rich or poor, slave or free, truly preached the same truth to all men and women. More than any man who ever lived Paul was the first and the most willing to step aside for that one who in the most complete and purest sense truly was all things for all, the ultimate "Man For All Seasons," Jesus Christ. For these past two millennia generally well-meaning men and women have endlessly attempted to co-opt the Master for their particular philosophy, manner of life and theology. Their spirit is good, but the ultimate effects have often run a bit awry of the actual truth and character of the Master.

A common descriptive and designation which many continue to apply to the humble man from Nazareth is that he was and yet so remains a "revolutionary." That term, though, is a powder keg with a lit fuse and often can mean just what the enunciator says it means. Likely, the first of life's arenas which comes to mind with the term revolutionary is that of the political, and well into the twenty-first century this shows no sign of abatement. Some political movements have claimed Christ as their heart, soul and leader and have attributed to Him words and conduct which are diametrically opposed to the real life and teachings of the Messiah. Strange and even bewildering as it may seem one of the most prominent are the Communists (or Marxists if it is preferred) and their pale pastel imitations, the socialists, who have for over a century and a half tried to sell the bizarre dogma that Jesus Himself was the first communist. From the famous Sermon on the Mount they extract the ideas that Christ was enunciating are of the fundamental bedrock truths of Marxism, i.e. the principle of "to each according to his need." In no single sentence can any person, especially the author, even begin to set forth a summary of the Sermon's spiritual message. We are on firm ground, though, when we claim that it was no economic treatise but rather the most brilliantly beautiful assertion of the Christian foundation of "Love thy neighbor as thyself." The underlying truths and moral principles of the Master's teachings ultimately leave in the dust the overriding and over emphasized lessons of any economic system. To this particular point we have omitted and save for its enumeration shall continue to omit the logical and spiritual absurdity of the compatibility of an economic and political system, communism, that posits that humans are nothing more than transiently existent material. Christ not only taught but demonstrated that man does not live by bread alone but is a permanently created spirit and soul made for the realm of eternity. To reduce, and with gross inaccuracy at that, that the Savior was some sort of political and material revolutionary is absurd to the point of the grotesque.

If not spiritually (but here maybe yes as well) the lunacy of Christ as a political revolutionary was at one time propagated by secular history's greatest villain, Adolf Hitler himself. In the grab bag of horrors that was national socialism (Nazism) was the murky, amorphous and patently absurd assertion that Christ, a figure with an almost endless genealogical line of Hebrew ancestors was Himself Aryan (read: German) blood, a belief of lunatic quality and absurd on its face. In other words Hitler even briefly toyed with the idea of Christ, the humble Prince of Peace, as a political agitator and a racial purist. Thankfully, Hitler and his followers provided ample evidence of their malevolence without harping on a patently absurd idea. Christ, as a type of racial savior and revolutionary, thankfully was an idea that never gained traction or even a real foothold.

At the polar opposite of earthly philosophies such as communism and fascism, both of which are fueled by continuous streams of hatred and violence, is that of non-violence, or its most pronounced form of pacifism. Here, Christ as a revolutionary comes somewhat closer to the mark of truth, although His life, teachings and God's Word from the beginning do not entirely support such a view. Still, a monument to Christ as a revolutionary pacifist will eventually crumble and fall because the life and attitudes of the Savior are not totally synchronized with such. The scriptures have never abrogated the basic, almost instinctual concept, that a person, or even a nation, has the right of self-defense, which usually necessitates violence. On two Biblical occasions Christ even violently drove the "money changers" and their desecrations from the Temple. Any fair-minded person, though, will acknowledge that the complete adoption of Christian precepts will lead a person to a practical personal pacifism that deplores violence.

All these ideas of Christ and His Mission are wrong, some more than others, but all have something in common, a stated or implied supposition that the Son of God came to earth to fulfill in whole or in part a political role. This is without exception false. Everything about the Savior from the millennia of Old Testament prophecy, through His own life chronicled in the four gospels to the early history of the Church in the New Testament dictates otherwise. The remainder of this chapter could be filled with instances where Christ eschewed the political realm and all attempts by trickery and/or coercion to trick Him into it. Instead, let us content ourselves with a couple of brief references and quotations from the Master Himself. The "closest" He ever came to a political statement was when the Pharisees sought to entrap Him by asking whether it was lawful to give tribute, or tax money, to Rome. Forever after He provided words which linger and are ever quoted:

> "Render unto Caesar the things which are Caesar's,
> and to God the things which are His."

Pay taxes, obey the civil laws, and seek to be compliant with civil authority, but give to the Father all else.

From the moment He began to be noticed multitudes of common people and even more relative to the present narrative so many of His skeptics, critics and outright enemies attempted to ensnare Him in private disputes and the great public and political questions of the day. Assiduously Jesus avoided them all until the final moments before His condemnation and crucifixion He was accused of being an insurrectionist against Rome and a revolutionary intent on bringing the mighty empire from the west to collapse. When Governor Pilate inquired of His possible station as the leader of a rebellion the Son of God replies with an answer of clarity and absolute truth:

> "My Kingdom is not of this world;

if My Kingdom were of this world then would
My servants fight."

He was not an earthly king, a statesman, a politician and certainly no revolutionary, or was He? A revolutionary in the well and often bitterly known sense of over twining, so often with the instruments of violence, existing governments and earthly powers, that He was not. Still, Jesus Christ was a revolutionary, a teacher, a messenger who sought to overthrow an existing power and replace it with another power. His was and remains a different sort of revolution. Christ seeks to not just uproot but to destroy an enemy power which will reside and take hold in every human heart marked by the absence of Christ. It is Satan and his power of sin and death, which is so tenaciously grasping, so powerful that it is capable of eradication and extinguishment by Christ and Christ alone. It is a revolution of the heart, a revolution of thinking, acting and just simply functioning in every human heart for which Christ aims. His entire life and every syllable of His teaching and ministering to humanity proclaims this, but nowhere more powerfully or beautifully than in perhaps the most famous of His parables.

Luke 10:25-37

Every incident, word, action and character of this story is at variance and at times adamantly and violently so with standard human thinking on the subject matter and character action breached by Christ's story. At first blush neither the story's setting nor its characters the least bit strange, but it is the striking surprise of at least three different men's reactions, radically different to the same situation that befalls each of them.

The physical setting of the story topographically at least has altered but little in the two thousand years since Jesus told the story. "A certain man went down from Jerusalem to Jericho," and this alone is the commencement point for a skeptic's cynicism since Jericho is, on the map seventeen miles north, or "up" from Jerusalem. Truly, a little knowledge is a dangerous thing. This is true, but the up and down refers to the striking difference in elevation between the two cities. Jericho is some 3,300 feet lower in elevation than Jerusalem, and such a distinction over seventeen miles makes for a severe gradient. It was a road, a rocky path, with twists, turns and constant plunges to which even modern travelers have reacted to its eerie foreboding atmosphere. Even today we associate certain areas, quite often decayed urban centers with violent crime, and the Jerusalem to Jericho road was a type of elongated path haunted by murderers, robbers, and assorted cutthroats. It is now the Master who assumes control and enunciates the story of a man traveling to Jericho who:

> "... fell among thieves, which stripped him of his raiment,
> and wounded him, and departed, leaving him half dead."

The piteous condition of an innocent traveler even two millennia later elicits the solicitude of any decent person, not least being the fact that each of us, while perhaps quite uncomfortable, can see ourselves in the abandoned condition of this traveler. We may find an entire thesaurus of adjectives to apply to this victimized man, but for the purposes of Christ's story let us focus on one – helpless. He was already half-dead, and the likelihood that nature, the elements, and/or more criminals would supply the other half was not minimal.

Time and the circumstances of who walked that treacherous path within a short period of time would determine life or death for the man. If he was conscious his heart likely would have leaped for joy if he had known the identity of two men who soon passed his way, a priest and a Levite, both men "of the cloth," highly respected and esteemed with the Jewish community as being a portion of the very spine of the Jewish religion. If he remained conscious how the wounded man would have rejoiced in the knowledge of, in its purest sense, a Godsend that the first two travelers to come his way were men known for their religious principles and professions of belief. Likely, Jesus's original audience momentarily was charged with this same emotion. Sadly, Jesus soon pulled the first blinders from their eyes and hearts when He explained:

> "And by chance there came down a certain priest that way:
> and when he saw him, he passed on the other side.
>
> And likewise a Levite, when he was at the place, came and looked on him, and passed by on the other side."

Astonishing, is it not? Two men, a Levite devoted to religious work and a priest himself passively refusing to offer any aid and succor to a man dying of his wounds? Human curiosity and moral substantive teaching requires that the reader pause and make further inquiry as to the rationale for such dispassionately callous behavior from two men publicly assumed to be moral exemplars. Such inquiry will be entirely speculative, for Christ's parable provides not a single syllable of explanation. This was two thousand years ago, in a basic, rather primitive culture inhabited not by modern twenty-first century Westerners but by Jews from the tiny province of Judea. Still, at whatever time and place and in whatever language human hearts operate with an astounding similarity. Shall we not be honest and ask rather "why would I have passed by this suffering and dying man with such a callous disregard?" Now, the natural kinship and bond among all humans will begin to assert itself as we lay bare the rationales in the first person, rather than the third person.

First of all, I do not even know this man, and certainly it is not I who is responsible for his lying on a pitiful, mangled heap in the roadway. Rather, I am a good person who seeks always to follow the precepts of God and the laws of men. His being attacked, brutalized and left for dead is unconscionable, inexplicable and unforgiveable. The violent and thuggish miscreants who perpetrated this horror should be apprehended and punished severely with the full rigors of the law. Law enforcement personnel trained medical people and others better suited to the moment will by any odds soon be here. They will know what to do, and I will simply be in their way. It is far better that I leave such a matter to the "professionals." Besides and perhaps most importantly I am a very busy person, and if I stop and get involved will I be able to meet my itinerary of important appointments with important persons scheduled for later today. I anticipate much good that potentially may come from them, not just material good but the spiritual blessings and benefits which in my role as a priest (or a Levite) I may endow upon others. With each footstep closer to the end point of my journey I feel more certain and satisfied with my decision to leave this situation for others better suited. It will not be a total loss, though, as I am already beginning to glean several thundering moral lessons from this despicable display of violence. Already, the horror of the dying man on the road begins to dim a bit.

The priest and the Levite continue on their journey, but Christ directs His listeners back to the innocent victim on the Jericho road. This is a man who moment by moment experiences the draining of the life-giving blood from his ravaged body. He, conscious or not, is dying and no human rationales, of whatever sophistication, will save him. Fortunately for him, though, the Jerusalem to Jericho road was a well-traveled corridor, and Jesus now introduces to us the most famous of the story's characters:

> "But a certain Samaritan, as he journeyed, came where he was:
> and when he saw him, he had compassion on him."

Likely, if we were among those either standing in the audience to whom Christ was first teaching this parable the most arresting word of His narrative was the "Samaritan" which He just spoken. The Master's immediate audience most probably was exclusively Jewish, a people historically who held a deep loathing for Samaritans, an emotion which generally was enthusiastically reciprocated by the Samaritans. Before our text advances any further into a discussion of the Jew/Samaritan dichotomy, let us examine an even more important and instructive word in Christ's sentence, "compassion." We shall eschew the dictionary entry on its meaning, though, and instead focus on the practical usage given to the word.

Compassion remains a very popular word, and generally all but the most hardened brutes wish to be known as compassionate. In everyday speech, though, it has generally come to signify tender emotion to one who is hurt, wounded, distressed or suffering in some manner. Almost all persons wish to be thought of as compassionate, sympathetic, soft hearted and tender. Even the political class, with its well-earned dubious reputation for character, morality and sincerity seeks to be known as compassionate. So is the nature of the compassion of the Samaritan on the roadway, a temporary ache in his heart and perhaps a tear in his eye as his journey continued. Not all matters of God or even men, however, go as we often suppose.

Let us activate the final word of the preceding paragraph, "suppose," and engage in a few worthy suppositions of our own about this Samaritan whose day was interrupted. Actually many of the suppositions are quite easy to make since they will be identical to those assumptions we make since they will be identical to those assumptions we make of the priest and the Levite. By definition he was in transit going from one point to another and was not out for a pleasant sojourn on a very treacherous road. He, too, had a schedule to keep, perhaps a business appointment, a family member to see or maybe he was on the welcome journey home after a long, arduous journey. Seeing a half-dead man on the roadway was a shock, an unexpected tremor, and to follow the possible demands of the situation could lead him to places and people to be avoided. Further, as a Samaritan he was walking in the foreign field of Judea, where his ordinary welcome would be frigid. Whether he did or did not overcome ethnic or national prejudice is beside the point because the Samaritan's actions swept by such concerns. He saw an unfortunate fellow man in the roadway, a man possibly dying, and one who needed help, not a need that could be fulfilled next week, or at 7:00 p.m., that evening, but here, now, at this moment and by this man. Samaritan or Jew mattered nothing, and chances are he did not even know as he acted in the factual scenario that a Jew and a Samaritan both looked and appeared rather similar. To the Master we defer as He explains the Samaritan's initial actions:

> "(He) went to him and bound up his wounds,
> pouring in oil and wine, and set him on his own beast,
> and brought him to an inn, and took care of him."

How remarkably rapid was the opening of the man's wallet and even more so his heart. The "oil and wine" were free gifts from no one, and the Samaritan was now the poorer by spending them on a complete stranger. More remarkably his heart was touched, and He saw before him not only a severely injured man but an opportunity and an obligation which the Samaritan alone chose to fulfill. Already he had done so much, and had he stopped at this point his conduct would have been exemplary for the ages. Just for a bit he could have delayed and hoped for a traveler (after all, the road was customarily busy) who was going to a nearby inn and passed responsibility to another person. Instead the Samaritan decided to make a journey of perhaps an extra mile or so and personally take the victim to an inn. There, the man could convalesce, receive rest and medical treatment and recover, all the while the Samaritan's journeying forward with the fulfilling knowledge of a job well done. This was not the man's character, and to borrow an allusion with which the Savior would soon become bitterly acquainted the Samaritan was not willing to wash his hands of the matter.

The Samaritan stayed the night at the inn with his newfound charge, and Christ recorded his conduct with an inspirational sweep that yet inspires us:

> "And on the morrow when he departed, he took out two pence,
> and gave them to the host, and said unto him,
> Take care of him, and whatsoever thou spendest more,
> when I come again, I will repay thee."

Such was the virtue, the goodness and the depth of the solidity of character of the Samaritan that he took a situation that had been suddenly and unexpectedly thrust upon him, willingly and with goodness shouldered the burden over two days of his own valuable time and then granted an open account to help him according to the man's necessity. With an extraordinary ease this Samaritan could have acted and performed differently at any juncture of his minimum two-day contact with the injured man. Easily he and his "beast," almost assuredly a donkey could have walked on by, eliminating any need for his even being in the parable, for this story was already seen in the conduct of the priest and the Levite.

Our story of this parable commenced with a somewhat extended discussion of the word "revolutionary." So, how is this really relevant to the parable which Christ has just related. The Samaritan appears as the polar opposite of the bomb throwing revolutionary, the terror of governments and authority everywhere and the willing, often to the point of enthusiasm shedder of copious quantities of blood. This man a revolutionary? Resoundingly, yes. The revolution, though, as Christ taught from His first utterance is to be in the heart of every man and woman. Well before this parable was offered, centuries early, the book of Proverbs recorded a simple statement that explains the source for practically all human behavior, good, bad or indifferent:

"For as he thinketh in his heart so is he."

This was and is Christ the "Revolutionary," a revolution that He seeks to effect in every human heart. This Samaritan provided not only one of the Bible's but all of history's greatest examples of the post-revolutionary Christian heart. A man's suffering was abated, his life saved and an example for all human history of a true Godly spirit.

The Samaritan is faced with the same dilemma and choices as were the priest and the Levite. He, too, was on his way somewhere and most assuredly was not traveling the Jerusalem to Jericho road, of all places, for a pleasure excursion. Likely, he had appointment(s) to keep, commercial meetings where goods and services would be exchanged for money. In other words, the daily grist of life. Or maybe he was returning home from a week's sojourn necessitated by that same business, and in the fore of his thinking was the domestic responsibilities which lay before, outweighed only by the joy of reuniting with his wife and children. All must wait, though, not on the bedraggled man in the roadway, not on the circumstances of the moment but on the heart of the Samaritan, who immediately recognized an unfulfilled need for which he would answer with his money and his time.

"He had compassion on him" related the parable in the words of the Savior Himself. "Compassion" remains a prevalent term, perhaps an overused one-word phrase, and it bears close attention when we are presented with such an explicit example. Jesus's story, other than this one word, is totally devoid of any mention of the Samaritan's emotions and his emotional equilibrium. He did not weep over the grisly scene, shed any tears or lament about the debased condition of the world. He was a man of action and knew that this beaten Jew (who for all the

Samaritan knew may have been a thief and a brigand himself) needed an immediate response. He needed care, respite, medical aid, primitive though it may have been, rest and convalescence so he took him to a stay at an inn, all expenses paid.

The nature of the Samaritan's personality is never offered. Yet, though, he may or may not have been quiet and unassuming, taciturn or garrulous, he met the challenge of the moment and provided the world with an everlasting definition of compassion, not by tears, emotional catharsis or lamentations but by doing and acting. Compassion, and love, the former being an essential component of the latter, in too many instances have had their definitions reduced to feelings, sentiments and emotions. Most certainly all these are essentialities to the love of those dearest to us, a wife, husband, mother, father, son, daughter, etc. Many persons (including the author) unashamedly and rightfully hold these feelings for cats, dogs, and other pets. Pitiable is a close family tie wherein these are lacking.

Yet, these relationships are few in number. As always without exception Christ finds the heart of the message, theologically and practically where he inquired of His audience:

> "Which now of these three; thinkest thou,
> was neighbor unto him that fell among the thieves?"

The Samaritan and the Jew had no prior connections, and nothing in Christ's story presupposes that even after the incident their paths ever crossed again. Maybe they never even learned each other's names, yet the Jew received from the Samaritan on that bloody crime scene the one thing he required, real love.

It is possible, perhaps even likely, that either the priest or the Levite, could have prepared and presented a sermon on the necessities and beauties of love, a sermon which in words, eloquence or presentation would have surpassed the efforts of the Samaritan. On the road to Jericho the time for sermons, for hypothesizing and debate had passed. Sentimental words dressed no wounds; sutured no cuts and healed the breaks in no bones. This truly victimized man whose life's blood was trickling from his body, needed immediate help. It came in the person of a stranger of a different, even hated ethnicity, a man whose life hung in the balance and who needed the love of a true neighbor, a man he had never seen before and likely never saw again. He was and still is technically anonymous, but history's gratitude, praise and admiration are found in countless cases on all continents. He is honored in the naming of hospitals, nursing centers, civil laws, sermons, Bible lessons and in the common speech and phraseology of humanity. He is an ever-undimmed beacon of light and love, as exemplary of the spirit of Jesus Christ as any man or woman who ever lived. He was and ever will remain – the Good Samaritan.

CONCLUSION

CHRIST, THE PRO-CHOICE SAVIOR

What? After sixteen chapters of discussion on the parables of Jesus Christ is the text suddenly to be diverted into the turbulent waters of perhaps the most intensive and bitter moral and political issue of our times? In a word, no, and in this book's conclusion we grant to ourselves a modicum of leeway in discussion and phraseology. The issue to which the words "choice" and "life" are invariably linked is always worthy of discussion, but to this we defer to another time. Jesus Christ as a "pro-choice" Savior is almost as applicable as His being a "pro-life" Savior, and was it not He who proclaimed that "I am the Way, the Truth and the Life" and that "I am the Resurrection and the Life." Also, it was He who fully demonstrated that the concepts and word choice and life are not antithetical one to another, but are actually complementary. In the literally dozens of parables which He told choice is central to the story of the protagonists action. As a sampling this conclusion will feature four of His most famous stories and offer what modern drama calls alternative endings if different choices had been made.

We ask the question, the same inquiry, repeatedly, of what of the main character had chosen differently? We begin with the ending of our narrative, and perhaps the most famous of the parables, that of the Good Samaritan.

On the day this poor, unnamed Jewish man was mugged and left for dead on the road to Jericho, many choices were made by many persons, and the exigency of the circumstances (as life invariably does) demanded that they be made quickly, almost in a moment. The priest and the Levite made their choices, one perhaps a bit quicker than the other, but they made them in the intense pressure of the moment. They walked on by and left the man to suffer the slow ebb of life from his body. The Samaritan came, saw a man "half-dead" and apparently made his first choice, which was to demount his donkey and make an initial assessment of the man's condition. The Samaritan had many choices to make, all tumbling with breakneck speed towards him. Just how far should I go with this man, he may have asked himself? Maybe I could stay with him just until someone better qualified and not as pressed for time happens by to relieve one of an increasingly heavy burden. Perhaps I will tend to him and take him to a local inn and hurriedly drop him off, trusting that he would now be in capable hands. Money is a bit tight this month, and I cannot pledge much beyond a token or two. Most definitely the Samaritan was confronted with an almost endless array of choices, each of which required an increasingly sacrificial commitment. The famed and fabled Good Samaritan, though, never appears to be a man who is hurried, in a rush, a choice made, perhaps even in part unconsciously, long before he set foot on this road, long before he had awakened that morning and certainly before he had ever encountered this Jewish crime victim. He had purposed in his heart, and was guided by a selfless spirit that he would serve others and thereby serve God. Hopefully the reader will forgive the phraseology, which is not meant either as a cliché or bombast, but the Samaritan was the Christian soldier prepared, always prepared, for battle. That day he had to combat the effects of plunder, looting and crime, and his choice had already been made before the rising of the morning sun. The Samaritan may not yet have known the Savior, but that day he chose not to walk the road to Jericho but rather the Way of Christ.

The parables discussed in Chapter Eleven herein concern forgiveness, and the choices in that venue which are presented to all men and women. Two men are debtors, one so deeply in debt that the possibility of paying it off on his own power, is not only a remote happening but practically impossible. His creditor and master, himself a man of means is moved by the horrible predicament into which his debtor has fallen. Moved by the man's situation he forgave him, not temporarily, not partially but entirely. Perhaps no element of time necessarily entered into the man's forgiving the debt, but certainly the element of exclusivity did. Only he could relieve his debtor. Neither government, institution, individual or other earthly being held the power to ease the man's catastrophic debt. His creditor alone held the power, and in those tersely descriptive words of the scriptures "... he frankly forgave all." But such beneficence, magnificence of character and yes, love, penetrated nary a millimeter of the forgiven man's heart, character and soul. Quickly this man morally pivoted from the grandeur of the mercy shown him and struck like a serpent towards a poor man who owed him but a few dollars, clutching him by the neck and spitting in his face the venomous demand to "pay me what thou owest." Surely, this moral abyss of a human being did not make the decision is the emotion of the moment, but rather he had chosen a life of heartlessness, void of mercy and compassion.

The rich fool (Chapter Twelve) was a man who in much of his life, his earthly endeavors, demonstrated that he was not a foolish, but rather an intelligent and quite diligent man. He was highly successful in what we might now call agri-business, continuing for who knows how long a consistent streak of success so great that he could no longer manage it by ordinary means. It is both purposeless and wrong to disparage the man's efforts. In Christ's parable nary a hint of corruption, dishonesty or sharp dealing appears. Any man or woman, be they situated in ancient Judea or modern America and all points between who is successful in business, a trade or a profession knows that with but a few exceptions the success is bought at the price of time, hard work, consistency and a determination that many individuals lack or simply wish not to possess. The honest and successful man or woman is not to be an object of contempt, scorn or hatred but rather is to be admired for certain exemplary qualities, traits which the scriptures land from beginning to end.

The man of Christ's parable is upbraided for a choice that he made. So successful was he that he could think of nothing better to do with his abundant surplus, his cornucopia of wealth, than to build bigger barns in which to store his bounty. With his newfound wealth, not just riches, but more and more abundant riches he was given a choice provided few persons, at least at this magnitude. The wealth could have been employed in the service of God and men, with still plenty remaining for him to lead a very comfortable life. Our present time of the twenty-first century furnishes examples aplenty, as now the recognized title of wealth is not "millionaire" but rather "billionaire." Some men and women handle such riches with some thought, wisdom and discretion. The rich fool of Christ's parable made the tragic mistake of being enamored y the lifestyle of eat, drink, and be merry with no regard for the status of his fellow men and women. His choices left him with nothing, as his own demise took from him his life, and all that remained was an eternity of bleakness.

The story of the prodigal son (Chapter Nine) is likely the most poignant and heart wrenching of all the Master's parables. The younger son, as most of us do, believed that with all life and its wonders before him he had so many choices that life could be an endless party and festival. He came from wealth, the riches that had been earned by others' labor and he chose to have it now while he was yet young and its advantages and rewards as great as could be imagined. Receiving his share of others' work he went into a far country and chose to waste and dissipate it all, as so presciently termed by Christ "... in riotous living" and was reduced to working in a pig sty feeding swine for a meager living. Still, even in the Stygian emotional gloom of that moment he was not deprived of choices. He could continue as he was and live out a wretched life in filth or degradation, or he could even take his own young life. For many, crime is always an option, but often it just merely delays the inevitable moral and spiritual collapse. Finally he chose the course wherein he had to admit his shame, to accept a reduced manhood and live as a lowly servant in his own father's house. Or so he thought, but his father had choices open to him.

Daily the father went to the same spot on his property and cast his eyes upon the same point on the horizon, hoping against all odds and hope itself to espy his lost son in the distance. Finally one day hope was rewarded, and the father, against all ancient cultural expectations for an older man ran to meet him, fell on the lost and beloved youth and heard the young son's confession of foolishness, pride and just plain stupidity. The father himself now had another choice to select. Although the young son had quickly and with pathos poured his heart dry with the confession that "Father, I have sinned against heaven, and in thy sight, and am no more worthy to be called thy son." He still awaited his father's verbal response. The author once knew a father whose prodigal child returned home, and the child was met with a substantive response of "... OK, but first we are going to establish the rules of your living again at home." That God (and most assuredly the father of this parable is a representation of God) this father chose a response from the other side of the spectrum, as he first effectively disregarded his son's confession and moved the emotional scene to a higher plane:

> "But the father said to his servants,
> Bring forth the best robe, and put it on him;
> and put a ring on his hand, and shoes on his feet."

The son's rebellion, youthful foolishness, greed, materialism, and sin had been washed away by the tears of the father's joy. A relationship between the father and son would now be built upon a foundation of love and forgiveness, an edifice which the father had chosen to begin to build.

The parables of Christ cast a wide net on the subjects which were covered, and amazingly spoken to an audience of first century Judeans now evolved into twenty-first century moderns outwardly living substantially different types of lives. The qualities of the parables, their occupations, dilemmas and moral dilemmas are universal, and Christ presented them in easily acceptable and understandable terms. The choices as to whether to accept their truths and moral directions are ours alone to make.

www.ingramcontent.com/pod-product-compliance
Lightning Source LLC
Chambersburg PA
CBHW071656090426

42738CB00009B/1551

Table of Contents

There is a companion book that goes hand in hand with this book and if you have not yet purchased it, you should. It is my book, **"Perceptions, Parables, and Pointers."** The book in your hands is the goal book and work book, and "Perceptions, Parables, and Pointers," contains the inspirational and motivational messages to keep you inspired as you set and achieve your goals this year.

Introduction..5
Discover Who You Are (Getting to Know Yourself).....................9
What is My Personal Mission in Life?.......................................13
What is My Life Plan?...15
Who do I want to be? (Describe the "You" you want to be)...........22
Formula for Success..25
Going for the Goal..27
My Personal Dream Map..29
Listing your Macro and Micro Goals for the year.....................30
Positively Positive Thinking Power..34
Skills, Principles, and Values..37
Good Habits, Self Discipline, and a Moral Compass................38
In the Habit of Forming Habits..39
List of Skills We Should Learn and Know How To Do.............41
The Power of Knowledge...46
Identifying Personal Strengths and Weaknesses.......................49
List of Virtues...51
Take Ownership of Your Actions..55
Make Today Count..59
Real Motivation..62
Daily To Do — Personal Improvement Outline.......................63
Summarize Your Year...430
About Music Motivation®...435
Jerald's Albums/CDs and Singles...436
Jerald's Music Books (for piano)...437
Jerald's Motivation/Inspiration Self Help Books.....................438
Make the Most of Each Minute..440

About the Author (Poet)
JERALD SIMON

http://musicmotivation.com
http://youtube.com/jeraldsimon
http://facebook.com/jeraldsimon
http://linkedin.com/in/jeraldsimon
http://twitter.com/jeraldsimon

"My purpose and mission in life is to motivate myself and others through my music and writing, to help others find their purpose and mission in life, and to teach values that encourage everyone everywhere to do and be their best." — JERALD SIMON

First and foremost, Jerald is a husband to his beautiful wife, Suzanne (Zanny), and a father to his wonderful children. Jerald Simon is the founder and president of Music Motivation®. He is a composer, author, poet, and Music Mentor/piano teacher (primarily focusing his piano teaching on music theory, improvisation, composition, and arranging). Jerald loves music, teaching, speaking, performing, playing sports, exercising, reading, writing poetry and self help books, gardening, and spending time with his wife, Zanny, and their children.

Jerald created **musicmotivation.com** as a resource for piano teachers, piano students, and parents of piano students. In 2014 he began creating his weekly "Cool Songs" to help teach music theory - the FUN way by putting FUN back into theory FUNdamentals. He is the author/poet of "The As If Principle" (motivational poetry), and the book "Perceptions, Parables, and Pointers." He is also the author of 21 music books from the Music Motivation® Series. He has also recorded and produced several albums and singles of original music.

Jerald also presents to various music schools, groups, and associations throughout the country doing workshops, music camps, master classes, concerts and firesides to inspire and motivate teens, adults, music students and teachers. He enjoys teaching piano students about music theory, improvisation, and composition. He refers to himself as a Music Mentor and encourages music students to get motivated by music and to motivate others through music of their own.

Welcome to "Who Are You" by JERALD SIMON

My wife and I, along with many of you, I'm sure, are constantly making checklists and to-do lists. Over the years I have filled up so many notebooks, loose pieces of paper and even napkins with ideas, goals, hopes, dreams, plans, projections, and thousands of other to-do items. I have had a difficult time keeping track of everything. Yes, I have folders and filing cabinets filled with these lists, and most of it is somewhat organized. But I have always wanted to have everything in one place both as a checklist and a handy road map. This way I can quickly see where I have been in life and I can map out where I am going.

As I was reviewing some of my past goals from previous years, I thought it would be helpful if I could organize everything into one book per year. In my mind I envisioned an entire bookshelf of my own books — not the books I have published for others, but my own life story mapped out day by day and month by month one year at a time. Each book would be one year filled with my goals, dreams, successes, failures, exercise logs, and a list of books I have read. I would then have within my hands my own personal motivational map to help me navigate my way through life on a day to day basis.

It is wonderful to have a desired destination where you would like to eventually end up. But you also need to know how you are going to get there. It requires repetitious practice and it demands discipline.

This book begins with getting to know yourself, and helping you discover who you are and who you can become. It then presents a simple formula for success to help you determine what you'd like to accomplish and how to go about doing it. You are then taught the importance of developing skills, understanding and following principles, and defining and living by your own values. The majority of the book features a personal improvement outline for you for every day of the year. There is a daily focus, a daily virtue, a biography, and a checklist of what to accomplish.

"YOU CAN DISCOVER WHO YOU ARE BY GETTING TO KNOW YOURSELF BETTER (SELF DISCOVERY)"

WHO ARE YOU? Do you know? What are your strengths? What are your weaknesses? How well do you really know yourself? What are your limitations? Do you have any? Do you feel you have too many? What are your goals, dreams, hopes, fears, and personal outlook on life? Have you ever taken the opportunity to sit down with yourself and have a "heart to heart" conversation about your true potential? What do you think you can accomplish in your life? What would you like to do, be, and become? What languages would you like to speak? What instruments would you like to be able to play? What sports would you like to participate in? What travels would you like to take? Who would you like to meet? What would you like to learn? Where are you currently, at this minute, with your goals, dreams, ambitions, talents, knowledge, and individual areas of expertise? What is your "dream destination?" How are you going to get there and what will it take for you to do everything you want to do and be everything you need to be?

The first step is to decide what you want. Dream a little or dream a lot. Write down anything and everything. You can decide what you like and don't like, what you would like to accomplish or not accomplish. Half the battle is knowing what you want out of life — the other half is doing what it takes to accomplish your goals. It takes being committed and determined to follow through, as well as sacrifice, work, and earning the rewards of your efforts. There are no free gifts handed out in life. We must earn what we receive by working for it. Talents, knowledge, skills, abilities, and expertise all require practice, patience, effort, discipline, focus, years of dedication, and constant commitment.

Who Are You? by JERALD SIMON

I hope that in purchasing this annual goal book, you will be committed to your future, to your dreams, and to your goals. I hope to show you that setting goals is only the first step in the wonderful journey of life. Each step is an exciting adventure and you can decide where you want to go in life. This book is about helping you discover what matters most to you and was written to encourage you to not only set goals and achieve them, but more importantly, to discover who you are, what you like and don't like, what you hope to accomplish, and what your own purpose and mission in life is and will be. This is what I feel my own purpose and mission in life is:

"My purpose and mission in life is to motivate myself and others through my music and writing, to help others find their purpose and mission in life, and to teach values that encourage everyone everywhere to do and be their best." - Jerald Simon

In this goal book, you can discover who you are by getting to know yourself better (this is self discovery). I hope you will create your own road map to success — a very personal and individual endeavor that will only be customized to you to fit your needs, wants, and ambitions in life. We will work on a **"Formula for Success"**, create your **"Personal Dream Map"**, and have you complete your **"Macro and Micro Goals"** for the year that you would like to do. In addition, you can create your own **"Personal Mission in Life Mission Statement."** There is a section on being **"In the Habit of Forming Habits"**, and another that has a list of **"120 Things You Should Learn and Know How to Do."** Then we will have you plan your year by creating your own **"Game Plan for the Year"** — what you hope to accomplish, what you will learn, and how you will help those around you to improve and be better. It's not only about you, your needs, and your wants — it's about helping those around you be the very best they can be. That is the only way you can truly be your best self and strive to be better — by giving back to others. Once you have determined who you are and who you want to become, then you must help those around you find themselves and discover their own potential. The power of possibility is humbling. Humans have continually been outdoing themselves and setting greater goals and accomplishing more with each passing year. The limits that bind us are those limitations of the mind that prevent us from performing at our peak potential. First, we must increase our understanding of what we can potentially do, believe in the power of our own possibility, and then commit to working as hard as we can to improve and continually outdo ourselves. We are not competing against anyone else around us. We must learn to look ourselves in the eye each day and ask ourselves these tough questions:

Am I doing my best?

Am I giving it my all?

Am I pushing myself to be better and improve?

Am I developing good habits and replacing bad habits?

Am I becoming a better person?

Am I making a difference in my home, community, school, and workplace? Am I helping those around me to be their best?

Who Are You? by Jerald Simon

Self Discovery
Discover Who <u>YOU</u> Are

> It's never too late to be who you might have been.
> George Eliot

Discovering who you are, also known as Self Discovery, is not an easy thing to do and does not happen overnight. It is a lifelong process and an enjoyable endeavor, or at least it should be. This book is all about "Getting to know yourself" (for who you are and more importantly, for who you can become). "Who ARE YOU?" Make it personal this time. "Who Am I? What are my strengths and weaknesses? What are my likes and dislikes? What are my goals and dreams? What are my fears and nightmares? What pushes me forward and what holds me back? What do I want to do with my time and my life? What is uniquely original about me? What would I change about myself? What would I never change about myself? How would I accurately describe myself to others? How would others describe me? When I look at myself in the mirror, what do I see? Who do I want to see? Who do I want to be and become? Do I counsel with or condemn myself when I make mistakes? How often do I honestly talk with myself to identify my weaknesses, faults, mistakes, corrections, and change? Do I follow up on myself and follow through with the improvements that must be made? How can I help myself improve in every area of my life?"

These are important questions to ask yourself. Only YOU can answer these questions. You do need to get to know yourself and figure out how you can be the best person you can be. With that being said, everything you do to help yourself become better should be done so that, in time, you will be able to help those around you. That should be the main focus. The best thing you or I can do is help those around us be their best. We need to get to know ourselves and work on improving ourselves so that we can help those around us. We must discover and rediscover ourselves each day!

Start today — right now! Answer the following questions about yourself:

WHO AM I? Write a brief summary of who you think you are — beliefs, talents, and interests.

_____
_____
_____
_____
_____

WHO DO I WANT TO BE? Realizing I must live with myself for the rest of my life — what kind of person do I want to be and strive to become each day?

_____
_____
_____
_____
_____

WHO AM I?

Now that you are warmed up, try to
write an entire page on who you think you are.

_____

_____

_____

_____

_____

_____

_____

_____

_____

_____

_____

_____

_____

_____

_____

_____

_____

_____

_____

_____

_____

_____

_____

_____

_____

Who Are You? by Jerald Simon

YOU
ARE
WONDERFUL!

You may not think so at times, and you may worry others don't think so as well, but you are wonderful. Part of this self discovery process is being comfortable with where you are on your process through life.

Everyone, if they are honest with themselves and others, wants to improve and be better. It is a natural part of life and one that is necessary for us to continually advance. We need change and it is a good thing because it forces us to push ourselves and stretch in ways that can be uncomfortable. The more we do it, however, the easier it becomes. As we change for the better, we naturally have moments of success or little accomplishments along the way that are a stamp of approval that we are on the right track and headed in the right direction. Everyone has areas where they are all-stars and other areas where they are just learning the ropes, so to speak. We are all beginners.

No matter where anyone is currently on their own personal journey in life, everyone has room for improvement. In fact, knowing that everyone is trying new hobbies, learning new skills, and attempting to improve and progress through this life experience is very comforting. We are all in this together. We are all learning and growing as we make it through each day.

Who Are You? by Jerald Simon

WHAT IS MY
PERSONAL MISSION IN LIFE?

"Your purpose in life is to find your purpose in life and give your whole life to it."

Buddha

What is YOUR personal mission in life? Everyone has purpose and meaning in life and everyone was born to do something. You can think of it as our calling, our destiny, our life's ambition, or our hope and desire to make a difference in the world. We all have something of value we can share with others: our time, talents, ideas, knowledge, perspective, beliefs, values, and love. Just knowing we believe in others is inspiring and powerful. Part of discovering our purpose in life is to educate, empower, and ennoble those around us and help them discover who they are and who they can become, without becoming lost or confused by all the mixed messages offered by the media. This is particularly pertinent to children and youth who are trying to discover who they are and what their own talents, abilities, and capabilities, are, and what direction they want to go in life. I encourage everyone to first create a **"Personal Mission Statement"** and also a **"Life Plan"** to help them think about their purpose and mission.

LIVE! Live intentionally. Live deliberately. Live purposefully. Live life to the fullest. Know what you want out of life. Know where you are going in life. Live life each day as if your life depended on it — because it does!

Everyone can and should create their own world and define their life the way they hope it will be and then work as hard as they can to make it happen. Yes, there are difficult disappointments in life, but you can make it. Everyone can.

Here is my own "Personal Mission Statement":

"My purpose and mission in life is to motivate myself and others through my music and writing, to help others find their purpose and mission in life, and to teach values that encourage everyone everywhere to do and be their best." — JERALD SIMON

It doesn't need to be long at all. Mine is very short, but to the point. First, discover who you want to be and become (we started this process on page 9). This is an ongoing discovery process and will continue to change throughout your life as you change, grow, and continue to learn, discover, and develop more interests and talents.

Now it's your turn. Create your own personal mission statement. This can evolve as you learn and grow. The main point is to start somewhere and give yourself a little direction. In the few lines below, create your own personal mission statement. This is yours and doesn't belong to anyone else. Personalize it to be true to who you are and what you hope to accomplish. Again, it doesn't need to be very long to be meaningful and make a difference in your life.

My "Personal Mission Statement"

_____
_____
_____
_____

Who Are You? by JERALD SIMON

WHAT IS MY
LIFE PLAN?

Some people think of careers or occupations as a life plan. They map out their life according to their education, degree, desired employment, and so on. But if we know what our mission in life is, then our focus will be directed on that life plan and our choices will change considerably.

Here is an example of my **Life Plan** in response to the question of what I want to do with my life and my time — again, this is my own and it is what I am striving for. I am working on it. I am striving to be better and this continually changes. You can customize your life plan to fit your needs, wants, interests, and personal outlook.

"I want to be with my family and teach my family values and truths. I want to leave a legacy for my family and serve and help and teach people from all over the world. I want to travel and visit as many countries, national parks, monuments, museums, historical sights, and religious centers as I can. I want to eat wonderful food in exceptional restaurants all over the world. I want to mentor others. I want to speak with groups. I want to write poetry, self help books, inspirational stories, and mini-motivational collections (short books) to help inspire and motivate people. I want to compose music and create my own original instrumental pieces in various styles and genres (for piano and all instruments): ballads, pop/rock pieces, new age music, classical, opera, Broadway/show tunes, hymns, meditation music, children's songs, and soundtrack scores. I want to teach music through on-line videos for world-wide distribution and streaming, and try to motivate others through my music and writing. I want to create short motivational movies that teach principles, values, and morals in an effort to uplift and edify others and make a difference in the world. I want to create children's books to teach values and principles, draw a music comic cartoon series, write essays on personal improvement, and create a lifelong personal development program for myself and others. In short, I want to help myself and others be better! That is what I want to do with my life and my time! I will always strive to put God and my family first and strive to serve those around me."

Now it's your turn. Create your own personal life plan. Again, this can evolve and change as you learn and grow in life. Start writing and see where it takes you.

MY PERSONAL "LIFE PLAN"

_____
_____
_____
_____
_____
_____
_____
_____
_____
_____

My Personal "Life Plan"
(Now that you are warmed up, try and write an
entire page describing what you'd like to do with your life)

Who Are You? by Jerald Simon

Now let us return to the main theme and focus of this book — **"Who are you?"** If you can answer that, then half the battle has already been fought and won. You're almost there! So, who are you?

First let me tell you who I believe I am in an effort to help you find out more about who you are.

I believe I am a son of God. Now, it does not matter whether or not you believe in God or a higher power — that is not the purpose of this book. But to better understand who I believe I am, I will tell you of my belief in God.

In believing I am a son of God, I believe He is my eternal father. I believe I was created in His image. I believe we as His children are brothers and sisters — one worldwide family. This belief of who I am impacts everything I do, say, think, believe, experience, view, everyone I meet, every place I visit, and every decision I make. I often ask myself: "Would a son or daughter of God act this way? Speak like this? Watch, view, read, participate in this activity? If I view myself as a son of God, as I do, then my perspective of myself and others changes. It has to because of my image of myself and my image of others.

Whether or not you believe in God, I think you may agree with some of my beliefs of who I am.

I am a human being who was born on earth to live life to the fullest and experience all the good that life has to offer. I was born into a family and began learning and growing day by day. Each new day brought with it life lessons — some good and some bad. I learned at an early age it is okay to fall down because I can always get back up. I learned to speak and communicate with others. I learned what small victories and personal success feels like. It feels great! I learned what huge set backs and personal failure feels like. It is horrible. I soon realized I had many individual strengths and began to excel and progress in certain areas. I also realized I had far too many individual weaknesses and noticed how they held me back and prevented me from progressing and improving. I have hopes and dreams and regrets and fears. As a child I had a little more caution, apprehension, and reluctance and at the same time had so much creativity, energy and a care-free attitude and outlook on life. As a teenager, I became less cautious, at times thinking I was invincible and indestructible — so not true. At the same time I became more focused and determined, goal oriented, and even more outgoing. I knew I had a purpose and mission on earth as everyone does. I wanted to find my mission and help others find theirs.

I developed more talents, tried to strengthen my strengths, and overcome the many weaknesses I had. I am still trying to overcome the many weaknesses I have. As a teenager I developed a life-long fascination with motivation, self help, goal-setting, positivity, and was drawn to personal improvement — the idea that I could look for the good in life and focus more on positivity than negativity. I wanted to genuinely be happy and help others be happy as well. I genuinely wanted to strive to be happy. I am still trying to do that and hope, in some small way, that I can help others experience and embrace true happiness. Some days are more challenging than others. We all have our individual struggles and personal bumps along the road of life. But, we are all on a personal journey through mortality and our lives are all connected. We interact with each other, verbally, non-verbally, musically, emotionally, scientifically, spiritually, and in every conceivable way possible. Our lives have become one beautifully and intricately woven human tapestry.

Who Are You? by Jerald Simon

We learn from each other, help each other, at times hurt each other, and collectively become connected with every human being with whom we come in contact. Even without knowing it, a simple smile from a stranger strengthens our spirits. It heals our hearts, and unifies and connects us to each other.

We belong to the brotherhood of humanity. Our earthly family extends beyond the color of anyone's skin, and beyond their beliefs and values. Everyone has potential and is brimming with possibility. Yes, we all have our many short-comings and individual deficits. That is what helps us realize that we are traveling through life together — not against each other, but with each other.

There are far too many ways to divide us into segregated groups. Differences have continued to divide us from the haves to the have-nots, the educated to the unlearned, the rich and poor, the good and the bad, to the believer and the unbeliever. We can celebrate our differences and know that we do not need to agree on everything in order for us to appreciate and respect each other.

In order to truly get to know yourself you must get to know those around you. We may all be unique, but we all share similar basic needs — the need to be loved, to be understood, to be accepted, to be appreciated, and to be respected. We all need that and thankfully we can all give that to others.

As you get to know yourself better, you can rediscover yourself on a daily basis. This can also help you to discover others.

Who Are You? by JERALD SIMON

Get to know yourself, your strengths, weaknesses, goals, dreams, hopes, fears, and potential. That is what we all must do if we are to make it through each day let alone a life time. It takes a certain amount of understanding, patience, practical application, faith, love, endurance, and determination to get up each morning and to make things happen.

Life is full of good experiences, but sometimes we get stuck in the rut on the wrong road that puts a wrinkle in our day. Any little problem can automatically turn us upside down. Each day brings with it the uncertainty of the unknown. We honestly don't know what will happen today let alone tomorrow. That is why it is so important to learn about ourselves and others so we can better face those challenges.

I have shared a little about me and who I believe I am. We all have had and will have similar experiences in life. Some may be extremely different and others will parallel what others around us are going through and enduring.

It is my hope that in sharing with you who I believe I am that you will discover who you are and believe in yourself, your present, and your future. On page 11 you wrote an entire page on who you think you are. Whether that page depicts someone who is confident and capable, qualified and content, or timid and shy, you have described who you believe you are at this moment. In order to know where you are going, you need to know where you have been and where you currently are at this moment in time. That is a good thing. You cannot improve and progress until you do this.

Who Are You? by Jerald Simon

Describe the
"You"
you want to be.

If you could look beyond the looking glass and see yourself in the future, not with your present problems — but picturing the great person you would like to become, who would you be? Describe yourself as if you are already that person.

What would you have that you don't have? What would you be doing that you are not doing right now? What would you not be doing that you are doing right now? What would you know? What would you be learning? What abilities, talents, accomplishments, characteristics, qualities, values, morals, ethics, and lifestyle would you have that you do not currently have? How would you act differently? Describe your speech, mannerisms, physique, outlook on life, and overall perspective you would have that you do not yet have. What does life look like as seen by the ideal you?

Life is all about perspective. It is about mental toughness — the ability to think about the you you'd like to become while continuing to live in the present with who you are now. You may be doing great as you are. But we can always do better. It is not about being complacent, satisfied, or apathetic in how we view ourselves and each day that comes our way. It is about bringing out the best within us and striving to help others to do the same.

Who Do I Want to Be?

(Now write an entire page on who you want to be and become)

_____
_____
_____
_____
_____
_____
_____
_____
_____
_____
_____
_____
_____
_____
_____
_____
_____
_____
_____
_____
_____
_____
_____
_____
_____

Who Are You? by JERALD SIMON

Continue writing about who you would like to become.

_____
_____
_____
_____
_____
_____
_____
_____
_____
_____
_____
_____
_____
_____
_____
_____
_____
_____
_____
_____
_____
_____
_____
_____
_____

Who Are You? by JERALD SIMON

FORMULA FOR SUCCESS

1. DREAM
2. PLAN AND PREPARE
3. GO TO WORK!

It may sound too simplistic, but when you break it down in its simplest form, this is the basic formula to help you accomplish anything!

1. DREAM — If you don't know what you want to obtain, you'll never obtain it. I ask people what they want to learn, accomplish, try, do, and become on a daily basis. The answers are interesting. Many people honestly haven't taken the time to dream and think about what they want out of life. So, go on and dream a little. Write down everything you would like to learn over the next year. What would you like to be able to do? What languages would you like to speak? Where would you like to go? Who would you like to meet? What new hobbies will you pursue? How much money would you like to earn? Save? Invest? Spend? How would you like to enrich your own life and the lives of those with whom you become acquainted? Write it all down. Decide what you *need* and *want* out of life. There's nothing wrong with that. Take a little time each day to dream, but always write your dreams down and look at them on a daily, weekly, and monthly basis. If you don't write them down and continually review and perfect them, they remain wishes. You cannot help your dreams become a reality unless you record them and review them often. Then and only then can you give yourself a deadline to turn your dreams into reality.

2. PLAN AND PREPARE — Dreaming is only the first step. Once you decide what you need and want out of life, you must create a plan or a map that will take you to your desired destination. Without a plan or a road map, people often end up stranded on the side of life. Take your list of dreams and begin creating a road map that will take you in the right direction. Choose five to ten of the dreams you'd most like to accomplish over the course of the next year and break the desired dreams (or goals) down into smaller, manageable parts. I often refer to this list of dreams as **Macro Goals** and the smaller goals as **Micro Goals**. These Micro Goals are really tasks, objectives, and the step-by-step daily to-do processes that turn your dreams into almost done projects. Then as soon as you start, you're almost finished. This is where you can give yourself a time-line. Plot out when you will accomplish each of the micro goals that will help to make your macro goal dream become a reality. Giving yourself a time-line and a deadline is the secret to completing your goals. If you don't give yourself a deadline, you'll never finish it because the end is not in sight. You'll always wait until tomorrow to do what you dream of doing. There are no tomorrows. They all become today. Start today!

3. GO TO WORK — Sometimes it is extremely difficult to follow through with your plan and turn your dreams into realities. Understand up front that it will require some effort on your part. Nothing worthwhile comes easily or freely. Often a price has to be paid. Many times, you will receive back tenfold what you paid in terms of your efforts, sacrifice, diligence, and hard work. Don't be afraid to work. Work is wonderful! Have fun and get things done. Now go to work!

Who Are You? by Jerald Simon

GOING FOR THE GOAL
(WHAT ARE GOALS AND WHY DO WE NEED TO ACTIVELY MAKE DAILY GOALS?)

So what is a goal? Why are they so important? Do we really need goals or can we get through life without them? Well, it all depends on what you want out of life. Let's define what a goal is and what it isn't. Let's assume the Webster (Merriam-Webster) dictionary is accurate in saying a goal is: "**1.** The mark set as limits to a race, **2.** AIM, Purpose, and **3.** An area or object toward which play is directed to score." The 1845 Winston dictionary defines a goal as: "**3.** any end aimed at"; and also, **4.** "The final purpose; one's desire or ambition. In the 1828 Noah Webster dictionary it states that a goal is: "**2.** Any starting post and **3.** The end or final purpose; the end to which design tends, or which a person aims to reach or accomplish."

We should each carefully examine, analyze, and dissect these definitions to more perfectly understand their intended meaning. Essentially, it is the end destination or accomplishment at which a person wants to arrive or what they hope to attain. If we set our sights on that which we hope to learn, understand, know, do, accomplish, experience, and become, then we are setting goals. But it is not enough to set a goal. The goal must be something that is primarily three things:

1. **DEFINABLE**
2. **MEASURABLE**
3. **OBTAINABLE**

Who Are You? by Jerald Simon

To define a goal we must state in meticulous, analytical detail exactly what we want to learn, understand, know, do, accomplish, experience, and become. For a goal to be measurable, we must have both macro and micro goals and must give ourselves a deadline to keep us on track and focused. The deadline gives us a measurable time frame with which to complete any of the little steps along the way that will help us accomplish our dreams. For a goal to be obtainable, it must be far enough beyond our reach to make us extend ourselves, but not so far-fetched that it is unrealistic, unimaginable, or unobtainable. When you think about your own goals, you should make sure that they are **1. Definable, 2. Measurable, and 3. Obtainable.** If they are not all three of these things, then the goal or dream does not have a very good chance of being accomplished.

When we define, measure, and obtain our goals, we see a change in who we are. We come alive. We change. But how can we continually do that every day of our lives? How can we know that we have truly been alive? We must have direction and purpose, something that is moving us forward and pushing us along. This is where good goals can help us. They give us something to live for, to look forward to, and to get up and get going for. We become alive because we have purpose! If we don't achieve a particular goal, it will be because we have found something that is more rewarding and meaningful to us. We will be living life!

Who Are You? by JERALD SIMON

My Personal
DREAM MAP

What do I want to learn and accomplish this year?

From the circle above, draw lines extending out — that list specific accomplishments you'd like to make this year. These are your ***Macro Goals***. From there, you can draw additional lines from the Macro Goals that list what steps you will need to take to accomplish each one. These are your ***Micro Goals.*** Try to come up with at least 10 Macro Goals and 3-5 Micro Goals to help you accomplish each Macro Goal.

Now that you have successfully come up with 10 **Macro Goals** and 3-5 **Micro Goals** for each Macro Goal, list them below in any order you'd like.

1. _____
    a. _____
    b. _____
    c. _____

2. _____
    a. _____
    b. _____
    c. _____

3. _____
    a. _____
    b. _____
    c. _____

4. _____
    a. _____
    b. _____
    c. _____

5. _____
    a. _____
    b. _____
    c. _____

As you go throughout this year and complete these macro and micro goals, come back to this page and page 31 and put a check mark next to your completed goals.

Who Are You? by Jerald Simon

Continue to list your *Macro* and *Micro* Goals below.

6. _____
    a. _____
    b. _____
    c. _____

7. _____
    a. _____
    b. _____
    c. _____

8. _____
    a. _____
    b. _____
    c. _____

9. _____
    a. _____
    b. _____
    c. _____

10. _____
    a. _____
    b. _____
    c. _____

Who Are You? by Jerald Simon

Now that you have listed your 10 *Macro Goals* and 3-5 *Micro Goals* for each of the Macro goals, simply place one of your Macro Goals next to the months listed below.

1. JANUARY _____
2. FEBRUARY _____
3. MARCH _____
4. APRIL _____
5. MAY _____
6. JUNE _____
7. JULY _____
8. AUGUST _____
9. SEPTEMBER _____
10. OCTOBER _____

This calendar only goes until October for a reason. Though it is good to have many different goals throughout the year, I believe November and December should specifically be goals for the good of others. Now, we can have goals for the good of others throughout the year, of course, but I believe this is the best way to end the year — by focusing on helping and serving those around us.

Add one Macro Goal for the month of November and one for the month of December that you will do for someone else. This will get you in the mode of thinking of serving and helping others throughout the year.

11. NOVEMBER _____
12. DECEMBER _____

Who Are You? by Jerald Simon

It's pretty simple, if you think about it. In the beginning, we really should simplify and primarily focus on one main (Macro) goal each month. If it is a one time Macro Goal, like writing a book, we can have one month be entirely dedicated to the writing of the book. Maybe the next month we can edit or proof it and then publish it. If we are trying to learn to play a musical instrument, we can set a Macro goal of trying to learn the names of the notes of the music, the rhythms, how many songs we would like to learn in a year, how many chords, scales, and so on we are going to learn.

Every goal has a specific deadline and we can break each Macro Goal down into small stages known as the Micro Goals. These are the little steps along the way. If, for instance, I wanted to learn how to play the guitar, I might give myself the Macro Goal to learn 50 chords on the guitar this year — simple triads, sixth and seventh chords, bar chords, and more. The Micro Goals might be to learn one new chord per week. Pretty simple, right? I would then write down which chord I am going to learn that week and know how to create it, play it and understand the theory of the intervals used to make it. I would make sure to learn and remember what the individual notes are that are used in the chord and how to play them as a blocked or strummed chord all together and how to play a picking pattern of a broken or arpeggiated chord.

You see, I am taking my main (Macro) goal and giving myself a little map with markers along the way telling me how far I've come and how much more I have left to do. If I want to get into better shape or lose so many pounds in a year, I would then determine how much I would need to workout to burn the needed calories to lose the weight and how many calories I could consume per day to stay healthy and see the results I want.

Who Are You? by Jerald Simon

POSITIVELY POSITIVE THINKING POWER
(WHY THINKING POSITIVELY IS SO POWERFUL!)

Wise men and women have been preaching about the power of positivity since the beginning of time. Here are some familiar quotes on positivity:

"We become what we think about." (Earl Nightingale)

"The mind is everything. What you think you become." (Buddha)

"If you can or you can't, you are right either way." (Henry Ford)

"A man is literally what he thinks, his character being the complete sum of all his thoughts." (James Allen)

Then Norman Vincent Peale, in his great literary masterpiece, titled, "The Power of Positive Thinking," said, "BELIEVE IN YOURSELF! Have faith in your abilities! Without a humble but reasonable confidence in your own powers you cannot be successful or happy. But with sound self-confidence you can succeed. A sense of inferiority and inadequacy interferes with the attainment of your hopes, but self-confidence leads to self-realization and successful achievement."

So, if we think negatively, those thoughts will automatically taint what we see, hear, feel, and experience, leaving us a little more negative and ultimately affecting everyone around us. These negative thoughts will turn into negative comments, sprinkled with sarcasm and cynicism. Thinking negatively impacts us drastically and passes the poison of pessimism on to others. In a sense, when we are thinking negatively, about anything or anyone, we become a deadly virus.

Our negativity not only darkens our day, it depresses everyone who comes our way. It is a deplorable disease and only we can stop it. Thankfully, it is treatable, curable, and even preventable. Instead of thinking negatively, we can think positively. Instead of finding what is wrong in a situation or person, we can find what is right. Instead of looking for the bad, we can discover the good. Instead of speaking about what we dislike about ourselves and others, we can speak about what we do like. Instead of cursing our burdens, why don't we count our blessings.

It's all in the way we think about things. We can either find opportunities in the problems we face or continually be faced with more problems because we don't look for the opportunities that surround us. Think positively and be optimistic in your outlook of life!

YOU CAN DO IT!

Don't ever let anyone tell you what you are not capable of accomplishing and becoming. Encourage yourself to learn more, do more, and become more than you currently are!

Too many people knowingly or unknowingly try to cut you down, make you feel foolish for dreaming big and for attempting to do what far too few will attempt to do themselves. These are the naysayers — the people who scoff or mock the dreams others dream. Don't let anyone destroy your dreams! Be realistic about what it will take to accomplish what you want to accomplish, but never let your fires of faith flicker because someone else says you won't, that you can't, or that you couldn't or shouldn't. You can make your dreams become a reality. You can and you should. Everyone else could as well if they were encouraged to learn more, do more, and become more than they currently are. For you to be the best that you can be, you must believe in yourself and know you can do it! That belief in yourself must overpower any negative thinking thrown at you by others. You must be honest with yourself and realistic about your abilities and potential, but, you must never give up!

NEVER GIVE UP ON YOU!

You can do difficult things. Know that about yourself. Things may be challenging or even overwhelming at times, but you can do anything you put your mind to. Believe in yourself. Know that you can face any challenge that comes your way.

I believe in you and in all that you can do. I believe that you were born to do amazing things!

You have so much to look forward to today and tomorrow. Every day is a gift and it should be treated as such. Don't let your dreams die. You have created a dream map and listed 10 Macro Goals and 3 accompanying Micro Goals for each of the goals. That is a great step in the right direction. It is not the final destination. Now that you have created a simple dream map to help you know what you want to accomplish this year, you must do what it takes to finish what you start.

Be positive! Be hopeful! Be cheerful and happy as you go about doing good each day. Life is too short to complain, get angry, or fret about daily problems.

Skills, Principles, and Values

As we mentioned before, this then becomes your formula for success: **1. DREAM, 2. PLAN AND PREPARE, and 3. GO TO WORK!** It really is that easy. First you need to decide what you want and then create a plan. If you are prepared, you will be ready to go to work. That is where you build your own personal dream map as we have done on the previous pages and follow it on a daily basis. If you prepare for something but don't follow through, then you are not allowing yourself to see the small successes along the way that give you the daily motivation you need to keep going.

In life, we must learn and develop *SKILLS*, understand and follow *PRINCIPLES*, and define and live by our *VALUES*. Let's define each of these.

1. SKILLS — According to the Noah Webster 1828 American Dictionary, the word SKILL means "To know; to understand — To be knowing in; to be dexterous in performance." Likewise, it states that SKILLED is: "Having familiar knowledge united with readiness and dexterity in the application of it; familiarly acquainted with."

2. PRINCIPLES — According to the Noah Webster 1828 American Dictionary, the word PRINCIPLES means, among other things "**5.** Ground; foundation; that which supports an assertion, an action, or a series of actions or of reasoning. **6.** A general truth; a law comprehending many subordinate truths, **8.** A principle of human nature, is a law of action in human beings; a constitutional propensity common to the human species."

3. VALUES — According to the Noah Webster 1828 American Dictionary, the word VALUES means, among other things "**1.** To estimate the worth of, **3.** To esteem; to hold in respect and estimation, **6.** To consider with respect to importance, **7.** To be worth."

So, as stated before, we must learn and develop *skills*, understand and follow *principles* and define and live by our *values*. To do this we must develop the following:

1. GOOD HABITS
2. SELF DISCIPLINE
3. A MORAL COMPASS

When we get in the habit of having good habits, we get in the habit of accomplishing and taking the daily small steps that help us improve. This helps us develop more skills. As we learn and develop more skills, we then better understand the principles of life. We realize our own value and begin to notice the value in others as well. We recognize potential and possibility within ourselves and those we meet. We see both the strengths and weaknesses we have and we choose to do our best and bring out the best in others. Having good habits requires self discipline. Our good habits and our self discipline help us to better define our moral compass.

We must learn skills, and the way we become more skilled is to develop good habits. We must learn about and follow guiding principles. This can only happen if we learn and practice self-discipline. In order for us to learn, understand, and live by values, we must have a guiding moral compass — a sense of right and wrong. These three pillars become our foundation for a more successful today and tomorrow. We must learn and teach others skills, principles, and values! In order to learn these we must develop good habits.

Who Are You? by Jerald Simon

In the Habit of Forming Habits

I am fascinated with words. It may sound weird, but I often read dictionaries like hopeless romantics read novels. I enjoy learning as much as I can about languages, meanings and origins. It completely fascinates me. I guess I'm odd in that way.

I thought I'd share one of my favorite word origins. The word **'ability'** comes from the Latin noun *'habilitas'*. The adjective is *'habilis'*, or *'habile'*, which is from the verb *'habere'* meaning **'habit'**. The original meaning is "to have, to hold (habeo)". The same Noah Webster 1828 American Dictionary defines a ***habit*** as:

"**1.** Garb; dress; clothes or garments in general, **3.** State of anything, implying some continuance or permanence; **4.** A disposition or condition of the mind or body acquired by custom or a frequent repetition of the same act. Habit is that which is held or retained, the effect of custom or frequent repetition. *Hence we speak of good habits and bad habits...We should endeavor to correct evil habits by a change of practice. A great point in the education of children, is to prevent the formation of bad habits.*"

The Noah Webster 1828 American Dictionary describes ***ability*** as:

"1. Physical power, whether bodily or mental; natural or acquired; force of understanding; skill in arts or science. Ability is active power, or power to perform; as opposed to capacity or power to receive. In the plural, abilities is much used in a like sense; and also for faculties of the mind, and acquired qualifications. 2. Riches, wealth, substance, which are the means, or which furnish the power, of doing certain acts. 3. Moral power depending on the will. 4. Civil or legal power; the power of right to do certain things, as an ability to transfer property or dispose of effects - ability to inherit."

I find it interesting that the words *habit* and *ability* essentially have the same origin. Their roots connect the two together so that they are, in a sense, inseparably connected. The one does not exist without the other. They are two halves that make a whole. The fascinating aspect of it all is how much the two work together in real life.

We may have good habits, and we may have bad habits. Our ability or inability to do anything in life depends on the habits we have formed. These habits can become addictions, but I would love to be addicted to good habits over bad habits any day, so addiction, in this case, does not necessarily denote anything negative. We basically need to reprogram our brains which, again, takes time and won't happen overnight.

So, what kinds of habits should we develop? I believe we should create habits that will push us, stretch us, and help us develop and grow as individuals. We should be in the habit of reading books, exercising, learning life skills, working, and developing our individual talents. We must be an example for others on how to work, serve, sacrifice, pray, obey, think for themselves, be creative, imagine, play, meditate, ponder, compliment others, be respectful, be honest, be kind, be grateful, and continually improve and work on being the best version of ourselves.

Who Are You? by JERALD SIMON

Here is a list of life skills we should learn and know how to do (in no particular order).

____Make your bed neatly
____Thoroughly brush your teeth
____Style your hair
____Deep clean your bedroom
____Vacuum
____Load/unload dishes for the dishwasher
____Do the wash (laundry) - washer and dryer
____Tie your shoes
____Have nice and legible handwriting/penmanship
____Speed read
____Fold and Iron Laundry
____Write poetry
____Write a story
____Write an essay
____Know and understand parliamentary procedure
____Recite the Pledge of Allegiance
____Effective stretching to increase flexibility
____Exercise
____Count to 10 in three to five different languages
____Read music
____Know how to lead/direct music
____Change a tire
____Change the oil in the car
____Replace a light-bulb
____Create and follow a budget (know where your money goes)
____Install a toilet flush system
____Plant flowers
____Plant vegetables
____Prune fruit trees
____Mow the lawn

Who Are You? by Jerald Simon

____Know how to save seeds for planting (flower, vegetable, and fruit seeds)
____Compost kitchen scraps for the garden
____Keep a steady beat on a drum
____Say hello in 10 different languages
____Know how to use Pages, Word, Excel, Power Point, Photoshop, Illustrator, and Indesign
____Know how to use i Movie, Final Cut or another video editing software program to create and edit your own movies.
____Climb a tree
____Start a fire (with and without matches)
____Ride a bike and scooter
____Ride a horse
____Use roller-skates or Rollerblades
____Play basketball, baseball, soccer, volleyball, tennis, football, badminton,
____Rock climb
____Learn to tie at least 25 different knots
____Know how to perform CPR
____Know how to do the Heimlich maneuver
____Do 25-50 push-ups in a row
____Do 25-50 jumping jacks in a row
____Do 25-50 pull-ups in a row
____Tie a tie (at least a full or double Windsor knot)
____Learn the alphabet in sign language
____Become an Eagle Scout
____Dress yourself (color coordinate as well)
____Compliment others
____Converse with others - look them in the eyes
____Don't speak about yourself
____Say "Yes, Sir," and "Yes, Ma'am" when speaking with adults and those older than you (like grandparents)
____Say "May I please..." When asking for anything
____Show everyone respect

Who Are You? by JERALD SIMON

____Say "Thank you" when others compliment you or when anything is offered/given to you
____Read at least 1 book per week (more if you can)
____If you are a man or a young man, hold the door open for all women, girls, and little boys
____Learn one new word every day (word of the day)
____Shoot a shot gun (rifle, 22, automatic, etc.)
____Shoot a hand gun (pistol)
____Shoot a bow and arrow
____Know how to use a sling shot
____Run a mile under 10 minutes
____Be able to play all hymns from your church's hymn book
____Say "I'm sorry" when you need to apologize
____Paint a picture
____Paint walls
____Swim
____Float on your back
____Tread water
____Canoe, kayak, row a rowboat
____Take pictures with a camera
____Dance (ballroom, cha-cha, foxtrot, tango, waltz, salsa, swing dance, country line dance, break dance
____Sing and stay on pitch
____Use woodworking tools
____Play the piano
____Play the recorder
____Play a stringed instrument (ukulele, guitar, violin, viola, cello, bass, or harp etc.)
____Play a wood wind instrument
____Play a brass instrument
____Learn survival skills, camping, homesteading, farming, wilderness survival, etc.

Who Are You? by Jerald Simon

This list is *not* complete. Add as many skills as you can!

____Woodworking (learn basic craftsman and shop techniques, and how to use basic wood tools and machinery)
____Learn how to hang shelves, fixtures, mirrors and pictures
____Identify at least 10 different trees from looking at them (i.e. leaves, branches, shape, fruit, etc.)
____Learn to draw
____Learn to measure with a ruler or measuring tape
____Know *how* to study
____Know how to prepare for and take tests
____Know how to prepare a talk or speech
____Know how to give a speech in front of an audience and be comfortable speaking in front of a group
____Learn and know how to do magic tricks
____Develop mathematical skills
____Develop industry specific skills according to the industry or career you would like to go into one day
____Do your own grocery shopping
____Clean the sink, bathroom, toilet
____Know how to cook your own meals
____Be able to identify and name 50 + tools for repair
____Learn to drive a manual transmission vehicle (stick shift)
____Learn sewing basics, such as sewing a button onto clothing
____Be able to jump start a car
____Know how to parallel park
____Learn to be able to drive safely in winter conditions

_____
_____
_____
_____
_____
_____
____

Who Are You? by JERALD SIMON

In addition to the list on the previous pages, here are some of the more important general **LIFE SKILLS** you should learn according to categories (some were mentioned before):

Here is a list of life skills for children to learn that was shared on (**MomJunction** — *momjunction.com*) - I think this is a great list for teens and young adults/adults as well!

1. **Cooking Skills**
2. **Wilderness Survival Skills**
3. **Home Gardening Basic Skills**
4. **First Aid Skills**
5. **Swimming Skills**
6. **Money Management Skills**
7. **Laundry Skills**
8. **Household repair Skills**
9. **Defense Skills**
10. **Time Management Skills**

To this list I would also add the following:

1. **Music Skills** (learn to read, write, sing, and play music — this can also be referred to as music literacy, music appreciation, and music mastery)
2. **Writing Skills** (writing essays, poetry, stories, letters, resumes, emails, and even text messages)
3. **Penmanship Skills**
4. **Analytical and Problem Solving Skills**
5. **Creative Thinking Skills**
6. **Computer and Technology Skills**
7. **Spiritual Skills**
8. **Leadership and Management Skills**
9. **Team-working Skills**
10. **Communication and People Skills**

Who Are You? by Jerald Simon

THE POWER OF KNOWLEDGE

Knowledge includes everything we learn, read, experience, see, do, and fervently believe. For this demonstration, we are going to talk about the knowledge we can gain from reading good books. This covers everything from our education, including philosophy, history, religion, music, medicine, self-help, poetry, sports, science, mathematics, the arts, astronomy, business, relationships, and any book that helps us improve and want to be better. How many books could you read in a lifetime if you read one book per week (assuming you live to be at least 80 and start at the age of 12)? Let's do the math. There are 52 weeks in a year so here is a little chart to help you out:

1 Book per week x 52 weeks x 68 years = 3,536
2 Books per week x 52 weeks x 68 years = 7,072
3 Books per week x 52 weeks x 68 years = 10,608
4 Books per week x 52 weeks x 68 years = 14,144
5 Books per week x 52 weeks x 68 years = 17,680
6 Books per week x 52 weeks x 68 years = 21,216
7 Books per week x 52 weeks x 68 years = 24,752
8 Books per week x 52 weeks x 68 years = 28,288
9 Books per week x 52 weeks x 68 years = 31,824
10 Books per week x 52 weeks x 68 years = 35,360

These numbers may surprise you! They certainly shocked me. I know several people who read on average 1-2 books per day so they would fall under the 7-10 books per week category. My personal goal is to get into the 7 books per week club, but I am currently in the 2-3 books per week group. Read for life!

Who Are You? by Jerald Simon

On track, on course, and headed in the right direction.

But are we really on track, on course, and headed in the right direction, or are we at times facing the wrong way?

Sometimes we're on track, but we're not on the right course. At other times, we might be headed in the right direction, but still be off track. We hear of getting our ducks in a row or hoping the stars will align. Sometimes we are in the right place at the wrong time. At other times, thankfully, we are in the wrong place at the right time when someone needs our help or someone is there to help us when we need it most. These little hiccups should not hinder us from continuing to put our best foot forward every step of the way.

Where we are right now is exactly where we ought to be for the moment. We must enjoy every step of the journey, but we must learn from our well-placed steps as well as our missteps. Each step is only a stepping stone. We are where we are and have arrived at our current position and place in our personal journey because of our day-to-day decisions. But it is not our final destination.

Think of your ultimate destination or where you would like to be. You must enjoy where you are or you will never be satisfied with where you are going, but in order to go anywhere you must have a destination in mind. Ask yourself the following five questions to better determine where you are and where you want to ultimately be. Be completely honest with your responses.

Who Are You? by JERALD SIMON

1. Am I currently on track and heading in the direction I want to go in life?
2. If I am not on track and striving to do better today than I did yesterday, what needs to change?
3. What new talents can I develop? What new skills can I learn? What new habits can I master that will help me improve and be better starting right now?
4. How can I change for the better and be the best I can be at everything I do?
5. What can I do today to make a difference for good? How can I bring out the best in myself and in others?

If you need to change course a little, ask for directions (it's okay to do that, men), or even turn around and go in a completely different direction altogether, do it! Don't hesitate. Don't put off doing today what will make you a better you. It can't wait until tomorrow, for there are only todays. Each new day becomes today and tomorrow continues to run away. Make the commitment today to always be heading down a path that would benefit you and those around you. It may be difficult and downright awful. But things will always get better as we do our best every day. We all must sacrifice a little here and there and give up a few momentary wants and needs for the greater good of a brighter tomorrow — which is today!

Have a glorious day today. Make it matter. Make it count. If you are not on track, on course, and headed in the right direction at this moment, do what it will take to live life deliberately, intentionally, and purposefully!

Who Are You? by Jerald Simon

Identifying Personal Strengths and Weaknesses

We all have strengths and weaknesses. What are we going to do to turn our weaknesses into strengths? That is the question we each must ask ourselves daily. You see, our weaknesses are essentially gifts and opportunities for growth, change, and learning to assess and re-assess what is and is not working in our lives. We all fall short of the person we want to be. We always will. We all feel, at times, as if we don't measure up — and we all have moments where we honestly don't.

With all of that being said, we are not a lost cause. Some of us may feel beaten, broken, weak, and worn out, but there is a reservoir of rejuvenating resources buried deep within us. We are stronger than our personal weaknesses, whatever they may be. Some of us may, on occasion, be lazy. We may procrastinate and put off the necessary changes that must be made in order to trade out our bad habits for good ones. We may have negative mental conditioning that needs to be reprogrammed or debugged because we currently think we don't have any strengths and aren't good at anything. That, of course, is wrong. This line of thinking does far too much damage because often times these destructive thoughts turn into deplorable beliefs that cripple our chances for change. We are better than that!

Break free from weaknesses and focus on strengths!

On the next page you can list your strengths and your weaknesses. List 10 of each. Don't list more than that because we are going to focus on making our strengths stronger and turning our weaknesses into strengths.

LIST 10 STRENGTHS YOU HAVE
(Focus on the positives)

1.
2.
3.
4.
5.
6.
7.
8.
9.
10.

LIST 10 WEAKNESSES YOU HAVE
(You will turn these into strengths this year)

1.
2.
3.
4.
5.
6.
7.
8.
9.
10.

Now that you have listed 10 strengths you have and 10 weaknesses you would like to turn into strengths, you can understand the importance of living by virtues. Most of the strengths we have are virtues. Most of the weaknesses we have represent a present lack of certain virtues.

LIST OF VIRTUES
DO YOU LIVE BY THESE VIRTUES?

Here is a list of virtues from **http://www.virtuescience.com/virtuelist.html**. Their list is fantastic so I had to include it here. I hope this inspires you to focus on the virtues you'd like to work on!

Acceptance	Diligence	Humor
Accountability	Discernment	Idealism
Ambition	Discretion	Integrity
Assertiveness	Discipline	Impartiality
Beauty	Eloquence	Industry
Benevolence	Empathy	Innocence
Bravery	Enthusiasm	Joyfulness
Caring	Excellence	Justice
Charity	Faith	Kindness
Chastity	Faithfulness	Knowledge
Caution	Flexibility	Liberality
Cleanliness	Focus	Love
Commitment	Forbearance	Loyalty
Compassion	Forgiveness	Magnanimity
Confidence	Fortitude	Majesty
Consideration	Friendliness	Meekness
Contentment	Frugality	Mercy
Cooperation	Generosity	Moderation
Courage	Gentleness	Modesty
Courtesy	Grace	Obedience
Creativity	Gratitude	Openness
Curiosity	Helpfulness	Orderliness
Defiance	Honesty	Patience
Dependability	Honor	Peace
Detachment	Hope	Perseverance
Determination	Humbleness	Persistence
Devotion	Humility	Piety

Who Are You? by Jerald Simon

Prudence	Self-sacrifice	Thrift
Punctuality	Service	Tolerance
Purity	Sensitivity	Toughness
Purposefulness	Silence	Tranquility
Reliability	Simplicity	Trust
Resoluteness	Sincerity	Trustworthiness
Resourcefulness	Sobriety	Truthfulness
Respect	Spontaneity	Understanding
Responsibility	Steadfastness	Unity
Restraint	Strength	Vitality
Reverence	Tact	Wisdom
Righteousness	Temperance	Wonder
Selflessness	Thankfulness	Zeal

This list of virtues is a great starting point. We should select a different virtue to work on each day during the week and throughout the month. By doing so, we continually keep at the forefront of our thoughts what we should be doing to improve. By focusing on principles and virtues, we learn behavioral life skills that then dictate how we should behave. We can select the principles and values that mean the most to us, and those that we believe will help us be our best.

CREATE YOUR OWN LIST OF VIRTUES!

In 1726, at the age of 20, Benjamin Franklin created a system to help him improve and develop his character. He actually selected 13 virtues that he wanted to work on every day. It became a lifelong quest for him. Here are the 13 virtues that Benjamin Franklin selected to work on throughout his life as he wrote them in his own words:

1. Temperance. Eat not to dullness; drink not to elevation.
2. Silence. Speak not but what may benefit others or yourself; avoid trifling conversation.
3. Order. Let all your things have their places; let each part of your business have its time.
4. Resolution. Resolve to perform what you ought; perform without fail what you resolve.
5. Frugality. Make no expense but to do good to others or yourself; i.e., waste nothing.
6. Industry. Lose no time; be always employ'd in something useful; cut off all unnecessary actions.
7. Sincerity. Use no hurtful deceit; think innocently and justly, and, if you speak, speak accordingly.
8. Justice. Wrong none by doing injuries, or omitting the benefits that are your duty.
9. Moderation. Avoid extremes; forbear resenting injuries so much as you think they deserve.
10. Cleanliness. Tolerate no uncleanliness in body, cloaths, or habitation.
11. Tranquillity. Be not disturbed at trifles, or at accidents common or unavoidable.
12. Chastity. Rarely use venery but for health or offspring, never to dullness, weakness, or the injury of your own or another's peace or reputation.
13. Humility. Imitate Jesus and Socrates.

This is what Benjamin Franklin said of his 13 virtues: "I propos'd to myself, for the sake of clearness, to use rather more names, with fewer ideas annex'd to each, than a few names with more ideas; and I included under thirteen names of virtues all that at that time occurr'd to me as necessary or desirable, and annexed to each a short precept, which fully express'd the extent I gave to its meaning."

Part of our purpose in life, is to find out which principles, values, and virtues we esteem as important to help carry us through this life. Some may speak in terms of religious morals and values, and others may speak about ethical or practical principles as they relate to relationships, careers, schooling and personal improvement.

In order to overcome the weaknesses we have, we must first understand and admit that they are weaknesses and that there is a need to improve. We must first realize that we need to change. This understanding and admitting requires us to take ownership of our actions.

Who Are You? by Jerald Simon

Take ownership of your actions!
You are the captain of your own ship!

Who Are You? by Jerald Simon

How often do we take ownership of our own faults, mistakes, wrong doings, misdeeds, and misspoken truths (lies of all shades and colors — white, gray, and even black)? Life is about learning and improving, and we make mistakes of all shapes and sizes. The key is what we learn from our past mistakes and if we can take ownership of missteps along the way.

Let's divide the word ownership in half. It now reads "owner ship". Think of that imagery. Who is at the helm of your own life? Do you call the shots? Are you in control? Are you willing to acknowledge when you are off course and take complete responsibility for the decisions you make? Remember, we must assume ownership for both the good and the bad outcomes in our life. Sometimes things naturally happen to us that are beyond our control. We all must do the best we can with the difficulties that come to us through no fault of our own. I am speaking of how we can pick ourselves up when we have been in the wrong and we are to blame. I believe that we should be in control of ourselves. Now, I personally believe in God and believe that He oversees my life. With that being said, I believe God has given us the birthright of choice, and once we reach an age of accountability when we can responsibly assume ownership for our choices and their consequences, He allows us to take the helm and direct ourselves, knowing we then are responsible for the decisions we make. He gives us the responsibility to be responsible for our choices and then allows us to choose what we would like to do or not do as the case may be. Because the choice is ours, we then must be accountable for those choices. Accepting ownership means realizing that we all have shortcomings and don't always make the best decisions. But we all have room to grow and improve. The most successful people in the world are generally the ones who have fallen down many times but continually stand up and move on after each fall. They learn from their own mistakes and from the mistakes of others. We are all students and teachers in the school of life. We learn from each other and we teach each other.

Let's think about the gift of choice. Being capable of choosing something allows us to experience the freedom of our decisions. It is empowering. We are free to make the choices, but the natural reaction or consequences — both the good and the bad — are not ours for the choosing. They happen as naturally as the sun sets. Any decision will ultimately lead to a reaction to our action. It may even lead to a chain reaction of hundreds of little ripple effects going on around us because of our choices. They are our choices and we must assume ownership of them. Again, they can be good or bad depending on what our initial choice was. It is wonderful to have good consequences or natural reactions to what we do. Some examples of this include feeling rested after getting a full night's sleep. After exercising every day, week in and week out, we are delighted when we feel more fit, are more healthy, and even lose weight along the way. It is the natural reaction to our action of exercising and being health conscious. On the other hand, it is sad when we have negative consequences, because deep down inside we know we could have and should have done things differently.

As a result of our ability to choose, we are then given the ability to either be responsible for what we have allowed to happen or what we created because of our decisions. We can also, if we choose, ignore the responsibility of our actions and blame others, essentially "passing the buck" to someone else. It's not what we should do, but sometimes we are all guilty of doing this. This is what I refer to as the "scapegoat sickness", when people refuse to take ownership for the reactions to their actions. They will not assume responsibility for their decisions and the outcome — generally when it is not in their favor. As president Harry S. Truman liked to say, "The buck stops here." That was a sign he had on his desk in the oval office of the White House. How would it be if everyone believed in that phrase, and took every opportunity to determine how they could fix the negative aspects of their life? It's not too late and it's not too much to ask. We can all work together on improving our lives and helping those around us. We can all work on being a little better and taking ownership of what we do, say, and think. If there are mistakes that need mending, we can do that. If there are wrongs that need righting, we can do that as well. Any unresolved unpleasantry can improve if we all will assume ownership of our faults, mistakes, wrong doings, misdeeds, and misspoken truths. We can turn the negatives into positives as we work together.

It's time to set sail on your very own ship of success. This is your "owner ship" and you are in command. Don't let anyone steer you in a wrong direction or try to take control of your life. You are at the helm and it is your turn to assume ownership for your choices. Carefully choose what you would like to do with today. It is your day and you can change course whenever you need to. Face the warmth of the sun. It is a new day and your adventure awaits. Make it count. Make today matter. Have a marvelous trip today. Set sail and succeed!

5 Steps to make the most of each day starting today!

Make Today Count!

Good days, bad days, and days that just won't go away! We all have them — the good, the bad, and the ugly. Some days are better than others. And, unfortunately, some are worse — much worse. In life, there are times when, despite our best efforts, we have terrible times. Bad things do happen to good people and we can't pretend they don't. But there are some things we can do to prepare ourselves physically, mentally, spiritually, and emotionally for tough times, and to help us make the most of each day.

Some people say we live in uncertain times and that is certainly true. No one knows what tomorrow will bring. In truth, no one knows what today will bring. We can look at the past and amuse ourselves, feel remorse, guilt, and frustration at the mistakes, sorrows, and problems of the past, but the present is where we must live today. Sadly, despite our best efforts, things don't always go the way we want them to. Oftentimes, they end up being much worse than we could have imagined. Each day must be given our full attention. If the days are jam-packed with problems, then we must put on our best problem-solving hats and come up with solutions.

Here are five steps we can take to make the most of each day starting today:

1. **PRAY** — whether you are religious or not, a prayer is hope for a better today and a brighter tomorrow.

2. **Create a daily game plan so you are prepared to face the day.** Know what you want to accomplish, where you are going, and what your purpose and goals are for each day. If you don't know where you are going today, you will never get there.

3. **ALWAYS BE PRESENT** — Don't waste away today (your present) by worrying about tomorrow or fretting about yesterday!

4. **Give each day your full attention!** — Especially the little things. Everything matters because everything is important.

5. **Focus on the most urgent/pressing problems and fix those first.** Every day has issues and problems. Start with the most pressing problems, get those resolved or moving in the right direction, and then move on to the next tasks to tackle. One at a time. Don't ever pile your plate full of all of your problems. If you do, then you'll not only eat the worst meal of your life, it will leave a bitter taste in your mouth for every sweet experience placed before you down the road.

This list could be arranged in any order you prefer. For myself, I listed prayer as the first step because I believe I need to start and end my day with prayer to get me going in the right direction. Some may refer to this as meditation, connecting with the universe, or simply being optimistic, hopeful, and positive. For me, prayer puts me on the correct path to face the challenges of each day.

What are you doing to make the most of each day TODAY? What steps are you taking right now to create your own game plan, be present, attentive, and completely focused on the issues you face? What can you do today to help others around you see the good in each day, be ready for the bad times when they come, and try to eliminate any ugly pessimism of the past or unproductive dreaming of the future they (and we) may have?

Create a daily mantra (a statement or slogan) that you can read to yourself. This can be as simple as saying "I will do my best today and help others." You could say more and be descriptive in listing qualities, characteristics, attributes, and even accomplishments for today. Make it personal. Make this an everyday statement you could read to yourself every morning when you wake up.

MY DAILY MANTRA

_____

_____

_____

_____

_____

REAL MOTIVATION

The two main types of motivation are *extrinsic motivation* (relying on others, objects, money, rewards, and incentives, to motivate you) and *intrinsic motivation* (relying on yourself to be motivated).

Real and lasting motivation is intrinsic motivation. I always reward myself after I've accomplished a new goal. My rewards usually consist of purchasing large quantities of books from thrift stores and second hand shops, as I have a weakness for books on history, religion, language, music, business, and self improvement. If you need to give yourself an incentive (and we all do), go ahead. Reward yourself. You deserve it and you've earned it. It will motivate you to dream a little more often and plan and prepare for your next goal. But remember, that is a form of extrinsic motivation and not intrinsic motivation. Learn to be a self-starter and motivate yourself because you *want* to. Don't let others make your decisions for you. Dream a little more often. Plan and prepare for what you want and deserve out of life and then go to work. You'll be surprised how good it makes you feel and what you are able to accomplish. There are no limits, and nothing can hold you back if you are committed. Dream and succeed.

Who Are You? by JERALD SIMON

Today is YOUR Day!   ———Date———
A **Personal Improvement Outline** for YOU.

Get up. Get going. Get ready! Your new life awaits you!

DAILY FOCUS (main goal for the day) _____

DAILY VIRTUE (choose a virtue from the list of virtues on pg. 51) _____

DAILY BIOGRAPHY (Who did you learn about today and how has their life influenced you?)
_____

3 MICRO GOALS TO BE ACCOMPLISHED TODAY (list 3 steps, actions, or projects you can complete today toward one of the macro goals listed on pages 30 and 31)

1. _____
2. _____
3. _____

Daily to-do checklist of chores, homework and activities to be done today! (list the three most important ones below - do these first and do more if you can)

1. _____
2. _____
3. _____

Book(s) to read and finish this week (you should read at least one book per week) List how many pages you will read from your book(s) today and check off when completed.

1. _____ 2. _____

What did I discover about myself today? (what worked and why):
_____
_____
_____
_____
_____

Who Are You? by Jerald Simon

Today is **YOUR** Day!

Date _____

A **Personal Improvement Outline** for YOU.

Do YOUR best! That is all you can do today!

DAILY FOCUS (main goal for the day) _____
DAILY VIRTUE (choose a virtue from the list of virtues on pg. 51) _____
DAILY BIOGRAPHY (Who did you learn about today and how has their life influenced you?)
_____

3 MICRO GOALS TO BE ACCOMPLISHED TODAY (list 3 steps, actions, or projects you can complete today toward one of the macro goals listed on pages 30 and 31)

1 _____
2 _____
3 _____

Daily to-do checklist of chores, homework and activities to be done today! (list the three most important ones below - do these first and do more if you can)

1 _____
2 _____
3 _____

Book(s) to read and finish this week (you should read at least one book per week) List how many pages you will read from your book(s) today and check off when completed.

1 _____ 2 _____

What did I discover about myself today? (what worked and why):
_____
_____
_____
_____
_____

Who Are You? by JERALD SIMON

Today is YOUR Day!   Date

A **Personal Improvement Outline** for YOU.

Don't worry if you don't know everything. No one does!

DAILY FOCUS (main goal for the day) _____
DAILY VIRTUE (choose a virtue from the list of virtues on pg. 51) _____
DAILY BIOGRAPHY (Who did you learn about today and how has their life influenced you?)
_____

3 MICRO GOALS TO BE ACCOMPLISHED TODAY (list 3 steps, actions, or projects you can complete today toward one of the macro goals listed on pages 30 and 31)

1 _____
2 _____
3 _____

Daily to-do checklist of chores, homework and activities to be done today! (list the three most important ones below - do these first and do more if you can)

1 _____
2 _____
3 _____

Book(s) to read and finish this week (you should read at least one book per week) List how many pages you will read from your book(s) today and check off when completed.

1 _____ 2 _____

What did I discover about myself today? (what worked and why):
_____
_____
_____
_____
_____

Who Are You? by Jerald Simon

Today is YOUR Day!
A **Personal Improvement Outline** for YOU.

Be your best today. That is all anyone can expect to do.

DAILY FOCUS (main goal for the day) _____
DAILY VIRTUE (choose a virtue from the list of virtues on pg. 51) _____
DAILY BIOGRAPHY (Who did you learn about today and how has their life influenced you?)
_____

3 MICRO GOALS TO BE ACCOMPLISHED TODAY (list 3 steps, actions, or projects you can complete today toward one of the macro goals listed on pages 30 and 31)

1 _____
2 _____
3 _____

Daily to-do checklist of chores, homework and activities to be done today! (list the three most important ones below - do these first and do more if you can)

1 _____
2 _____
3 _____

Book(s) to read and finish this week (you should read at least one book per week) List how many pages you will read from your book(s) today and check off when completed.

1 _____ 2 _____

What did I discover about myself today? (what worked and why):
_____
_____
_____
_____
_____

Who Are You? by JERALD SIMON

Today is YOUR Day!
_____ Date

A **Personal Improvement Outline** for YOU.

Smile all the while!

DAILY FOCUS (main goal for the day) _____

DAILY VIRTUE (choose a virtue from the list of virtues on pg. 51) _____

DAILY BIOGRAPHY (Who did you learn about today and how has their life influenced you?)
_____

3 MICRO GOALS TO BE ACCOMPLISHED TODAY (list 3 steps, actions, or projects you can complete today toward one of the macro goals listed on pages 30 and 31)

1 _____
2 _____
3 _____

Daily to-do checklist of chores, homework and activities to be done today! (list the three most important ones below - do these first and do more if you can)

1 _____
2 _____
3 _____

Book(s) to read and finish this week (you should read at least one book per week) List how many pages you will read from your book(s) today and check off when completed.

1 _____ 2 _____

What did I discover about myself today? (what worked and why):
_____
_____
_____
_____
_____

Who Are You? by Jerald Simon

Date _____

Today is **YOUR** Day!
A **Personal Improvement Outline** for YOU.

Happiness is an inside job!

DAILY FOCUS (main goal for the day) _____
DAILY VIRTUE (choose a virtue from the list of virtues on pg. 51) _____
DAILY BIOGRAPHY (Who did you learn about today and how has their life influenced you?)
_____

3 MICRO GOALS TO BE ACCOMPLISHED TODAY (list 3 steps, actions, or projects you can complete today toward one of the macro goals listed on pages 30 and 31)

1 _____
2 _____
3 _____

Daily to-do checklist of chores, homework and activities to be done today! (list the three most important ones below - do these first and do more if you can)

1 _____
2 _____
3 _____

Book(s) to read and finish this week (you should read at least one book per week) List how many pages you will read from your book(s) today and check off when completed.

1 _____ 2 _____

What did I discover about myself today? (what worked and why):
_____
_____
_____
_____

Who Are You? by Jerald Simon

Today is YOUR Day!

Date

A **Personal Improvement Outline** for YOU.

Smile at a stranger today and say a friendly hello.

DAILY FOCUS (main goal for the day) _____
DAILY VIRTUE (choose a virtue from the list of virtues on pg. 51) _____
DAILY BIOGRAPHY (Who did you learn about today and how has their life influenced you?)
_____

3 MICRO GOALS TO BE ACCOMPLISHED TODAY (list 3 steps, actions, or projects you can complete today toward one of the macro goals listed on pages 30 and 31)

1 _____
2 _____
3 _____

Daily to-do checklist of chores, homework and activities to be done today! (list the three most important ones below - do these first and do more if you can)

1 _____
2 _____
3 _____

Book(s) to read and finish this week (you should read at least one book per week) List how many pages you will read from your book(s) today and check off when completed.

1 _____ 2 _____

What did I discover about myself today? (what worked and why):
_____
_____
_____
_____
_____

Who Are You? by JERALD SIMON

___ Date

Today is YOUR Day!
A **Personal Improvement Outline** for YOU.

Serve someone anonymously today.

DAILY FOCUS (main goal for the day) _____
DAILY VIRTUE (choose a virtue from the list of virtues on pg. 51) _____
DAILY BIOGRAPHY (Who did you learn about today and how has their life influenced you?)
_____

3 MICRO GOALS TO BE ACCOMPLISHED TODAY (list 3 steps, actions, or projects you can complete today toward one of the macro goals listed on pages 30 and 31)

1. _____
2. _____
3. _____

Daily to-do checklist of chores, homework and activities to be done today! (list the three most important ones below - do these first and do more if you can)

1. _____
2. _____
3. _____

Book(s) to read and finish this week (you should read at least one book per week) List how many pages you will read from your book(s) today and check off when completed.

1. _____ 2. _____

What did I discover about myself today? (what worked and why):

_____
_____
_____
_____
_____

Who Are You? by Jerald Simon

Today is YOUR Day!
Date _____

A **Personal Improvement Outline** for YOU.

Talk with an old friend today and find out how they are doing.

DAILY FOCUS (main goal for the day) _____

DAILY VIRTUE (choose a virtue from the list of virtues on pg. 51) _____

DAILY BIOGRAPHY (Who did you learn about today and how has their life influenced you?)
_____

3 MICRO GOALS TO BE ACCOMPLISHED TODAY (list 3 steps, actions, or projects you can complete today toward one of the macro goals listed on pages 30 and 31)

1. _____
2. _____
3. _____

Daily to-do checklist of chores, homework and activities to be done today! (list the three most important ones below - do these first and do more if you can)

1. _____
2. _____
3. _____

Book(s) to read and finish this week (you should read at least one book per week) List how many pages you will read from your book(s) today and check off when completed.

1. _____ 2. _____

What did I discover about myself today? (what worked and why):
_____
_____
_____
_____
_____

Who Are You? by JERALD SIMON

_____ Date   # Today is **YOUR** Day!
A **Personal Improvement Outline** for YOU.

Write a letter to a loved one today.

DAILY FOCUS (main goal for the day) _____
DAILY VIRTUE (choose a virtue from the list of virtues on pg. 51) _____
DAILY BIOGRAPHY (Who did you learn about today and how has their life influenced you?)
_____

3 MICRO GOALS TO BE ACCOMPLISHED TODAY (list 3 steps, actions, or projects you can complete today toward one of the macro goals listed on pages 30 and 31)

1 _____
2 _____
3 _____

Daily to-do checklist of chores, homework and activities to be done today!
(list the three most important ones below - do these first and do more if you can)

1 _____
2 _____
3 _____

Book(s) to read and finish this week
(you should read at least one book per week) List how many pages you will read from your book(s) today and check off when completed.

1 _____ 2 _____

What did I discover about myself today? (what worked and why):
_____
_____
_____
_____

Who Are You? by Jerald Simon

Today is YOUR Day!
A **Personal Improvement Outline** for YOU.

Date _____

Purchase a single flower (or cut one) and give it to a stranger.

DAILY FOCUS (main goal for the day) _____
DAILY VIRTUE (choose a virtue from the list of virtues on pg. 51) _____
DAILY BIOGRAPHY (Who did you learn about today and how has their life influenced you?)
_____

3 MICRO GOALS TO BE ACCOMPLISHED TODAY (list 3 steps, actions, or projects you can complete today toward one of the macro goals listed on pages 30 and 31)

1 _____
2 _____
3 _____

Daily to-do checklist of chores, homework and activities to be done today! (list the three most important ones below - do these first and do more if you can)

1 _____
2 _____
3 _____

Book(s) to read and finish this week (you should read at least one book per week) List how many pages you will read from your book(s) today and check off when completed.

1 _____ 2 _____

What did I discover about myself today? (what worked and why):

_____
_____
_____
_____
_____

Who Are You? by Jerald Simon

Date _____

Today is YOUR Day!
A **Personal Improvement Outline** for YOU.

Think about your childhood and tell someone a story about you.

DAILY FOCUS (main goal for the day) _____
DAILY VIRTUE (choose a virtue from the list of virtues on pg. 51) _____
DAILY BIOGRAPHY (Who did you learn about today and how has their life influenced you?)
_____

3 MICRO GOALS TO BE ACCOMPLISHED TODAY (list 3 steps, actions, or projects you can complete today toward one of the macro goals listed on pages 30 and 31)

1 _____
2 _____
3 _____

Daily to-do checklist of chores, homework and activities to be done today! (list the three most important ones below - do these first and do more if you can)

1 _____
2 _____
3 _____

Book(s) to read and finish this week (you should read at least one book per week) List how many pages you will read from your book(s) today and check off when completed.

1 _____ 2 _____

What did I discover about myself today? (what worked and why):
_____
_____
_____
_____
_____

Who Are You? by JERALD SIMON

Today is YOUR Day!

Date

A **Personal Improvement Outline** for YOU.

Ask a neighbor to show you how to do something new.

DAILY FOCUS (main goal for the day) _____
DAILY VIRTUE (choose a virtue from the list of virtues on pg. 51) _____
DAILY BIOGRAPHY (Who did you learn about today and how has their life influenced you?)
_____

3 MICRO GOALS TO BE ACCOMPLISHED TODAY (list 3 steps, actions, or projects you can complete today toward one of the macro goals listed on pages 30 and 31)

1 _____
2 _____
3 _____

Daily to-do checklist of chores, homework and activities to be done today! (list the three most important ones below - do these first and do more if you can)

1 _____
2 _____
3 _____

Book(s) to read and finish this week (you should read at least one book per week) List how many pages you will read from your book(s) today and check off when completed.

1 _____ 2 _____

What did I discover about myself today? (what worked and why):

_____
_____
_____
_____
_____

Who Are You? by Jerald Simon

_____ Date _____ # Today is YOUR Day!
A **Personal Improvement Outline** for YOU.

Ask your neighbor how they are doing. See if you can help out.

DAILY FOCUS (main goal for the day) _____
DAILY VIRTUE (choose a virtue from the list of virtues on pg. 51) _____
DAILY BIOGRAPHY (Who did you learn about today and how has their life influenced you?)
_____

3 MICRO GOALS TO BE ACCOMPLISHED TODAY (list 3 steps, actions, or projects you can complete today toward one of the macro goals listed on pages 30 and 31)

1 _____
2 _____
3 _____

Daily to-do checklist of chores, homework and activities to be done today! (list the three most important ones below - do these first and do more if you can)

1 _____
2 _____
3 _____

Book(s) to read and finish this week (you should read at least one book per week) List how many pages you will read from your book(s) today and check off when completed.

1 _____ 2 _____

What did I discover about myself today? (what worked and why):
_____
_____
_____
_____
_____

Who Are You? by Jerald Simon

Today is YOUR Day!   ———Date———
A **Personal Improvement Outline** for YOU.

Learn a magic trick today.

DAILY FOCUS (main goal for the day) _____
DAILY VIRTUE (choose a virtue from the list of virtues on pg. 51) _____
DAILY BIOGRAPHY (Who did you learn about today and how has their life influenced you?)
_____

3 MICRO GOALS TO BE ACCOMPLISHED TODAY (list 3 steps, actions, or projects you can complete today toward one of the macro goals listed on pages 30 and 31)

1 _____
2 _____
3 _____

Daily to-do checklist of chores, homework and activities to be done today! (list the three most important ones below - do these first and do more if you can)

1 _____
2 _____
3 _____

Book(s) to read and finish this week (you should read at least one book per week) List how many pages you will read from your book(s) today and check off when completed.

1 _____ 2 _____

What did I discover about myself today? (what worked and why):
_____
_____
_____
_____
_____

Who Are You? by JERALD SIMON

___Date___ # Today is YOUR Day!
A **Personal Improvement Outline** for YOU.

Bake cookies today and share them with friends.

DAILY FOCUS (main goal for the day) _____
DAILY VIRTUE (choose a virtue from the list of virtues on pg. 51) _____
DAILY BIOGRAPHY (Who did you learn about today and how has their life influenced you?)
_____

3 MICRO GOALS TO BE ACCOMPLISHED TODAY (list 3 steps, actions, or projects you can complete today toward one of the macro goals listed on pages 30 and 31)

1 _____
2 _____
3 _____

Daily to-do checklist of chores, homework and activities to be done today! (list the three most important ones below - do these first and do more if you can)

1 _____
2 _____
3 _____

Book(s) to read and finish this week (you should read at least one book per week) List how many pages you will read from your book(s) today and check off when completed.

1 _____ 2 _____

What did I discover about myself today? (what worked and why):
_____
_____
_____
_____

Who Are You? by JERALD SIMON

Today is YOUR Day!
Date
A **Personal Improvement Outline** for YOU.

Don't get frustrated if today has not gone well. Learn from it.

DAILY FOCUS (main goal for the day) _____
DAILY VIRTUE (choose a virtue from the list of virtues on pg. 51) _____
DAILY BIOGRAPHY (Who did you learn about today and how has their life influenced you?)
_____

3 MICRO GOALS TO BE ACCOMPLISHED TODAY (list 3 steps, actions, or projects you can complete today toward one of the macro goals listed on pages 30 and 31)

1 _____
2 _____
3 _____

Daily to-do checklist of chores, homework and activities to be done today! (list the three most important ones below - do these first and do more if you can)

1 _____
2 _____
3 _____

Book(s) to read and finish this week (you should read at least one book per week) List how many pages you will read from your book(s) today and check off when completed.

1 _____ 2 _____

What did I discover about myself today? (what worked and why):
_____
_____
_____
_____
_____

Who Are You? by JERALD SIMON

Today is YOUR Day!
Date

A **Personal Improvement Outline** for YOU.

How can you be a better friend today?

DAILY FOCUS (main goal for the day) _____
DAILY VIRTUE (choose a virtue from the list of virtues on pg. 51) _____
DAILY BIOGRAPHY (Who did you learn about today and how has their life influenced you?)
_____

3 MICRO GOALS TO BE ACCOMPLISHED TODAY (list 3 steps, actions, or projects you can complete today toward one of the macro goals listed on pages 30 and 31)

1 _____
2 _____
3 _____

Daily to-do checklist of chores, homework and activities to be done today! (list the three most important ones below - do these first and do more if you can)

1 _____
2 _____
3 _____

Book(s) to read and finish this week (you should read at least one book per week) List how many pages you will read from your book(s) today and check off when completed.

1 _____ 2 _____

What did I discover about myself today? (what worked and why):
_____
_____
_____
_____

Who Are You? by JERALD SIMON

Today is YOUR Day!   ⸻ Date
A **Personal Improvement Outline** for YOU.

Find a need and fill it!

DAILY FOCUS (main goal for the day) _____

DAILY VIRTUE (choose a virtue from the list of virtues on pg. 51) _____

DAILY BIOGRAPHY (Who did you learn about today and how has their life influenced you?)
_____

3 MICRO GOALS TO BE ACCOMPLISHED TODAY (list 3 steps, actions, or projects you can complete today toward one of the macro goals listed on pages 30 and 31)

1 _____
2 _____
3 _____

Daily to-do checklist of chores, homework and activities to be done today! (list the three most important ones below - do these first and do more if you can)

1 _____
2 _____
3 _____

Book(s) to read and finish this week (you should read at least one book per week) List how many pages you will read from your book(s) today and check off when completed.

1 _____ 2 _____

What did I discover about myself today? (what worked and why):
_____
_____
_____
_____
_____

Who Are You? by Jerald Simon

Today is YOUR Day!
__Date__

A **Personal Improvement Outline** for YOU.

When you speak with others today look them in the eyes.

DAILY FOCUS (main goal for the day) _____
DAILY VIRTUE (choose a virtue from the list of virtues on pg. 51) _____
DAILY BIOGRAPHY (Who did you learn about today and how has their life influenced you?)
_____

3 MICRO GOALS TO BE ACCOMPLISHED TODAY (list 3 steps, actions, or projects you can complete today toward one of the macro goals listed on pages 30 and 31)

1 _____
2 _____
3 _____

Daily to-do checklist of chores, homework and activities to be done today! (list the three most important ones below - do these first and do more if you can)

1 _____
2 _____
3 _____

Book(s) to read and finish this week (you should read at least one book per week) List how many pages you will read from your book(s) today and check off when completed.

1 _____ 2 _____

What did I discover about myself today? (what worked and why):
_____
_____
_____
_____
_____

Who Are You? by JERALD SIMON

Today is YOUR Day! _____
Date
A **Personal Improvement Outline** for YOU.

Set aside some money today for a rainy day slush fund.

DAILY FOCUS (main goal for the day) _____
DAILY VIRTUE (choose a virtue from the list of virtues on pg. 51) _____
DAILY BIOGRAPHY (Who did you learn about today and how has their life influenced you?)
_____

3 MICRO GOALS TO BE ACCOMPLISHED TODAY (list 3 steps, actions, or projects you can complete today toward one of the macro goals listed on pages 30 and 31)

1 _____
2 _____
3 _____

Daily to-do checklist of chores, homework and activities to be done today! (list the three most important ones below - do these first and do more if you can)

1 _____
2 _____
3 _____

Book(s) to read and finish this week (you should read at least one book per week) List how many pages you will read from your book(s) today and check off when completed.

1 _____ 2 _____

What did I discover about myself today? (what worked and why):
_____
_____
_____
_____
_____

Who Are You? by Jerald Simon

___Date___ ## Today is **YOUR** Day!
A **Personal Improvement Outline** for YOU.

Paint a picture today with someone you care about.

DAILY FOCUS (main goal for the day) _____
DAILY VIRTUE (choose a virtue from the list of virtues on pg. 51) _____
DAILY BIOGRAPHY (Who did you learn about today and how has their life influenced you?)
_____

3 MICRO GOALS TO BE ACCOMPLISHED TODAY (list 3 steps, actions, or projects you can complete today toward one of the macro goals listed on pages 30 and 31)

1 _____
2 _____
3 _____

Daily to-do checklist of chores, homework and activities to be done today!
(list the three most important ones below - do these first and do more if you can)

1 _____
2 _____
3 _____

Book(s) to read and finish this week (you should read at least one book per week) List how many pages you will read from your book(s) today and check off when completed.

1 _____ 2 _____

What did I discover about myself today? (what worked and why):
_____
_____
_____
_____

Who Are You? by JERALD SIMON

Today is YOUR Day!   ___Date___
A **Personal Improvement Outline** for YOU.

Watch a video tutorial on how to fix an appliance or machine.

DAILY FOCUS (main goal for the day) _____

DAILY VIRTUE (choose a virtue from the list of virtues on pg. 51) _____

DAILY BIOGRAPHY (Who did you learn about today and how has their life influenced you?)
_____

3 MICRO GOALS TO BE ACCOMPLISHED TODAY (list 3 steps, actions, or projects you can complete today toward one of the macro goals listed on pages 30 and 31)

1 _____
2 _____
3 _____

Daily to-do checklist of chores, homework and activities to be done today! (list the three most important ones below - do these first and do more if you can)

1 _____
2 _____
3 _____

Book(s) to read and finish this week (you should read at least one book per week) List how many pages you will read from your book(s) today and check off when completed.

1 _____ 2 _____

What did I discover about myself today? (what worked and why):
_____
_____
_____
_____
_____

Who Are You? by Jerald Simon

<u>　　　　　</u>   ## Today is **YOUR** Day!
　　Date
A **Personal Improvement Outline** for YOU.

Listen to a classical masterpiece by Beethoven today.

DAILY FOCUS (main goal for the day) _____

DAILY VIRTUE (choose a virtue from the list of virtues on pg. 51) _____

DAILY BIOGRAPHY (Who did you learn about today and how has their life influenced you?)
_____

3 MICRO GOALS TO BE ACCOMPLISHED TODAY (list 3 steps, actions, or projects you can complete today toward one of the macro goals listed on pages 30 and 31)

1 _____
2 _____
3 _____

Daily to-do checklist of chores, homework and activities to be done today! (list the three most important ones below - do these first and do more if you can)

1 _____
2 _____
3 _____

Book(s) to read and finish this week (you should read at least one book per week) List how many pages you will read from your book(s) today and check off when completed.

1 _____ 2 _____

What did I discover about myself today? (what worked and why):
_____
_____
_____
_____
_____

Who Are You? by JERALD SIMON

Today is YOUR Day!   ___Date___
A **Personal Improvement Outline** for YOU.

Sit in a dark room with the lights off and breathe slowly.

DAILY FOCUS (main goal for the day) _____
DAILY VIRTUE (choose a virtue from the list of virtues on pg. 51) _____
DAILY BIOGRAPHY (Who did you learn about today and how has their life influenced you?)
_____

3 MICRO GOALS TO BE ACCOMPLISHED TODAY (list 3 steps, actions, or projects you can complete today toward one of the macro goals listed on pages 30 and 31)

1 _____
2 _____
3 _____

Daily to-do checklist of chores, homework and activities to be done today! (list the three most important ones below - do these first and do more if you can)

1 _____
2 _____
3 _____

Book(s) to read and finish this week (you should read at least one book per week) List how many pages you will read from your book(s) today and check off when completed.

1 _____ 2 _____

What did I discover about myself today? (what worked and why):
_____
_____
_____
_____
_____

Who Are You? by JERALD SIMON

___Date___ # Today is **YOUR** Day!
A **Personal Improvement Outline** for YOU.

Eat a new fruit you've never eaten before.

DAILY FOCUS (main goal for the day) _____
DAILY VIRTUE (choose a virtue from the list of virtues on pg. 51) _____
DAILY BIOGRAPHY (Who did you learn about today and how has their life influenced you?)
_____

3 MICRO GOALS TO BE ACCOMPLISHED TODAY (list 3 steps, actions, or projects you can complete today toward one of the macro goals listed on pages 30 and 31)

1 _____
2 _____
3 _____

Daily to-do checklist of chores, homework and activities to be done today! (list the three most important ones below - do these first and do more if you can)

1 _____
2 _____
3 _____

Book(s) to read and finish this week (you should read at least one book per week) List how many pages you will read from your book(s) today and check off when completed.

1 _____ 2 _____

What did I discover about myself today? (what worked and why):
_____
_____
_____
_____
_____

Who Are You? by JERALD SIMON

Today is YOUR Day!
Date

A **Personal Improvement Outline** for YOU.

Watch an Opera today!

DAILY FOCUS (main goal for the day) _____

DAILY VIRTUE (choose a virtue from the list of virtues on pg. 51) _____

DAILY BIOGRAPHY (Who did you learn about today and how has their life influenced you?)
_____

3 MICRO GOALS TO BE ACCOMPLISHED TODAY (list 3 steps, actions, or projects you can complete today toward one of the macro goals listed on pages 30 and 31)

1 _____
2 _____
3 _____

Daily to-do checklist of chores, homework and activities to be done today! (list the three most important ones below - do these first and do more if you can)

1 _____
2 _____
3 _____

Book(s) to read and finish this week (you should read at least one book per week) List how many pages you will read from your book(s) today and check off when completed.

1 _____ 2 _____

What did I discover about myself today? (what worked and why):
_____
_____
_____
_____
_____

Who Are You? by Jerald Simon

_____ Date

Today is YOUR Day!
A **Personal Improvement Outline** for YOU.

Write a simple poem today that rhymes (ABAB format).

DAILY FOCUS (main goal for the day) _____
DAILY VIRTUE (choose a virtue from the list of virtues on pg. 51) _____
DAILY BIOGRAPHY (Who did you learn about today and how has their life influenced you?)
_____

3 MICRO GOALS TO BE ACCOMPLISHED TODAY (list 3 steps, actions, or projects you can complete today toward one of the macro goals listed on pages 30 and 31)

1 _____
2 _____
3 _____

Daily to-do checklist of chores, homework and activities to be done today! (list the three most important ones below - do these first and do more if you can)

1 _____
2 _____
3 _____

Book(s) to read and finish this week (you should read at least one book per week) List how many pages you will read from your book(s) today and check off when completed.

1 _____ 2 _____

What did I discover about myself today? (what worked and why):
_____
_____
_____
_____
_____

Who Are You? by Jerald Simon

Today is YOUR Day!
Date

A **Personal Improvement Outline** for YOU.

Take a picture of the sunrise or sunset today.

DAILY FOCUS (main goal for the day) _____

DAILY VIRTUE (choose a virtue from the list of virtues on pg. 51) _____

DAILY BIOGRAPHY (Who did you learn about today and how has their life influenced you?)
_____

3 MICRO GOALS TO BE ACCOMPLISHED TODAY (list 3 steps, actions, or projects you can complete today toward one of the macro goals listed on pages 30 and 31)

1 _____
2 _____
3 _____

Daily to-do checklist of chores, homework and activities to be done today! (list the three most important ones below - do these first and do more if you can)

1 _____
2 _____
3 _____

Book(s) to read and finish this week (you should read at least one book per week) List how many pages you will read from your book(s) today and check off when completed.

1 _____ 2 _____

What did I discover about myself today? (what worked and why):
_____
_____
_____
_____
_____

Who Are You? by Jerald Simon

_____Date_____ # Today is **YOUR** Day!
A **Personal Improvement Outline** for YOU.

Take one room in your house and thoroughly clean it today.

DAILY FOCUS (main goal for the day) _____
DAILY VIRTUE (choose a virtue from the list of virtues on pg. 51) _____
DAILY BIOGRAPHY (Who did you learn about today and how has their life influenced you?)
_____

3 MICRO GOALS TO BE ACCOMPLISHED TODAY (list 3 steps, actions, or projects you can complete today toward one of the macro goals listed on pages 30 and 31)

1 _____
2 _____
3 _____

Daily to-do checklist of chores, homework and activities to be done today! (list the three most important ones below - do these first and do more if you can)

1 _____
2 _____
3 _____

Book(s) to read and finish this week (you should read at least one book per week) List how many pages you will read from your book(s) today and check off when completed.

1 _____ 2 _____

What did I discover about myself today? (what worked and why):
_____
_____
_____
_____

Who Are You? by JERALD SIMON

Today is YOUR Day!

Date _____

A **Personal Improvement Outline** for YOU.

Learn 2 chords on a guitar today (even if you don't have one).

DAILY FOCUS (main goal for the day) _____

DAILY VIRTUE (choose a virtue from the list of virtues on pg. 51) _____

DAILY BIOGRAPHY (Who did you learn about today and how has their life influenced you?)
_____

3 MICRO GOALS TO BE ACCOMPLISHED TODAY (list 3 steps, actions, or projects you can complete today toward one of the macro goals listed on pages 30 and 31)

1 _____
2 _____
3 _____

Daily to-do checklist of chores, homework and activities to be done today! (list the three most important ones below - do these first and do more if you can)

1 _____
2 _____
3 _____

Book(s) to read and finish this week (you should read at least one book per week) List how many pages you will read from your book(s) today and check off when completed.

1 _____ 2 _____

What did I discover about myself today? (what worked and why):

_____
_____
_____
_____

Who Are You? by Jerald Simon

Date _____

Today is **YOUR** Day!
A **Personal Improvement Outline** for YOU.

Play with little children today — your own or relatives.

DAILY FOCUS (main goal for the day) _____

DAILY VIRTUE (choose a virtue from the list of virtues on pg. 51) _____

DAILY BIOGRAPHY (Who did you learn about today and how has their life influenced you?)
_____

3 MICRO GOALS TO BE ACCOMPLISHED TODAY (list 3 steps, actions, or projects you can complete today toward one of the macro goals listed on pages 30 and 31)

1 _____
2 _____
3 _____

Daily to-do checklist of chores, homework and activities to be done today! (list the three most important ones below - do these first and do more if you can)

1 _____
2 _____
3 _____

Book(s) to read and finish this week (you should read at least one book per week) List how many pages you will read from your book(s) today and check off when completed.

1 _____ 2 _____

What did I discover about myself today? (what worked and why):

_____
_____
_____
_____
_____

Who Are You? by JERALD SIMON

Today is YOUR Day!
Date _____

A **Personal Improvement Outline** for YOU.

Try to draw a cartoon comic strip today.

DAILY FOCUS (main goal for the day) _____
DAILY VIRTUE (choose a virtue from the list of virtues on pg. 51) _____
DAILY BIOGRAPHY (Who did you learn about today and how has their life influenced you?)
_____

3 MICRO GOALS TO BE ACCOMPLISHED TODAY (list 3 steps, actions, or projects you can complete today toward one of the macro goals listed on pages 30 and 31)

1 _____
2 _____
3 _____

Daily to-do checklist of chores, homework and activities to be done today! (list the three most important ones below - do these first and do more if you can)

1 _____
2 _____
3 _____

Book(s) to read and finish this week (you should read at least one book per week) List how many pages you will read from your book(s) today and check off when completed.

1 _____ 2 _____

What did I discover about myself today? (what worked and why):

_____
_____
_____
_____
_____

Who Are You? by Jerald Simon

___Date___ ## Today is **YOUR** Day!
A **Personal Improvement Outline** for YOU.

Write the title to a book you'd like to write. If you want, start it.

DAILY FOCUS (main goal for the day) _____
DAILY VIRTUE (choose a virtue from the list of virtues on pg. 51) _____
DAILY BIOGRAPHY (Who did you learn about today and how has their life influenced you?)
_____

3 MICRO GOALS TO BE ACCOMPLISHED TODAY (list 3 steps, actions, or projects you can complete today toward one of the macro goals listed on pages 30 and 31)

1 _____
2 _____
3 _____

Daily to-do checklist of chores, homework and activities to be done today! (list the three most important ones below - do these first and do more if you can)

1 _____
2 _____
3 _____

Book(s) to read and finish this week (you should read at least one book per week) List how many pages you will read from your book(s) today and check off when completed.

1 _____ 2 _____

What did I discover about myself today? (what worked and why):
_____
_____
_____
_____

Who Are You? by Jerald Simon

Today is YOUR Day! ⎯⎯ Date ⎯⎯
A **Personal Improvement Outline** for YOU.

Learn a little of the history of the Mayan civilization today.

DAILY FOCUS (main goal for the day) _____

DAILY VIRTUE (choose a virtue from the list of virtues on pg. 51) _____

DAILY BIOGRAPHY (Who did you learn about today and how has their life influenced you?)
_____

3 MICRO GOALS TO BE ACCOMPLISHED TODAY (list 3 steps, actions, or projects you can complete today toward one of the macro goals listed on pages 30 and 31)

1 _____
2 _____
3 _____

Daily to-do checklist of chores, homework and activities to be done today! (list the three most important ones below - do these first and do more if you can)

1 _____
2 _____
3 _____

Book(s) to read and finish this week (you should read at least one book per week) List how many pages you will read from your book(s) today and check off when completed.

1 _____ 2 _____

What did I discover about myself today? (what worked and why):

_____
_____
_____
_____
_____

Who Are You? by Jerald Simon

<u>   Date   </u> # Today is **YOUR** Day!
A **Personal Improvement Outline** for YOU.

Watch a documentary about how things are made.

DAILY FOCUS (main goal for the day) _____
DAILY VIRTUE (choose a virtue from the list of virtues on pg. 51) _____
DAILY BIOGRAPHY (Who did you learn about today and how has their life influenced you?)
_____

3 MICRO GOALS TO BE ACCOMPLISHED TODAY (list 3 steps, actions, or projects you can complete today toward one of the macro goals listed on pages 30 and 31)

1. _____
2. _____
3. _____

Daily to-do checklist of chores, homework and activities to be done today! (list the three most important ones below - do these first and do more if you can)

1. _____
2. _____
3. _____

Book(s) to read and finish this week (you should read at least one book per week) List how many pages you will read from your book(s) today and check off when completed.

1. _____ 2. _____

What did I discover about myself today? (what worked and why):
_____
_____
_____
_____
_____

Who Are You? by JERALD SIMON

Today is YOUR Day! ___Date___
A **Personal Improvement Outline** for YOU.

Write a Haiku today (5/7/5 syllable count form).

DAILY FOCUS (main goal for the day) _____
DAILY VIRTUE (choose a virtue from the list of virtues on pg. 51) _____
DAILY BIOGRAPHY (Who did you learn about today and how has their life influenced you?)
_____

3 MICRO GOALS TO BE ACCOMPLISHED TODAY (list 3 steps, actions, or projects you can complete today toward one of the macro goals listed on pages 30 and 31)

1 _____
2 _____
3 _____

Daily to-do checklist of chores, homework and activities to be done today! (list the three most important ones below - do these first and do more if you can)

1 _____
2 _____
3 _____

Book(s) to read and finish this week (you should read at least one book per week) List how many pages you will read from your book(s) today and check off when completed.

1 _____ 2 _____

What did I discover about myself today? (what worked and why):
_____
_____
_____
_____
_____

Who Are You? by JERALD SIMON

___Date___ ## Today is **YOUR** Day!
A **Personal Improvement Outline** for YOU.

Read a short biography about Leonardo Da Vinci today.

DAILY FOCUS (main goal for the day) _____
DAILY VIRTUE (choose a virtue from the list of virtues on pg. 51) _____
DAILY BIOGRAPHY (Who did you learn about today and how has their life influenced you?)
_____

3 MICRO GOALS TO BE ACCOMPLISHED TODAY (list 3 steps, actions, or projects you can complete today toward one of the macro goals listed on pages 30 and 31)

1. _____
2. _____
3. _____

Daily to-do checklist of chores, homework and activities to be done today! (list the three most important ones below - do these first and do more if you can)

1. _____
2. _____
3. _____

Book(s) to read and finish this week (you should read at least one book per week) List how many pages you will read from your book(s) today and check off when completed.

1. _____ 2. _____

What did I discover about myself today? (what worked and why):
_____
_____
_____
_____
_____

Who Are You? by Jerald Simon

Today is YOUR Day!
Date

A **Personal Improvement Outline** for YOU.

Play a game of checkers or chess today to challenge your brain.

DAILY FOCUS (main goal for the day) _____

DAILY VIRTUE (choose a virtue from the list of virtues on pg. 51) _____

DAILY BIOGRAPHY (Who did you learn about today and how has their life influenced you?)
_____

3 MICRO GOALS TO BE ACCOMPLISHED TODAY (list 3 steps, actions, or projects you can complete today toward one of the macro goals listed on pages 30 and 31)

1 _____
2 _____
3 _____

Daily to-do checklist of chores, homework and activities to be done today! (list the three most important ones below - do these first and do more if you can)

1 _____
2 _____
3 _____

Book(s) to read and finish this week (you should read at least one book per week) List how many pages you will read from your book(s) today and check off when completed.

1 _____ 2 _____

What did I discover about myself today? (what worked and why):

_____
_____
_____
_____
_____

Who Are You? by Jerald Simon

___Date___

Today is YOUR Day!
A **Personal Improvement Outline** for YOU.

Teach a sibling, child, or even parent something today.

DAILY FOCUS (main goal for the day) _____
DAILY VIRTUE (choose a virtue from the list of virtues on pg. 51) _____
DAILY BIOGRAPHY (Who did you learn about today and how has their life influenced you?)
_____

3 MICRO GOALS TO BE ACCOMPLISHED TODAY (list 3 steps, actions, or projects you can complete today toward one of the macro goals listed on pages 30 and 31)

1. _____
2. _____
3. _____

Daily to-do checklist of chores, homework and activities to be done today! (list the three most important ones below - do these first and do more if you can)

1. _____
2. _____
3. _____

Book(s) to read and finish this week (you should read at least one book per week) List how many pages you will read from your book(s) today and check off when completed.

1. _____ 2. _____

What did I discover about myself today? (what worked and why):
_____
_____
_____
_____
_____

Who Are You? by Jerald Simon

Today is **YOUR** Day!   Date _____

A **Personal Improvement Outline** for YOU.

Listen to some blues or jazz music today.

DAILY FOCUS (main goal for the day) _____
DAILY VIRTUE (choose a virtue from the list of virtues on pg. 51) _____
DAILY BIOGRAPHY (Who did you learn about today and how has their life influenced you?)
_____

3 MICRO GOALS TO BE ACCOMPLISHED TODAY (list 3 steps, actions, or projects you can complete today toward one of the macro goals listed on pages 30 and 31)

1 _____
2 _____
3 _____

Daily to-do checklist of chores, homework and activities to be done today! (list the three most important ones below - do these first and do more if you can)

1 _____
2 _____
3 _____

Book(s) to read and finish this week (you should read at least one book per week) List how many pages you will read from your book(s) today and check off when completed.

1 _____ 2 _____

What did I discover about myself today? (what worked and why):
_____
_____
_____
_____
_____

Who Are You? by Jerald Simon

Today is YOUR Day!
Date

A **Personal Improvement Outline** for YOU.

Read a short biography about Benjamin Franklin today.

DAILY FOCUS (main goal for the day) _____

DAILY VIRTUE (choose a virtue from the list of virtues on pg. 51) _____

DAILY BIOGRAPHY (Who did you learn about today and how has their life influenced you?)
_____

3 MICRO GOALS TO BE ACCOMPLISHED TODAY (list 3 steps, actions, or projects you can complete today toward one of the macro goals listed on pages 30 and 31)

1 _____
2 _____
3 _____

Daily to-do checklist of chores, homework and activities to be done today! (list the three most important ones below - do these first and do more if you can)

1 _____
2 _____
3 _____

Book(s) to read and finish this week (you should read at least one book per week) List how many pages you will read from your book(s) today and check off when completed.

1 _____ 2 _____

What did I discover about myself today? (what worked and why):
_____
_____
_____
_____

Who Are You? by JERALD SIMON

Today is YOUR Day!   ⎯ Date ⎯
A **Personal Improvement Outline** for YOU.

Learn a little about philosophy today. Who is Plato? Socrates?

DAILY FOCUS (main goal for the day) _____
DAILY VIRTUE (choose a virtue from the list of virtues on pg. 51) _____
DAILY BIOGRAPHY (Who did you learn about today and how has their life influenced you?)
_____

3 MICRO GOALS TO BE ACCOMPLISHED TODAY (list 3 steps, actions, or projects you can complete today toward one of the macro goals listed on pages 30 and 31)

1 _____
2 _____
3 _____

Daily to-do checklist of chores, homework and activities to be done today! (list the three most important ones below - do these first and do more if you can)

1 _____
2 _____
3 _____

Book(s) to read and finish this week (you should read at least one book per week) List how many pages you will read from your book(s) today and check off when completed.

1 _____ 2 _____

What did I discover about myself today? (what worked and why):

_____
_____
_____
_____
_____

Who Are You? by JERALD SIMON

Today is **YOUR** Day!
_{Date}

A **Personal Improvement Outline** for YOU.

Write an essay on personal development today.

DAILY FOCUS (main goal for the day) _____
DAILY VIRTUE (choose a virtue from the list of virtues on pg. 51) _____
DAILY BIOGRAPHY (Who did you learn about today and how has their life influenced you?)
_____

3 MICRO GOALS TO BE ACCOMPLISHED TODAY (list 3 steps, actions, or projects you can complete today toward one of the macro goals listed on pages 30 and 31)

1 _____
2 _____
3 _____

Daily to-do checklist of chores, homework and activities to be done today! (list the three most important ones below - do these first and do more if you can)

1 _____
2 _____
3 _____

Book(s) to read and finish this week (you should read at least one book per week) List how many pages you will read from your book(s) today and check off when completed.

1 _____ 2 _____

What did I discover about myself today? (what worked and why):
_____
_____
_____
_____
_____

Who Are You? by JERALD SIMON

Today is YOUR Day!   ———— Date

A **Personal Improvement Outline** for YOU.

Get in the habit of stretching and exercising everyday.

DAILY FOCUS (main goal for the day) _____

DAILY VIRTUE (choose a virtue from the list of virtues on pg. 51) _____

DAILY BIOGRAPHY (Who did you learn about today and how has their life influenced you?)
_____

3 MICRO GOALS TO BE ACCOMPLISHED TODAY (list 3 steps, actions, or projects you can complete today toward one of the macro goals listed on pages 30 and 31)

1 _____
2 _____
3 _____

Daily to-do checklist of chores, homework and activities to be done today! (list the three most important ones below - do these first and do more if you can)

1 _____
2 _____
3 _____

Book(s) to read and finish this week (you should read at least one book per week) List how many pages you will read from your book(s) today and check off when completed.

1 _____ 2 _____

What did I discover about myself today? (what worked and why):
_____
_____
_____
_____

Who Are You? by Jerald Simon

<u>   </u>
Date

Today is **YOUR** Day!
A **Personal Improvement Outline** for YOU.

Study about the original 13 colonies of America.

DAILY FOCUS (main goal for the day) _____
DAILY VIRTUE (choose a virtue from the list of virtues on pg. 51) _____
DAILY BIOGRAPHY (Who did you learn about today and how has their life influenced you?)
_____

3 MICRO GOALS TO BE ACCOMPLISHED TODAY (list 3 steps, actions, or projects you can complete today toward one of the macro goals listed on pages 30 and 31)

1 _____
2 _____
3 _____

Daily to-do checklist of chores, homework and activities to be done today! (list the three most important ones below - do these first and do more if you can)

1 _____
2 _____
3 _____

Book(s) to read and finish this week (you should read at least one book per week) List how many pages you will read from your book(s) today and check off when completed.

1 _____ 2 _____

What did I discover about myself today? (what worked and why):
_____
_____
_____
_____
_____

Who Are You? by Jerald Simon

Today is YOUR Day!   _____
Date
A **Personal Improvement Outline** for YOU.

Try to write for 30 minutes with your non-dominant hand.

DAILY FOCUS (main goal for the day) _____

DAILY VIRTUE (choose a virtue from the list of virtues on pg. 51) _____

DAILY BIOGRAPHY (Who did you learn about today and how has their life influenced you?)
_____

3 MICRO GOALS TO BE ACCOMPLISHED TODAY (list 3 steps, actions, or projects you can complete today toward one of the macro goals listed on pages 30 and 31)

1 _____
2 _____
3 _____

Daily to-do checklist of chores, homework and activities to be done today! (list the three most important ones below - do these first and do more if you can)

1 _____
2 _____
3 _____

Book(s) to read and finish this week (you should read at least one book per week) List how many pages you will read from your book(s) today and check off when completed.

1 _____ 2 _____

What did I discover about myself today? (what worked and why):
_____
_____
_____
_____
_____

Who Are You? by Jerald Simon

<u>   Date   </u> # Today is YOUR Day!
A **Personal Improvement Outline** for YOU.

Learn about the Boy Scouts and the Girl Scouts today.

DAILY FOCUS (main goal for the day) _____
DAILY VIRTUE (choose a virtue from the list of virtues on pg. 51) _____
DAILY BIOGRAPHY (Who did you learn about today and how has their life influenced you?)
_____

3 MICRO GOALS TO BE ACCOMPLISHED TODAY (list 3 steps, actions, or projects you can complete today toward one of the macro goals listed on pages 30 and 31)

1 _____
2 _____
3 _____

Daily to-do checklist of chores, homework and activities to be done today! (list the three most important ones below - do these first and do more if you can)

1 _____
2 _____
3 _____

Book(s) to read and finish this week (you should read at least one book per week) List how many pages you will read from your book(s) today and check off when completed.

1 _____ 2 _____

What did I discover about myself today? (what worked and why):
_____
_____
_____
_____

Who Are You? by Jerald Simon

Today is YOUR Day!
_____ Date

A **Personal Improvement Outline** for YOU.

Write a letter to a parent or sibling and thank them.

DAILY FOCUS (main goal for the day) _____
DAILY VIRTUE (choose a virtue from the list of virtues on pg. 51) _____
DAILY BIOGRAPHY (Who did you learn about today and how has their life influenced you?)
_____

3 MICRO GOALS TO BE ACCOMPLISHED TODAY (list 3 steps, actions, or projects you can complete today toward one of the macro goals listed on pages 30 and 31)

1 _____
2 _____
3 _____

Daily to-do checklist of chores, homework and activities to be done today! (list the three most important ones below - do these first and do more if you can)

1 _____
2 _____
3 _____

Book(s) to read and finish this week (you should read at least one book per week) List how many pages you will read from your book(s) today and check off when completed.

1 _____ 2 _____

What did I discover about myself today? (what worked and why):
_____
_____
_____
_____
_____

Who Are You? by Jerald Simon

___Date___ # Today is **YOUR** Day!
A **Personal Improvement Outline** for YOU.

Learn to count to 10 in Spanish or Portuguese today.

DAILY FOCUS (main goal for the day) _____
DAILY VIRTUE (choose a virtue from the list of virtues on pg. 51) _____
DAILY BIOGRAPHY (Who did you learn about today and how has their life influenced you?)
_____

3 MICRO GOALS TO BE ACCOMPLISHED TODAY (list 3 steps, actions, or projects you can complete today toward one of the macro goals listed on pages 30 and 31)

1 _____
2 _____
3 _____

Daily to-do checklist of chores, homework and activities to be done today! (list the three most important ones below - do these first and do more if you can)

1 _____
2 _____
3 _____

Book(s) to read and finish this week (you should read at least one book per week) List how many pages you will read from your book(s) today and check off when completed.

1 _____ 2 _____

What did I discover about myself today? (what worked and why):
_____
_____
_____
_____
_____

Who Are You? by JERALD SIMON

Today is YOUR Day!
Date

A **Personal Improvement Outline** for YOU.

Practice the art of meditating today. Learn about it and try it.

DAILY FOCUS (main goal for the day) _____
DAILY VIRTUE (choose a virtue from the list of virtues on pg. 51) _____
DAILY BIOGRAPHY (Who did you learn about today and how has their life influenced you?)
_____

3 MICRO GOALS TO BE ACCOMPLISHED TODAY (list 3 steps, actions, or projects you can complete today toward one of the macro goals listed on pages 30 and 31)

1 _____
2 _____
3 _____

Daily to-do checklist of chores, homework and activities to be done today! (list the three most important ones below - do these first and do more if you can)

1 _____
2 _____
3 _____

Book(s) to read and finish this week (you should read at least one book per week) List how many pages you will read from your book(s) today and check off when completed.

1 _____ 2 _____

What did I discover about myself today? (what worked and why):
_____
_____
_____
_____
_____

Who Are You? by Jerald Simon

<u>   Date   </u> # Today is **YOUR** Day!
A **Personal Improvement Outline** for YOU.

Look at the artwork of Rembrandt today.

DAILY FOCUS (main goal for the day) _____

DAILY VIRTUE (choose a virtue from the list of virtues on pg. 51) _____

DAILY BIOGRAPHY (Who did you learn about today and how has their life influenced you?)
_____

3 MICRO GOALS TO BE ACCOMPLISHED TODAY (list 3 steps, actions, or projects you can complete today toward one of the macro goals listed on pages 30 and 31)

1. _____
2. _____
3. _____

Daily to-do checklist of chores, homework and activities to be done today! (list the three most important ones below - do these first and do more if you can)

1. _____
2. _____
3. _____

Book(s) to read and finish this week (you should read at least one book per week) List how many pages you will read from your book(s) today and check off when completed.

1. _____ 2. _____

What did I discover about myself today? (what worked and why):
_____
_____
_____
_____

Who Are You? by Jerald Simon

Today is YOUR Day!   ———— Date

A **Personal Improvement Outline** for YOU.

Listen to music by Mozart today.

DAILY FOCUS (main goal for the day) _____

DAILY VIRTUE (choose a virtue from the list of virtues on pg. 51) _____

DAILY BIOGRAPHY (Who did you learn about today and how has their life influenced you?)
_____

3 MICRO GOALS TO BE ACCOMPLISHED TODAY (list 3 steps, actions, or projects you can complete today toward one of the macro goals listed on pages 30 and 31)

1 _____
2 _____
3 _____

Daily to-do checklist of chores, homework and activities to be done today! (list the three most important ones below - do these first and do more if you can)

1 _____
2 _____
3 _____

Book(s) to read and finish this week (you should read at least one book per week) List how many pages you will read from your book(s) today and check off when completed.

1 _____ 2 _____

What did I discover about myself today? (what worked and why):

_____
_____
_____
_____
_____

Who Are You? by Jerald Simon

___Date___ # Today is **YOUR** Day!
A **Personal Improvement Outline** for YOU.

If you don't have one, purchase a musical recorder and play it.

DAILY FOCUS (main goal for the day) _____
DAILY VIRTUE (choose a virtue from the list of virtues on pg. 51) _____
DAILY BIOGRAPHY (Who did you learn about today and how has their life influenced you?)
_____

3 MICRO GOALS TO BE ACCOMPLISHED TODAY (list 3 steps, actions, or projects you can complete today toward one of the macro goals listed on pages 30 and 31)

1 _____
2 _____
3 _____

Daily to-do checklist of chores, homework and activities to be done today! (list the three most important ones below - do these first and do more if you can)

1 _____
2 _____
3 _____

Book(s) to read and finish this week (you should read at least one book per week) List how many pages you will read from your book(s) today and check off when completed.

1 _____ 2 _____

What did I discover about myself today? (what worked and why):

_____
_____
_____
_____

Who Are You? by Jerald Simon

Today is YOUR Day! Date _____
A **Personal Improvement Outline** for YOU.

Create your own personal wish list of what you'd like to do.

DAILY FOCUS (main goal for the day) _____
DAILY VIRTUE (choose a virtue from the list of virtues on pg. 51) _____
DAILY BIOGRAPHY (Who did you learn about today and how has their life influenced you?)
_____

3 MICRO GOALS TO BE ACCOMPLISHED TODAY (list 3 steps, actions, or projects you can complete today toward one of the macro goals listed on pages 30 and 31)

1 _____
2 _____
3 _____

Daily to-do checklist of chores, homework and activities to be done today! (list the three most important ones below - do these first and do more if you can)

1 _____
2 _____
3 _____

Book(s) to read and finish this week (you should read at least one book per week) List how many pages you will read from your book(s) today and check off when completed.

1 _____ 2 _____

What did I discover about myself today? (what worked and why):
_____
_____
_____
_____
_____

Who Are You? by JERALD SIMON

Date

Today is YOUR Day!
A **Personal Improvement Outline** for YOU.

Make a meal for your family and learn more about cooking.

DAILY FOCUS (main goal for the day) _____

DAILY VIRTUE (choose a virtue from the list of virtues on pg. 51) _____

DAILY BIOGRAPHY (Who did you learn about today and how has their life influenced you?)
_____

3 MICRO GOALS TO BE ACCOMPLISHED TODAY (list 3 steps, actions, or projects you can complete today toward one of the macro goals listed on pages 30 and 31)

1 _____
2 _____
3 _____

Daily to-do checklist of chores, homework and activities to be done today! (list the three most important ones below - do these first and do more if you can)

1 _____
2 _____
3 _____

Book(s) to read and finish this week (you should read at least one book per week) List how many pages you will read from your book(s) today and check off when completed.

1 _____ 2 _____

What did I discover about myself today? (what worked and why):
_____
_____
_____
_____
_____

Who Are You? by JERALD SIMON

Today is YOUR Day!   ———Date———
A **Personal Improvement Outline** for YOU.

Go for a "walk and talk" with a friend. Walk around the block.

DAILY FOCUS (main goal for the day) _____

DAILY VIRTUE (choose a virtue from the list of virtues on pg. 51) _____

DAILY BIOGRAPHY (Who did you learn about today and how has their life influenced you?)
_____

3 MICRO GOALS TO BE ACCOMPLISHED TODAY (list 3 steps, actions, or projects you can complete today toward one of the macro goals listed on pages 30 and 31)

1 _____
2 _____
3 _____

Daily to-do checklist of chores, homework and activities to be done today! (list the three most important ones below - do these first and do more if you can)

1 _____
2 _____
3 _____

Book(s) to read and finish this week (you should read at least one book per week) List how many pages you will read from your book(s) today and check off when completed.

1 _____ 2 _____

What did I discover about myself today? (what worked and why):
_____
_____
_____
_____
_____

Who Are You? by Jerald Simon

_____ Date

Today is **YOUR** Day!
A **Personal Improvement Outline** for YOU.

Learn about George Washington today.

DAILY FOCUS (main goal for the day) _____

DAILY VIRTUE (choose a virtue from the list of virtues on pg. 51) _____

DAILY BIOGRAPHY (Who did you learn about today and how has their life influenced you?)
_____

3 MICRO GOALS TO BE ACCOMPLISHED TODAY (list 3 steps, actions, or projects you can complete today toward one of the macro goals listed on pages 30 and 31)

1 _____
2 _____
3 _____

Daily to-do checklist of chores, homework and activities to be done today! (list the three most important ones below - do these first and do more if you can)

1 _____
2 _____
3 _____

Book(s) to read and finish this week (you should read at least one book per week) List how many pages you will read from your book(s) today and check off when completed.

1 _____ 2 _____

What did I discover about myself today? (what worked and why):
_____
_____
_____
_____

Who Are You? by JERALD SIMON

Today is YOUR Day! ___Date___
A **Personal Improvement Outline** for YOU.

Watch an old black and white movie from the early 1900s.

DAILY FOCUS (main goal for the day) _____

DAILY VIRTUE (choose a virtue from the list of virtues on pg. 51) _____

DAILY BIOGRAPHY (Who did you learn about today and how has their life influenced you?)
_____

3 MICRO GOALS TO BE ACCOMPLISHED TODAY (list 3 steps, actions, or projects you can complete today toward one of the macro goals listed on pages 30 and 31)

1 _____
2 _____
3 _____

Daily to-do checklist of chores, homework and activities to be done today! (list the three most important ones below - do these first and do more if you can)

1 _____
2 _____
3 _____

Book(s) to read and finish this week (you should read at least one book per week) List how many pages you will read from your book(s) today and check off when completed.

1 _____ 2 _____

What did I discover about myself today? (what worked and why):
_____
_____
_____
_____
_____

Who Are You? by Jerald Simon

Date _____

Today is YOUR Day!
A **Personal Improvement Outline** for YOU.

Don't eat any sugar today.

DAILY FOCUS (main goal for the day) _____
DAILY VIRTUE (choose a virtue from the list of virtues on pg. 51) _____
DAILY BIOGRAPHY (Who did you learn about today and how has their life influenced you?)
_____

3 MICRO GOALS TO BE ACCOMPLISHED TODAY (list 3 steps, actions, or projects you can complete today toward one of the macro goals listed on pages 30 and 31)

1. _____
2. _____
3. _____

Daily to-do checklist of chores, homework and activities to be done today! (list the three most important ones below - do these first and do more if you can)

1. _____
2. _____
3. _____

Book(s) to read and finish this week (you should read at least one book per week) List how many pages you will read from your book(s) today and check off when completed.

1. _____ 2. _____

What did I discover about myself today? (what worked and why):
_____
_____
_____
_____
_____

Who Are You? by Jerald Simon

Today is YOUR Day!   ____Date____
A **Personal Improvement Outline** for YOU.

Learn something new about Australia today.

DAILY FOCUS (main goal for the day) _____
DAILY VIRTUE (choose a virtue from the list of virtues on pg. 51) _____
DAILY BIOGRAPHY (Who did you learn about today and how has their life influenced you?)
_____

3 MICRO GOALS TO BE ACCOMPLISHED TODAY (list 3 steps, actions, or projects you can complete today toward one of the macro goals listed on pages 30 and 31)

1 _____
2 _____
3 _____

Daily to-do checklist of chores, homework and activities to be done today! (list the three most important ones below - do these first and do more if you can)

1 _____
2 _____
3 _____

Book(s) to read and finish this week (you should read at least one book per week) List how many pages you will read from your book(s) today and check off when completed.

1 _____ 2 _____

What did I discover about myself today? (what worked and why):
_____
_____
_____
_____
_____

Who Are You? by Jerald Simon

___Date___ # Today is **YOUR** Day!
A **Personal Improvement Outline** for YOU.

Start a journal and write at least one paragraph every day.

DAILY FOCUS (main goal for the day) _____

DAILY VIRTUE (choose a virtue from the list of virtues on pg. 51) _____

DAILY BIOGRAPHY (Who did you learn about today and how has their life influenced you?)
_____

3 MICRO GOALS TO BE ACCOMPLISHED TODAY (list 3 steps, actions, or projects you can complete today toward one of the macro goals listed on pages 30 and 31)

1 _____
2 _____
3 _____

Daily to-do checklist of chores, homework and activities to be done today! (list the three most important ones below - do these first and do more if you can)

1 _____
2 _____
3 _____

Book(s) to read and finish this week (you should read at least one book per week) List how many pages you will read from your book(s) today and check off when completed.

1 _____ 2 _____

What did I discover about myself today? (what worked and why):
_____
_____
_____
_____
_____

Who Are You? by JERALD SIMON

Today is YOUR Day!   ___Date___
A **Personal Improvement Outline** for YOU.

Learn about the Middle Ages today.

DAILY FOCUS (main goal for the day) _____
DAILY VIRTUE (choose a virtue from the list of virtues on pg. 51) _____
DAILY BIOGRAPHY (Who did you learn about today and how has their life influenced you?)
_____

3 MICRO GOALS TO BE ACCOMPLISHED TODAY (list 3 steps, actions, or projects you can complete today toward one of the macro goals listed on pages 30 and 31)

1 _____
2 _____
3 _____

Daily to-do checklist of chores, homework and activities to be done today! (list the three most important ones below - do these first and do more if you can)

1 _____
2 _____
3 _____

Book(s) to read and finish this week (you should read at least one book per week) List how many pages you will read from your book(s) today and check off when completed.

1 _____ 2 _____

What did I discover about myself today? (what worked and why):
_____
_____
_____
_____
_____

Who Are You? by Jerald Simon

___Date___ ## Today is **YOUR** Day!
A **Personal Improvement Outline** for YOU.

If you don't know how already, learn to read music.

DAILY FOCUS (main goal for the day) _____
DAILY VIRTUE (choose a virtue from the list of virtues on pg. 51) _____
DAILY BIOGRAPHY (Who did you learn about today and how has their life influenced you?)
_____

3 MICRO GOALS TO BE ACCOMPLISHED TODAY (list 3 steps, actions, or projects you can complete today toward one of the macro goals listed on pages 30 and 31)

1 _____
2 _____
3 _____

Daily to-do checklist of chores, homework and activities to be done today! (list the three most important ones below - do these first and do more if you can)

1 _____
2 _____
3 _____

Book(s) to read and finish this week (you should read at least one book per week) List how many pages you will read from your book(s) today and check off when completed.

1 _____ 2 _____

What did I discover about myself today? (what worked and why):
_____
_____
_____
_____

Who Are You? by Jerald Simon

Today is YOUR Day! ⎯ Date ⎯
A **Personal Improvement Outline** for YOU.

Learn about homesteading and farming today.

DAILY FOCUS (main goal for the day) _____
DAILY VIRTUE (choose a virtue from the list of virtues on pg. 51) _____
DAILY BIOGRAPHY (Who did you learn about today and how has their life influenced you?)
_____

3 MICRO GOALS TO BE ACCOMPLISHED TODAY (list 3 steps, actions, or projects you can complete today toward one of the macro goals listed on pages 30 and 31)

1 _____
2 _____
3 _____

Daily to-do checklist of chores, homework and activities to be done today! (list the three most important ones below - do these first and do more if you can)

1 _____
2 _____
3 _____

Book(s) to read and finish this week (you should read at least one book per week) List how many pages you will read from your book(s) today and check off when completed.

1 _____ 2 _____

What did I discover about myself today? (what worked and why):
_____
_____
_____
_____
_____

Who Are You? by JERALD SIMON

Today is YOUR Day!
Date

A **Personal Improvement Outline** for YOU.

Learn how to dance. Learn at least two simple dance steps.

DAILY FOCUS (main goal for the day) _____
DAILY VIRTUE (choose a virtue from the list of virtues on pg. 51) _____
DAILY BIOGRAPHY (Who did you learn about today and how has their life influenced you?)
_____

3 MICRO GOALS TO BE ACCOMPLISHED TODAY (list 3 steps, actions, or projects you can complete today toward one of the macro goals listed on pages 30 and 31)

1 _____
2 _____
3 _____

Daily to-do checklist of chores, homework and activities to be done today! (list the three most important ones below - do these first and do more if you can)

1 _____
2 _____
3 _____

Book(s) to read and finish this week (you should read at least one book per week) List how many pages you will read from your book(s) today and check off when completed.

1 _____ 2 _____

What did I discover about myself today? (what worked and why):
_____
_____
_____
_____
_____

Who Are You? by Jerald Simon

Today is YOUR Day!   ——Date——
A **Personal Improvement Outline** for YOU.

Be positive. There is good in everyone and every situation.

DAILY FOCUS (main goal for the day) _____
DAILY VIRTUE (choose a virtue from the list of virtues on pg. 51) _____
DAILY BIOGRAPHY (Who did you learn about today and how has their life influenced you?)
_____

3 MICRO GOALS TO BE ACCOMPLISHED TODAY (list 3 steps, actions, or projects you can complete today toward one of the macro goals listed on pages 30 and 31)

1 _____
2 _____
3 _____

Daily to-do checklist of chores, homework and activities to be done today! (list the three most important ones below - do these first and do more if you can)

1 _____
2 _____
3 _____

Book(s) to read and finish this week (you should read at least one book per week) List how many pages you will read from your book(s) today and check off when completed.

1 _____ 2 _____

What did I discover about myself today? (what worked and why):
_____
_____
_____
_____
_____

Who Are You? by Jerald Simon

Date _____

Today is YOUR Day!
A **Personal Improvement Outline** for YOU.

Work hard, play hard, and learn and grow in between.

DAILY FOCUS (main goal for the day) _____
DAILY VIRTUE (choose a virtue from the list of virtues on pg. 51) _____
DAILY BIOGRAPHY (Who did you learn about today and how has their life influenced you?)
_____

3 MICRO GOALS TO BE ACCOMPLISHED TODAY (list 3 steps, actions, or projects you can complete today toward one of the macro goals listed on pages 30 and 31)

1 _____
2 _____
3 _____

Daily to-do checklist of chores, homework and activities to be done today! (list the three most important ones below - do these first and do more if you can)

1 _____
2 _____
3 _____

Book(s) to read and finish this week (you should read at least one book per week) List how many pages you will read from your book(s) today and check off when completed.

1 _____ 2 _____

What did I discover about myself today? (what worked and why):
_____
_____
_____
_____
_____

Who Are You? by JERALD SIMON

Today is YOUR Day!   ———Date———
A **Personal Improvement Outline** for YOU.

Pick one or two topics and learn everything you can about it.

DAILY FOCUS (main goal for the day) _____

DAILY VIRTUE (choose a virtue from the list of virtues on pg. 51) _____

DAILY BIOGRAPHY (Who did you learn about today and how has their life influenced you?)
_____

3 MICRO GOALS TO BE ACCOMPLISHED TODAY (list 3 steps, actions, or projects you can complete today toward one of the macro goals listed on pages 30 and 31)

1 _____
2 _____
3 _____

Daily to-do checklist of chores, homework and activities to be done today! (list the three most important ones below - do these first and do more if you can)

1 _____
2 _____
3 _____

Book(s) to read and finish this week (you should read at least one book per week) List how many pages you will read from your book(s) today and check off when completed.

1 _____ 2 _____

What did I discover about myself today? (what worked and why):

_____
_____
_____
_____
_____

Who Are You? by Jerald Simon

___Date___   Today is **YOUR** Day!
A **Personal Improvement Outline** for YOU.

Have a poetry evening and read and recite poetry with family.

DAILY FOCUS (main goal for the day) _____

DAILY VIRTUE (choose a virtue from the list of virtues on pg. 51) _____

DAILY BIOGRAPHY (Who did you learn about today and how has their life influenced you?)
_____

3 MICRO GOALS TO BE ACCOMPLISHED TODAY (list 3 steps, actions, or projects you can complete today toward one of the macro goals listed on pages 30 and 31)

1 _____
2 _____
3 _____

Daily to-do checklist of chores, homework and activities to be done today! (list the three most important ones below - do these first and do more if you can)

1 _____
2 _____
3 _____

Book(s) to read and finish this week (you should read at least one book per week) List how many pages you will read from your book(s) today and check off when completed.

1 _____ 2 _____

What did I discover about myself today? (what worked and why):
_____
_____
_____
_____
_____

Who Are You? by JERALD SIMON

Today is YOUR Day! _____
Date
A **Personal Improvement Outline** for YOU.

Learn the names and identify 10 different work tools

DAILY FOCUS (main goal for the day) _____
DAILY VIRTUE (choose a virtue from the list of virtues on pg. 51) _____
DAILY BIOGRAPHY (Who did you learn about today and how has their life influenced you?)
_____

3 MICRO GOALS TO BE ACCOMPLISHED TODAY (list 3 steps, actions, or projects you can complete today toward one of the macro goals listed on pages 30 and 31)

1 _____
2 _____
3 _____

Daily to-do checklist of chores, homework and activities to be done today! (list the three most important ones below - do these first and do more if you can)

1 _____
2 _____
3 _____

Book(s) to read and finish this week (you should read at least one book per week) List how many pages you will read from your book(s) today and check off when completed.

1 _____ 2 _____

What did I discover about myself today? (what worked and why):

_____
_____
_____
_____
_____

Who Are You? by Jerald Simon

___Date___

Today is YOUR Day!
A **Personal Improvement Outline** for YOU.

Learn the rules of one sporting event or activity.

DAILY FOCUS (main goal for the day)_____
DAILY VIRTUE (choose a virtue from the list of virtues on pg. 51)_____
DAILY BIOGRAPHY (Who did you learn about today and how has their life influenced you?)
_____

3 MICRO GOALS TO BE ACCOMPLISHED TODAY (list 3 steps, actions, or projects you can complete today toward one of the macro goals listed on pages 30 and 31)

1 _____
2 _____
3 _____

Daily to-do checklist of chores, homework and activities to be done today! (list the three most important ones below - do these first and do more if you can)

1 _____
2 _____
3 _____

Book(s) to read and finish this week (you should read at least one book per week) List how many pages you will read from your book(s) today and check off when completed.

1 _____ 2 _____

What did I discover about myself today? (what worked and why):
_____
_____
_____
_____
_____

Who Are You? by JERALD SIMON

Today is YOUR Day! _____Date

A **Personal Improvement Outline** for YOU.

Go on a hike by yourself or with family and friends.

DAILY FOCUS (main goal for the day) _____
DAILY VIRTUE (choose a virtue from the list of virtues on pg. 51) _____
DAILY BIOGRAPHY (Who did you learn about today and how has their life influenced you?)
_____

3 MICRO GOALS TO BE ACCOMPLISHED TODAY (list 3 steps, actions, or projects you can complete today toward one of the macro goals listed on pages 30 and 31)

1. _____
2. _____
3. _____

Daily to-do checklist of chores, homework and activities to be done today! (list the three most important ones below - do these first and do more if you can)

1. _____
2. _____
3. _____

Book(s) to read and finish this week (you should read at least one book per week) List how many pages you will read from your book(s) today and check off when completed.

1. _____ 2. _____

What did I discover about myself today? (what worked and why):
_____
_____
_____
_____
_____

Who Are You? by Jerald Simon

___Date___ ## Today is YOUR Day!
A **Personal Improvement Outline** for YOU.

Build something out of wood today.

DAILY FOCUS (main goal for the day) _____
DAILY VIRTUE (choose a virtue from the list of virtues on pg. 51) _____
DAILY BIOGRAPHY (Who did you learn about today and how has their life influenced you?)
_____

3 MICRO GOALS TO BE ACCOMPLISHED TODAY (list 3 steps, actions, or projects you can complete today toward one of the macro goals listed on pages 30 and 31)

1 _____
2 _____
3 _____

Daily to-do checklist of chores, homework and activities to be done today! (list the three most important ones below - do these first and do more if you can)

1 _____
2 _____
3 _____

Book(s) to read and finish this week (you should read at least one book per week) List how many pages you will read from your book(s) today and check off when completed.

1 _____ 2 _____

What did I discover about myself today? (what worked and why):
_____
_____
_____
_____
_____

Who Are You? by JERALD SIMON

Today is YOUR Day!

Date

A **Personal Improvement Outline** for YOU.

Visit an assisted living center and help serve others.

DAILY FOCUS (main goal for the day) _____

DAILY VIRTUE (choose a virtue from the list of virtues on pg. 51) _____

DAILY BIOGRAPHY (Who did you learn about today and how has their life influenced you?)

_____

3 MICRO GOALS TO BE ACCOMPLISHED TODAY (list 3 steps, actions, or projects you can complete today toward one of the macro goals listed on pages 30 and 31)

1 _____
2 _____
3 _____

Daily to-do checklist of chores, homework and activities to be done today! (list the three most important ones below - do these first and do more if you can)

1 _____
2 _____
3 _____

Book(s) to read and finish this week (you should read at least one book per week) List how many pages you will read from your book(s) today and check off when completed.

1 _____ 2 _____

What did I discover about myself today? (what worked and why):

_____
_____
_____
_____
_____

Who Are You? by Jerald Simon

___Date___

Today is YOUR Day!
A Personal Improvement Outline for YOU.

Learn about Albert Einstein today.

DAILY FOCUS (main goal for the day) _____

DAILY VIRTUE (choose a virtue from the list of virtues on pg. 51) _____

DAILY BIOGRAPHY (Who did you learn about today and how has their life influenced you?)
_____

3 MICRO GOALS TO BE ACCOMPLISHED TODAY (list 3 steps, actions, or projects you can complete today toward one of the macro goals listed on pages 30 and 31)

1 _____
2 _____
3 _____

Daily to-do checklist of chores, homework and activities to be done today! (list the three most important ones below - do these first and do more if you can)

1 _____
2 _____
3 _____

Book(s) to read and finish this week (you should read at least one book per week) List how many pages you will read from your book(s) today and check off when completed.

1 _____ 2 _____

What did I discover about myself today? (what worked and why):
_____
_____
_____
_____
_____

Who Are You? by Jerald Simon

Today is YOUR Day! ___Date___
A **Personal Improvement Outline** for YOU.

Make up a game today and play it with family and friends.

DAILY FOCUS (main goal for the day) _____
DAILY VIRTUE (choose a virtue from the list of virtues on pg. 51) _____
DAILY BIOGRAPHY (Who did you learn about today and how has their life influenced you?)
_____

3 MICRO GOALS TO BE ACCOMPLISHED TODAY (list 3 steps, actions, or projects you can complete today toward one of the macro goals listed on pages 30 and 31)

1 _____
2 _____
3 _____

Daily to-do checklist of chores, homework and activities to be done today! (list the three most important ones below - do these first and do more if you can)

1 _____
2 _____
3 _____

Book(s) to read and finish this week (you should read at least one book per week) List how many pages you will read from your book(s) today and check off when completed.

1 _____ 2 _____

What did I discover about myself today? (what worked and why):
_____
_____
_____
_____
_____

Who Are You? by JERALD SIMON

---Date---   # Today is YOUR Day!
A **Personal Improvement Outline** for YOU.

Find out about 5 different world religions.

DAILY FOCUS (main goal for the day) _____
DAILY VIRTUE (choose a virtue from the list of virtues on pg. 51) _____
DAILY BIOGRAPHY (Who did you learn about today and how has their life influenced you?)
_____

3 MICRO GOALS TO BE ACCOMPLISHED TODAY (list 3 steps, actions, or projects you can complete today toward one of the macro goals listed on pages 30 and 31)

1 _____
2 _____
3 _____

Daily to-do checklist of chores, homework and activities to be done today! (list the three most important ones below - do these first and do more if you can)

1 _____
2 _____
3 _____

Book(s) to read and finish this week (you should read at least one book per week) List how many pages you will read from your book(s) today and check off when completed.

1 _____ 2 _____

What did I discover about myself today? (what worked and why):
_____
_____
_____
_____
_____

Who Are You? by JERALD SIMON

Today is YOUR Day!   ___Date___
A **Personal Improvement Outline** for YOU.

Create an exercise program and commit to follow it for 30 days.

DAILY FOCUS (main goal for the day) _____

DAILY VIRTUE (choose a virtue from the list of virtues on pg. 51) _____

DAILY BIOGRAPHY (Who did you learn about today and how has their life influenced you?)
_____

3 MICRO GOALS TO BE ACCOMPLISHED TODAY (list 3 steps, actions, or projects you can complete today toward one of the macro goals listed on pages 30 and 31)

1 _____
2 _____
3 _____

Daily to-do checklist of chores, homework and activities to be done today! (list the three most important ones below - do these first and do more if you can)

1 _____
2 _____
3 _____

Book(s) to read and finish this week (you should read at least one book per week) List how many pages you will read from your book(s) today and check off when completed.

1 _____ 2 _____

What did I discover about myself today? (what worked and why):
_____
_____
_____
_____
_____

Who Are You? by Jerald Simon

___Date___ # Today is YOUR Day!
A **Personal Improvement Outline** for YOU.

Don't watch any T.V. today or use phones/tablets/etc..

DAILY FOCUS (main goal for the day) _____
DAILY VIRTUE (choose a virtue from the list of virtues on pg. 51) _____
DAILY BIOGRAPHY (Who did you learn about today and how has their life influenced you?)
_____

3 MICRO GOALS TO BE ACCOMPLISHED TODAY (list 3 steps, actions, or projects you can complete today toward one of the macro goals listed on pages 30 and 31)

1 _____
2 _____
3 _____

Daily to-do checklist of chores, homework and activities to be done today! (list the three most important ones below - do these first and do more if you can)

1 _____
2 _____
3 _____

Book(s) to read and finish this week (you should read at least one book per week) List how many pages you will read from your book(s) today and check off when completed.

1 _____ 2 _____

What did I discover about myself today? (what worked and why):
_____
_____
_____
_____

Who Are You? by JERALD SIMON

Today is YOUR Day!   ____Date____
A **Personal Improvement Outline** for YOU.

Learn about gardening today.

DAILY FOCUS (main goal for the day) _____

DAILY VIRTUE (choose a virtue from the list of virtues on pg. 51) _____

DAILY BIOGRAPHY (Who did you learn about today and how has their life influenced you?)
_____

3 MICRO GOALS TO BE ACCOMPLISHED TODAY (list 3 steps, actions, or projects you can complete today toward one of the macro goals listed on pages 30 and 31)

1 _____
2 _____
3 _____

Daily to-do checklist of chores, homework and activities to be done today! (list the three most important ones below - do these first and do more if you can)

1 _____
2 _____
3 _____

Book(s) to read and finish this week (you should read at least one book per week) List how many pages you will read from your book(s) today and check off when completed.

1 _____ 2 _____

What did I discover about myself today? (what worked and why):
_____
_____
_____
_____
_____

Who Are You? by Jerald Simon

<u>　　　　</u> # Today is **YOUR** Day!
Date

A **Personal Improvement Outline** for YOU.

Be polite and sincere when speaking with everyone.

DAILY FOCUS (main goal for the day) _____

DAILY VIRTUE (choose a virtue from the list of virtues on pg. 51) _____

DAILY BIOGRAPHY (Who did you learn about today and how has their life influenced you?)
_____

3 MICRO GOALS TO BE ACCOMPLISHED TODAY (list 3 steps, actions, or projects you can complete today toward one of the macro goals listed on pages 30 and 31)

1. _____
2. _____
3. _____

Daily to-do checklist of chores, homework and activities to be done today! (list the three most important ones below - do these first and do more if you can)

1. _____
2. _____
3. _____

Book(s) to read and finish this week (you should read at least one book per week) List how many pages you will read from your book(s) today and check off when completed.

1. _____ 2. _____

What did I discover about myself today? (what worked and why):

_____
_____
_____
_____

WHO ARE YOU? by JERALD SIMON

Today is YOUR Day!   ___Date___
A **Personal Improvement Outline** for YOU.

Work on your posture today. Stand up straight.

DAILY FOCUS (main goal for the day) _____
DAILY VIRTUE (choose a virtue from the list of virtues on pg. 51) _____
DAILY BIOGRAPHY (Who did you learn about today and how has their life influenced you?)
_____

3 MICRO GOALS TO BE ACCOMPLISHED TODAY (list 3 steps, actions, or projects you can complete today toward one of the macro goals listed on pages 30 and 31)

1 _____
2 _____
3 _____

Daily to-do checklist of chores, homework and activities to be done today! (list the three most important ones below - do these first and do more if you can)

1 _____
2 _____
3 _____

Book(s) to read and finish this week (you should read at least one book per week) List how many pages you will read from your book(s) today and check off when completed.

1 _____ 2 _____

What did I discover about myself today? (what worked and why):
_____
_____
_____
_____
_____

Who Are You? by Jerald Simon

___Date___ # Today is YOUR Day!
A **Personal Improvement Outline** for YOU.

Find out about your ancestors today.

DAILY FOCUS (main goal for the day) _____
DAILY VIRTUE (choose a virtue from the list of virtues on pg. 51) _____
DAILY BIOGRAPHY (Who did you learn about today and how has their life influenced you?)
_____

3 MICRO GOALS TO BE ACCOMPLISHED TODAY (list 3 steps, actions, or projects you can complete today toward one of the macro goals listed on pages 30 and 31)

1 _____
2 _____
3 _____

Daily to-do checklist of chores, homework and activities to be done today! (list the three most important ones below - do these first and do more if you can)

1 _____
2 _____
3 _____

Book(s) to read and finish this week (you should read at least one book per week) List how many pages you will read from your book(s) today and check off when completed.

1 _____ 2 _____

What did I discover about myself today? (what worked and why):
_____
_____
_____
_____

Who Are You? by JERALD SIMON

Today is YOUR Day! _____Date
A **Personal Improvement Outline** for YOU.

Learn the alphabet in sign language, if you don't know it yet.

DAILY FOCUS (main goal for the day) _____
DAILY VIRTUE (choose a virtue from the list of virtues on pg. 51) _____
DAILY BIOGRAPHY (Who did you learn about today and how has their life influenced you?)
_____

3 MICRO GOALS TO BE ACCOMPLISHED TODAY (list 3 steps, actions, or projects you can complete today toward one of the macro goals listed on pages 30 and 31)

1 _____
2 _____
3 _____

Daily to-do checklist of chores, homework and activities to be done today! (list the three most important ones below - do these first and do more if you can)

1 _____
2 _____
3 _____

Book(s) to read and finish this week (you should read at least one book per week) List how many pages you will read from your book(s) today and check off when completed.

1 _____ 2 _____

What did I discover about myself today? (what worked and why):
_____
_____
_____
_____
_____

Who Are You? by Jerald Simon

―― Date ―― ## Today is **YOUR** Day!
A **Personal Improvement Outline** for YOU.

You are wonderful! Don't ever forget that.

DAILY FOCUS (main goal for the day) _____
DAILY VIRTUE (choose a virtue from the list of virtues on pg. 51) _____
DAILY BIOGRAPHY (Who did you learn about today and how has their life influenced you?)
_____

3 MICRO GOALS TO BE ACCOMPLISHED TODAY (list 3 steps, actions, or projects you can complete today toward one of the macro goals listed on pages 30 and 31)

1 _____
2 _____
3 _____

Daily to-do checklist of chores, homework and activities to be done today! (list the three most important ones below - do these first and do more if you can)

1 _____
2 _____
3 _____

Book(s) to read and finish this week (you should read at least one book per week) List how many pages you will read from your book(s) today and check off when completed.

1 _____ 2 _____

What did I discover about myself today? (what worked and why):
_____
_____
_____
_____
_____

Who Are You? by JERALD SIMON

Today is YOUR Day!

Date

A **Personal Improvement Outline** for YOU.

Don't give up on your dreams. Keep on keeping on!

DAILY FOCUS (main goal for the day) _____

DAILY VIRTUE (choose a virtue from the list of virtues on pg. 51) _____

DAILY BIOGRAPHY (Who did you learn about today and how has their life influenced you?)
_____

3 MICRO GOALS TO BE ACCOMPLISHED TODAY (list 3 steps, actions, or projects you can complete today toward one of the macro goals listed on pages 30 and 31)

1 _____
2 _____
3 _____

Daily to-do checklist of chores, homework and activities to be done today! (list the three most important ones below - do these first and do more if you can)

1 _____
2 _____
3 _____

Book(s) to read and finish this week (you should read at least one book per week) List how many pages you will read from your book(s) today and check off when completed.

1 _____ 2 _____

What did I discover about myself today? (what worked and why):

_____
_____
_____
_____
_____

Who Are You? by JERALD SIMON

Date _____

Today is **YOUR** Day!
A **Personal Improvement Outline** for YOU.

Interview a neighbor, relative, or friend, and learn about them.

DAILY FOCUS (main goal for the day) _____
DAILY VIRTUE (choose a virtue from the list of virtues on pg. 51) _____
DAILY BIOGRAPHY (Who did you learn about today and how has their life influenced you?)
_____

3 MICRO GOALS TO BE ACCOMPLISHED TODAY (list 3 steps, actions, or projects you can complete today toward one of the macro goals listed on pages 30 and 31)

1 _____
2 _____
3 _____

Daily to-do checklist of chores, homework and activities to be done today! (list the three most important ones below - do these first and do more if you can)

1 _____
2 _____
3 _____

Book(s) to read and finish this week (you should read at least one book per week) List how many pages you will read from your book(s) today and check off when completed.

1 _____ 2 _____

What did I discover about myself today? (what worked and why):
_____
_____
_____
_____
_____

Who Are You? by JERALD SIMON

Today is YOUR Day!   ⎯⎯⎯⎯
                                                       Date

A **Personal Improvement Outline** for YOU.

Be yourself. Don't try to be someone you aren't.

DAILY FOCUS (main goal for the day) _____

DAILY VIRTUE (choose a virtue from the list of virtues on pg. 51) _____

DAILY BIOGRAPHY (Who did you learn about today and how has their life influenced you?)
_____

3 MICRO GOALS TO BE ACCOMPLISHED TODAY (list 3 steps, actions, or projects you can complete today toward one of the macro goals listed on pages 30 and 31)

1 _____
2 _____
3 _____

Daily to-do checklist of chores, homework and activities to be done today! (list the three most important ones below - do these first and do more if you can)

1 _____
2 _____
3 _____

Book(s) to read and finish this week (you should read at least one book per week) List how many pages you will read from your book(s) today and check off when completed.

1 _____ 2 _____

What did I discover about myself today? (what worked and why):
_____
_____
_____
_____
_____

Who Are You? by JERALD SIMON

___Date___ **Today is YOUR Day!**
A **Personal Improvement Outline** for YOU.

Be honest in everything you say and do.

DAILY FOCUS (main goal for the day) _____
DAILY VIRTUE (choose a virtue from the list of virtues on pg. 51) _____
DAILY BIOGRAPHY (Who did you learn about today and how has their life influenced you?)
_____

3 MICRO GOALS TO BE ACCOMPLISHED TODAY (list 3 steps, actions, or projects you can complete today toward one of the macro goals listed on pages 30 and 31)

1 _____
2 _____
3 _____

Daily to-do checklist of chores, homework and activities to be done today! (list the three most important ones below - do these first and do more if you can)

1 _____
2 _____
3 _____

Book(s) to read and finish this week (you should read at least one book per week) List how many pages you will read from your book(s) today and check off when completed.

1 _____ 2 _____

What did I discover about myself today? (what worked and why):
_____
_____
_____
_____

Who Are You? by JERALD SIMON

Today is YOUR Day!   ___Date___
A **Personal Improvement Outline** for YOU.

Read a children's story or a fairytale today.

DAILY FOCUS (main goal for the day) _____

DAILY VIRTUE (choose a virtue from the list of virtues on pg. 51) _____

DAILY BIOGRAPHY (Who did you learn about today and how has their life influenced you?)
_____

3 MICRO GOALS TO BE ACCOMPLISHED TODAY (list 3 steps, actions, or projects you can complete today toward one of the macro goals listed on pages 30 and 31)

1 _____
2 _____
3 _____

Daily to-do checklist of chores, homework and activities to be done today! (list the three most important ones below - do these first and do more if you can)

1 _____
2 _____
3 _____

Book(s) to read and finish this week (you should read at least one book per week) List how many pages you will read from your book(s) today and check off when completed.

1 _____ 2 _____

What did I discover about myself today? (what worked and why):

_____
_____
_____
_____
_____

Who Are You? by Jerald Simon

___Date___

Today is **YOUR** Day!
A **Personal Improvement Outline** for YOU.

Read the Preamble to the Constitution of the United States.

DAILY FOCUS (main goal for the day) _____
DAILY VIRTUE (choose a virtue from the list of virtues on pg. 51) _____
DAILY BIOGRAPHY (Who did you learn about today and how has their life influenced you?)
_____

3 MICRO GOALS TO BE ACCOMPLISHED TODAY (list 3 steps, actions, or projects you can complete today toward one of the macro goals listed on pages 30 and 31)

1. _____
2. _____
3. _____

Daily to-do checklist of chores, homework and activities to be done today! (list the three most important ones below - do these first and do more if you can)

1. _____
2. _____
3. _____

Book(s) to read and finish this week (you should read at least one book per week) List how many pages you will read from your book(s) today and check off when completed.

1. _____ 2. _____

What did I discover about myself today? (what worked and why):
_____
_____
_____
_____

Who Are You? by JERALD SIMON

Today is YOUR Day!
Date

A **Personal Improvement Outline** for YOU.

Listen more than you speak.

DAILY FOCUS (main goal for the day) _____

DAILY VIRTUE (choose a virtue from the list of virtues on pg. 51) _____

DAILY BIOGRAPHY (Who did you learn about today and how has their life influenced you?)
_____

3 MICRO GOALS TO BE ACCOMPLISHED TODAY (list 3 steps, actions, or projects you can complete today toward one of the macro goals listed on pages 30 and 31)

1 _____
2 _____
3 _____

Daily to-do checklist of chores, homework and activities to be done today! (list the three most important ones below - do these first and do more if you can)

1 _____
2 _____
3 _____

Book(s) to read and finish this week (you should read at least one book per week) List how many pages you will read from your book(s) today and check off when completed.

1 _____ 2 _____

What did I discover about myself today? (what worked and why):

_____
_____
_____
_____
_____

Who Are You? by JERALD SIMON

___Date___ ## Today is **YOUR** Day!
A **Personal Improvement Outline** for YOU.

Hang in there! You'll get there eventually.

DAILY FOCUS (main goal for the day) _____
DAILY VIRTUE (choose a virtue from the list of virtues on pg. 51) _____
DAILY BIOGRAPHY (Who did you learn about today and how has their life influenced you?)
_____

3 MICRO GOALS TO BE ACCOMPLISHED TODAY (list 3 steps, actions, or projects you can complete today toward one of the macro goals listed on pages 30 and 31)

1 _____
2 _____
3 _____

Daily to-do checklist of chores, homework and activities to be done today! (list the three most important ones below - do these first and do more if you can)

1 _____
2 _____
3 _____

Book(s) to read and finish this week (you should read at least one book per week) List how many pages you will read from your book(s) today and check off when completed.

1 _____ 2 _____

What did I discover about myself today? (what worked and why):

_____
_____
_____
_____
_____

Who Are You? by Jerald Simon

Today is YOUR Day!   _____ Date

A **Personal Improvement Outline** for YOU.

Believe in yourself and all you can do!

DAILY FOCUS (main goal for the day) _____
DAILY VIRTUE (choose a virtue from the list of virtues on pg. 51) _____
DAILY BIOGRAPHY (Who did you learn about today and how has their life influenced you?)
_____

3 MICRO GOALS TO BE ACCOMPLISHED TODAY (list 3 steps, actions, or projects you can complete today toward one of the macro goals listed on pages 30 and 31)

1 _____
2 _____
3 _____

Daily to-do checklist of chores, homework and activities to be done today!
(list the three most important ones below - do these first and do more if you can)

1 _____
2 _____
3 _____

Book(s) to read and finish this week (you should read at least one book per week) List how many pages you will read from your book(s) today and check off when completed.

1 _____ 2 _____

What did I discover about myself today? (what worked and why):
_____
_____
_____
_____
_____

Who Are You? by Jerald Simon

<u>　　　　　</u> Date

Today is YOUR Day!
A **Personal Improvement Outline** for YOU.

Listen to music by Sergei Rachmaninoff.

DAILY FOCUS (main goal for the day) _____
DAILY VIRTUE (choose a virtue from the list of virtues on pg. 51) _____
DAILY BIOGRAPHY (Who did you learn about today and how has their life influenced you?)
_____

3 MICRO GOALS TO BE ACCOMPLISHED TODAY (list 3 steps, actions, or projects you can complete today toward one of the macro goals listed on pages 30 and 31)

1 _____
2 _____
3 _____

Daily to-do checklist of chores, homework and activities to be done today! (list the three most important ones below - do these first and do more if you can)

1 _____
2 _____
3 _____

Book(s) to read and finish this week (you should read at least one book per week) List how many pages you will read from your book(s) today and check off when completed.

1 _____ 2 _____

What did I discover about myself today? (what worked and why):
_____
_____
_____
_____
_____

Who Are You? by JERALD SIMON

Today is YOUR Day!   Date _____
A **Personal Improvement Outline** for YOU.

Learn about the Renaissance.

DAILY FOCUS (main goal for the day) _____
DAILY VIRTUE (choose a virtue from the list of virtues on pg. 51) _____
DAILY BIOGRAPHY (Who did you learn about today and how has their life influenced you?)
_____

3 MICRO GOALS TO BE ACCOMPLISHED TODAY (list 3 steps, actions, or projects you can complete today toward one of the macro goals listed on pages 30 and 31)

1 _____
2 _____
3 _____

Daily to-do checklist of chores, homework and activities to be done today! (list the three most important ones below - do these first and do more if you can)

1 _____
2 _____
3 _____

Book(s) to read and finish this week (you should read at least one book per week) List how many pages you will read from your book(s) today and check off when completed.

1 _____   2 _____

What did I discover about myself today? (what worked and why):

_____
_____
_____
_____
_____

Who Are You? by JERALD SIMON

<u>_____</u> # Today is YOUR Day!
Date

A **Personal Improvement Outline** for YOU.

Paint a picture with complimentary colors.

DAILY FOCUS (main goal for the day) _____
DAILY VIRTUE (choose a virtue from the list of virtues on pg. 51) _____
DAILY BIOGRAPHY (Who did you learn about today and how has their life influenced you?)
_____

3 MICRO GOALS TO BE ACCOMPLISHED TODAY (list 3 steps, actions, or projects you can complete today toward one of the macro goals listed on pages 30 and 31)

1 _____
2 _____
3 _____

Daily to-do checklist of chores, homework and activities to be done today! (list the three most important ones below - do these first and do more if you can)

1 _____
2 _____
3 _____

Book(s) to read and finish this week (you should read at least one book per week) List how many pages you will read from your book(s) today and check off when completed.

1 _____ 2 _____

What did I discover about myself today? (what worked and why):
_____
_____
_____
_____

Who Are You? by Jerald Simon

Today is YOUR Day!   ⎯⎯Date⎯⎯
A **Personal Improvement Outline** for YOU.

Keep a notebook next to your bed and write down ideas.

DAILY FOCUS (main goal for the day) _____

DAILY VIRTUE (choose a virtue from the list of virtues on pg. 51) _____

DAILY BIOGRAPHY (Who did you learn about today and how has their life influenced you?)
_____

3 MICRO GOALS TO BE ACCOMPLISHED TODAY (list 3 steps, actions, or projects you can complete today toward one of the macro goals listed on pages 30 and 31)

1 _____
2 _____
3 _____

Daily to-do checklist of chores, homework and activities to be done today! (list the three most important ones below - do these first and do more if you can)

1 _____
2 _____
3 _____

Book(s) to read and finish this week (you should read at least one book per week) List how many pages you will read from your book(s) today and check off when completed.

1 _____ 2 _____

What did I discover about myself today? (what worked and why):
_____
_____
_____
_____
_____

Who Are You? by JERALD SIMON

Date _____

Today is **YOUR** Day!
A **Personal Improvement Outline** for YOU.

Follow the Boy Scouts and BE PREPARED.

DAILY FOCUS (main goal for the day) _____
DAILY VIRTUE (choose a virtue from the list of virtues on pg. 51) _____
DAILY BIOGRAPHY (Who did you learn about today and how has their life influenced you?)
_____

3 MICRO GOALS TO BE ACCOMPLISHED TODAY (list 3 steps, actions, or projects you can complete today toward one of the macro goals listed on pages 30 and 31)

1 _____
2 _____
3 _____

Daily to-do checklist of chores, homework and activities to be done today! (list the three most important ones below - do these first and do more if you can)

1 _____
2 _____
3 _____

Book(s) to read and finish this week (you should read at least one book per week) List how many pages you will read from your book(s) today and check off when completed.

1 _____ 2 _____

What did I discover about myself today? (what worked and why):
_____
_____
_____
_____
_____

Who Are You? by Jerald Simon

Today is YOUR Day!   <u>_____</u>
                                                                     Date

A **Personal Improvement Outline** for YOU.

Go on a hike in the mountains today.

DAILY FOCUS (main goal for the day) _____

DAILY VIRTUE (choose a virtue from the list of virtues on pg. 51) _____

DAILY BIOGRAPHY (Who did you learn about today and how has their life influenced you?)
_____

3 MICRO GOALS TO BE ACCOMPLISHED TODAY (list 3 steps, actions, or projects you can complete today toward one of the macro goals listed on pages 30 and 31)

1 _____
2 _____
3 _____

Daily to-do checklist of chores, homework and activities to be done today! (list the three most important ones below - do these first and do more if you can)

1 _____
2 _____
3 _____

Book(s) to read and finish this week (you should read at least one book per week) List how many pages you will read from your book(s) today and check off when completed.

1 _____ 2 _____

What did I discover about myself today? (what worked and why):
_____
_____
_____
_____
_____

Who Are You? by JERALD SIMON

Date

Today is **YOUR** Day!
A **Personal Improvement Outline** for YOU.

Look in the mirror and say 10 kind things about yourself.

DAILY FOCUS (main goal for the day) _____

DAILY VIRTUE (choose a virtue from the list of virtues on pg. 51) _____

DAILY BIOGRAPHY (Who did you learn about today and how has their life influenced you?)
_____

3 MICRO GOALS TO BE ACCOMPLISHED TODAY (list 3 steps, actions, or projects you can complete today toward one of the macro goals listed on pages 30 and 31)

1 _____
2 _____
3 _____

Daily to-do checklist of chores, homework and activities to be done today! (list the three most important ones below - do these first and do more if you can)

1 _____
2 _____
3 _____

Book(s) to read and finish this week (you should read at least one book per week) List how many pages you will read from your book(s) today and check off when completed.

1 _____ 2 _____

What did I discover about myself today? (what worked and why):
_____
_____
_____
_____
_____

Who Are You? by JERALD SIMON

Today is **YOUR** Day!   Date
A **Personal Improvement Outline** for YOU.

Compliment someone today. Say something nice to a stranger.

DAILY FOCUS (main goal for the day) _____
DAILY VIRTUE (choose a virtue from the list of virtues on pg. 51) _____
DAILY BIOGRAPHY (Who did you learn about today and how has their life influenced you?)
_____

3 MICRO GOALS TO BE ACCOMPLISHED TODAY (list 3 steps, actions, or projects you can complete today toward one of the macro goals listed on pages 30 and 31)

1 _____
2 _____
3 _____

Daily to-do checklist of chores, homework and activities to be done today! (list the three most important ones below - do these first and do more if you can)

1 _____
2 _____
3 _____

Book(s) to read and finish this week (you should read at least one book per week) List how many pages you will read from your book(s) today and check off when completed.

1 _____ 2 _____

What did I discover about myself today? (what worked and why):
_____
_____
_____
_____
_____

Who Are You? by Jerald Simon

<u>   Date   </u> # Today is **YOUR** Day!
A **Personal Improvement Outline** for YOU.

Go for a run today.

DAILY FOCUS (main goal for the day) _____

DAILY VIRTUE (choose a virtue from the list of virtues on pg. 51) _____

DAILY BIOGRAPHY (Who did you learn about today and how has their life influenced you?)
_____

3 MICRO GOALS TO BE ACCOMPLISHED TODAY (list 3 steps, actions, or projects you can complete today toward one of the macro goals listed on pages 30 and 31)

1 _____
2 _____
3 _____

Daily to-do checklist of chores, homework and activities to be done today!
(list the three most important ones below - do these first and do more if you can)

1 _____
2 _____
3 _____

Book(s) to read and finish this week
(you should read at least one book per week) List how many pages you will read from your book(s) today and check off when completed.

1 _____ 2 _____

What did I discover about myself today? (what worked and why):
_____
_____
_____
_____
_____

Who Are You? by Jerald Simon

Today is YOUR Day! _____
Date

A **Personal Improvement Outline** for YOU.

Go to the back yard and throw the baseball or football.

DAILY FOCUS (main goal for the day) _____
DAILY VIRTUE (choose a virtue from the list of virtues on pg. 51) _____
DAILY BIOGRAPHY (Who did you learn about today and how has their life influenced you?)
_____

3 MICRO GOALS TO BE ACCOMPLISHED TODAY (list 3 steps, actions, or projects you can complete today toward one of the macro goals listed on pages 30 and 31)

1 _____
2 _____
3 _____

Daily to-do checklist of chores, homework and activities to be done today! (list the three most important ones below - do these first and do more if you can)

1 _____
2 _____
3 _____

Book(s) to read and finish this week (you should read at least one book per week) List how many pages you will read from your book(s) today and check off when completed.

1 _____ 2 _____

What did I discover about myself today? (what worked and why):
_____
_____
_____
_____
_____

Who Are You? by JERALD SIMON

___Date___ # Today is **YOUR** Day!
A **Personal Improvement Outline** for YOU.

Learn about Abraham Lincoln.

DAILY FOCUS (main goal for the day) _____

DAILY VIRTUE (choose a virtue from the list of virtues on pg. 51) _____

DAILY BIOGRAPHY (Who did you learn about today and how has their life influenced you?)
_____

3 MICRO GOALS TO BE ACCOMPLISHED TODAY (list 3 steps, actions, or projects you can complete today toward one of the macro goals listed on pages 30 and 31)

1 _____
2 _____
3 _____

Daily to-do checklist of chores, homework and activities to be done today!
(list the three most important ones below - do these first and do more if you can)

1 _____
2 _____
3 _____

Book(s) to read and finish this week (you should read at least one book per week) List how many pages you will read from your book(s) today and check off when completed.

1 _____ 2 _____

What did I discover about myself today? (what worked and why):

_____
_____
_____
_____

Who Are You? by Jerald Simon

Today is YOUR Day! _____Date

A **Personal Improvement Outline** for YOU.

Help someone who needs your help today.

DAILY FOCUS (main goal for the day) _____
DAILY VIRTUE (choose a virtue from the list of virtues on pg. 51) _____
DAILY BIOGRAPHY (Who did you learn about today and how has their life influenced you?)
_____

3 MICRO GOALS TO BE ACCOMPLISHED TODAY (list 3 steps, actions, or projects you can complete today toward one of the macro goals listed on pages 30 and 31)

1 _____
2 _____
3 _____

Daily to-do checklist of chores, homework and activities to be done today! (list the three most important ones below - do these first and do more if you can)

1 _____
2 _____
3 _____

Book(s) to read and finish this week (you should read at least one book per week) List how many pages you will read from your book(s) today and check off when completed.

1 _____ 2 _____

What did I discover about myself today? (what worked and why):
_____
_____
_____
_____
_____

Who Are You? by JERALD SIMON

Date _____

Today is YOUR Day!
A **Personal Improvement Outline** for YOU.

Watch a musical today.

DAILY FOCUS (main goal for the day) _____

DAILY VIRTUE (choose a virtue from the list of virtues on pg. 51) _____

DAILY BIOGRAPHY (Who did you learn about today and how has their life influenced you?)
_____

3 MICRO GOALS TO BE ACCOMPLISHED TODAY (list 3 steps, actions, or projects you can complete today toward one of the macro goals listed on pages 30 and 31)

1 _____
2 _____
3 _____

Daily to-do checklist of chores, homework and activities to be done today! (list the three most important ones below - do these first and do more if you can)

1 _____
2 _____
3 _____

Book(s) to read and finish this week (you should read at least one book per week) List how many pages you will read from your book(s) today and check off when completed.

1 _____ 2 _____

What did I discover about myself today? (what worked and why):
_____
_____
_____
_____
_____

Who Are You? by JERALD SIMON

Today is YOUR Day!   Date
A **Personal Improvement Outline** for YOU.

Write an essay titled, "All about Me", and get to know yourself.

DAILY FOCUS (main goal for the day) _____

DAILY VIRTUE (choose a virtue from the list of virtues on pg. 51) _____

DAILY BIOGRAPHY (Who did you learn about today and how has their life influenced you?)
_____

3 MICRO GOALS TO BE ACCOMPLISHED TODAY (list 3 steps, actions, or projects you can complete today toward one of the macro goals listed on pages 30 and 31)

1 _____
2 _____
3 _____

Daily to-do checklist of chores, homework and activities to be done today! (list the three most important ones below - do these first and do more if you can)

1 _____
2 _____
3 _____

Book(s) to read and finish this week (you should read at least one book per week) List how many pages you will read from your book(s) today and check off when completed.

1 _____ 2 _____

What did I discover about myself today? (what worked and why):
_____
_____
_____
_____
_____

Who Are You? by Jerald Simon

___Date___ # Today is YOUR Day!
A **Personal Improvement Outline** for YOU.

Practice breathing techniques to improve your health.

DAILY FOCUS (main goal for the day) _____
DAILY VIRTUE (choose a virtue from the list of virtues on pg. 51) _____
DAILY BIOGRAPHY (Who did you learn about today and how has their life influenced you?)
_____

3 MICRO GOALS TO BE ACCOMPLISHED TODAY (list 3 steps, actions, or projects you can complete today toward one of the macro goals listed on pages 30 and 31)

1 _____
2 _____
3 _____

Daily to-do checklist of chores, homework and activities to be done today! (list the three most important ones below - do these first and do more if you can)

1 _____
2 _____
3 _____

Book(s) to read and finish this week (you should read at least one book per week) List how many pages you will read from your book(s) today and check off when completed.

1 _____ 2 _____

What did I discover about myself today? (what worked and why):

_____
_____
_____
_____

Who Are You? by JERALD SIMON

Today is YOUR Day!
Date

A **Personal Improvement Outline** for YOU.

Learn a simple drum beat today.

DAILY FOCUS (main goal for the day) _____
DAILY VIRTUE (choose a virtue from the list of virtues on pg. 51) _____
DAILY BIOGRAPHY (Who did you learn about today and how has their life influenced you?)
_____

3 MICRO GOALS TO BE ACCOMPLISHED TODAY (list 3 steps, actions, or projects you can complete today toward one of the macro goals listed on pages 30 and 31)

1 _____
2 _____
3 _____

Daily to-do checklist of chores, homework and activities to be done today! (list the three most important ones below - do these first and do more if you can)

1 _____
2 _____
3 _____

Book(s) to read and finish this week (you should read at least one book per week) List how many pages you will read from your book(s) today and check off when completed.

1 _____ 2 _____

What did I discover about myself today? (what worked and why):
_____
_____
_____
_____
_____

Who Are You? by Jerald Simon

<u>   </u> # Today is **YOUR** Day!
   Date

A **Personal Improvement Outline** for YOU.

Be generous and help others.

DAILY FOCUS (main goal for the day) _____
DAILY VIRTUE (choose a virtue from the list of virtues on pg. 51) _____
DAILY BIOGRAPHY (Who did you learn about today and how has their life influenced you?)
_____

3 MICRO GOALS TO BE ACCOMPLISHED TODAY (list 3 steps, actions, or projects you can complete today toward one of the macro goals listed on pages 30 and 31)

1 _____
2 _____
3 _____

Daily to-do checklist of chores, homework and activities to be done today! (list the three most important ones below - do these first and do more if you can)

1 _____
2 _____
3 _____

Book(s) to read and finish this week (you should read at least one book per week) List how many pages you will read from your book(s) today and check off when completed.

1 _____ 2 _____

What did I discover about myself today? (what worked and why):

_____
_____
_____
_____

Who Are You? by Jerald Simon

Today is YOUR Day!   _____
Date

A **Personal Improvement Outline** for YOU.

Your attitude can change everything.

DAILY FOCUS (main goal for the day) _____
DAILY VIRTUE (choose a virtue from the list of virtues on pg. 51) _____
DAILY BIOGRAPHY (Who did you learn about today and how has their life influenced you?)
_____

3 MICRO GOALS TO BE ACCOMPLISHED TODAY (list 3 steps, actions, or projects you can complete today toward one of the macro goals listed on pages 30 and 31)

1 _____
2 _____
3 _____

Daily to-do checklist of chores, homework and activities to be done today! (list the three most important ones below - do these first and do more if you can)

1 _____
2 _____
3 _____

Book(s) to read and finish this week (you should read at least one book per week) List how many pages you will read from your book(s) today and check off when completed.

1 _____ 2 _____

What did I discover about myself today? (what worked and why):
_____
_____
_____
_____

Who Are You? by JERALD SIMON

——Date—— # Today is YOUR Day!
A **Personal Improvement Outline** for YOU.

Look for the good and you will find it.

DAILY FOCUS (main goal for the day) _____
DAILY VIRTUE (choose a virtue from the list of virtues on pg. 51) _____
DAILY BIOGRAPHY (Who did you learn about today and how has their life influenced you?)
_____

3 MICRO GOALS TO BE ACCOMPLISHED TODAY (list 3 steps, actions, or projects you can complete today toward one of the macro goals listed on pages 30 and 31)

1 _____
2 _____
3 _____

Daily to-do checklist of chores, homework and activities to be done today!
(list the three most important ones below - do these first and do more if you can)

1 _____
2 _____
3 _____

Book(s) to read and finish this week (you should read at least one book per week) List how many pages you will read from your book(s) today and check off when completed.

1 _____ 2 _____

What did I discover about myself today? (what worked and why):
_____
_____
_____
_____

Who Are You? by Jerald Simon

Today is YOUR Day!   ___Date___
A **Personal Improvement Outline** for YOU.

Learn about Voltaire (François Marie Arouet).

DAILY FOCUS (main goal for the day) _____

DAILY VIRTUE (choose a virtue from the list of virtues on pg. 51) _____

DAILY BIOGRAPHY (Who did you learn about today and how has their life influenced you?)
_____

3 MICRO GOALS TO BE ACCOMPLISHED TODAY (list 3 steps, actions, or projects you can complete today toward one of the macro goals listed on pages 30 and 31)

1 _____
2 _____
3 _____

Daily to-do checklist of chores, homework and activities to be done today! (list the three most important ones below - do these first and do more if you can)

1 _____
2 _____
3 _____

Book(s) to read and finish this week (you should read at least one book per week) List how many pages you will read from your book(s) today and check off when completed.

1 _____ 2 _____

What did I discover about myself today? (what worked and why):
_____
_____
_____
_____
_____

Who Are You? by JERALD SIMON

<u>   </u> Date

Today is **YOUR** Day!
A **Personal Improvement Outline** for YOU.

Try an activity you've never tried before.

DAILY FOCUS (main goal for the day) _____
DAILY VIRTUE (choose a virtue from the list of virtues on pg. 51) _____
DAILY BIOGRAPHY (Who did you learn about today and how has their life influenced you?)
_____

3 MICRO GOALS TO BE ACCOMPLISHED TODAY (list 3 steps, actions, or projects you can complete today toward one of the macro goals listed on pages 30 and 31)

1 _____
2 _____
3 _____

Daily to-do checklist of chores, homework and activities to be done today!
(list the three most important ones below - do these first and do more if you can)

1 _____
2 _____
3 _____

Book(s) to read and finish this week (you should read at least one book per week) List how many pages you will read from your book(s) today and check off when completed.

1 _____ 2 _____

What did I discover about myself today? (what worked and why):
_____
_____
_____
_____
_____

Who Are You? by Jerald Simon

Today is YOUR Day!   Date
A **Personal Improvement Outline** for YOU.

Don't worry or stress out about today. Everything will be fine.

DAILY FOCUS (main goal for the day) _____

DAILY VIRTUE (choose a virtue from the list of virtues on pg. 51) _____

DAILY BIOGRAPHY (Who did you learn about today and how has their life influenced you?)
_____

3 MICRO GOALS TO BE ACCOMPLISHED TODAY (list 3 steps, actions, or projects you can complete today toward one of the macro goals listed on pages 30 and 31)

1 _____
2 _____
3 _____

Daily to-do checklist of chores, homework and activities to be done today! (list the three most important ones below - do these first and do more if you can)

1 _____
2 _____
3 _____

Book(s) to read and finish this week (you should read at least one book per week) List how many pages you will read from your book(s) today and check off when completed.

1 _____ 2 _____

What did I discover about myself today? (what worked and why):
_____
_____
_____
_____
_____

Who Are You? by JERALD SIMON

Date _____

Today is YOUR Day!
A **Personal Improvement Outline** for YOU.

Go to the park today and play games.

DAILY FOCUS (main goal for the day) _____
DAILY VIRTUE (choose a virtue from the list of virtues on pg. 51) _____
DAILY BIOGRAPHY (Who did you learn about today and how has their life influenced you?)
_____

3 MICRO GOALS TO BE ACCOMPLISHED TODAY (list 3 steps, actions, or projects you can complete today toward one of the macro goals listed on pages 30 and 31)

1 _____
2 _____
3 _____

Daily to-do checklist of chores, homework and activities to be done today! (list the three most important ones below - do these first and do more if you can)

1 _____
2 _____
3 _____

Book(s) to read and finish this week (you should read at least one book per week) List how many pages you will read from your book(s) today and check off when completed.

1 _____ 2 _____

What did I discover about myself today? (what worked and why):
_____
_____
_____
_____
_____

Who Are You? by Jerald Simon

Today is YOUR Day! ⎯⎯Date⎯⎯
A **Personal Improvement Outline** for YOU.

Learn about Greek Mythology today.

DAILY FOCUS (main goal for the day) _____
DAILY VIRTUE (choose a virtue from the list of virtues on pg. 51) _____
DAILY BIOGRAPHY (Who did you learn about today and how has their life influenced you?)
_____

3 MICRO GOALS TO BE ACCOMPLISHED TODAY (list 3 steps, actions, or projects you can complete today toward one of the macro goals listed on pages 30 and 31)

1 _____
2 _____
3 _____

Daily to-do checklist of chores, homework and activities to be done today! (list the three most important ones below - do these first and do more if you can)

1 _____
2 _____
3 _____

Book(s) to read and finish this week (you should read at least one book per week) List how many pages you will read from your book(s) today and check off when completed.

1 _____ 2 _____

What did I discover about myself today? (what worked and why):
_____
_____
_____
_____
_____

Who Are You? by Jerald Simon

___Date___ # Today is YOUR Day!
A **Personal Improvement Outline** for YOU.

Learn about various inventions throughout history.

DAILY FOCUS (main goal for the day) _____
DAILY VIRTUE (choose a virtue from the list of virtues on pg. 51) _____
DAILY BIOGRAPHY (Who did you learn about today and how has their life influenced you?)
_____

3 MICRO GOALS TO BE ACCOMPLISHED TODAY (list 3 steps, actions, or projects you can complete today toward one of the macro goals listed on pages 30 and 31)

1 _____
2 _____
3 _____

Daily to-do checklist of chores, homework and activities to be done today!
(list the three most important ones below - do these first and do more if you can)

1 _____
2 _____
3 _____

Book(s) to read and finish this week
(you should read at least one book per week) List how many pages you will read from your book(s) today and check off when completed.

1 _____ 2 _____

What did I discover about myself today? (what worked and why):
_____
_____
_____
_____
_____

Who Are You? by JERALD SIMON

Today is YOUR Day!   ___Date___
A **Personal Improvement Outline** for YOU.

Learn the Parliamentary Procedure.

DAILY FOCUS (main goal for the day) _____
DAILY VIRTUE (choose a virtue from the list of virtues on pg. 51) _____
DAILY BIOGRAPHY (Who did you learn about today and how has their life influenced you?)
_____

3 MICRO GOALS TO BE ACCOMPLISHED TODAY (list 3 steps, actions, or projects you can complete today toward one of the macro goals listed on pages 30 and 31)

1 _____
2 _____
3 _____

Daily to-do checklist of chores, homework and activities to be done today! (list the three most important ones below - do these first and do more if you can)

1 _____
2 _____
3 _____

Book(s) to read and finish this week (you should read at least one book per week) List how many pages you will read from your book(s) today and check off when completed.

1 _____ 2 _____

What did I discover about myself today? (what worked and why):
_____
_____
_____
_____
_____

Who Are You? by JERALD SIMON

<u>   </u> # Today is **YOUR** Day!
   Date

A **Personal Improvement Outline** for YOU.

Be grateful for the gifts of life!

DAILY FOCUS (main goal for the day) _____
DAILY VIRTUE (choose a virtue from the list of virtues on pg. 51) _____
DAILY BIOGRAPHY (Who did you learn about today and how has their life influenced you?)
_____

3 MICRO GOALS TO BE ACCOMPLISHED TODAY (list 3 steps, actions, or projects you can complete today toward one of the macro goals listed on pages 30 and 31)

1 _____
2 _____
3 _____

Daily to-do checklist of chores, homework and activities to be done today!
(list the three most important ones below - do these first and do more if you can)

1 _____
2 _____
3 _____

Book(s) to read and finish this week (you should read at least one book per week) List how many pages you will read from your book(s) today and check off when completed.

1 _____ 2 _____

What did I discover about myself today? (what worked and why):
_____
_____
_____
_____
_____

Who Are You? by Jerald Simon

Today is YOUR Day!   _Date_
A **Personal Improvement Outline** for YOU.

Look at the stars at night tonight and learn about them.

DAILY FOCUS (main goal for the day) _____

DAILY VIRTUE (choose a virtue from the list of virtues on pg. 51) _____

DAILY BIOGRAPHY (Who did you learn about today and how has their life influenced you?)
_____

3 MICRO GOALS TO BE ACCOMPLISHED TODAY (list 3 steps, actions, or projects you can complete today toward one of the macro goals listed on pages 30 and 31)

1 _____
2 _____
3 _____

Daily to-do checklist of chores, homework and activities to be done today! (list the three most important ones below - do these first and do more if you can)

1 _____
2 _____
3 _____

Book(s) to read and finish this week (you should read at least one book per week) List how many pages you will read from your book(s) today and check off when completed.

1 _____ 2 _____

What did I discover about myself today? (what worked and why):
_____
_____
_____
_____
_____

Who Are You? by Jerald Simon

Date _____

Today is YOUR Day!
A **Personal Improvement Outline** for YOU.

Take time to visit with a friend who needs you.

DAILY FOCUS (main goal for the day) _____
DAILY VIRTUE (choose a virtue from the list of virtues on pg. 51) _____
DAILY BIOGRAPHY (Who did you learn about today and how has their life influenced you?)
_____

3 MICRO GOALS TO BE ACCOMPLISHED TODAY (list 3 steps, actions, or projects you can complete today toward one of the macro goals listed on pages 30 and 31)

1. _____
2. _____
3. _____

Daily to-do checklist of chores, homework and activities to be done today! (list the three most important ones below - do these first and do more if you can)

1. _____
2. _____
3. _____

Book(s) to read and finish this week (you should read at least one book per week) List how many pages you will read from your book(s) today and check off when completed.

1. _____ 2. _____

What did I discover about myself today? (what worked and why):
_____
_____
_____
_____
_____

Who Are You? by Jerald Simon

Today is YOUR Day! ___Date___
A **Personal Improvement Outline** for YOU.

Have a paper air plane making contest today.

DAILY FOCUS (main goal for the day) _____
DAILY VIRTUE (choose a virtue from the list of virtues on pg. 51) _____
DAILY BIOGRAPHY (Who did you learn about today and how has their life influenced you?)
_____

3 MICRO GOALS TO BE ACCOMPLISHED TODAY (list 3 steps, actions, or projects you can complete today toward one of the macro goals listed on pages 30 and 31)

1 _____
2 _____
3 _____

Daily to-do checklist of chores, homework and activities to be done today! (list the three most important ones below - do these first and do more if you can)

1 _____
2 _____
3 _____

Book(s) to read and finish this week (you should read at least one book per week) List how many pages you will read from your book(s) today and check off when completed.

1 _____ 2 _____

What did I discover about myself today? (what worked and why):
_____
_____
_____
_____
_____

Who Are You? by Jerald Simon

<u>   Date   </u> # Today is YOUR Day!
A **Personal Improvement Outline** for YOU.

Get out and work in the yard today.

DAILY FOCUS (main goal for the day) _____

DAILY VIRTUE (choose a virtue from the list of virtues on pg. 51) _____

DAILY BIOGRAPHY (Who did you learn about today and how has their life influenced you?)
_____

3 MICRO GOALS TO BE ACCOMPLISHED TODAY (list 3 steps, actions, or projects you can complete today toward one of the macro goals listed on pages 30 and 31)

1 _____
2 _____
3 _____

Daily to-do checklist of chores, homework and activities to be done today! (list the three most important ones below - do these first and do more if you can)

1 _____
2 _____
3 _____

Book(s) to read and finish this week (you should read at least one book per week) List how many pages you will read from your book(s) today and check off when completed.

1 _____ 2 _____

What did I discover about myself today? (what worked and why):

_____
_____
_____
_____

Who Are You? by Jerald Simon

Today is YOUR Day!   Date _____
A **Personal Improvement Outline** for YOU.

Learn how to change a tire today.

DAILY FOCUS (main goal for the day) _____

DAILY VIRTUE (choose a virtue from the list of virtues on pg. 51) _____

DAILY BIOGRAPHY (Who did you learn about today and how has their life influenced you?)
_____

3 MICRO GOALS TO BE ACCOMPLISHED TODAY (list 3 steps, actions, or projects you can complete today toward one of the macro goals listed on pages 30 and 31)

1 _____
2 _____
3 _____

Daily to-do checklist of chores, homework and activities to be done today!
(list the three most important ones below - do these first and do more if you can)

1 _____
2 _____
3 _____

Book(s) to read and finish this week (you should read at least one book per week) List how many pages you will read from your book(s) today and check off when completed.

1 _____ 2 _____

What did I discover about myself today? (what worked and why):
_____
_____
_____
_____
_____

Who Are You? by Jerald Simon

Date —————

Today is **YOUR** Day!
A **Personal Improvement Outline** for YOU.

Learn about pruning fruit trees and go try it.

DAILY FOCUS (main goal for the day) _____
DAILY VIRTUE (choose a virtue from the list of virtues on pg. 51) _____
DAILY BIOGRAPHY (Who did you learn about today and how has their life influenced you?)
_____

3 MICRO GOALS TO BE ACCOMPLISHED TODAY (list 3 steps, actions, or projects you can complete today toward one of the macro goals listed on pages 30 and 31)

1 _____
2 _____
3 _____

Daily to-do checklist of chores, homework and activities to be done today! (list the three most important ones below - do these first and do more if you can)

1 _____
2 _____
3 _____

Book(s) to read and finish this week (you should read at least one book per week) List how many pages you will read from your book(s) today and check off when completed.

1 _____ 2 _____

What did I discover about myself today? (what worked and why):
_____
_____
_____
_____

Who Are You? by JERALD SIMON

Today is YOUR Day!
Date
A **Personal Improvement Outline** for YOU.

Learn to keep a steady beat on a drum (quarter notes).

DAILY FOCUS (main goal for the day) _____

DAILY VIRTUE (choose a virtue from the list of virtues on pg. 51) _____

DAILY BIOGRAPHY (Who did you learn about today and how has their life influenced you?)
_____

3 MICRO GOALS TO BE ACCOMPLISHED TODAY (list 3 steps, actions, or projects you can complete today toward one of the macro goals listed on pages 30 and 31)

1 _____
2 _____
3 _____

Daily to-do checklist of chores, homework and activities to be done today! (list the three most important ones below - do these first and do more if you can)

1 _____
2 _____
3 _____

Book(s) to read and finish this week (you should read at least one book per week) List how many pages you will read from your book(s) today and check off when completed.

1 _____ 2 _____

What did I discover about myself today? (what worked and why):
_____
_____
_____
_____
_____

Who Are You? by Jerald Simon

<u>   Date   </u> # Today is YOUR Day!
A **Personal Improvement Outline** for YOU.

Go outside today and climb a tree.

DAILY FOCUS (main goal for the day) _____
DAILY VIRTUE (choose a virtue from the list of virtues on pg. 51) _____
DAILY BIOGRAPHY (Who did you learn about today and how has their life influenced you?)
_____

3 MICRO GOALS TO BE ACCOMPLISHED TODAY (list 3 steps, actions, or projects you can complete today toward one of the macro goals listed on pages 30 and 31)

1 _____
2 _____
3 _____

Daily to-do checklist of chores, homework and activities to be done today! (list the three most important ones below - do these first and do more if you can)

1 _____
2 _____
3 _____

Book(s) to read and finish this week (you should read at least one book per week) List how many pages you will read from your book(s) today and check off when completed.

1 _____ 2 _____

What did I discover about myself today? (what worked and why):
_____
_____
_____
_____
_____

Who Are You? by Jerald Simon

Today is YOUR Day!
Date

A **Personal Improvement Outline** for YOU.

Say hello to everyone you see today — even those don't know.

DAILY FOCUS (main goal for the day) _____

DAILY VIRTUE (choose a virtue from the list of virtues on pg. 51) _____

DAILY BIOGRAPHY (Who did you learn about today and how has their life influenced you?)
_____

3 MICRO GOALS TO BE ACCOMPLISHED TODAY (list 3 steps, actions, or projects you can complete today toward one of the macro goals listed on pages 30 and 31)

1 _____
2 _____
3 _____

Daily to-do checklist of chores, homework and activities to be done today! (list the three most important ones below - do these first and do more if you can)

1 _____
2 _____
3 _____

Book(s) to read and finish this week (you should read at least one book per week) List how many pages you will read from your book(s) today and check off when completed.

1 _____ 2 _____

What did I discover about myself today? (what worked and why):
_____
_____
_____
_____
_____

Who Are You? by JERALD SIMON

<u>　　Date　　</u> # Today is YOUR Day!
A **Personal Improvement Outline** for YOU.

Plant seeds of positivity every where you go today.

DAILY FOCUS (main goal for the day) _____
DAILY VIRTUE (choose a virtue from the list of virtues on pg. 51) _____
DAILY BIOGRAPHY (Who did you learn about today and how has their life influenced you?)
_____

3 MICRO GOALS TO BE ACCOMPLISHED TODAY (list 3 steps, actions, or projects you can complete today toward one of the macro goals listed on pages 30 and 31)

1 _____
2 _____
3 _____

Daily to-do checklist of chores, homework and activities to be done today! (list the three most important ones below - do these first and do more if you can)

1 _____
2 _____
3 _____

Book(s) to read and finish this week (you should read at least one book per week) List how many pages you will read from your book(s) today and check off when completed.

1 _____ 2 _____

What did I discover about myself today? (what worked and why):
_____
_____
_____
_____

Who Are You? by JERALD SIMON

Today is YOUR Day! ___Date___
A **Personal Improvement Outline** for YOU.

Be kind to everyone — even those who are unkind to you.

DAILY FOCUS (main goal for the day) _____
DAILY VIRTUE (choose a virtue from the list of virtues on pg. 51) _____
DAILY BIOGRAPHY (Who did you learn about today and how has their life influenced you?)
_____

3 MICRO GOALS TO BE ACCOMPLISHED TODAY (list 3 steps, actions, or projects you can complete today toward one of the macro goals listed on pages 30 and 31)

1 _____
2 _____
3 _____

Daily to-do checklist of chores, homework and activities to be done today! (list the three most important ones below - do these first and do more if you can)

1 _____
2 _____
3 _____

Book(s) to read and finish this week (you should read at least one book per week) List how many pages you will read from your book(s) today and check off when completed.

1 _____ 2 _____

What did I discover about myself today? (what worked and why):
_____
_____
_____
_____
_____

Who Are You? by JERALD SIMON

Today is YOUR Day!
Date

A **Personal Improvement Outline** for YOU.

Learn CPR today. Know what it means and how to do it.

DAILY FOCUS (main goal for the day) _____

DAILY VIRTUE (choose a virtue from the list of virtues on pg. 51) _____

DAILY BIOGRAPHY (Who did you learn about today and how has their life influenced you?)
_____

3 MICRO GOALS TO BE ACCOMPLISHED TODAY (list 3 steps, actions, or projects you can complete today toward one of the macro goals listed on pages 30 and 31)

1 _____
2 _____
3 _____

Daily to-do checklist of chores, homework and activities to be done today! (list the three most important ones below - do these first and do more if you can)

1 _____
2 _____
3 _____

Book(s) to read and finish this week (you should read at least one book per week) List how many pages you will read from your book(s) today and check off when completed.

1 _____ 2 _____

What did I discover about myself today? (what worked and why):
_____
_____
_____
_____

Who Are You? by Jerald Simon

Today is YOUR Day!   ──Date──
A **Personal Improvement Outline** for YOU.

Go swing on swings at a playground today.

DAILY FOCUS (main goal for the day) _____
DAILY VIRTUE (choose a virtue from the list of virtues on pg. 51) _____
DAILY BIOGRAPHY (Who did you learn about today and how has their life influenced you?)
_____

3 MICRO GOALS TO BE ACCOMPLISHED TODAY (list 3 steps, actions, or projects you can complete today toward one of the macro goals listed on pages 30 and 31)

1 _____
2 _____
3 _____

Daily to-do checklist of chores, homework and activities to be done today! (list the three most important ones below - do these first and do more if you can)

1 _____
2 _____
3 _____

Book(s) to read and finish this week (you should read at least one book per week) List how many pages you will read from your book(s) today and check off when completed.

1 _____ 2 _____

What did I discover about myself today? (what worked and why):
_____
_____
_____
_____
_____

Who Are You? by Jerald Simon

___Date___ # Today is YOUR Day!
A **Personal Improvement Outline** for YOU.

All you can do is to do your best. Leave the rest alone.

DAILY FOCUS (main goal for the day) _____
DAILY VIRTUE (choose a virtue from the list of virtues on pg. 51) _____
DAILY BIOGRAPHY (Who did you learn about today and how has their life influenced you?)
_____

3 MICRO GOALS TO BE ACCOMPLISHED TODAY (list 3 steps, actions, or projects you can complete today toward one of the macro goals listed on pages 30 and 31)

1 _____
2 _____
3 _____

Daily to-do checklist of chores, homework and activities to be done today!
(list the three most important ones below - do these first and do more if you can)

1 _____
2 _____
3 _____

Book(s) to read and finish this week
(you should read at least one book per week) List how many pages you will read from your book(s) today and check off when completed.

1 _____ 2 _____

What did I discover about myself today? (what worked and why):

_____
_____
_____
_____

Who Are You? by Jerald Simon

Today is YOUR Day! ⎯ Date

A **Personal Improvement Outline** for YOU.

Always finish what you start. Don't start and stop. FINISH!

DAILY FOCUS (main goal for the day) _____
DAILY VIRTUE (choose a virtue from the list of virtues on pg. 51) _____
DAILY BIOGRAPHY (Who did you learn about today and how has their life influenced you?)
_____

3 MICRO GOALS TO BE ACCOMPLISHED TODAY (list 3 steps, actions, or projects you can complete today toward one of the macro goals listed on pages 30 and 31)

1 _____
2 _____
3 _____

Daily to-do checklist of chores, homework and activities to be done today! (list the three most important ones below - do these first and do more if you can)

1 _____
2 _____
3 _____

Book(s) to read and finish this week (you should read at least one book per week) List how many pages you will read from your book(s) today and check off when completed.

1 _____ 2 _____

What did I discover about myself today? (what worked and why):
_____
_____
_____
_____
_____

Who Are You? by Jerald Simon

___Date___ # Today is YOUR Day!
A **Personal Improvement Outline** for YOU.

How can you help your father, mother, sister, or brother today?

DAILY FOCUS (main goal for the day) _____

DAILY VIRTUE (choose a virtue from the list of virtues on pg. 51) _____

DAILY BIOGRAPHY (Who did you learn about today and how has their life influenced you?)
_____

3 MICRO GOALS TO BE ACCOMPLISHED TODAY (list 3 steps, actions, or projects you can complete today toward one of the macro goals listed on pages 30 and 31)

1 _____
2 _____
3 _____

Daily to-do checklist of chores, homework and activities to be done today! (list the three most important ones below - do these first and do more if you can)

1 _____
2 _____
3 _____

Book(s) to read and finish this week (you should read at least one book per week) List how many pages you will read from your book(s) today and check off when completed.

1 _____ 2 _____

What did I discover about myself today? (what worked and why):
_____
_____
_____
_____

Who Are You? by Jerald Simon

Today is YOUR Day! ___Date___
A **Personal Improvement Outline** for YOU.

Do a random act of kindness today for a stranger.

DAILY FOCUS (main goal for the day) _____
DAILY VIRTUE (choose a virtue from the list of virtues on pg. 51) _____
DAILY BIOGRAPHY (Who did you learn about today and how has their life influenced you?)
_____

3 MICRO GOALS TO BE ACCOMPLISHED TODAY (list 3 steps, actions, or projects you can complete today toward one of the macro goals listed on pages 30 and 31)

1 _____
2 _____
3 _____

Daily to-do checklist of chores, homework and activities to be done today! (list the three most important ones below - do these first and do more if you can)

1 _____
2 _____
3 _____

Book(s) to read and finish this week (you should read at least one book per week) List how many pages you will read from your book(s) today and check off when completed.

1 _____ 2 _____

What did I discover about myself today? (what worked and why):
_____
_____
_____
_____
_____

Who Are You? by JERALD SIMON

Date _____

Today is **YOUR** Day!

A **Personal Improvement Outline** for YOU.

Believe and have faith in your future.

DAILY FOCUS (main goal for the day) _____

DAILY VIRTUE (choose a virtue from the list of virtues on pg. 51) _____

DAILY BIOGRAPHY (Who did you learn about today and how has their life influenced you?)
_____

3 MICRO GOALS TO BE ACCOMPLISHED TODAY (list 3 steps, actions, or projects you can complete today toward one of the macro goals listed on pages 30 and 31)

1. _____
2. _____
3. _____

Daily to-do checklist of chores, homework and activities to be done today! (list the three most important ones below - do these first and do more if you can)

1. _____
2. _____
3. _____

Book(s) to read and finish this week (you should read at least one book per week) List how many pages you will read from your book(s) today and check off when completed.

1. _____ 2. _____

What did I discover about myself today? (what worked and why):
_____
_____
_____
_____

Who Are You? by JERALD SIMON

Today is YOUR Day!   ――――― Date
A **Personal Improvement Outline** for YOU.

When problems seem to be too much you can always pray.

DAILY FOCUS (main goal for the day) _____

DAILY VIRTUE (choose a virtue from the list of virtues on pg. 51) _____

DAILY BIOGRAPHY (Who did you learn about today and how has their life influenced you?)

_____

3 MICRO GOALS TO BE ACCOMPLISHED TODAY (list 3 steps, actions, or projects you can complete today toward one of the macro goals listed on pages 30 and 31)

1 _____
2 _____
3 _____

Daily to-do checklist of chores, homework and activities to be done today! (list the three most important ones below - do these first and do more if you can)

1 _____
2 _____
3 _____

Book(s) to read and finish this week (you should read at least one book per week) List how many pages you will read from your book(s) today and check off when completed.

1 _____ 2 _____

What did I discover about myself today? (what worked and why):

_____
_____
_____
_____
_____

Who Are You? by Jerald Simon

Date _____

Today is **YOUR** Day!
A **Personal Improvement Outline** for YOU.

Watch a movie with the volume turned off and create the dialog.

DAILY FOCUS (main goal for the day) _____
DAILY VIRTUE (choose a virtue from the list of virtues on pg. 51) _____
DAILY BIOGRAPHY (Who did you learn about today and how has their life influenced you?)
_____

3 MICRO GOALS TO BE ACCOMPLISHED TODAY (list 3 steps, actions, or projects you can complete today toward one of the macro goals listed on pages 30 and 31)

1 _____
2 _____
3 _____

Daily to-do checklist of chores, homework and activities to be done today! (list the three most important ones below - do these first and do more if you can)

1 _____
2 _____
3 _____

Book(s) to read and finish this week (you should read at least one book per week) List how many pages you will read from your book(s) today and check off when completed.

1 _____ 2 _____

What did I discover about myself today? (what worked and why):
_____
_____
_____
_____

Who Are You? by JERALD SIMON

Today is YOUR Day!
Date
A **Personal Improvement Outline** for YOU.

Make breakfast for dinner tonight.

DAILY FOCUS (main goal for the day) _____
DAILY VIRTUE (choose a virtue from the list of virtues on pg. 51) _____
DAILY BIOGRAPHY (Who did you learn about today and how has their life influenced you?)
_____

3 MICRO GOALS TO BE ACCOMPLISHED TODAY (list 3 steps, actions, or projects you can complete today toward one of the macro goals listed on pages 30 and 31)

1 _____
2 _____
3 _____

Daily to-do checklist of chores, homework and activities to be done today! (list the three most important ones below - do these first and do more if you can)

1 _____
2 _____
3 _____

Book(s) to read and finish this week (you should read at least one book per week) List how many pages you will read from your book(s) today and check off when completed.

1 _____ 2 _____

What did I discover about myself today? (what worked and why):
_____
_____
_____
_____
_____

Who Are You? by JERALD SIMON

Today is **YOUR** Day!
Date

A **Personal Improvement Outline** for YOU.

Focus on one of your weaknesses and make it a strength.

DAILY FOCUS (main goal for the day) _____
DAILY VIRTUE (choose a virtue from the list of virtues on pg. 51) _____
DAILY BIOGRAPHY (Who did you learn about today and how has their life influenced you?)
_____

3 MICRO GOALS TO BE ACCOMPLISHED TODAY (list 3 steps, actions, or projects you can complete today toward one of the macro goals listed on pages 30 and 31)

1 _____
2 _____
3 _____

Daily to-do checklist of chores, homework and activities to be done today! (list the three most important ones below - do these first and do more if you can)

1 _____
2 _____
3 _____

Book(s) to read and finish this week (you should read at least one book per week) List how many pages you will read from your book(s) today and check off when completed.

1 _____ 2 _____

What did I discover about myself today? (what worked and why):
_____
_____
_____
_____
_____

Who Are You? by JERALD SIMON

Today is YOUR Day!   ‾‾Date‾‾
A **Personal Improvement Outline** for YOU.

Do the unexpected today. Be spontaneous!

DAILY FOCUS (main goal for the day) _____
DAILY VIRTUE (choose a virtue from the list of virtues on pg. 51) _____
DAILY BIOGRAPHY (Who did you learn about today and how has their life influenced you?)
_____

3 MICRO GOALS TO BE ACCOMPLISHED TODAY (list 3 steps, actions, or projects you can complete today toward one of the macro goals listed on pages 30 and 31)

1 _____
2 _____
3 _____

Daily to-do checklist of chores, homework and activities to be done today! (list the three most important ones below - do these first and do more if you can)

1 _____
2 _____
3 _____

Book(s) to read and finish this week (you should read at least one book per week) List how many pages you will read from your book(s) today and check off when completed.

1 _____ 2 _____

What did I discover about myself today? (what worked and why):
_____
_____
_____
_____
_____

Who Are You? by JERALD SIMON

<u>Date</u>   # Today is **YOUR** Day!
A **Personal Improvement Outline** for YOU.

Visit a used bookstore today and spend time reading old books.

DAILY FOCUS (main goal for the day) _____

DAILY VIRTUE (choose a virtue from the list of virtues on pg. 51) _____

DAILY BIOGRAPHY (Who did you learn about today and how has their life influenced you?)
_____

3 MICRO GOALS TO BE ACCOMPLISHED TODAY (list 3 steps, actions, or projects you can complete today toward one of the macro goals listed on pages 30 and 31)

1. _____
2. _____
3. _____

Daily to-do checklist of chores, homework and activities to be done today! (list the three most important ones below - do these first and do more if you can)

1. _____
2. _____
3. _____

Book(s) to read and finish this week (you should read at least one book per week) List how many pages you will read from your book(s) today and check off when completed.

1. _____ 2. _____

What did I discover about myself today? (what worked and why):
_____
_____
_____
_____

Who Are You? by JERALD SIMON

Today is YOUR Day! ⎯⎯Date⎯⎯
A **Personal Improvement Outline** for YOU.

Visit a thrift store today and find lost treasures.

DAILY FOCUS (main goal for the day) _____
DAILY VIRTUE (choose a virtue from the list of virtues on pg. 51) _____
DAILY BIOGRAPHY (Who did you learn about today and how has their life influenced you?)
_____

3 MICRO GOALS TO BE ACCOMPLISHED TODAY (list 3 steps, actions, or projects you can complete today toward one of the macro goals listed on pages 30 and 31)

1 _____
2 _____
3 _____

Daily to-do checklist of chores, homework and activities to be done today! (list the three most important ones below - do these first and do more if you can)

1 _____
2 _____
3 _____

Book(s) to read and finish this week (you should read at least one book per week) List how many pages you will read from your book(s) today and check off when completed.

1 _____ 2 _____

What did I discover about myself today? (what worked and why):
_____
_____
_____
_____
_____

Who Are You? by Jerald Simon

Today is YOUR Day!
Date

A Personal Improvement Outline for YOU.

Don't talk about yourself at all today. Not once! Don't do it!

DAILY FOCUS (main goal for the day) _____
DAILY VIRTUE (choose a virtue from the list of virtues on pg. 51) _____
DAILY BIOGRAPHY (Who did you learn about today and how has their life influenced you?)
_____

3 MICRO GOALS TO BE ACCOMPLISHED TODAY (list 3 steps, actions, or projects you can complete today toward one of the macro goals listed on pages 30 and 31)

1 _____
2 _____
3 _____

Daily to-do checklist of chores, homework and activities to be done today! (list the three most important ones below - do these first and do more if you can)

1 _____
2 _____
3 _____

Book(s) to read and finish this week (you should read at least one book per week) List how many pages you will read from your book(s) today and check off when completed.

1 _____ 2 _____

What did I discover about myself today? (what worked and why):
_____
_____
_____
_____

Who Are You? by JERALD SIMON

Today is YOUR Day!   ⎯Date⎯

A **Personal Improvement Outline** for YOU.

Take a dog for a walk even if you don't have one.

DAILY FOCUS (main goal for the day) _____
DAILY VIRTUE (choose a virtue from the list of virtues on pg. 51) _____
DAILY BIOGRAPHY (Who did you learn about today and how has their life influenced you?)
_____

3 MICRO GOALS TO BE ACCOMPLISHED TODAY (list 3 steps, actions, or projects you can complete today toward one of the macro goals listed on pages 30 and 31)

1 _____
2 _____
3 _____

Daily to-do checklist of chores, homework and activities to be done today! (list the three most important ones below - do these first and do more if you can)

1 _____
2 _____
3 _____

Book(s) to read and finish this week (you should read at least one book per week) List how many pages you will read from your book(s) today and check off when completed.

1 _____   2 _____

What did I discover about myself today? (what worked and why):
_____
_____
_____
_____
_____

Who Are You? by Jerald Simon

Date _____

Today is YOUR Day!
A **Personal Improvement Outline** for YOU.

Turn the music on in the kitchen or living room and dance!

DAILY FOCUS (main goal for the day) _____
DAILY VIRTUE (choose a virtue from the list of virtues on pg. 51) _____
DAILY BIOGRAPHY (Who did you learn about today and how has their life influenced you?)
_____

3 MICRO GOALS TO BE ACCOMPLISHED TODAY (list 3 steps, actions, or projects you can complete today toward one of the macro goals listed on pages 30 and 31)

1 _____
2 _____
3 _____

Daily to-do checklist of chores, homework and activities to be done today! (list the three most important ones below - do these first and do more if you can)

1 _____
2 _____
3 _____

Book(s) to read and finish this week (you should read at least one book per week) List how many pages you will read from your book(s) today and check off when completed.

1 _____ 2 _____

What did I discover about myself today? (what worked and why):
_____
_____
_____
_____

Who Are You? by Jerald Simon

Today is YOUR Day!   ___Date___
A **Personal Improvement Outline** for YOU.

Write a story with your family. Everyone writes one paragraph.

DAILY FOCUS (main goal for the day) _____
DAILY VIRTUE (choose a virtue from the list of virtues on pg. 51) _____
DAILY BIOGRAPHY (Who did you learn about today and how has their life influenced you?)
_____

3 MICRO GOALS TO BE ACCOMPLISHED TODAY (list 3 steps, actions, or projects you can complete today toward one of the macro goals listed on pages 30 and 31)

1 _____
2 _____
3 _____

Daily to-do checklist of chores, homework and activities to be done today! (list the three most important ones below - do these first and do more if you can)

1 _____
2 _____
3 _____

Book(s) to read and finish this week (you should read at least one book per week) List how many pages you will read from your book(s) today and check off when completed.

1 _____ 2 _____

What did I discover about myself today? (what worked and why):
_____
_____
_____
_____

Who Are You? by JERALD SIMON

---Date--- ## Today is **YOUR** Day!
A **Personal Improvement Outline** for YOU.

Trust yourself. The world wants to drown you out. Don't listen.

DAILY FOCUS (main goal for the day) _____
DAILY VIRTUE (choose a virtue from the list of virtues on pg. 51) _____
DAILY BIOGRAPHY (Who did you learn about today and how has their life influenced you?)
_____

3 MICRO GOALS TO BE ACCOMPLISHED TODAY (list 3 steps, actions, or projects you can complete today toward one of the macro goals listed on pages 30 and 31)

1 _____
2 _____
3 _____

Daily to-do checklist of chores, homework and activities to be done today! (list the three most important ones below - do these first and do more if you can)

1 _____
2 _____
3 _____

Book(s) to read and finish this week (you should read at least one book per week) List how many pages you will read from your book(s) today and check off when completed.

1 _____ 2 _____

What did I discover about myself today? (what worked and why):

_____
_____
_____
_____

Who Are You? by JERALD SIMON

Today is YOUR Day! ___Date___
A **Personal Improvement Outline** for YOU.

Visit a hospital and ask if you can read stories to children.

DAILY FOCUS (main goal for the day) _____
DAILY VIRTUE (choose a virtue from the list of virtues on pg. 51) _____
DAILY BIOGRAPHY (Who did you learn about today and how has their life influenced you?)
_____

3 MICRO GOALS TO BE ACCOMPLISHED TODAY (list 3 steps, actions, or projects you can complete today toward one of the macro goals listed on pages 30 and 31)

1 _____
2 _____
3 _____

Daily to-do checklist of chores, homework and activities to be done today! (list the three most important ones below - do these first and do more if you can)

1 _____
2 _____
3 _____

Book(s) to read and finish this week (you should read at least one book per week) List how many pages you will read from your book(s) today and check off when completed.

1 _____ 2 _____

What did I discover about myself today? (what worked and why):
_____
_____
_____
_____
_____

Who Are You? by Jerald Simon

____Date____ # Today is YOUR Day!
A **Personal Improvement Outline** for YOU.

Focus on the best within everyone. Bring out their strengths.

DAILY FOCUS (main goal for the day) _____
DAILY VIRTUE (choose a virtue from the list of virtues on pg. 51) _____
DAILY BIOGRAPHY (Who did you learn about today and how has their life influenced you?)
_____

3 MICRO GOALS TO BE ACCOMPLISHED TODAY (list 3 steps, actions, or projects you can complete today toward one of the macro goals listed on pages 30 and 31)

1 _____
2 _____
3 _____

Daily to-do checklist of chores, homework and activities to be done today! (list the three most important ones below - do these first and do more if you can)

1 _____
2 _____
3 _____

Book(s) to read and finish this week (you should read at least one book per week)
List how many pages you will read from your book(s) today and check off when completed.

1 _____ 2 _____

What did I discover about myself today? (what worked and why):

_____
_____
_____
_____

Who Are You? by JERALD SIMON

Today is YOUR Day! ⎯⎯ Date
A **Personal Improvement Outline** for YOU.

Look at the world differently today. Use binoculars.

DAILY FOCUS (main goal for the day) _____
DAILY VIRTUE (choose a virtue from the list of virtues on pg. 51) _____
DAILY BIOGRAPHY (Who did you learn about today and how has their life influenced you?)
_____

3 MICRO GOALS TO BE ACCOMPLISHED TODAY (list 3 steps, actions, or projects you can complete today toward one of the macro goals listed on pages 30 and 31)

1 _____
2 _____
3 _____

Daily to-do checklist of chores, homework and activities to be done today! (list the three most important ones below - do these first and do more if you can)

1 _____
2 _____
3 _____

Book(s) to read and finish this week (you should read at least one book per week) List how many pages you will read from your book(s) today and check off when completed.

1 _____ 2 _____

What did I discover about myself today? (what worked and why):
_____
_____
_____
_____
_____

Who Are You? by Jerald Simon

Date _____

Today is **YOUR** Day!
A **Personal Improvement Outline** for YOU.

Sing your favorite song out loud today at the top of your lungs.

DAILY FOCUS (main goal for the day) _____
DAILY VIRTUE (choose a virtue from the list of virtues on pg. 51) _____
DAILY BIOGRAPHY (Who did you learn about today and how has their life influenced you?)
_____

3 MICRO GOALS TO BE ACCOMPLISHED TODAY (list 3 steps, actions, or projects you can complete today toward one of the macro goals listed on pages 30 and 31)

1 _____
2 _____
3 _____

Daily to-do checklist of chores, homework and activities to be done today! (list the three most important ones below - do these first and do more if you can)

1 _____
2 _____
3 _____

Book(s) to read and finish this week (you should read at least one book per week) List how many pages you will read from your book(s) today and check off when completed.

1 _____ 2 _____

What did I discover about myself today? (what worked and why):
_____
_____
_____
_____
_____

Who Are You? by Jerald Simon

Today is YOUR Day! _____Date_____
A **Personal Improvement Outline** for YOU.

Make a wish list of 100 things you'd like to do this year.

DAILY FOCUS (main goal for the day) _____
DAILY VIRTUE (choose a virtue from the list of virtues on pg. 51) _____
DAILY BIOGRAPHY (Who did you learn about today and how has their life influenced you?)
_____

3 MICRO GOALS TO BE ACCOMPLISHED TODAY (list 3 steps, actions, or projects you can complete today toward one of the macro goals listed on pages 30 and 31)

1 _____
2 _____
3 _____

Daily to-do checklist of chores, homework and activities to be done today! (list the three most important ones below - do these first and do more if you can)

1 _____
2 _____
3 _____

Book(s) to read and finish this week (you should read at least one book per week) List how many pages you will read from your book(s) today and check off when completed.

1 _____ 2 _____

What did I discover about myself today? (what worked and why):
_____
_____
_____
_____
_____

Who Are You? by JERALD SIMON

___Date___ ## Today is **YOUR** Day!
A **Personal Improvement Outline** for YOU.

Learn about trains today and, if you can, take a ride on a train.

DAILY FOCUS (main goal for the day) _____
DAILY VIRTUE (choose a virtue from the list of virtues on pg. 51) _____
DAILY BIOGRAPHY (Who did you learn about today and how has their life influenced you?)
_____

3 MICRO GOALS TO BE ACCOMPLISHED TODAY (list 3 steps, actions, or projects you can complete today toward one of the macro goals listed on pages 30 and 31)

1 _____
2 _____
3 _____

Daily to-do checklist of chores, homework and activities to be done today! (list the three most important ones below - do these first and do more if you can)

1 _____
2 _____
3 _____

Book(s) to read and finish this week (you should read at least one book per week) List how many pages you will read from your book(s) today and check off when completed.

1 _____ 2 _____

What did I discover about myself today? (what worked and why):
_____
_____
_____
_____
_____

Who Are You? by JERALD SIMON

Today is YOUR Day!   Date
A **Personal Improvement Outline** for YOU.

Plant flowers in the yard. Make your path before you beautiful.

DAILY FOCUS (main goal for the day) _____
DAILY VIRTUE (choose a virtue from the list of virtues on pg. 51) _____
DAILY BIOGRAPHY (Who did you learn about today and how has their life influenced you?)
_____

3 MICRO GOALS TO BE ACCOMPLISHED TODAY (list 3 steps, actions, or projects you can complete today toward one of the macro goals listed on pages 30 and 31)

1 _____
2 _____
3 _____

Daily to-do checklist of chores, homework and activities to be done today! (list the three most important ones below - do these first and do more if you can)

1 _____
2 _____
3 _____

Book(s) to read and finish this week (you should read at least one book per week) List how many pages you will read from your book(s) today and check off when completed.

1 _____ 2 _____

What did I discover about myself today? (what worked and why):
_____
_____
_____
_____

Who Are You? by Jerald Simon

<u>   Date   </u> # Today is YOUR Day!
A **Personal Improvement Outline** for YOU.

Laugh today! A lot. Find a funny movie and laugh out loud.

DAILY FOCUS (main goal for the day) _____
DAILY VIRTUE (choose a virtue from the list of virtues on pg. 51) _____
DAILY BIOGRAPHY (Who did you learn about today and how has their life influenced you?)
_____

3 MICRO GOALS TO BE ACCOMPLISHED TODAY (list 3 steps, actions, or projects you can complete today toward one of the macro goals listed on pages 30 and 31)

1 _____
2 _____
3 _____

Daily to-do checklist of chores, homework and activities to be done today! (list the three most important ones below - do these first and do more if you can)

1 _____
2 _____
3 _____

Book(s) to read and finish this week (you should read at least one book per week) List how many pages you will read from your book(s) today and check off when completed.

1 _____ 2 _____

What did I discover about myself today? (what worked and why):

_____
_____
_____
_____

Who Are You? by JERALD SIMON

Today is YOUR Day! ⎯⎯ Date ⎯⎯
A **Personal Improvement Outline** for YOU.

Practice what you preach. But don't preach, though. LOVE.

DAILY FOCUS (main goal for the day) _____
DAILY VIRTUE (choose a virtue from the list of virtues on pg. 51) _____
DAILY BIOGRAPHY (Who did you learn about today and how has their life influenced you?)
_____

3 MICRO GOALS TO BE ACCOMPLISHED TODAY (list 3 steps, actions, or projects you can complete today toward one of the macro goals listed on pages 30 and 31)

1 _____
2 _____
3 _____

Daily to-do checklist of chores, homework and activities to be done today! (list the three most important ones below - do these first and do more if you can)

1 _____
2 _____
3 _____

Book(s) to read and finish this week (you should read at least one book per week) List how many pages you will read from your book(s) today and check off when completed.

1 _____ 2 _____

What did I discover about myself today? (what worked and why):
_____
_____
_____
_____
_____

Who Are You? by JERALD SIMON

<u>Date</u>   # Today is **YOUR** Day!
A **Personal Improvement Outline** for YOU.

Learn about computers today. The what, why, how, and when.

DAILY FOCUS (main goal for the day) _____

DAILY VIRTUE (choose a virtue from the list of virtues on pg. 51) _____

DAILY BIOGRAPHY (Who did you learn about today and how has their life influenced you?)
_____

3 MICRO GOALS TO BE ACCOMPLISHED TODAY (list 3 steps, actions, or projects you can complete today toward one of the macro goals listed on pages 30 and 31)

1 _____
2 _____
3 _____

Daily to-do checklist of chores, homework and activities to be done today! (list the three most important ones below - do these first and do more if you can)

1 _____
2 _____
3 _____

Book(s) to read and finish this week (you should read at least one book per week) List how many pages you will read from your book(s) today and check off when completed.

1 _____   2 _____

What did I discover about myself today? (what worked and why):
_____
_____
_____
_____

Who Are You? by JERALD SIMON

Today is YOUR Day!
Date
A **Personal Improvement Outline** for YOU.

Don't listen with your ears. Listen with your head and heart.

DAILY FOCUS (main goal for the day) _____

DAILY VIRTUE (choose a virtue from the list of virtues on pg. 51) _____

DAILY BIOGRAPHY (Who did you learn about today and how has their life influenced you?)
_____

3 MICRO GOALS TO BE ACCOMPLISHED TODAY (list 3 steps, actions, or projects you can complete today toward one of the macro goals listed on pages 30 and 31)

1 _____
2 _____
3 _____

Daily to-do checklist of chores, homework and activities to be done today! (list the three most important ones below - do these first and do more if you can)

1 _____
2 _____
3 _____

Book(s) to read and finish this week (you should read at least one book per week) List how many pages you will read from your book(s) today and check off when completed.

1 _____ 2 _____

What did I discover about myself today? (what worked and why):
_____
_____
_____
_____
_____

Who Are You? by Jerald Simon

| Date | # Today is **YOUR** Day! |

A **Personal Improvement Outline** for YOU.

It's okay to fall down every now and then. Just get back up!

DAILY FOCUS (main goal for the day) _____
DAILY VIRTUE (choose a virtue from the list of virtues on pg. 51) _____
DAILY BIOGRAPHY (Who did you learn about today and how has their life influenced you?)
_____

3 MICRO GOALS TO BE ACCOMPLISHED TODAY (list 3 steps, actions, or projects you can complete today toward one of the macro goals listed on pages 30 and 31)

1 _____
2 _____
3 _____

Daily to-do checklist of chores, homework and activities to be done today! (list the three most important ones below - do these first and do more if you can)

1 _____
2 _____
3 _____

Book(s) to read and finish this week (you should read at least one book per week) List how many pages you will read from your book(s) today and check off when completed.

1 _____ 2 _____

What did I discover about myself today? (what worked and why):
_____
_____
_____
_____
_____

Who Are You? by JERALD SIMON

Today is YOUR Day! ───Date───
A **Personal Improvement Outline** for YOU.

Believe in yourself — especially when others do not.

DAILY FOCUS (main goal for the day) _____
DAILY VIRTUE (choose a virtue from the list of virtues on pg. 51) _____
DAILY BIOGRAPHY (Who did you learn about today and how has their life influenced you?)
_____

3 MICRO GOALS TO BE ACCOMPLISHED TODAY (list 3 steps, actions, or projects you can complete today toward one of the macro goals listed on pages 30 and 31)

1 _____
2 _____
3 _____

Daily to-do checklist of chores, homework and activities to be done today! (list the three most important ones below - do these first and do more if you can)

1 _____
2 _____
3 _____

Book(s) to read and finish this week (you should read at least one book per week) List how many pages you will read from your book(s) today and check off when completed.

1 _____ 2 _____

What did I discover about myself today? (what worked and why):

_____
_____
_____
_____

Who Are You? by JERALD SIMON

Today is **YOUR** Day!
Date
A **Personal Improvement Outline** for YOU.

Live the life you want to live. Be who you were born to be.

DAILY FOCUS (main goal for the day) _____
DAILY VIRTUE (choose a virtue from the list of virtues on pg. 51) _____
DAILY BIOGRAPHY (Who did you learn about today and how has their life influenced you?)
_____

3 MICRO GOALS TO BE ACCOMPLISHED TODAY (list 3 steps, actions, or projects you can complete today toward one of the macro goals listed on pages 30 and 31)

1 _____
2 _____
3 _____

Daily to-do checklist of chores, homework and activities to be done today! (list the three most important ones below - do these first and do more if you can)

1 _____
2 _____
3 _____

Book(s) to read and finish this week (you should read at least one book per week) List how many pages you will read from your book(s) today and check off when completed.

1 _____ 2 _____

What did I discover about myself today? (what worked and why):
_____
_____
_____
_____
_____

Who Are You? by Jerald Simon

Today is YOUR Day!   ⎯⎯ Date

A **Personal Improvement Outline** for YOU.

Be hopeful. Be helpful. BE HAPPY!

DAILY FOCUS (main goal for the day) _____
DAILY VIRTUE (choose a virtue from the list of virtues on pg. 51) _____
DAILY BIOGRAPHY (Who did you learn about today and how has their life influenced you?)
_____

3 MICRO GOALS TO BE ACCOMPLISHED TODAY (list 3 steps, actions, or projects you can complete today toward one of the macro goals listed on pages 30 and 31)

1 _____
2 _____
3 _____

Daily to-do checklist of chores, homework and activities to be done today! (list the three most important ones below - do these first and do more if you can)

1 _____
2 _____
3 _____

Book(s) to read and finish this week (you should read at least one book per week) List how many pages you will read from your book(s) today and check off when completed.

1 _____ 2 _____

What did I discover about myself today? (what worked and why):
_____
_____
_____
_____
_____

Who Are You? by JERALD SIMON

Today is YOUR Day!
Date

A **Personal Improvement Outline** for YOU.

Don't let life slip by you because you're asleep at the wheel.

DAILY FOCUS (main goal for the day) _____
DAILY VIRTUE (choose a virtue from the list of virtues on pg. 51) _____
DAILY BIOGRAPHY (Who did you learn about today and how has their life influenced you?)
_____

3 MICRO GOALS TO BE ACCOMPLISHED TODAY (list 3 steps, actions, or projects you can complete today toward one of the macro goals listed on pages 30 and 31)

1. _____
2. _____
3. _____

Daily to-do checklist of chores, homework and activities to be done today! (list the three most important ones below - do these first and do more if you can)

1. _____
2. _____
3. _____

Book(s) to read and finish this week (you should read at least one book per week) List how many pages you will read from your book(s) today and check off when completed.

1. _____   2. _____

What did I discover about myself today? (what worked and why):
_____
_____
_____
_____
_____

Who Are You? by JERALD SIMON

Today is YOUR Day! ___Date___
A **Personal Improvement Outline** for YOU.

STOP and smell the flowers today.

DAILY FOCUS (main goal for the day) _____

DAILY VIRTUE (choose a virtue from the list of virtues on pg. 51) _____

DAILY BIOGRAPHY (Who did you learn about today and how has their life influenced you?)

_____

3 MICRO GOALS TO BE ACCOMPLISHED TODAY (list 3 steps, actions, or projects you can complete today toward one of the macro goals listed on pages 30 and 31)

1 _____
2 _____
3 _____

Daily to-do checklist of chores, homework and activities to be done today! (list the three most important ones below - do these first and do more if you can)

1 _____
2 _____
3 _____

Book(s) to read and finish this week (you should read at least one book per week) List how many pages you will read from your book(s) today and check off when completed.

1 _____ 2 _____

What did I discover about myself today? (what worked and why):

_____
_____
_____
_____
_____

Who Are You? by Jerald Simon

Date _____

Today is YOUR Day!
A **Personal Improvement Outline** for YOU.

Lie down on the grass and look up at the clouds today.

DAILY FOCUS (main goal for the day) _____
DAILY VIRTUE (choose a virtue from the list of virtues on pg. 51) _____
DAILY BIOGRAPHY (Who did you learn about today and how has their life influenced you?)
_____

3 MICRO GOALS TO BE ACCOMPLISHED TODAY (list 3 steps, actions, or projects you can complete today toward one of the macro goals listed on pages 30 and 31)

1 _____
2 _____
3 _____

Daily to-do checklist of chores, homework and activities to be done today! (list the three most important ones below - do these first and do more if you can)

1 _____
2 _____
3 _____

Book(s) to read and finish this week (you should read at least one book per week) List how many pages you will read from your book(s) today and check off when completed.

1 _____ 2 _____

What did I discover about myself today? (what worked and why):

_____
_____
_____
_____
_____

Who Are You? by JERALD SIMON

Today is YOUR Day!   ——— Date ———
A **Personal Improvement Outline** for YOU.

Learn survival skills today. Could you survive in the wilderness?

DAILY FOCUS (main goal for the day) _____

DAILY VIRTUE (choose a virtue from the list of virtues on pg. 51) _____

DAILY BIOGRAPHY (Who did you learn about today and how has their life influenced you?)
_____

3 MICRO GOALS TO BE ACCOMPLISHED TODAY (list 3 steps, actions, or projects you can complete today toward one of the macro goals listed on pages 30 and 31)

1 _____
2 _____
3 _____

Daily to-do checklist of chores, homework and activities to be done today!
(list the three most important ones below - do these first and do more if you can)

1 _____
2 _____
3 _____

Book(s) to read and finish this week
(you should read at least one book per week) List how many pages you will read from your book(s) today and check off when completed.

1 _____   2 _____

What did I discover about myself today? (what worked and why):
_____
_____
_____
_____
_____

Who Are You? by Jerald Simon

Date _____

Today is **YOUR** Day!
A **Personal Improvement Outline** for YOU.

Work on your personal and family budget today.

DAILY FOCUS (main goal for the day) _____
DAILY VIRTUE (choose a virtue from the list of virtues on pg. 51) _____
DAILY BIOGRAPHY (Who did you learn about today and how has their life influenced you?)
_____

3 MICRO GOALS TO BE ACCOMPLISHED TODAY (list 3 steps, actions, or projects you can complete today toward one of the macro goals listed on pages 30 and 31)

1 _____
2 _____
3 _____

Daily to-do checklist of chores, homework and activities to be done today! (list the three most important ones below - do these first and do more if you can)

1 _____
2 _____
3 _____

Book(s) to read and finish this week (you should read at least one book per week) List how many pages you will read from your book(s) today and check off when completed.

1 _____ 2 _____

What did I discover about myself today? (what worked and why):

_____
_____
_____
_____

Who Are You? by JERALD SIMON

Today is YOUR Day! _____Date
A **Personal Improvement Outline** for YOU.

Learn to use a pocket knife today. Carve something with it.

DAILY FOCUS (main goal for the day) _____
DAILY VIRTUE (choose a virtue from the list of virtues on pg. 51) _____
DAILY BIOGRAPHY (Who did you learn about today and how has their life influenced you?)
_____

3 MICRO GOALS TO BE ACCOMPLISHED TODAY (list 3 steps, actions, or projects you can complete today toward one of the macro goals listed on pages 30 and 31)

1 _____
2 _____
3 _____

Daily to-do checklist of chores, homework and activities to be done today! (list the three most important ones below - do these first and do more if you can)

1 _____
2 _____
3 _____

Book(s) to read and finish this week (you should read at least one book per week) List how many pages you will read from your book(s) today and check off when completed.

1 _____ 2 _____

What did I discover about myself today? (what worked and why):
_____
_____
_____
_____
_____

Who Are You? by Jerald Simon

Today is YOUR Day!
Date

A **Personal Improvement Outline** for YOU.

Be part of the solution and not part of the problem.

DAILY FOCUS (main goal for the day) _____

DAILY VIRTUE (choose a virtue from the list of virtues on pg. 51) _____

DAILY BIOGRAPHY (Who did you learn about today and how has their life influenced you?)
_____

3 MICRO GOALS TO BE ACCOMPLISHED TODAY (list 3 steps, actions, or projects you can complete today toward one of the macro goals listed on pages 30 and 31)

1. _____
2. _____
3. _____

Daily to-do checklist of chores, homework and activities to be done today! (list the three most important ones below - do these first and do more if you can)

1. _____
2. _____
3. _____

Book(s) to read and finish this week (you should read at least one book per week) List how many pages you will read from your book(s) today and check off when completed.

1. _____ 2. _____

What did I discover about myself today? (what worked and why):

_____
_____
_____
_____

Who Are You? by JERALD SIMON

Today is YOUR Day! _____
Date

A **Personal Improvement Outline** for YOU.

How can you help the members of your family today?

DAILY FOCUS (main goal for the day) _____

DAILY VIRTUE (choose a virtue from the list of virtues on pg. 51) _____

DAILY BIOGRAPHY (Who did you learn about today and how has their life influenced you?)
_____

3 MICRO GOALS TO BE ACCOMPLISHED TODAY (list 3 steps, actions, or projects you can complete today toward one of the macro goals listed on pages 30 and 31)

1 _____
2 _____
3 _____

Daily to-do checklist of chores, homework and activities to be done today! (list the three most important ones below - do these first and do more if you can)

1 _____
2 _____
3 _____

Book(s) to read and finish this week (you should read at least one book per week) List how many pages you will read from your book(s) today and check off when completed.

1 _____ 2 _____

What did I discover about myself today? (what worked and why):
_____
_____
_____
_____
_____

Who Are You? by Jerald Simon

___Date___ # Today is YOUR Day!
A Personal Improvement Outline for YOU.

Learn about woodworking today.

DAILY FOCUS (main goal for the day) _____
DAILY VIRTUE (choose a virtue from the list of virtues on pg. 51) _____
DAILY BIOGRAPHY (Who did you learn about today and how has their life influenced you?)
_____

3 MICRO GOALS TO BE ACCOMPLISHED TODAY (list 3 steps, actions, or projects you can complete today toward one of the macro goals listed on pages 30 and 31)

1. _____
2. _____
3. _____

Daily to-do checklist of chores, homework and activities to be done today! (list the three most important ones below - do these first and do more if you can)

1. _____
2. _____
3. _____

Book(s) to read and finish this week (you should read at least one book per week) List how many pages you will read from your book(s) today and check off when completed.

1. _____ 2. _____

What did I discover about myself today? (what worked and why):
_____
_____
_____
_____
_____

Who Are You? by JERALD SIMON

Today is YOUR Day! Date
A **Personal Improvement Outline** for YOU.

Choose a favorite author and learn everything about them.

DAILY FOCUS (main goal for the day) _____
DAILY VIRTUE (choose a virtue from the list of virtues on pg. 51) _____
DAILY BIOGRAPHY (Who did you learn about today and how has their life influenced you?)
_____

3 MICRO GOALS TO BE ACCOMPLISHED TODAY (list 3 steps, actions, or projects you can complete today toward one of the macro goals listed on pages 30 and 31)

1 _____
2 _____
3 _____

Daily to-do checklist of chores, homework and activities to be done today! (list the three most important ones below - do these first and do more if you can)

1 _____
2 _____
3 _____

Book(s) to read and finish this week (you should read at least one book per week) List how many pages you will read from your book(s) today and check off when completed.

1 _____ 2 _____

What did I discover about myself today? (what worked and why):
_____
_____
_____
_____
_____

Who Are You? by JERALD SIMON

Date _____

Today is YOUR Day!
A **Personal Improvement Outline** for YOU.

Finger paint today.

DAILY FOCUS (main goal for the day) _____
DAILY VIRTUE (choose a virtue from the list of virtues on pg. 51) _____
DAILY BIOGRAPHY (Who did you learn about today and how has their life influenced you?)
_____

3 MICRO GOALS TO BE ACCOMPLISHED TODAY (list 3 steps, actions, or projects you can complete today toward one of the macro goals listed on pages 30 and 31)

1 _____
2 _____
3 _____

Daily to-do checklist of chores, homework and activities to be done today! (list the three most important ones below - do these first and do more if you can)

1 _____
2 _____
3 _____

Book(s) to read and finish this week (you should read at least one book per week) List how many pages you will read from your book(s) today and check off when completed.

1 _____ 2 _____

What did I discover about myself today? (what worked and why):
_____
_____
_____
_____

Who Are You? by JERALD SIMON

Today is YOUR Day!
Date

A **Personal Improvement Outline** for YOU.

Be patient but persistent.

DAILY FOCUS (main goal for the day) _____

DAILY VIRTUE (choose a virtue from the list of virtues on pg. 51) _____

DAILY BIOGRAPHY (Who did you learn about today and how has their life influenced you?)
_____

3 MICRO GOALS TO BE ACCOMPLISHED TODAY (list 3 steps, actions, or projects you can complete today toward one of the macro goals listed on pages 30 and 31)

1 _____
2 _____
3 _____

Daily to-do checklist of chores, homework and activities to be done today! (list the three most important ones below - do these first and do more if you can)

1 _____
2 _____
3 _____

Book(s) to read and finish this week (you should read at least one book per week) List how many pages you will read from your book(s) today and check off when completed.

1 _____ 2 _____

What did I discover about myself today? (what worked and why):
_____
_____
_____
_____
_____

Who Are You? by Jerald Simon

<u>   Date   </u> # Today is YOUR Day!
A **Personal Improvement Outline** for YOU.

Focus on self control today.

DAILY FOCUS (main goal for the day) _____
DAILY VIRTUE (choose a virtue from the list of virtues on pg. 51) _____
DAILY BIOGRAPHY (Who did you learn about today and how has their life influenced you?)
_____

3 MICRO GOALS TO BE ACCOMPLISHED TODAY (list 3 steps, actions, or projects you can complete today toward one of the macro goals listed on pages 30 and 31)

1 _____
2 _____
3 _____

Daily to-do checklist of chores, homework and activities to be done today! (list the three most important ones below - do these first and do more if you can)

1 _____
2 _____
3 _____

Book(s) to read and finish this week (you should read at least one book per week) List how many pages you will read from your book(s) today and check off when completed.

1 _____ 2 _____

What did I discover about myself today? (what worked and why):
_____
_____
_____
_____
_____

Who Are You? by Jerald Simon

Today is YOUR Day! _____ Date
A **Personal Improvement Outline** for YOU.

If you feel depressed or sad, help someone else. Serve today.

DAILY FOCUS (main goal for the day) _____

DAILY VIRTUE (choose a virtue from the list of virtues on pg. 51) _____

DAILY BIOGRAPHY (Who did you learn about today and how has their life influenced you?)
_____

3 MICRO GOALS TO BE ACCOMPLISHED TODAY (list 3 steps, actions, or projects you can complete today toward one of the macro goals listed on pages 30 and 31)

1 _____
2 _____
3 _____

Daily to-do checklist of chores, homework and activities to be done today! (list the three most important ones below - do these first and do more if you can)

1 _____
2 _____
3 _____

Book(s) to read and finish this week (you should read at least one book per week) List how many pages you will read from your book(s) today and check off when completed.

1 _____ 2 _____

What did I discover about myself today? (what worked and why):
_____
_____
_____
_____
_____

Who Are You? by Jerald Simon

Date _____

Today is YOUR Day!
A **Personal Improvement Outline** for YOU.

If you haven't already, create an exercise regime and follow it.

DAILY FOCUS (main goal for the day) _____
DAILY VIRTUE (choose a virtue from the list of virtues on pg. 51) _____
DAILY BIOGRAPHY (Who did you learn about today and how has their life influenced you?)
_____

3 MICRO GOALS TO BE ACCOMPLISHED TODAY (list 3 steps, actions, or projects you can complete today toward one of the macro goals listed on pages 30 and 31)

1 _____
2 _____
3 _____

Daily to-do checklist of chores, homework and activities to be done today! (list the three most important ones below - do these first and do more if you can)

1 _____
2 _____
3 _____

Book(s) to read and finish this week (you should read at least one book per week) List how many pages you will read from your book(s) today and check off when completed.

1 _____ 2 _____

What did I discover about myself today? (what worked and why):
_____
_____
_____
_____
_____

Who Are You? by JERALD SIMON

Today is YOUR Day! — Date —
A **Personal Improvement Outline** for YOU.

Look up today. The sky has many secrets to share.

DAILY FOCUS (main goal for the day) _____

DAILY VIRTUE (choose a virtue from the list of virtues on pg. 51) _____

DAILY BIOGRAPHY (Who did you learn about today and how has their life influenced you?)
_____

3 MICRO GOALS TO BE ACCOMPLISHED TODAY (list 3 steps, actions, or projects you can complete today toward one of the macro goals listed on pages 30 and 31)

1 _____
2 _____
3 _____

Daily to-do checklist of chores, homework and activities to be done today! (list the three most important ones below - do these first and do more if you can)

1 _____
2 _____
3 _____

Book(s) to read and finish this week (you should read at least one book per week) List how many pages you will read from your book(s) today and check off when completed.

1 _____ 2 _____

What did I discover about myself today? (what worked and why):
_____
_____
_____
_____
_____

Who Are You? by JERALD SIMON

_____Date_____ # Today is **YOUR** Day!
A **Personal Improvement Outline** for YOU.

Clean the entire house today. It's a good feeling!

DAILY FOCUS (main goal for the day) _____
DAILY VIRTUE (choose a virtue from the list of virtues on pg. 51) _____
DAILY BIOGRAPHY (Who did you learn about today and how has their life influenced you?)
_____

3 MICRO GOALS TO BE ACCOMPLISHED TODAY (list 3 steps, actions, or projects you can complete today toward one of the macro goals listed on pages 30 and 31)

1. _____
2. _____
3. _____

Daily to-do checklist of chores, homework and activities to be done today! (list the three most important ones below - do these first and do more if you can)

1. _____
2. _____
3. _____

Book(s) to read and finish this week (you should read at least one book per week) List how many pages you will read from your book(s) today and check off when completed.

1. _____ 2. _____

What did I discover about myself today? (what worked and why):
_____
_____
_____
_____
_____

Who Are You? by Jerald Simon

Today is YOUR Day!   ___Date___
A **Personal Improvement Outline** for YOU.

Life is wonderful!

DAILY FOCUS (main goal for the day) _____

DAILY VIRTUE (choose a virtue from the list of virtues on pg. 51) _____

DAILY BIOGRAPHY (Who did you learn about today and how has their life influenced you?)
_____

3 MICRO GOALS TO BE ACCOMPLISHED TODAY (list 3 steps, actions, or projects you can complete today toward one of the macro goals listed on pages 30 and 31)

1 _____
2 _____
3 _____

Daily to-do checklist of chores, homework and activities to be done today! (list the three most important ones below - do these first and do more if you can)

1 _____
2 _____
3 _____

Book(s) to read and finish this week (you should read at least one book per week) List how many pages you will read from your book(s) today and check off when completed.

1 _____ 2 _____

What did I discover about myself today? (what worked and why):

_____
_____
_____
_____
_____

Who Are You? by Jerald Simon

Date	# Today is **YOUR** Day!

A **Personal Improvement Outline** for YOU.

Take an old appliance apart and see what's inside.

DAILY FOCUS (main goal for the day) _____
DAILY VIRTUE (choose a virtue from the list of virtues on pg. 51) _____
DAILY BIOGRAPHY (Who did you learn about today and how has their life influenced you?)
_____

3 MICRO GOALS TO BE ACCOMPLISHED TODAY (list 3 steps, actions, or projects you can complete today toward one of the macro goals listed on pages 30 and 31)

1. _____
2. _____
3. _____

Daily to-do checklist of chores, homework and activities to be done today! (list the three most important ones below - do these first and do more if you can)

1. _____
2. _____
3. _____

Book(s) to read and finish this week (you should read at least one book per week) List how many pages you will read from your book(s) today and check off when completed.

1. _____ 2. _____

What did I discover about myself today? (what worked and why):

_____
_____
_____
_____

Who Are You? by JERALD SIMON

Today is YOUR Day!   _{Date}
A **Personal Improvement Outline** for YOU.

Make a new friend today.

DAILY FOCUS (main goal for the day) _____

DAILY VIRTUE (choose a virtue from the list of virtues on pg. 51) _____

DAILY BIOGRAPHY (Who did you learn about today and how has their life influenced you?)
_____

3 MICRO GOALS TO BE ACCOMPLISHED TODAY (list 3 steps, actions, or projects you can complete today toward one of the macro goals listed on pages 30 and 31)

1 _____
2 _____
3 _____

Daily to-do checklist of chores, homework and activities to be done today! (list the three most important ones below - do these first and do more if you can)

1 _____
2 _____
3 _____

Book(s) to read and finish this week (you should read at least one book per week) List how many pages you will read from your book(s) today and check off when completed.

1 _____ 2 _____

What did I discover about myself today? (what worked and why):
_____
_____
_____
_____

Who Are You? by Jerald Simon

<u>Date</u>

Today is YOUR Day!
A **Personal Improvement Outline** for YOU.

Have a pillow fight today.

DAILY FOCUS (main goal for the day) _____

DAILY VIRTUE (choose a virtue from the list of virtues on pg. 51) _____

DAILY BIOGRAPHY (Who did you learn about today and how has their life influenced you?)
_____

3 MICRO GOALS TO BE ACCOMPLISHED TODAY (list 3 steps, actions, or projects you can complete today toward one of the macro goals listed on pages 30 and 31)

1 _____
2 _____
3 _____

Daily to-do checklist of chores, homework and activities to be done today! (list the three most important ones below - do these first and do more if you can)

1 _____
2 _____
3 _____

Book(s) to read and finish this week (you should read at least one book per week) List how many pages you will read from your book(s) today and check off when completed.

1 _____ 2 _____

What did I discover about myself today? (what worked and why):
_____
_____
_____
_____
_____

Who Are You? by JERALD SIMON

Today is YOUR Day!
Date

A **Personal Improvement Outline** for YOU.

Try a new vegetable today.

DAILY FOCUS (main goal for the day) _____

DAILY VIRTUE (choose a virtue from the list of virtues on pg. 51) _____

DAILY BIOGRAPHY (Who did you learn about today and how has their life influenced you?)
_____

3 MICRO GOALS TO BE ACCOMPLISHED TODAY (list 3 steps, actions, or projects you can complete today toward one of the macro goals listed on pages 30 and 31)

1 _____
2 _____
3 _____

Daily to-do checklist of chores, homework and activities to be done today!
(list the three most important ones below - do these first and do more if you can)

1 _____
2 _____
3 _____

Book(s) to read and finish this week (you should read at least one book per week) List how many pages you will read from your book(s) today and check off when completed.

1 _____ 2 _____

What did I discover about myself today? (what worked and why):
_____
_____
_____
_____
_____

Who Are You? by Jerald Simon

___Date___   # Today is **YOUR** Day!
A **Personal Improvement Outline** for YOU.

Find a new street you have never been down before and explore.

DAILY FOCUS (main goal for the day) _____
DAILY VIRTUE (choose a virtue from the list of virtues on pg. 51) _____
DAILY BIOGRAPHY (Who did you learn about today and how has their life influenced you?)
_____

3 MICRO GOALS TO BE ACCOMPLISHED TODAY (list 3 steps, actions, or projects you can complete today toward one of the macro goals listed on pages 30 and 31)

1 _____
2 _____
3 _____

Daily to-do checklist of chores, homework and activities to be done today! (list the three most important ones below - do these first and do more if you can)

1 _____
2 _____
3 _____

Book(s) to read and finish this week (you should read at least one book per week) List how many pages you will read from your book(s) today and check off when completed.

1 _____ 2 _____

What did I discover about myself today? (what worked and why):
_____
_____
_____
_____

Who Are You? by Jerald Simon

Today is YOUR Day!   _____
                          Date
A **Personal Improvement Outline** for YOU.

Go on a bike ride today.

DAILY FOCUS (main goal for the day) _____
DAILY VIRTUE (choose a virtue from the list of virtues on pg. 51) _____
DAILY BIOGRAPHY (Who did you learn about today and how has their life influenced you?)
_____

3 MICRO GOALS TO BE ACCOMPLISHED TODAY (list 3 steps, actions, or projects you can complete today toward one of the macro goals listed on pages 30 and 31)

1 _____
2 _____
3 _____

Daily to-do checklist of chores, homework and activities to be done today! (list the three most important ones below - do these first and do more if you can)

1 _____
2 _____
3 _____

Book(s) to read and finish this week (you should read at least one book per week) List how many pages you will read from your book(s) today and check off when completed.

1 _____   2 _____

What did I discover about myself today? (what worked and why):
_____
_____
_____
_____
_____

Who Are You? by Jerald Simon

___Date___   Today is **YOUR** Day!
A **Personal Improvement Outline** for YOU.

Learn about Michelangelo (the sculptor/artist).

DAILY FOCUS (main goal for the day) _____
DAILY VIRTUE (choose a virtue from the list of virtues on pg. 51) _____
DAILY BIOGRAPHY (Who did you learn about today and how has their life influenced you?)
_____

3 MICRO GOALS TO BE ACCOMPLISHED TODAY (list 3 steps, actions, or projects you can complete today toward one of the macro goals listed on pages 30 and 31)

1 _____
2 _____
3 _____

Daily to-do checklist of chores, homework and activities to be done today! (list the three most important ones below - do these first and do more if you can)

1 _____
2 _____
3 _____

Book(s) to read and finish this week (you should read at least one book per week) List how many pages you will read from your book(s) today and check off when completed.

1 _____ 2 _____

What did I discover about myself today? (what worked and why):
_____
_____
_____
_____

Who Are You? by Jerald Simon

Today is YOUR Day!   ———Date———
A **Personal Improvement Outline** for YOU.

Watch fish swim in a fish tank today. It's calming.

DAILY FOCUS (main goal for the day) _____
DAILY VIRTUE (choose a virtue from the list of virtues on pg. 51) _____
DAILY BIOGRAPHY (Who did you learn about today and how has their life influenced you?)
_____

3 MICRO GOALS TO BE ACCOMPLISHED TODAY (list 3 steps, actions, or projects you can complete today toward one of the macro goals listed on pages 30 and 31)

1 _____
2 _____
3 _____

Daily to-do checklist of chores, homework and activities to be done today! (list the three most important ones below - do these first and do more if you can)

1 _____
2 _____
3 _____

Book(s) to read and finish this week (you should read at least one book per week) List how many pages you will read from your book(s) today and check off when completed.

1 _____ 2 _____

What did I discover about myself today? (what worked and why):
_____
_____
_____
_____
_____

Who Are You? by JERALD SIMON

Date _____ # Today is **YOUR** Day!
A **Personal Improvement Outline** for YOU.

What would you change about yourself, if you could?

DAILY FOCUS (main goal for the day) _____
DAILY VIRTUE (choose a virtue from the list of virtues on pg. 51) _____
DAILY BIOGRAPHY (Who did you learn about today and how has their life influenced you?)
_____

3 MICRO GOALS TO BE ACCOMPLISHED TODAY (list 3 steps, actions, or projects you can complete today toward one of the macro goals listed on pages 30 and 31)

1 _____
2 _____
3 _____

Daily to-do checklist of chores, homework and activities to be done today! (list the three most important ones below - do these first and do more if you can)

1 _____
2 _____
3 _____

Book(s) to read and finish this week (you should read at least one book per week) List how many pages you will read from your book(s) today and check off when completed.

1 _____ 2 _____

What did I discover about myself today? (what worked and why):
_____
_____
_____
_____
_____

Who Are You? by Jerald Simon

Today is YOUR Day!   <u>   </u>
                                                                                  Date

A **Personal Improvement Outline** for YOU.

Choose a street and walk down it. Pick up any trash you see.

DAILY FOCUS (main goal for the day) _____

DAILY VIRTUE (choose a virtue from the list of virtues on pg. 51) _____

DAILY BIOGRAPHY (Who did you learn about today and how has their life influenced you?)

_____

3 MICRO GOALS TO BE ACCOMPLISHED TODAY (list 3 steps, actions, or projects you can complete today toward one of the macro goals listed on pages 30 and 31)

1 _____
2 _____
3 _____

Daily to-do checklist of chores, homework and activities to be done today! (list the three most important ones below - do these first and do more if you can)

1 _____
2 _____
3 _____

Book(s) to read and finish this week (you should read at least one book per week) List how many pages you will read from your book(s) today and check off when completed.

1 _____ 2 _____

What did I discover about myself today? (what worked and why):

_____
_____
_____
_____
_____

Who Are You? by Jerald Simon

___Date___ ## Today is **YOUR** Day!
A **Personal Improvement Outline** for YOU.

Talk to a grandparent or other older friend. Learn from them.

DAILY FOCUS (main goal for the day) _____
DAILY VIRTUE (choose a virtue from the list of virtues on pg. 51) _____
DAILY BIOGRAPHY (Who did you learn about today and how has their life influenced you?)
_____

3 MICRO GOALS TO BE ACCOMPLISHED TODAY (list 3 steps, actions, or projects you can complete today toward one of the macro goals listed on pages 30 and 31)

1 _____
2 _____
3 _____

Daily to-do checklist of chores, homework and activities to be done today! (list the three most important ones below - do these first and do more if you can)

1 _____
2 _____
3 _____

Book(s) to read and finish this week (you should read at least one book per week) List how many pages you will read from your book(s) today and check off when completed.

1 _____ 2 _____

What did I discover about myself today? (what worked and why):
_____
_____
_____
_____
_____

Who Are You? by JERALD SIMON

Today is YOUR Day!   Date

A **Personal Improvement Outline** for YOU.

Go to the park and throw a frisbee today.

DAILY FOCUS (main goal for the day) _____

DAILY VIRTUE (choose a virtue from the list of virtues on pg. 51) _____

DAILY BIOGRAPHY (Who did you learn about today and how has their life influenced you?)
_____

3 MICRO GOALS TO BE ACCOMPLISHED TODAY (list 3 steps, actions, or projects you can complete today toward one of the macro goals listed on pages 30 and 31)

1 _____
2 _____
3 _____

Daily to-do checklist of chores, homework and activities to be done today! (list the three most important ones below - do these first and do more if you can)

1 _____
2 _____
3 _____

Book(s) to read and finish this week (you should read at least one book per week) List how many pages you will read from your book(s) today and check off when completed.

1 _____ 2 _____

What did I discover about myself today? (what worked and why):
_____
_____
_____
_____
_____

Who Are You? by Jerald Simon

___Date___ ## Today is YOUR Day!
A Personal Improvement Outline for YOU.

Learn how to cha-cha today. (Dance)

DAILY FOCUS (main goal for the day) _____

DAILY VIRTUE (choose a virtue from the list of virtues on pg. 51) _____

DAILY BIOGRAPHY (Who did you learn about today and how has their life influenced you?)
_____

3 MICRO GOALS TO BE ACCOMPLISHED TODAY (list 3 steps, actions, or projects you can complete today toward one of the macro goals listed on pages 30 and 31)

1 _____
2 _____
3 _____

Daily to-do checklist of chores, homework and activities to be done today! (list the three most important ones below - do these first and do more if you can)

1 _____
2 _____
3 _____

Book(s) to read and finish this week (you should read at least one book per week) List how many pages you will read from your book(s) today and check off when completed.

1 _____ 2 _____

What did I discover about myself today? (what worked and why):

_____
_____
_____
_____
_____

Who Are You? by JERALD SIMON

Today is YOUR Day!
Date

A Personal Improvement Outline for YOU.

Learn how a pencil is made.

DAILY FOCUS (main goal for the day) _____
DAILY VIRTUE (choose a virtue from the list of virtues on pg. 51) _____
DAILY BIOGRAPHY (Who did you learn about today and how has their life influenced you?)
_____

3 MICRO GOALS TO BE ACCOMPLISHED TODAY (list 3 steps, actions, or projects you can complete today toward one of the macro goals listed on pages 30 and 31)

1 _____
2 _____
3 _____

Daily to-do checklist of chores, homework and activities to be done today! (list the three most important ones below - do these first and do more if you can)

1 _____
2 _____
3 _____

Book(s) to read and finish this week (you should read at least one book per week) List how many pages you will read from your book(s) today and check off when completed.

1 _____ 2 _____

What did I discover about myself today? (what worked and why):
_____
_____
_____
_____
_____

Who Are You? by Jerald Simon

___Date___ ## Today is **YOUR** Day!
A **Personal Improvement Outline** for YOU.

Be a tourist in your town today and go exploring.

DAILY FOCUS (main goal for the day) _____

DAILY VIRTUE (choose a virtue from the list of virtues on pg. 51) _____

DAILY BIOGRAPHY (Who did you learn about today and how has their life influenced you?)
_____

3 MICRO GOALS TO BE ACCOMPLISHED TODAY (list 3 steps, actions, or projects you can complete today toward one of the macro goals listed on pages 30 and 31)

1 _____
2 _____
3 _____

Daily to-do checklist of chores, homework and activities to be done today! (list the three most important ones below - do these first and do more if you can)

1 _____
2 _____
3 _____

Book(s) to read and finish this week (you should read at least one book per week) List how many pages you will read from your book(s) today and check off when completed.

1 _____ 2 _____

What did I discover about myself today? (what worked and why):

_____
_____
_____
_____
_____

Who Are You? by JERALD SIMON

Today is YOUR Day! Date
A **Personal Improvement Outline** for YOU.

Don't ever give up on yourself!

DAILY FOCUS (main goal for the day) _____

DAILY VIRTUE (choose a virtue from the list of virtues on pg. 51) _____

DAILY BIOGRAPHY (Who did you learn about today and how has their life influenced you?)
_____

3 MICRO GOALS TO BE ACCOMPLISHED TODAY (list 3 steps, actions, or projects you can complete today toward one of the macro goals listed on pages 30 and 31)

1 _____
2 _____
3 _____

Daily to-do checklist of chores, homework and activities to be done today! (list the three most important ones below - do these first and do more if you can)

1 _____
2 _____
3 _____

Book(s) to read and finish this week (you should read at least one book per week) List how many pages you will read from your book(s) today and check off when completed.

1 _____ 2 _____

What did I discover about myself today? (what worked and why):
_____
_____
_____
_____
_____

Who Are You? by Jerald Simon

___Date___ # Today is **YOUR** Day!
A **Personal Improvement Outline** for YOU.

Be careful what you tell yourself. You will believe it and live it.

DAILY FOCUS (main goal for the day) _____
DAILY VIRTUE (choose a virtue from the list of virtues on pg. 51) _____
DAILY BIOGRAPHY (Who did you learn about today and how has their life influenced you?)
_____

3 MICRO GOALS TO BE ACCOMPLISHED TODAY (list 3 steps, actions, or projects you can complete today toward one of the macro goals listed on pages 30 and 31)

1 _____
2 _____
3 _____

Daily to-do checklist of chores, homework and activities to be done today! (list the three most important ones below - do these first and do more if you can)

1 _____
2 _____
3 _____

Book(s) to read and finish this week (you should read at least one book per week) List how many pages you will read from your book(s) today and check off when completed.

1 _____ 2 _____

What did I discover about myself today? (what worked and why):
_____
_____
_____
_____
_____

Who Are You? by JERALD SIMON

Today is YOUR Day!   Date _____

A **Personal Improvement Outline** for YOU.

Go out of your way to make a new friend today.

DAILY FOCUS (main goal for the day) _____
DAILY VIRTUE (choose a virtue from the list of virtues on pg. 51) _____
DAILY BIOGRAPHY (Who did you learn about today and how has their life influenced you?)
_____

3 MICRO GOALS TO BE ACCOMPLISHED TODAY (list 3 steps, actions, or projects you can complete today toward one of the macro goals listed on pages 30 and 31)

1 _____
2 _____
3 _____

Daily to-do checklist of chores, homework and activities to be done today! (list the three most important ones below - do these first and do more if you can)

1 _____
2 _____
3 _____

Book(s) to read and finish this week (you should read at least one book per week) List how many pages you will read from your book(s) today and check off when completed.

1 _____ 2 _____

What did I discover about myself today? (what worked and why):
_____
_____
_____
_____
_____

Who Are You? by Jerald Simon

___Date___ # Today is YOUR Day!
A Personal Improvement Outline for YOU.

Go outside today and listen as the birds sing and the bees buzz.

DAILY FOCUS (main goal for the day) _____

DAILY VIRTUE (choose a virtue from the list of virtues on pg. 51) _____

DAILY BIOGRAPHY (Who did you learn about today and how has their life influenced you?)
_____

3 MICRO GOALS TO BE ACCOMPLISHED TODAY (list 3 steps, actions, or projects you can complete today toward one of the macro goals listed on pages 30 and 31)

1. _____
2. _____
3. _____

Daily to-do checklist of chores, homework and activities to be done today! (list the three most important ones below - do these first and do more if you can)

1. _____
2. _____
3. _____

Book(s) to read and finish this week (you should read at least one book per week) List how many pages you will read from your book(s) today and check off when completed.

1. _____ 2. _____

What did I discover about myself today? (what worked and why):

_____
_____
_____
_____

Who Are You? by Jerald Simon

Today is YOUR Day!   Date
A Personal Improvement Outline for YOU.

Only listen to Baroque classical music today.

DAILY FOCUS (main goal for the day) _____
DAILY VIRTUE (choose a virtue from the list of virtues on pg. 51) _____
DAILY BIOGRAPHY (Who did you learn about today and how has their life influenced you?)
_____

3 MICRO GOALS TO BE ACCOMPLISHED TODAY (list 3 steps, actions, or projects you can complete today toward one of the macro goals listed on pages 30 and 31)

1 _____
2 _____
3 _____

Daily to-do checklist of chores, homework and activities to be done today! (list the three most important ones below - do these first and do more if you can)

1 _____
2 _____
3 _____

Book(s) to read and finish this week (you should read at least one book per week) List how many pages you will read from your book(s) today and check off when completed.

1 _____ 2 _____

What did I discover about myself today? (what worked and why):
_____
_____
_____
_____
_____

Who Are You? by Jerald Simon

<u>Date</u>

Today is YOUR Day!
A **Personal Improvement Outline** for YOU.

Study about the Romanticism period of art (1790-1800s).

DAILY FOCUS (main goal for the day) _____

DAILY VIRTUE (choose a virtue from the list of virtues on pg. 51) _____

DAILY BIOGRAPHY (Who did you learn about today and how has their life influenced you?)
_____

3 MICRO GOALS TO BE ACCOMPLISHED TODAY (list 3 steps, actions, or projects you can complete today toward one of the macro goals listed on pages 30 and 31)

1. _____
2. _____
3. _____

Daily to-do checklist of chores, homework and activities to be done today!
(list the three most important ones below - do these first and do more if you can)

1. _____
2. _____
3. _____

Book(s) to read and finish this week
(you should read at least one book per week) List how many pages you will read from your book(s) today and check off when completed.

1. _____ 2. _____

What did I discover about myself today? (what worked and why):
_____
_____
_____
_____
_____

Who Are You? by JERALD SIMON

Today is YOUR Day! _____Date

A **Personal Improvement Outline** for YOU.

Face one of your biggest fears today.

DAILY FOCUS (main goal for the day) _____

DAILY VIRTUE (choose a virtue from the list of virtues on pg. 51) _____

DAILY BIOGRAPHY (Who did you learn about today and how has their life influenced you?)
_____

3 MICRO GOALS TO BE ACCOMPLISHED TODAY (list 3 steps, actions, or projects you can complete today toward one of the macro goals listed on pages 30 and 31)

1 _____
2 _____
3 _____

Daily to-do checklist of chores, homework and activities to be done today! (list the three most important ones below - do these first and do more if you can)

1 _____
2 _____
3 _____

Book(s) to read and finish this week (you should read at least one book per week) List how many pages you will read from your book(s) today and check off when completed.

1 _____ 2 _____

What did I discover about myself today? (what worked and why):
_____
_____
_____
_____
_____

Who Are You? by Jerald Simon

___Date___ # Today is YOUR Day!
A **Personal Improvement Outline** for YOU.

Meditate for 15 minutes in the morning and 15 minutes at night.

DAILY FOCUS (main goal for the day) _____
DAILY VIRTUE (choose a virtue from the list of virtues on pg. 51) _____
DAILY BIOGRAPHY (Who did you learn about today and how has their life influenced you?)
_____

3 MICRO GOALS TO BE ACCOMPLISHED TODAY (list 3 steps, actions, or projects you can complete today toward one of the macro goals listed on pages 30 and 31)

1 _____
2 _____
3 _____

Daily to-do checklist of chores, homework and activities to be done today! (list the three most important ones below - do these first and do more if you can)

1 _____
2 _____
3 _____

Book(s) to read and finish this week (you should read at least one book per week) List how many pages you will read from your book(s) today and check off when completed.

1 _____ 2 _____

What did I discover about myself today? (what worked and why):
_____
_____
_____
_____

Who Are You? by Jerald Simon

Today is YOUR Day!   _Date_
A **Personal Improvement Outline** for YOU.

You may feel discouraged. That is okay. Know you are not alone.

DAILY FOCUS (main goal for the day) _____

DAILY VIRTUE (choose a virtue from the list of virtues on pg. 51) _____

DAILY BIOGRAPHY (Who did you learn about today and how has their life influenced you?)
_____

3 MICRO GOALS TO BE ACCOMPLISHED TODAY (list 3 steps, actions, or projects you can complete today toward one of the macro goals listed on pages 30 and 31)

1 _____
2 _____
3 _____

Daily to-do checklist of chores, homework and activities to be done today! (list the three most important ones below - do these first and do more if you can)

1 _____
2 _____
3 _____

Book(s) to read and finish this week (you should read at least one book per week) List how many pages you will read from your book(s) today and check off when completed.

1 _____ 2 _____

What did I discover about myself today? (what worked and why):
_____
_____
_____
_____
_____

Who Are You? by Jerald Simon

Date _____

Today is YOUR Day!

A **Personal Improvement Outline** for YOU.

What do you want to do with your life?

DAILY FOCUS (main goal for the day) _____
DAILY VIRTUE (choose a virtue from the list of virtues on pg. 51) _____
DAILY BIOGRAPHY (Who did you learn about today and how has their life influenced you?)
_____

3 MICRO GOALS TO BE ACCOMPLISHED TODAY (list 3 steps, actions, or projects you can complete today toward one of the macro goals listed on pages 30 and 31)

1 _____
2 _____
3 _____

Daily to-do checklist of chores, homework and activities to be done today! (list the three most important ones below - do these first and do more if you can)

1 _____
2 _____
3 _____

Book(s) to read and finish this week (you should read at least one book per week) List how many pages you will read from your book(s) today and check off when completed.

1 _____ 2 _____

What did I discover about myself today? (what worked and why):

_____
_____
_____
_____
_____

Who Are You? by Jerald Simon

Today is YOUR Day! ___Date___
A **Personal Improvement Outline** for YOU.

Build a model car, airplane, or train today.

DAILY FOCUS (main goal for the day) _____
DAILY VIRTUE (choose a virtue from the list of virtues on pg. 51) _____
DAILY BIOGRAPHY (Who did you learn about today and how has their life influenced you?)
_____

3 MICRO GOALS TO BE ACCOMPLISHED TODAY (list 3 steps, actions, or projects you can complete today toward one of the macro goals listed on pages 30 and 31)

1 _____
2 _____
3 _____

Daily to-do checklist of chores, homework and activities to be done today! (list the three most important ones below - do these first and do more if you can)

1 _____
2 _____
3 _____

Book(s) to read and finish this week (you should read at least one book per week) List how many pages you will read from your book(s) today and check off when completed.

1 _____ 2 _____

What did I discover about myself today? (what worked and why):
_____
_____
_____
_____
_____

Who Are You? by JERALD SIMON

<u>   Date   </u> # Today is **YOUR** Day!
A **Personal Improvement Outline** for YOU.

Write down the feelings you are having right now.

DAILY FOCUS (main goal for the day) _____
DAILY VIRTUE (choose a virtue from the list of virtues on pg. 51) _____
DAILY BIOGRAPHY (Who did you learn about today and how has their life influenced you?)
_____

3 MICRO GOALS TO BE ACCOMPLISHED TODAY (list 3 steps, actions, or projects you can complete today toward one of the macro goals listed on pages 30 and 31)

1 _____
2 _____
3 _____

Daily to-do checklist of chores, homework and activities to be done today! (list the three most important ones below - do these first and do more if you can)

1 _____
2 _____
3 _____

Book(s) to read and finish this week (you should read at least one book per week) List how many pages you will read from your book(s) today and check off when completed.

1 _____ 2 _____

What did I discover about myself today? (what worked and why):
_____
_____
_____
_____

Who Are You? by Jerald Simon

Today is YOUR Day!

Date

A **Personal Improvement Outline** for YOU.

Create a list of 100+ places you would like to visit in your life.

DAILY FOCUS (main goal for the day) _____

DAILY VIRTUE (choose a virtue from the list of virtues on pg. 51) _____

DAILY BIOGRAPHY (Who did you learn about today and how has their life influenced you?)

_____

3 MICRO GOALS TO BE ACCOMPLISHED TODAY (list 3 steps, actions, or projects you can complete today toward one of the macro goals listed on pages 30 and 31)

1 _____
2 _____
3 _____

Daily to-do checklist of chores, homework and activities to be done today! (list the three most important ones below - do these first and do more if you can)

1 _____
2 _____
3 _____

Book(s) to read and finish this week (you should read at least one book per week) List how many pages you will read from your book(s) today and check off when completed.

1 _____ 2 _____

What did I discover about myself today? (what worked and why):

_____
_____
_____
_____
_____

Who Are You? by Jerald Simon

___Date___ # Today is **YOUR** Day!
A **Personal Improvement Outline** for YOU.

Learn to whistle today if you don't know how.

DAILY FOCUS (main goal for the day) _____
DAILY VIRTUE (choose a virtue from the list of virtues on pg. 51) _____
DAILY BIOGRAPHY (Who did you learn about today and how has their life influenced you?)
_____

3 MICRO GOALS TO BE ACCOMPLISHED TODAY (list 3 steps, actions, or projects you can complete today toward one of the macro goals listed on pages 30 and 31)

1 _____
2 _____
3 _____

Daily to-do checklist of chores, homework and activities to be done today! (list the three most important ones below - do these first and do more if you can)

1 _____
2 _____
3 _____

Book(s) to read and finish this week (you should read at least one book per week) List how many pages you will read from your book(s) today and check off when completed.

1 _____ 2 _____

What did I discover about myself today? (what worked and why):

_____
_____
_____
_____
_____

Who Are You? by Jerald Simon

Today is YOUR Day! ___Date___
A **Personal Improvement Outline** for YOU.

Start studying about great lost civilizations (Incas, Easter Islands, etc.)

DAILY FOCUS (main goal for the day) _____
DAILY VIRTUE (choose a virtue from the list of virtues on pg. 51) _____
DAILY BIOGRAPHY (Who did you learn about today and how has their life influenced you?)
_____

3 MICRO GOALS TO BE ACCOMPLISHED TODAY (list 3 steps, actions, or projects you can complete today toward one of the macro goals listed on pages 30 and 31)

1 _____
2 _____
3 _____

Daily to-do checklist of chores, homework and activities to be done today! (list the three most important ones below - do these first and do more if you can)

1 _____
2 _____
3 _____

Book(s) to read and finish this week (you should read at least one book per week) List how many pages you will read from your book(s) today and check off when completed.

1 _____ 2 _____

What did I discover about myself today? (what worked and why):
_____
_____
_____
_____
_____

Who Are You? by Jerald Simon

___Date___ ## Today is **YOUR** Day!
A **Personal Improvement Outline** for YOU.

Focus on what you'd like to accomplish today. Only today!

DAILY FOCUS (main goal for the day) _____
DAILY VIRTUE (choose a virtue from the list of virtues on pg. 51) _____
DAILY BIOGRAPHY (Who did you learn about today and how has their life influenced you?)
_____

3 MICRO GOALS TO BE ACCOMPLISHED TODAY (list 3 steps, actions, or projects you can complete today toward one of the macro goals listed on pages 30 and 31)

1 _____
2 _____
3 _____

Daily to-do checklist of chores, homework and activities to be done today! (list the three most important ones below - do these first and do more if you can)

1 _____
2 _____
3 _____

Book(s) to read and finish this week (you should read at least one book per week) List how many pages you will read from your book(s) today and check off when completed.

1 _____ 2 _____

What did I discover about myself today? (what worked and why):
_____
_____
_____
_____

Who Are You? by JERALD SIMON

Today is YOUR Day! ___Date___
A **Personal Improvement Outline** for YOU.

Go to bed early and get up early. Get 8 hours of sleep.

DAILY FOCUS (main goal for the day) _____

DAILY VIRTUE (choose a virtue from the list of virtues on pg. 51) _____

DAILY BIOGRAPHY (Who did you learn about today and how has their life influenced you?)
_____

3 MICRO GOALS TO BE ACCOMPLISHED TODAY (list 3 steps, actions, or projects you can complete today toward one of the macro goals listed on pages 30 and 31)

1 _____
2 _____
3 _____

Daily to-do checklist of chores, homework and activities to be done today! (list the three most important ones below - do these first and do more if you can)

1 _____
2 _____
3 _____

Book(s) to read and finish this week (you should read at least one book per week) List how many pages you will read from your book(s) today and check off when completed.

1 _____ 2 _____

What did I discover about myself today? (what worked and why):
_____
_____
_____
_____
_____

Who Are You? by Jerald Simon

___Date___ ## Today is **YOUR** Day!
A **Personal Improvement Outline** for YOU.

Spend one hour today pretending you are blind. What happens?

DAILY FOCUS (main goal for the day) _____
DAILY VIRTUE (choose a virtue from the list of virtues on pg. 51) _____
DAILY BIOGRAPHY (Who did you learn about today and how has their life influenced you?)
_____

3 MICRO GOALS TO BE ACCOMPLISHED TODAY (list 3 steps, actions, or projects you can complete today toward one of the macro goals listed on pages 30 and 31)

1 _____
2 _____
3 _____

Daily to-do checklist of chores, homework and activities to be done today! (list the three most important ones below - do these first and do more if you can)

1 _____
2 _____
3 _____

Book(s) to read and finish this week (you should read at least one book per week) List how many pages you will read from your book(s) today and check off when completed.

1 _____ 2 _____

What did I discover about myself today? (what worked and why):
_____
_____
_____
_____

Who Are You? by JERALD SIMON

Today is YOUR Day!   ──Date──
A **Personal Improvement Outline** for YOU.

Drink 8 full glasses of water today. Water is wonderful!

DAILY FOCUS (main goal for the day) _____

DAILY VIRTUE (choose a virtue from the list of virtues on pg. 51) _____

DAILY BIOGRAPHY (Who did you learn about today and how has their life influenced you?)
_____

3 MICRO GOALS TO BE ACCOMPLISHED TODAY (list 3 steps, actions, or projects you can complete today toward one of the macro goals listed on pages 30 and 31)

1 _____
2 _____
3 _____

Daily to-do checklist of chores, homework and activities to be done today! (list the three most important ones below - do these first and do more if you can)

1 _____
2 _____
3 _____

Book(s) to read and finish this week (you should read at least one book per week) List how many pages you will read from your book(s) today and check off when completed.

1 _____ 2 _____

What did I discover about myself today? (what worked and why):
_____
_____
_____
_____
_____

Who Are You? by Jerald Simon

___Date___ ## Today is **YOUR** Day!
A **Personal Improvement Outline** for YOU.

Put yourself in someone else's shoes and see the world anew.

DAILY FOCUS (main goal for the day) _____
DAILY VIRTUE (choose a virtue from the list of virtues on pg. 51) _____
DAILY BIOGRAPHY (Who did you learn about today and how has their life influenced you?)
_____

3 MICRO GOALS TO BE ACCOMPLISHED TODAY (list 3 steps, actions, or projects you can complete today toward one of the macro goals listed on pages 30 and 31)

1 _____
2 _____
3 _____

Daily to-do checklist of chores, homework and activities to be done today! (list the three most important ones below - do these first and do more if you can)

1 _____
2 _____
3 _____

Book(s) to read and finish this week (you should read at least one book per week) List how many pages you will read from your book(s) today and check off when completed.

1 _____ 2 _____

What did I discover about myself today? (what worked and why):

_____
_____
_____
_____

Who Are You? by Jerald Simon

Today is YOUR Day! ⎯⎯Date⎯⎯
A **Personal Improvement Outline** for YOU.

Do nothing today (or as little as possible). Relax. Enjoy it!

DAILY FOCUS (main goal for the day) _____
DAILY VIRTUE (choose a virtue from the list of virtues on pg. 51) _____
DAILY BIOGRAPHY (Who did you learn about today and how has their life influenced you?)
_____

3 MICRO GOALS TO BE ACCOMPLISHED TODAY (list 3 steps, actions, or projects you can complete today toward one of the macro goals listed on pages 30 and 31)

1 _____
2 _____
3 _____

Daily to-do checklist of chores, homework and activities to be done today! (list the three most important ones below - do these first and do more if you can)

1 _____
2 _____
3 _____

Book(s) to read and finish this week (you should read at least one book per week) List how many pages you will read from your book(s) today and check off when completed.

1 _____ 2 _____

What did I discover about myself today? (what worked and why):
_____
_____
_____
_____
_____

Who Are You? by Jerald Simon

_____Date_____ # Today is **YOUR** Day!
A **Personal Improvement Outline** for YOU.

Never give up on your dreams!

DAILY FOCUS (main goal for the day) _____
DAILY VIRTUE (choose a virtue from the list of virtues on pg. 51) _____
DAILY BIOGRAPHY (Who did you learn about today and how has their life influenced you?)
_____

3 MICRO GOALS TO BE ACCOMPLISHED TODAY (list 3 steps, actions, or projects you can complete today toward one of the macro goals listed on pages 30 and 31)

1 _____
2 _____
3 _____

Daily to-do checklist of chores, homework and activities to be done today! (list the three most important ones below - do these first and do more if you can)

1 _____
2 _____
3 _____

Book(s) to read and finish this week (you should read at least one book per week) List how many pages you will read from your book(s) today and check off when completed.

1 _____ 2 _____

What did I discover about myself today? (what worked and why):
_____
_____
_____
_____
_____

Who Are You? by JERALD SIMON

Today is YOUR Day!
_____ Date

A **Personal Improvement Outline** for YOU.

Try to write a non-fiction book today (or at least start it).

DAILY FOCUS (main goal for the day) _____
DAILY VIRTUE (choose a virtue from the list of virtues on pg. 51) _____
DAILY BIOGRAPHY (Who did you learn about today and how has their life influenced you?)
_____

3 MICRO GOALS TO BE ACCOMPLISHED TODAY (list 3 steps, actions, or projects you can complete today toward one of the macro goals listed on pages 30 and 31)

1 _____
2 _____
3 _____

Daily to-do checklist of chores, homework and activities to be done today! (list the three most important ones below - do these first and do more if you can)

1 _____
2 _____
3 _____

Book(s) to read and finish this week (you should read at least one book per week) List how many pages you will read from your book(s) today and check off when completed.

1 _____ 2 _____

What did I discover about myself today? (what worked and why):
_____
_____
_____
_____
_____

Who Are You? by JERALD SIMON

Today is **YOUR** Day!
<u>   </u> Date

A **Personal Improvement Outline** for YOU.

Play tennis today.

DAILY FOCUS (main goal for the day) _____
DAILY VIRTUE (choose a virtue from the list of virtues on pg. 51) _____
DAILY BIOGRAPHY (Who did you learn about today and how has their life influenced you?)
_____

3 MICRO GOALS TO BE ACCOMPLISHED TODAY (list 3 steps, actions, or projects you can complete today toward one of the macro goals listed on pages 30 and 31)

1 _____
2 _____
3 _____

Daily to-do checklist of chores, homework and activities to be done today! (list the three most important ones below - do these first and do more if you can)

1 _____
2 _____
3 _____

Book(s) to read and finish this week (you should read at least one book per week) List how many pages you will read from your book(s) today and check off when completed.

1 _____ 2 _____

What did I discover about myself today? (what worked and why):

_____
_____
_____
_____

Who Are You? by JERALD SIMON

Today is YOUR Day! ———Date———
A **Personal Improvement Outline** for YOU.

Plant a garden and grow your own vegetables and fruit.

DAILY FOCUS (main goal for the day) _____
DAILY VIRTUE (choose a virtue from the list of virtues on pg. 51) _____
DAILY BIOGRAPHY (Who did you learn about today and how has their life influenced you?)
_____

3 MICRO GOALS TO BE ACCOMPLISHED TODAY (list 3 steps, actions, or projects you can complete today toward one of the macro goals listed on pages 30 and 31)

1 _____
2 _____
3 _____

Daily to-do checklist of chores, homework and activities to be done today! (list the three most important ones below - do these first and do more if you can)

1 _____
2 _____
3 _____

Book(s) to read and finish this week (you should read at least one book per week) List how many pages you will read from your book(s) today and check off when completed.

1 _____ 2 _____

What did I discover about myself today? (what worked and why):
_____
_____
_____
_____

Who Are You? by JERALD SIMON

Date _____

Today is YOUR Day!
A **Personal Improvement Outline** for YOU.

Learn about Andrew Carnegie today.

DAILY FOCUS (main goal for the day) _____

DAILY VIRTUE (choose a virtue from the list of virtues on pg. 51) _____

DAILY BIOGRAPHY (Who did you learn about today and how has their life influenced you?)
_____

3 MICRO GOALS TO BE ACCOMPLISHED TODAY (list 3 steps, actions, or projects you can complete today toward one of the macro goals listed on pages 30 and 31)

1 _____
2 _____
3 _____

Daily to-do checklist of chores, homework and activities to be done today! (list the three most important ones below - do these first and do more if you can)

1 _____
2 _____
3 _____

Book(s) to read and finish this week (you should read at least one book per week) List how many pages you will read from your book(s) today and check off when completed.

1 _____ 2 _____

What did I discover about myself today? (what worked and why):
_____
_____
_____
_____
_____

Who Are You? by Jerald Simon

Today is YOUR Day!
Date

A **Personal Improvement Outline** for YOU.

What is the scientific method?

DAILY FOCUS (main goal for the day) _____

DAILY VIRTUE (choose a virtue from the list of virtues on pg. 51) _____

DAILY BIOGRAPHY (Who did you learn about today and how has their life influenced you?)
_____

3 MICRO GOALS TO BE ACCOMPLISHED TODAY (list 3 steps, actions, or projects you can complete today toward one of the macro goals listed on pages 30 and 31)

1 _____
2 _____
3 _____

Daily to-do checklist of chores, homework and activities to be done today! (list the three most important ones below - do these first and do more if you can)

1 _____
2 _____
3 _____

Book(s) to read and finish this week (you should read at least one book per week) List how many pages you will read from your book(s) today and check off when completed.

1 _____ 2 _____

What did I discover about myself today? (what worked and why):
_____
_____
_____
_____
_____

Who Are You? by JERALD SIMON

Date
Today is **YOUR** Day!
A **Personal Improvement Outline** for YOU.

How does the internet work? When and why was it created?

DAILY FOCUS (main goal for the day) _____
DAILY VIRTUE (choose a virtue from the list of virtues on pg. 51) _____
DAILY BIOGRAPHY (Who did you learn about today and how has their life influenced you?)
_____

3 MICRO GOALS TO BE ACCOMPLISHED TODAY (list 3 steps, actions, or projects you can complete today toward one of the macro goals listed on pages 30 and 31)

1 _____
2 _____
3 _____

Daily to-do checklist of chores, homework and activities to be done today! (list the three most important ones below - do these first and do more if you can)

1 _____
2 _____
3 _____

Book(s) to read and finish this week (you should read at least one book per week) List how many pages you will read from your book(s) today and check off when completed.

1 _____ 2 _____

What did I discover about myself today? (what worked and why):
_____
_____
_____
_____
_____

Who Are You? by Jerald Simon

Today is YOUR Day!
Date

A **Personal Improvement Outline** for YOU.

What do you fear most?

DAILY FOCUS (main goal for the day) _____
DAILY VIRTUE (choose a virtue from the list of virtues on pg. 51) _____
DAILY BIOGRAPHY (Who did you learn about today and how has their life influenced you?)
_____

3 MICRO GOALS TO BE ACCOMPLISHED TODAY (list 3 steps, actions, or projects you can complete today toward one of the macro goals listed on pages 30 and 31)

1. _____
2. _____
3. _____

Daily to-do checklist of chores, homework and activities to be done today! (list the three most important ones below - do these first and do more if you can)

1. _____
2. _____
3. _____

Book(s) to read and finish this week (you should read at least one book per week) List how many pages you will read from your book(s) today and check off when completed.

1. _____ 2. _____

What did I discover about myself today? (what worked and why):

_____
_____
_____
_____
_____

Who Are You? by JERALD SIMON

Today is **YOUR** Day!
Date

A Personal Improvement Outline for YOU.

Read something written by a spiritual leader.

DAILY FOCUS (main goal for the day) _____
DAILY VIRTUE (choose a virtue from the list of virtues on pg. 51) _____
DAILY BIOGRAPHY (Who did you learn about today and how has their life influenced you?)
_____

3 MICRO GOALS TO BE ACCOMPLISHED TODAY (list 3 steps, actions, or projects you can complete today toward one of the macro goals listed on pages 30 and 31)

1. _____
2. _____
3. _____

Daily to-do checklist of chores, homework and activities to be done today! (list the three most important ones below - do these first and do more if you can)

1. _____
2. _____
3. _____

Book(s) to read and finish this week (you should read at least one book per week) List how many pages you will read from your book(s) today and check off when completed.

1. _____ 2. _____

What did I discover about myself today? (what worked and why):

_____
_____
_____
_____

Who Are You? by Jerald Simon

Today is YOUR Day! ⎯⎯Date⎯⎯
A **Personal Improvement Outline** for YOU.

Learn about Galileo Galilei

DAILY FOCUS (main goal for the day) _____

DAILY VIRTUE (choose a virtue from the list of virtues on pg. 51) _____

DAILY BIOGRAPHY (Who did you learn about today and how has their life influenced you?)
_____

3 MICRO GOALS TO BE ACCOMPLISHED TODAY (list 3 steps, actions, or projects you can complete today toward one of the macro goals listed on pages 30 and 31)

1 _____
2 _____
3 _____

Daily to-do checklist of chores, homework and activities to be done today! (list the three most important ones below - do these first and do more if you can)

1 _____
2 _____
3 _____

Book(s) to read and finish this week (you should read at least one book per week) List how many pages you will read from your book(s) today and check off when completed.

1 _____ 2 _____

What did I discover about myself today? (what worked and why):
_____
_____
_____
_____
_____

Who Are You? by JERALD SIMON

___Date___ # Today is **YOUR** Day!
A **Personal Improvement Outline** for YOU.

Who is Democritus?

DAILY FOCUS (main goal for the day) _____
DAILY VIRTUE (choose a virtue from the list of virtues on pg. 51) _____
DAILY BIOGRAPHY (Who did you learn about today and how has their life influenced you?)
_____

3 MICRO GOALS TO BE ACCOMPLISHED TODAY (list 3 steps, actions, or projects you can complete today toward one of the macro goals listed on pages 30 and 31)

1 _____
2 _____
3 _____

Daily to-do checklist of chores, homework and activities to be done today! (list the three most important ones below - do these first and do more if you can)

1 _____
2 _____
3 _____

Book(s) to read and finish this week (you should read at least one book per week) List how many pages you will read from your book(s) today and check off when completed.

1 _____ 2 _____

What did I discover about myself today? (what worked and why):
_____
_____
_____
_____

Who Are You? by Jerald Simon

Today is YOUR Day!
Date

A **Personal Improvement Outline** for YOU.

What are your hopes and dreams for today? This month?

DAILY FOCUS (main goal for the day) _____

DAILY VIRTUE (choose a virtue from the list of virtues on pg. 51) _____

DAILY BIOGRAPHY (Who did you learn about today and how has their life influenced you?)
_____

3 MICRO GOALS TO BE ACCOMPLISHED TODAY (list 3 steps, actions, or projects you can complete today toward one of the macro goals listed on pages 30 and 31)

1 _____
2 _____
3 _____

Daily to-do checklist of chores, homework and activities to be done today! (list the three most important ones below - do these first and do more if you can)

1 _____
2 _____
3 _____

Book(s) to read and finish this week (you should read at least one book per week) List how many pages you will read from your book(s) today and check off when completed.

1 _____ 2 _____

What did I discover about myself today? (what worked and why):
_____
_____
_____
_____
_____

Who Are You? by Jerald Simon

---Date--- **Today is YOUR Day!**
A **Personal Improvement Outline** for YOU.

Study the great writings of past and present philosophers.

DAILY FOCUS (main goal for the day) _____
DAILY VIRTUE (choose a virtue from the list of virtues on pg. 51) _____
DAILY BIOGRAPHY (Who did you learn about today and how has their life influenced you?)
_____

3 MICRO GOALS TO BE ACCOMPLISHED TODAY (list 3 steps, actions, or projects you can complete today toward one of the macro goals listed on pages 30 and 31)

1 _____
2 _____
3 _____

Daily to-do checklist of chores, homework and activities to be done today! (list the three most important ones below - do these first and do more if you can)

1 _____
2 _____
3 _____

Book(s) to read and finish this week (you should read at least one book per week) List how many pages you will read from your book(s) today and check off when completed.

1 _____ 2 _____

What did I discover about myself today? (what worked and why):

_____
_____
_____
_____
_____

Who Are You? by Jerald Simon

Today is YOUR Day! ___Date___
A **Personal Improvement Outline** for YOU.

Who is Lucretius?

DAILY FOCUS (main goal for the day) _____
DAILY VIRTUE (choose a virtue from the list of virtues on pg. 51) _____
DAILY BIOGRAPHY (Who did you learn about today and how has their life influenced you?)
_____

3 MICRO GOALS TO BE ACCOMPLISHED TODAY (list 3 steps, actions, or projects you can complete today toward one of the macro goals listed on pages 30 and 31)

1 _____
2 _____
3 _____

Daily to-do checklist of chores, homework and activities to be done today! (list the three most important ones below - do these first and do more if you can)

1 _____
2 _____
3 _____

Book(s) to read and finish this week (you should read at least one book per week) List how many pages you will read from your book(s) today and check off when completed.

1 _____ 2 _____

What did I discover about myself today? (what worked and why):
_____
_____
_____
_____
_____

Who Are You? by Jerald Simon

___Date___ ## Today is **YOUR** Day!
A **Personal Improvement Outline** for YOU.

Listen to music by Frédéric François Chopin today.

DAILY FOCUS (main goal for the day) _____
DAILY VIRTUE (choose a virtue from the list of virtues on pg. 51) _____
DAILY BIOGRAPHY (Who did you learn about today and how has their life influenced you?)
_____

3 MICRO GOALS TO BE ACCOMPLISHED TODAY (list 3 steps, actions, or projects you can complete today toward one of the macro goals listed on pages 30 and 31)

1 _____
2 _____
3 _____

Daily to-do checklist of chores, homework and activities to be done today! (list the three most important ones below - do these first and do more if you can)

1 _____
2 _____
3 _____

Book(s) to read and finish this week (you should read at least one book per week) List how many pages you will read from your book(s) today and check off when completed.

1 _____ 2 _____

What did I discover about myself today? (what worked and why):
_____
_____
_____
_____

Who Are You? by Jerald Simon

Today is **YOUR** Day! ⎯⎯Date⎯⎯
A **Personal Improvement Outline** for YOU.

Learn how to lead music today.

DAILY FOCUS (main goal for the day) _____
DAILY VIRTUE (choose a virtue from the list of virtues on pg. 51) _____
DAILY BIOGRAPHY (Who did you learn about today and how has their life influenced you?)
_____

3 MICRO GOALS TO BE ACCOMPLISHED TODAY (list 3 steps, actions, or projects you can complete today toward one of the macro goals listed on pages 30 and 31)

1 _____
2 _____
3 _____

Daily to-do checklist of chores, homework and activities to be done today! (list the three most important ones below - do these first and do more if you can)

1 _____
2 _____
3 _____

Book(s) to read and finish this week (you should read at least one book per week) List how many pages you will read from your book(s) today and check off when completed.

1 _____ 2 _____

What did I discover about myself today? (what worked and why):
_____
_____
_____
_____
_____

Who Are You? by Jerald Simon

Date _____

Today is YOUR Day!
A **Personal Improvement Outline** for YOU.

Build something out of clay today.

DAILY FOCUS (main goal for the day) _____

DAILY VIRTUE (choose a virtue from the list of virtues on pg. 51) _____

DAILY BIOGRAPHY (Who did you learn about today and how has their life influenced you?)
_____

3 MICRO GOALS TO BE ACCOMPLISHED TODAY (list 3 steps, actions, or projects you can complete today toward one of the macro goals listed on pages 30 and 31)

1. _____
2. _____
3. _____

Daily to-do checklist of chores, homework and activities to be done today! (list the three most important ones below - do these first and do more if you can)

1. _____
2. _____
3. _____

Book(s) to read and finish this week (you should read at least one book per week) List how many pages you will read from your book(s) today and check off when completed.

1. _____   2. _____

What did I discover about myself today? (what worked and why):
_____
_____
_____
_____

Who Are You? by JERALD SIMON

Today is YOUR Day!
Date
A **Personal Improvement Outline** for YOU.

Learn how to sew on a button today.

DAILY FOCUS (main goal for the day) _____

DAILY VIRTUE (choose a virtue from the list of virtues on pg. 51) _____

DAILY BIOGRAPHY (Who did you learn about today and how has their life influenced you?)
_____

3 MICRO GOALS TO BE ACCOMPLISHED TODAY (list 3 steps, actions, or projects you can complete today toward one of the macro goals listed on pages 30 and 31)

1 _____
2 _____
3 _____

Daily to-do checklist of chores, homework and activities to be done today! (list the three most important ones below - do these first and do more if you can)

1 _____
2 _____
3 _____

Book(s) to read and finish this week (you should read at least one book per week) List how many pages you will read from your book(s) today and check off when completed.

1 _____ 2 _____

What did I discover about myself today? (what worked and why):
_____
_____
_____
_____
_____

Who Are You? by JERALD SIMON

___Date___ ## Today is **YOUR** Day!
A **Personal Improvement Outline** for YOU.

Make breakfast, lunch, and dinner today.

DAILY FOCUS (main goal for the day) _____
DAILY VIRTUE (choose a virtue from the list of virtues on pg. 51) _____
DAILY BIOGRAPHY (Who did you learn about today and how has their life influenced you?)
_____

3 MICRO GOALS TO BE ACCOMPLISHED TODAY (list 3 steps, actions, or projects you can complete today toward one of the macro goals listed on pages 30 and 31)

1 _____
2 _____
3 _____

Daily to-do checklist of chores, homework and activities to be done today! (list the three most important ones below - do these first and do more if you can)

1 _____
2 _____
3 _____

Book(s) to read and finish this week (you should read at least one book per week) List how many pages you will read from your book(s) today and check off when completed.

1 _____ 2 _____

What did I discover about myself today? (what worked and why):
_____
_____
_____
_____

Who Are You? by JERALD SIMON

Today is YOUR Day!   ___Date___
A **Personal Improvement Outline** for YOU.

Try to come up with an invention today. Maybe you can sell it.

DAILY FOCUS (main goal for the day) _____

DAILY VIRTUE (choose a virtue from the list of virtues on pg. 51) _____

DAILY BIOGRAPHY (Who did you learn about today and how has their life influenced you?)
_____

3 MICRO GOALS TO BE ACCOMPLISHED TODAY (list 3 steps, actions, or projects you can complete today toward one of the macro goals listed on pages 30 and 31)

1 _____
2 _____
3 _____

Daily to-do checklist of chores, homework and activities to be done today! (list the three most important ones below - do these first and do more if you can)

1 _____
2 _____
3 _____

Book(s) to read and finish this week (you should read at least one book per week) List how many pages you will read from your book(s) today and check off when completed.

1 _____ 2 _____

What did I discover about myself today? (what worked and why):
_____
_____
_____
_____
_____

Who Are You? by JERALD SIMON

Date _____

Today is YOUR Day!
A **Personal Improvement Outline** for YOU.

Who is James Allen? What did he do?

DAILY FOCUS (main goal for the day) _____
DAILY VIRTUE (choose a virtue from the list of virtues on pg. 51) _____
DAILY BIOGRAPHY (Who did you learn about today and how has their life influenced you?)
_____

3 MICRO GOALS TO BE ACCOMPLISHED TODAY (list 3 steps, actions, or projects you can complete today toward one of the macro goals listed on pages 30 and 31)

1 _____
2 _____
3 _____

Daily to-do checklist of chores, homework and activities to be done today! (list the three most important ones below - do these first and do more if you can)

1 _____
2 _____
3 _____

Book(s) to read and finish this week (you should read at least one book per week) List how many pages you will read from your book(s) today and check off when completed.

1 _____ 2 _____

What did I discover about myself today? (what worked and why):
_____
_____
_____
_____

Who Are You? by Jerald Simon

Today is **YOUR** Day! ———Date———
A **Personal Improvement Outline** for YOU.

Dream. Imagine. Create!

DAILY FOCUS (main goal for the day) _____

DAILY VIRTUE (choose a virtue from the list of virtues on pg. 51) _____

DAILY BIOGRAPHY (Who did you learn about today and how has their life influenced you?)
_____

3 MICRO GOALS TO BE ACCOMPLISHED TODAY (list 3 steps, actions, or projects you can complete today toward one of the macro goals listed on pages 30 and 31)

1 _____
2 _____
3 _____

Daily to-do checklist of chores, homework and activities to be done today! (list the three most important ones below - do these first and do more if you can)

1 _____
2 _____
3 _____

Book(s) to read and finish this week (you should read at least one book per week) List how many pages you will read from your book(s) today and check off when completed.

1 _____ 2 _____

What did I discover about myself today? (what worked and why):
_____
_____
_____
_____
_____

Who Are You? by JERALD SIMON

---Date--- ## Today is **YOUR** Day!
A **Personal Improvement Outline** for YOU.

Spread sunshine wherever you go.

DAILY FOCUS (main goal for the day) _____
DAILY VIRTUE (choose a virtue from the list of virtues on pg. 51) _____
DAILY BIOGRAPHY (Who did you learn about today and how has their life influenced you?)
_____

3 MICRO GOALS TO BE ACCOMPLISHED TODAY (list 3 steps, actions, or projects you can complete today toward one of the macro goals listed on pages 30 and 31)

1 _____
2 _____
3 _____

Daily to-do checklist of chores, homework and activities to be done today! (list the three most important ones below - do these first and do more if you can)

1 _____
2 _____
3 _____

Book(s) to read and finish this week (you should read at least one book per week) List how many pages you will read from your book(s) today and check off when completed.

1 _____ 2 _____

What did I discover about myself today? (what worked and why):
_____
_____
_____
_____
_____

Who Are You? by JERALD SIMON

Today is YOUR Day! ___Date___
A **Personal Improvement Outline** for YOU.

Always tell the truth. Be true to who you really are.

DAILY FOCUS (main goal for the day) _____
DAILY VIRTUE (choose a virtue from the list of virtues on pg. 51) _____
DAILY BIOGRAPHY (Who did you learn about today and how has their life influenced you?)
_____

3 MICRO GOALS TO BE ACCOMPLISHED TODAY (list 3 steps, actions, or projects you can complete today toward one of the macro goals listed on pages 30 and 31)

1 _____
2 _____
3 _____

Daily to-do checklist of chores, homework and activities to be done today! (list the three most important ones below - do these first and do more if you can)

1 _____
2 _____
3 _____

Book(s) to read and finish this week (you should read at least one book per week) List how many pages you will read from your book(s) today and check off when completed.

1 _____ 2 _____

What did I discover about myself today? (what worked and why):
_____
_____
_____
_____
_____

Who Are You? by Jerald Simon

Date _____

Today is **YOUR** Day!
A **Personal Improvement Outline** for YOU.

Don't stop when the going gets tough. You are tougher!

DAILY FOCUS (main goal for the day) _____
DAILY VIRTUE (choose a virtue from the list of virtues on pg. 51) _____
DAILY BIOGRAPHY (Who did you learn about today and how has their life influenced you?)
_____

3 MICRO GOALS TO BE ACCOMPLISHED TODAY (list 3 steps, actions, or projects you can complete today toward one of the macro goals listed on pages 30 and 31)

1 _____
2 _____
3 _____

Daily to-do checklist of chores, homework and activities to be done today! (list the three most important ones below - do these first and do more if you can)

1 _____
2 _____
3 _____

Book(s) to read and finish this week (you should read at least one book per week) List how many pages you will read from your book(s) today and check off when completed.

1 _____ 2 _____

What did I discover about myself today? (what worked and why):
_____
_____
_____
_____
_____

Who Are You? by Jerald Simon

Today is YOUR Day!   ——Date——
A **Personal Improvement Outline** for YOU.

Be the kind of friend you would like to have.

DAILY FOCUS (main goal for the day) _____
DAILY VIRTUE (choose a virtue from the list of virtues on pg. 51) _____
DAILY BIOGRAPHY (Who did you learn about today and how has their life influenced you?)
_____

3 MICRO GOALS TO BE ACCOMPLISHED TODAY (list 3 steps, actions, or projects you can complete today toward one of the macro goals listed on pages 30 and 31)

1 _____
2 _____
3 _____

Daily to-do checklist of chores, homework and activities to be done today! (list the three most important ones below - do these first and do more if you can)

1 _____
2 _____
3 _____

Book(s) to read and finish this week (you should read at least one book per week) List how many pages you will read from your book(s) today and check off when completed.

1 _____ 2 _____

What did I discover about myself today? (what worked and why):
_____
_____
_____
_____
_____

Who Are You? by Jerald Simon

Date _____

Today is YOUR Day!
A **Personal Improvement Outline** for YOU.

Life is good! Do what it takes to have a good life!

DAILY FOCUS (main goal for the day) _____

DAILY VIRTUE (choose a virtue from the list of virtues on pg. 51) _____

DAILY BIOGRAPHY (Who did you learn about today and how has their life influenced you?)
_____

3 MICRO GOALS TO BE ACCOMPLISHED TODAY (list 3 steps, actions, or projects you can complete today toward one of the macro goals listed on pages 30 and 31)

1. _____
2. _____
3. _____

Daily to-do checklist of chores, homework and activities to be done today! (list the three most important ones below - do these first and do more if you can)

1. _____
2. _____
3. _____

Book(s) to read and finish this week (you should read at least one book per week) List how many pages you will read from your book(s) today and check off when completed.

1. _____ 2. _____

What did I discover about myself today? (what worked and why):
_____
_____
_____
_____

Who Are You? by Jerald Simon

Today is YOUR Day!
Date

A **Personal Improvement Outline** for YOU.

Who is Alexander Graham Bell?

DAILY FOCUS (main goal for the day) _____
DAILY VIRTUE (choose a virtue from the list of virtues on pg. 51) _____
DAILY BIOGRAPHY (Who did you learn about today and how has their life influenced you?)
_____

3 MICRO GOALS TO BE ACCOMPLISHED TODAY (list 3 steps, actions, or projects you can complete today toward one of the macro goals listed on pages 30 and 31)

1 _____
2 _____
3 _____

Daily to-do checklist of chores, homework and activities to be done today! (list the three most important ones below - do these first and do more if you can)

1 _____
2 _____
3 _____

Book(s) to read and finish this week (you should read at least one book per week) List how many pages you will read from your book(s) today and check off when completed.

1 _____ 2 _____

What did I discover about myself today? (what worked and why):
_____
_____
_____
_____
_____

Who Are You? by Jerald Simon

Date _____

Today is YOUR Day!
A Personal Improvement Outline for YOU.

What can you do today to help those around you?

DAILY FOCUS (main goal for the day) _____
DAILY VIRTUE (choose a virtue from the list of virtues on pg. 51) _____
DAILY BIOGRAPHY (Who did you learn about today and how has their life influenced you?)
_____

3 MICRO GOALS TO BE ACCOMPLISHED TODAY (list 3 steps, actions, or projects you can complete today toward one of the macro goals listed on pages 30 and 31)

1. _____
2. _____
3. _____

Daily to-do checklist of chores, homework and activities to be done today! (list the three most important ones below - do these first and do more if you can)

1. _____
2. _____
3. _____

Book(s) to read and finish this week (you should read at least one book per week) List how many pages you will read from your book(s) today and check off when completed.

1. _____ 2. _____

What did I discover about myself today? (what worked and why):

_____
_____
_____
_____

Who Are You? by Jerald Simon

Today is YOUR Day!
Date
A Personal Improvement Outline for YOU.

Listen to criticism. It often carries much truth.

DAILY FOCUS (main goal for the day) _____

DAILY VIRTUE (choose a virtue from the list of virtues on pg. 51) _____

DAILY BIOGRAPHY (Who did you learn about today and how has their life influenced you?)
_____

3 MICRO GOALS TO BE ACCOMPLISHED TODAY (list 3 steps, actions, or projects you can complete today toward one of the macro goals listed on pages 30 and 31)

1 _____
2 _____
3 _____

Daily to-do checklist of chores, homework and activities to be done today! (list the three most important ones below - do these first and do more if you can)

1 _____
2 _____
3 _____

Book(s) to read and finish this week (you should read at least one book per week) List how many pages you will read from your book(s) today and check off when completed.

1 _____ 2 _____

What did I discover about myself today? (what worked and why):
_____
_____
_____
_____
_____

Who Are You? by Jerald Simon

___Date___   # Today is **YOUR** Day!
A **Personal Improvement Outline** for YOU.

Life is about sacrificing what we want to fulfill others' needs.

DAILY FOCUS (main goal for the day) _____

DAILY VIRTUE (choose a virtue from the list of virtues on pg. 51) _____

DAILY BIOGRAPHY (Who did you learn about today and how has their life influenced you?)
_____

3 MICRO GOALS TO BE ACCOMPLISHED TODAY (list 3 steps, actions, or projects you can complete today toward one of the macro goals listed on pages 30 and 31)

1 _____
2 _____
3 _____

Daily to-do checklist of chores, homework and activities to be done today! (list the three most important ones below - do these first and do more if you can)

1 _____
2 _____
3 _____

Book(s) to read and finish this week (you should read at least one book per week) List how many pages you will read from your book(s) today and check off when completed.

1 _____ 2 _____

What did I discover about myself today? (what worked and why):
_____
_____
_____
_____

Who Are You? by Jerald Simon

Today is YOUR Day!
Date

A **Personal Improvement Outline** for YOU.

Listen to music by Antonín Leopold Dvořák today.

DAILY FOCUS (main goal for the day) _____

DAILY VIRTUE (choose a virtue from the list of virtues on pg. 51) _____

DAILY BIOGRAPHY (Who did you learn about today and how has their life influenced you?)
_____

3 MICRO GOALS TO BE ACCOMPLISHED TODAY (list 3 steps, actions, or projects you can complete today toward one of the macro goals listed on pages 30 and 31)

1 _____
2 _____
3 _____

Daily to-do checklist of chores, homework and activities to be done today! (list the three most important ones below - do these first and do more if you can)

1 _____
2 _____
3 _____

Book(s) to read and finish this week (you should read at least one book per week) List how many pages you will read from your book(s) today and check off when completed.

1 _____ 2 _____

What did I discover about myself today? (what worked and why):
_____
_____
_____
_____
_____

Who Are You? by JERALD SIMON

<u>   Date   </u> # Today is **YOUR** Day!
A **Personal Improvement Outline** for YOU.

Who is Lao Tzu and what did he do?

DAILY FOCUS (main goal for the day) _____
DAILY VIRTUE (choose a virtue from the list of virtues on pg. 51) _____
DAILY BIOGRAPHY (Who did you learn about today and how has their life influenced you?)
_____

3 MICRO GOALS TO BE ACCOMPLISHED TODAY (list 3 steps, actions, or projects you can complete today toward one of the macro goals listed on pages 30 and 31)

1. _____
2. _____
3. _____

Daily to-do checklist of chores, homework and activities to be done today! (list the three most important ones below - do these first and do more if you can)

1. _____
2. _____
3. _____

Book(s) to read and finish this week (you should read at least one book per week) List how many pages you will read from your book(s) today and check off when completed.

1. _____ 2. _____

What did I discover about myself today? (what worked and why):

_____
_____
_____
_____

Who Are You? by Jerald Simon

Today is YOUR Day! — Date —
A **Personal Improvement Outline** for YOU.

Who is Alexander the Great? Why is he important?

DAILY FOCUS (main goal for the day) _____
DAILY VIRTUE (choose a virtue from the list of virtues on pg. 51) _____
DAILY BIOGRAPHY (Who did you learn about today and how has their life influenced you?)
_____

3 MICRO GOALS TO BE ACCOMPLISHED TODAY (list 3 steps, actions, or projects you can complete today toward one of the macro goals listed on pages 30 and 31)

1 _____
2 _____
3 _____

Daily to-do checklist of chores, homework and activities to be done today! (list the three most important ones below - do these first and do more if you can)

1 _____
2 _____
3 _____

Book(s) to read and finish this week (you should read at least one book per week) List how many pages you will read from your book(s) today and check off when completed.

1 _____ 2 _____

What did I discover about myself today? (what worked and why):
_____
_____
_____
_____
_____

Who Are You? by Jerald Simon

Date _____

Today is YOUR Day!
A **Personal Improvement Outline** for YOU.

Learn what it takes to be an entrepreneur today.

DAILY FOCUS (main goal for the day) _____
DAILY VIRTUE (choose a virtue from the list of virtues on pg. 51) _____
DAILY BIOGRAPHY (Who did you learn about today and how has their life influenced you?)
_____

3 MICRO GOALS TO BE ACCOMPLISHED TODAY (list 3 steps, actions, or projects you can complete today toward one of the macro goals listed on pages 30 and 31)

1 _____
2 _____
3 _____

Daily to-do checklist of chores, homework and activities to be done today! (list the three most important ones below - do these first and do more if you can)

1 _____
2 _____
3 _____

Book(s) to read and finish this week (you should read at least one book per week) List how many pages you will read from your book(s) today and check off when completed.

1 _____ 2 _____

What did I discover about myself today? (what worked and why):

_____
_____
_____
_____
_____

Who Are You? by Jerald Simon

Today is YOUR Day!   _Date_
A **Personal Improvement Outline** for YOU.

Listen to the music of Joseph Hayden today.

DAILY FOCUS (main goal for the day) _____

DAILY VIRTUE (choose a virtue from the list of virtues on pg. 51) _____

DAILY BIOGRAPHY (Who did you learn about today and how has their life influenced you?)
_____

3 MICRO GOALS TO BE ACCOMPLISHED TODAY (list 3 steps, actions, or projects you can complete today toward one of the macro goals listed on pages 30 and 31)

1. _____
2. _____
3. _____

Daily to-do checklist of chores, homework and activities to be done today! (list the three most important ones below - do these first and do more if you can)

1. _____
2. _____
3. _____

Book(s) to read and finish this week (you should read at least one book per week) List how many pages you will read from your book(s) today and check off when completed.

1. _____ 2. _____

What did I discover about myself today? (what worked and why):
_____
_____
_____
_____

Who Are You? by JERALD SIMON

Date _____

Today is **YOUR** Day!
A **Personal Improvement Outline** for YOU.

Learn about Baltasar Gracián. Who was he? What did he do?

DAILY FOCUS (main goal for the day) _____
DAILY VIRTUE (choose a virtue from the list of virtues on pg. 51) _____
DAILY BIOGRAPHY (Who did you learn about today and how has their life influenced you?)
_____

3 MICRO GOALS TO BE ACCOMPLISHED TODAY (list 3 steps, actions, or projects you can complete today toward one of the macro goals listed on pages 30 and 31)

1 _____
2 _____
3 _____

Daily to-do checklist of chores, homework and activities to be done today! (list the three most important ones below - do these first and do more if you can)

1 _____
2 _____
3 _____

Book(s) to read and finish this week (you should read at least one book per week) List how many pages you will read from your book(s) today and check off when completed.

1 _____ 2 _____

What did I discover about myself today? (what worked and why):

_____
_____
_____
_____
_____

Who Are You? by Jerald Simon

Today is YOUR Day! — Date

A **Personal Improvement Outline** for YOU.

Who is Aesop? Read some of his fables today.

DAILY FOCUS (main goal for the day) _____

DAILY VIRTUE (choose a virtue from the list of virtues on pg. 51) _____

DAILY BIOGRAPHY (Who did you learn about today and how has their life influenced you?)
_____

3 MICRO GOALS TO BE ACCOMPLISHED TODAY (list 3 steps, actions, or projects you can complete today toward one of the macro goals listed on pages 30 and 31)

1 _____
2 _____
3 _____

Daily to-do checklist of chores, homework and activities to be done today! (list the three most important ones below - do these first and do more if you can)

1 _____
2 _____
3 _____

Book(s) to read and finish this week (you should read at least one book per week) List how many pages you will read from your book(s) today and check off when completed.

1 _____ 2 _____

What did I discover about myself today? (what worked and why):
_____
_____
_____
_____
_____

Who Are You? by Jerald Simon

<u>Date</u> ## Today is **YOUR** Day!
A **Personal Improvement Outline** for YOU.

Make a goal to learn one new word every day!

DAILY FOCUS (main goal for the day) _____
DAILY VIRTUE (choose a virtue from the list of virtues on pg. 51) _____
DAILY BIOGRAPHY (Who did you learn about today and how has their life influenced you?)
_____

3 MICRO GOALS TO BE ACCOMPLISHED TODAY (list 3 steps, actions, or projects you can complete today toward one of the macro goals listed on pages 30 and 31)

1 _____
2 _____
3 _____

Daily to-do checklist of chores, homework and activities to be done today! (list the three most important ones below - do these first and do more if you can)

1 _____
2 _____
3 _____

Book(s) to read and finish this week (you should read at least one book per week) List how many pages you will read from your book(s) today and check off when completed.

1 _____ 2 _____

What did I discover about myself today? (what worked and why):
_____
_____
_____
_____

Who Are You? by Jerald Simon

Today is YOUR Day!   Date _____
A **Personal Improvement Outline** for YOU.

Learn how to use a sling shot today.

DAILY FOCUS (main goal for the day) _____

DAILY VIRTUE (choose a virtue from the list of virtues on pg. 51) _____

DAILY BIOGRAPHY (Who did you learn about today and how has their life influenced you?)
_____

3 MICRO GOALS TO BE ACCOMPLISHED TODAY (list 3 steps, actions, or projects you can complete today toward one of the macro goals listed on pages 30 and 31)

1 _____
2 _____
3 _____

Daily to-do checklist of chores, homework and activities to be done today! (list the three most important ones below - do these first and do more if you can)

1 _____
2 _____
3 _____

Book(s) to read and finish this week (you should read at least one book per week) List how many pages you will read from your book(s) today and check off when completed.

1 _____ 2 _____

What did I discover about myself today? (what worked and why):
_____
_____
_____
_____
_____

Who Are You? by Jerald Simon

<u>   Date   </u>   Today is **YOUR** Day!
A **Personal Improvement Outline** for YOU.

Who is Sir Walter Scott?

DAILY FOCUS (main goal for the day) _____

DAILY VIRTUE (choose a virtue from the list of virtues on pg. 51) _____

DAILY BIOGRAPHY (Who did you learn about today and how has their life influenced you?)
_____

3 MICRO GOALS TO BE ACCOMPLISHED TODAY (list 3 steps, actions, or projects you can complete today toward one of the macro goals listed on pages 30 and 31)

1 _____
2 _____
3 _____

Daily to-do checklist of chores, homework and activities to be done today! (list the three most important ones below - do these first and do more if you can)

1 _____
2 _____
3 _____

Book(s) to read and finish this week (you should read at least one book per week) List how many pages you will read from your book(s) today and check off when completed.

1 _____ 2 _____

What did I discover about myself today? (what worked and why):
_____
_____
_____
_____
_____

Who Are You? by Jerald Simon

Today is YOUR Day! ___Date___
A **Personal Improvement Outline** for YOU.

When things don't go your way, please don't complain!

DAILY FOCUS (main goal for the day) _____
DAILY VIRTUE (choose a virtue from the list of virtues on pg. 51) _____
DAILY BIOGRAPHY (Who did you learn about today and how has their life influenced you?)
_____

3 MICRO GOALS TO BE ACCOMPLISHED TODAY (list 3 steps, actions, or projects you can complete today toward one of the macro goals listed on pages 30 and 31)

1 _____
2 _____
3 _____

Daily to-do checklist of chores, homework and activities to be done today! (list the three most important ones below - do these first and do more if you can)

1 _____
2 _____
3 _____

Book(s) to read and finish this week (you should read at least one book per week) List how many pages you will read from your book(s) today and check off when completed.

1 _____ 2 _____

What did I discover about myself today? (what worked and why):
_____
_____
_____
_____
_____

Who Are You? by Jerald Simon

Date _____

Today is **YOUR** Day!
A **Personal Improvement Outline** for YOU.

Learn about Epictetus today. Who was he? What did he do?

DAILY FOCUS (main goal for the day) _____
DAILY VIRTUE (choose a virtue from the list of virtues on pg. 51) _____
DAILY BIOGRAPHY (Who did you learn about today and how has their life influenced you?)
_____

3 MICRO GOALS TO BE ACCOMPLISHED TODAY (list 3 steps, actions, or projects you can complete today toward one of the macro goals listed on pages 30 and 31)

1 _____
2 _____
3 _____

Daily to-do checklist of chores, homework and activities to be done today! (list the three most important ones below - do these first and do more if you can)

1 _____
2 _____
3 _____

Book(s) to read and finish this week (you should read at least one book per week) List how many pages you will read from your book(s) today and check off when completed.

1 _____ 2 _____

What did I discover about myself today? (what worked and why):
_____
_____
_____
_____
_____

Who Are You? by Jerald Simon

Today is YOUR Day! _____Date

A **Personal Improvement Outline** for YOU.

Don't worry about those things over which you have no control.

DAILY FOCUS (main goal for the day) _____
DAILY VIRTUE (choose a virtue from the list of virtues on pg. 51) _____
DAILY BIOGRAPHY (Who did you learn about today and how has their life influenced you?)
_____

3 MICRO GOALS TO BE ACCOMPLISHED TODAY (list 3 steps, actions, or projects you can complete today toward one of the macro goals listed on pages 30 and 31)

1 _____
2 _____
3 _____

Daily to-do checklist of chores, homework and activities to be done today! (list the three most important ones below - do these first and do more if you can)

1 _____
2 _____
3 _____

Book(s) to read and finish this week (you should read at least one book per week) List how many pages you will read from your book(s) today and check off when completed.

1 _____ 2 _____

What did I discover about myself today? (what worked and why):
_____
_____
_____
_____
_____

Who Are You? by Jerald Simon

___Date___ # Today is YOUR Day!
A **Personal Improvement Outline** for YOU.

Visit a local fire station today and learn about safety!

DAILY FOCUS (main goal for the day) _____
DAILY VIRTUE (choose a virtue from the list of virtues on pg. 51) _____
DAILY BIOGRAPHY (Who did you learn about today and how has their life influenced you?)
_____

3 MICRO GOALS TO BE ACCOMPLISHED TODAY (list 3 steps, actions, or projects you can complete today toward one of the macro goals listed on pages 30 and 31)

1 _____
2 _____
3 _____

Daily to-do checklist of chores, homework and activities to be done today! (list the three most important ones below - do these first and do more if you can)

1 _____
2 _____
3 _____

Book(s) to read and finish this week (you should read at least one book per week) List how many pages you will read from your book(s) today and check off when completed.

1 _____ 2 _____

What did I discover about myself today? (what worked and why):
_____
_____
_____
_____

Who Are You? by JERALD SIMON

Today is YOUR Day! ⎯⎯Date⎯⎯
A **Personal Improvement Outline** for YOU.

Learn a few self defense procedures to protect yourself.

DAILY FOCUS (main goal for the day) _____
DAILY VIRTUE (choose a virtue from the list of virtues on pg. 51) _____
DAILY BIOGRAPHY (Who did you learn about today and how has their life influenced you?)
_____

3 MICRO GOALS TO BE ACCOMPLISHED TODAY (list 3 steps, actions, or projects you can complete today toward one of the macro goals listed on pages 30 and 31)

1 _____
2 _____
3 _____

Daily to-do checklist of chores, homework and activities to be done today! (list the three most important ones below - do these first and do more if you can)

1 _____
2 _____
3 _____

Book(s) to read and finish this week (you should read at least one book per week) List how many pages you will read from your book(s) today and check off when completed.

1 _____ 2 _____

What did I discover about myself today? (what worked and why):
_____
_____
_____
_____
_____

Who Are You? by JERALD SIMON

___Date___   # Today is YOUR Day!
A **Personal Improvement Outline** for YOU.

Create a "Creativity Notebook" today.

DAILY FOCUS (main goal for the day) _____
DAILY VIRTUE (choose a virtue from the list of virtues on pg. 51) _____
DAILY BIOGRAPHY (Who did you learn about today and how has their life influenced you?)
_____

3 MICRO GOALS TO BE ACCOMPLISHED TODAY (list 3 steps, actions, or projects you can complete today toward one of the macro goals listed on pages 30 and 31)

1 _____
2 _____
3 _____

Daily to-do checklist of chores, homework and activities to be done today! (list the three most important ones below - do these first and do more if you can)

1 _____
2 _____
3 _____

Book(s) to read and finish this week (you should read at least one book per week) List how many pages you will read from your book(s) today and check off when completed.

1 _____ 2 _____

What did I discover about myself today? (what worked and why):
_____
_____
_____
_____
_____

Who Are You? by JERALD SIMON

Today is YOUR Day!   ——— Date

A **Personal Improvement Outline** for YOU.

Create your own Think Tank group with family and friends.

DAILY FOCUS (main goal for the day) _____

DAILY VIRTUE (choose a virtue from the list of virtues on pg. 51) _____

DAILY BIOGRAPHY (Who did you learn about today and how has their life influenced you?)
_____

3 MICRO GOALS TO BE ACCOMPLISHED TODAY (list 3 steps, actions, or projects you can complete today toward one of the macro goals listed on pages 30 and 31)

1 _____
2 _____
3 _____

Daily to-do checklist of chores, homework and activities to be done today! (list the three most important ones below - do these first and do more if you can)

1 _____
2 _____
3 _____

Book(s) to read and finish this week (you should read at least one book per week) List how many pages you will read from your book(s) today and check off when completed.

1 _____   2 _____

What did I discover about myself today? (what worked and why):
_____
_____
_____
_____
_____

Who Are You? by Jerald Simon

---Date--- ## Today is **YOUR** Day!
A **Personal Improvement Outline** for YOU.

Visit the library today and checkout books and videos on bugs.

DAILY FOCUS (main goal for the day) _____
DAILY VIRTUE (choose a virtue from the list of virtues on pg. 51) _____
DAILY BIOGRAPHY (Who did you learn about today and how has their life influenced you?)
_____

3 MICRO GOALS TO BE ACCOMPLISHED TODAY (list 3 steps, actions, or projects you can complete today toward one of the macro goals listed on pages 30 and 31)

1 _____
2 _____
3 _____

Daily to-do checklist of chores, homework and activities to be done today! (list the three most important ones below - do these first and do more if you can)

1 _____
2 _____
3 _____

Book(s) to read and finish this week (you should read at least one book per week) List how many pages you will read from your book(s) today and check off when completed.

1 _____ 2 _____

What did I discover about myself today? (what worked and why):
_____
_____
_____
_____

Who Are You? by Jerald Simon

Today is YOUR Day! ——Date——
A **Personal Improvement Outline** for YOU.

Start a collection of anything you'd like to collect today.

DAILY FOCUS (main goal for the day) _____

DAILY VIRTUE (choose a virtue from the list of virtues on pg. 51) _____

DAILY BIOGRAPHY (Who did you learn about today and how has their life influenced you?)
_____

3 MICRO GOALS TO BE ACCOMPLISHED TODAY (list 3 steps, actions, or projects you can complete today toward one of the macro goals listed on pages 30 and 31)

1 _____
2 _____
3 _____

Daily to-do checklist of chores, homework and activities to be done today! (list the three most important ones below - do these first and do more if you can)

1 _____
2 _____
3 _____

Book(s) to read and finish this week (you should read at least one book per week) List how many pages you will read from your book(s) today and check off when completed.

1 _____ 2 _____

What did I discover about myself today? (what worked and why):
_____
_____
_____
_____
_____

Who Are You? by Jerald Simon

_____Date_____ ## Today is **YOUR** Day!
A **Personal Improvement Outline** for YOU.

Learn everything you can about computers today.

DAILY FOCUS (main goal for the day) _____
DAILY VIRTUE (choose a virtue from the list of virtues on pg. 51) _____
DAILY BIOGRAPHY (Who did you learn about today and how has their life influenced you?)
_____

3 MICRO GOALS TO BE ACCOMPLISHED TODAY (list 3 steps, actions, or projects you can complete today toward one of the macro goals listed on pages 30 and 31)

1 _____
2 _____
3 _____

Daily to-do checklist of chores, homework and activities to be done today! (list the three most important ones below - do these first and do more if you can)

1 _____
2 _____
3 _____

Book(s) to read and finish this week (you should read at least one book per week) List how many pages you will read from your book(s) today and check off when completed.

1 _____ 2 _____

What did I discover about myself today? (what worked and why):
_____
_____
_____
_____

Who Are You? by Jerald Simon

Today is YOUR Day!   ———— Date

A **Personal Improvement Outline** for YOU.

What is the Theory of Relativity?

DAILY FOCUS (main goal for the day) _____
DAILY VIRTUE (choose a virtue from the list of virtues on pg. 51) _____
DAILY BIOGRAPHY (Who did you learn about today and how has their life influenced you?)
_____

3 MICRO GOALS TO BE ACCOMPLISHED TODAY (list 3 steps, actions, or projects you can complete today toward one of the macro goals listed on pages 30 and 31)

1 _____
2 _____
3 _____

Daily to-do checklist of chores, homework and activities to be done today! (list the three most important ones below - do these first and do more if you can)

1 _____
2 _____
3 _____

Book(s) to read and finish this week (you should read at least one book per week) List how many pages you will read from your book(s) today and check off when completed.

1 _____ 2 _____

What did I discover about myself today? (what worked and why):
_____
_____
_____
_____
_____

Who Are You? by Jerald Simon

<u>   Date   </u> # Today is YOUR Day!
A **Personal Improvement Outline** for YOU.

Learn about Quantum Physics today.

DAILY FOCUS (main goal for the day) _____

DAILY VIRTUE (choose a virtue from the list of virtues on pg. 51) _____

DAILY BIOGRAPHY (Who did you learn about today and how has their life influenced you?)
_____

3 MICRO GOALS TO BE ACCOMPLISHED TODAY (list 3 steps, actions, or projects you can complete today toward one of the macro goals listed on pages 30 and 31)

1 _____
2 _____
3 _____

Daily to-do checklist of chores, homework and activities to be done today! (list the three most important ones below - do these first and do more if you can)

1 _____
2 _____
3 _____

Book(s) to read and finish this week (you should read at least one book per week) List how many pages you will read from your book(s) today and check off when completed.

1 _____ 2 _____

What did I discover about myself today? (what worked and why):
_____
_____
_____
_____

Who Are You? by Jerald Simon

Today is YOUR Day! _____
Date
A **Personal Improvement Outline** for YOU.

Find out about stars, constellations, super novas, and space.

DAILY FOCUS (main goal for the day) _____

DAILY VIRTUE (choose a virtue from the list of virtues on pg. 51) _____

DAILY BIOGRAPHY (Who did you learn about today and how has their life influenced you?)
_____

3 MICRO GOALS TO BE ACCOMPLISHED TODAY (list 3 steps, actions, or projects you can complete today toward one of the macro goals listed on pages 30 and 31)

1 _____
2 _____
3 _____

Daily to-do checklist of chores, homework and activities to be done today! (list the three most important ones below - do these first and do more if you can)

1 _____
2 _____
3 _____

Book(s) to read and finish this week (you should read at least one book per week) List how many pages you will read from your book(s) today and check off when completed.

1 _____   2 _____

What did I discover about myself today? (what worked and why):
_____
_____
_____
_____
_____

Who Are You? by Jerald Simon

Date _____

Today is YOUR Day!
A **Personal Improvement Outline** for YOU.

How can you create compost and mulch for the garden?

DAILY FOCUS (main goal for the day) _____
DAILY VIRTUE (choose a virtue from the list of virtues on pg. 51) _____
DAILY BIOGRAPHY (Who did you learn about today and how has their life influenced you?)
_____

3 MICRO GOALS TO BE ACCOMPLISHED TODAY (list 3 steps, actions, or projects you can complete today toward one of the macro goals listed on pages 30 and 31)

1. _____
2. _____
3. _____

Daily to-do checklist of chores, homework and activities to be done today! (list the three most important ones below - do these first and do more if you can)

1. _____
2. _____
3. _____

Book(s) to read and finish this week (you should read at least one book per week) List how many pages you will read from your book(s) today and check off when completed.

1. _____ 2. _____

What did I discover about myself today? (what worked and why):
_____
_____
_____
_____
_____

Who Are You? by JERALD SIMON

Today is YOUR Day!   _____
Date

A **Personal Improvement Outline** for YOU.

Work on team-working skills today.

DAILY FOCUS (main goal for the day) _____
DAILY VIRTUE (choose a virtue from the list of virtues on pg. 51) _____
DAILY BIOGRAPHY (Who did you learn about today and how has their life influenced you?)
_____

3 MICRO GOALS TO BE ACCOMPLISHED TODAY (list 3 steps, actions, or projects you can complete today toward one of the macro goals listed on pages 30 and 31)

1 _____
2 _____
3 _____

Daily to-do checklist of chores, homework and activities to be done today! (list the three most important ones below - do these first and do more if you can)

1 _____
2 _____
3 _____

Book(s) to read and finish this week (you should read at least one book per week) List how many pages you will read from your book(s) today and check off when completed.

1 _____ 2 _____

What did I discover about myself today? (what worked and why):
_____
_____
_____
_____
_____

Who Are You? by Jerald Simon

---Date--- ## Today is YOUR Day!
A **Personal Improvement Outline** for YOU.

Improve your music skills today. If you don't have any - start!

DAILY FOCUS (main goal for the day) _____

DAILY VIRTUE (choose a virtue from the list of virtues on pg. 51) _____

DAILY BIOGRAPHY (Who did you learn about today and how has their life influenced you?)
_____

3 MICRO GOALS TO BE ACCOMPLISHED TODAY (list 3 steps, actions, or projects you can complete today toward one of the macro goals listed on pages 30 and 31)

1 _____
2 _____
3 _____

Daily to-do checklist of chores, homework and activities to be done today! (list the three most important ones below - do these first and do more if you can)

1 _____
2 _____
3 _____

Book(s) to read and finish this week (you should read at least one book per week) List how many pages you will read from your book(s) today and check off when completed.

1 _____ 2 _____

What did I discover about myself today? (what worked and why):
_____
_____
_____
_____
_____

Who Are You? by JERALD SIMON

Today is YOUR Day!
Date

A **Personal Improvement Outline** for YOU.

What and when were the Punic Wars?

DAILY FOCUS (main goal for the day) _____

DAILY VIRTUE (choose a virtue from the list of virtues on pg. 51) _____

DAILY BIOGRAPHY (Who did you learn about today and how has their life influenced you?)

_____

3 MICRO GOALS TO BE ACCOMPLISHED TODAY (list 3 steps, actions, or projects you can complete today toward one of the macro goals listed on pages 30 and 31)

1 _____
2 _____
3 _____

Daily to-do checklist of chores, homework and activities to be done today!
(list the three most important ones below - do these first and do more if you can)

1 _____
2 _____
3 _____

Book(s) to read and finish this week (you should read at least one book per week) List how many pages you will read from your book(s) today and check off when completed.

1 _____ 2 _____

What did I discover about myself today? (what worked and why):

_____
_____
_____
_____
_____

Who Are You? by Jerald Simon

Date _____

Today is YOUR Day!
A **Personal Improvement Outline** for YOU.

Who is Hannibal?

DAILY FOCUS (main goal for the day) _____
DAILY VIRTUE (choose a virtue from the list of virtues on pg. 51) _____
DAILY BIOGRAPHY (Who did you learn about today and how has their life influenced you?)
_____

3 MICRO GOALS TO BE ACCOMPLISHED TODAY (list 3 steps, actions, or projects you can complete today toward one of the macro goals listed on pages 30 and 31)

1. _____
2. _____
3. _____

Daily to-do checklist of chores, homework and activities to be done today! (list the three most important ones below - do these first and do more if you can)

1. _____
2. _____
3. _____

Book(s) to read and finish this week (you should read at least one book per week) List how many pages you will read from your book(s) today and check off when completed.

1. _____ 2. _____

What did I discover about myself today? (what worked and why):
_____
_____
_____
_____
_____

Who Are You? by Jerald Simon

Today is YOUR Day! ___Date___
A **Personal Improvement Outline** for YOU.

Learn about Pericles, often called the Father of Democracy.

DAILY FOCUS (main goal for the day) _____

DAILY VIRTUE (choose a virtue from the list of virtues on pg. 51) _____

DAILY BIOGRAPHY (Who did you learn about today and how has their life influenced you?)
_____

3 MICRO GOALS TO BE ACCOMPLISHED TODAY (list 3 steps, actions, or projects you can complete today toward one of the macro goals listed on pages 30 and 31)

1 _____
2 _____
3 _____

Daily to-do checklist of chores, homework and activities to be done today! (list the three most important ones below - do these first and do more if you can)

1 _____
2 _____
3 _____

Book(s) to read and finish this week (you should read at least one book per week) List how many pages you will read from your book(s) today and check off when completed.

1 _____ 2 _____

What did I discover about myself today? (what worked and why):
_____
_____
_____
_____
_____

Who Are You? by Jerald Simon

Date _____

Today is **YOUR** Day!
A **Personal Improvement Outline** for YOU.

How and when did the Olympics begin?

DAILY FOCUS (main goal for the day) _____
DAILY VIRTUE (choose a virtue from the list of virtues on pg. 51) _____
DAILY BIOGRAPHY (Who did you learn about today and how has their life influenced you?)
_____

3 MICRO GOALS TO BE ACCOMPLISHED TODAY (list 3 steps, actions, or projects you can complete today toward one of the macro goals listed on pages 30 and 31)

1 _____
2 _____
3 _____

Daily to-do checklist of chores, homework and activities to be done today! (list the three most important ones below - do these first and do more if you can)

1 _____
2 _____
3 _____

Book(s) to read and finish this week (you should read at least one book per week) List how many pages you will read from your book(s) today and check off when completed.

1 _____ 2 _____

What did I discover about myself today? (what worked and why):
_____
_____
_____
_____

Who Are You? by Jerald Simon

Today is YOUR Day!
Date

A **Personal Improvement Outline** for YOU.

Who are the Knights Templar? What did they do?

DAILY FOCUS (main goal for the day) _____

DAILY VIRTUE (choose a virtue from the list of virtues on pg. 51) _____

DAILY BIOGRAPHY (Who did you learn about today and how has their life influenced you?)
_____

3 MICRO GOALS TO BE ACCOMPLISHED TODAY (list 3 steps, actions, or projects you can complete today toward one of the macro goals listed on pages 30 and 31)

1 _____
2 _____
3 _____

Daily to-do checklist of chores, homework and activities to be done today! (list the three most important ones below - do these first and do more if you can)

1 _____
2 _____
3 _____

Book(s) to read and finish this week (you should read at least one book per week) List how many pages you will read from your book(s) today and check off when completed.

1 _____ 2 _____

What did I discover about myself today? (what worked and why):
_____
_____
_____
_____
_____

Who Are You? by Jerald Simon

<u>　　　Date　　　</u>
Today is YOUR Day!
A **Personal Improvement Outline** for YOU.

Learn about the Freemasons today? Can you name any?

DAILY FOCUS (main goal for the day) _____
DAILY VIRTUE (choose a virtue from the list of virtues on pg. 51) _____
DAILY BIOGRAPHY (Who did you learn about today and how has their life influenced you?)
_____

3 MICRO GOALS TO BE ACCOMPLISHED TODAY (list 3 steps, actions, or projects you can complete today toward one of the macro goals listed on pages 30 and 31)

1 _____
2 _____
3 _____

Daily to-do checklist of chores, homework and activities to be done today! (list the three most important ones below - do these first and do more if you can)

1 _____
2 _____
3 _____

Book(s) to read and finish this week (you should read at least one book per week) List how many pages you will read from your book(s) today and check off when completed.

1 _____ 2 _____

What did I discover about myself today? (what worked and why):
_____
_____
_____
_____
_____

Who Are You? by Jerald Simon

Today is YOUR Day!
Date
A **Personal Improvement Outline** for YOU.

Who are Romulus and Remus?

DAILY FOCUS (main goal for the day) _____
DAILY VIRTUE (choose a virtue from the list of virtues on pg. 51) _____
DAILY BIOGRAPHY (Who did you learn about today and how has their life influenced you?)
_____

3 MICRO GOALS TO BE ACCOMPLISHED TODAY (list 3 steps, actions, or projects you can complete today toward one of the macro goals listed on pages 30 and 31)

1 _____
2 _____
3 _____

Daily to-do checklist of chores, homework and activities to be done today!
(list the three most important ones below - do these first and do more if you can)

1 _____
2 _____
3 _____

Book(s) to read and finish this week
(you should read at least one book per week) List how many pages you will read from your book(s) today and check off when completed.

1 _____ 2 _____

What did I discover about myself today? (what worked and why):
_____
_____
_____
_____
_____

Who Are You? by JERALD SIMON

Date	# Today is **YOUR** Day!

A **Personal Improvement Outline** for YOU.

Learn about the Middle Ages today? What do you know?

DAILY FOCUS (main goal for the day) _____

DAILY VIRTUE (choose a virtue from the list of virtues on pg. 51) _____

DAILY BIOGRAPHY (Who did you learn about today and how has their life influenced you?)
_____

3 MICRO GOALS TO BE ACCOMPLISHED TODAY (list 3 steps, actions, or projects you can complete today toward one of the macro goals listed on pages 30 and 31)

1. _____
2. _____
3. _____

Daily to-do checklist of chores, homework and activities to be done today! (list the three most important ones below - do these first and do more if you can)

1. _____
2. _____
3. _____

Book(s) to read and finish this week (you should read at least one book per week) List how many pages you will read from your book(s) today and check off when completed.

1. _____ 2. _____

What did I discover about myself today? (what worked and why):
_____
_____
_____
_____
_____

Who Are You? by JERALD SIMON

Today is YOUR Day!
Date

A **Personal Improvement Outline** for YOU.

Watch your thoughts, your words, and your actions!

DAILY FOCUS (main goal for the day) _____

DAILY VIRTUE (choose a virtue from the list of virtues on pg. 51) _____

DAILY BIOGRAPHY (Who did you learn about today and how has their life influenced you?)
_____

3 MICRO GOALS TO BE ACCOMPLISHED TODAY (list 3 steps, actions, or projects you can complete today toward one of the macro goals listed on pages 30 and 31)

1 _____
2 _____
3 _____

Daily to-do checklist of chores, homework and activities to be done today!
(list the three most important ones below - do these first and do more if you can)

1 _____
2 _____
3 _____

Book(s) to read and finish this week (you should read at least one book per week) List how many pages you will read from your book(s) today and check off when completed.

1 _____ 2 _____

What did I discover about myself today? (what worked and why):
_____
_____
_____
_____
_____

Who Are You? by Jerald Simon

<u>   Date   </u> **Today is YOUR Day!**
A Personal Improvement Outline for YOU.

Learn everything you can about Thomas Jefferson today.

DAILY FOCUS (main goal for the day) _____
DAILY VIRTUE (choose a virtue from the list of virtues on pg. 51) _____
DAILY BIOGRAPHY (Who did you learn about today and how has their life influenced you?)
_____

3 MICRO GOALS TO BE ACCOMPLISHED TODAY (list 3 steps, actions, or projects you can complete today toward one of the macro goals listed on pages 30 and 31)

1 _____
2 _____
3 _____

Daily to-do checklist of chores, homework and activities to be done today! (list the three most important ones below - do these first and do more if you can)

1 _____
2 _____
3 _____

Book(s) to read and finish this week (you should read at least one book per week) List how many pages you will read from your book(s) today and check off when completed.

1 _____ 2 _____

What did I discover about myself today? (what worked and why):
_____
_____
_____
_____
_____

Who Are You? by Jerald Simon

Today is **YOUR** Day!   _{Date}
A **Personal Improvement Outline** for YOU.

Listen to music composed by Antonio Vivaldi today.

DAILY FOCUS (main goal for the day) _____

DAILY VIRTUE (choose a virtue from the list of virtues on pg. 51) _____

DAILY BIOGRAPHY (Who did you learn about today and how has their life influenced you?)
_____

3 MICRO GOALS TO BE ACCOMPLISHED TODAY (list 3 steps, actions, or projects you can complete today toward one of the macro goals listed on pages 30 and 31)

1 _____
2 _____
3 _____

Daily to-do checklist of chores, homework and activities to be done today! (list the three most important ones below - do these first and do more if you can)

1 _____
2 _____
3 _____

Book(s) to read and finish this week (you should read at least one book per week) List how many pages you will read from your book(s) today and check off when completed.

1 _____ 2 _____

What did I discover about myself today? (what worked and why):
_____
_____
_____
_____
_____

Who Are You? by Jerald Simon

Date _____   ## Today is **YOUR** Day!
A **Personal Improvement Outline** for YOU.

Learn about the artwork of Albrecht Dürer today.

DAILY FOCUS (main goal for the day) _____
DAILY VIRTUE (choose a virtue from the list of virtues on pg. 51) _____
DAILY BIOGRAPHY (Who did you learn about today and how has their life influenced you?)
_____

3 MICRO GOALS TO BE ACCOMPLISHED TODAY (list 3 steps, actions, or projects you can complete today toward one of the macro goals listed on pages 30 and 31)

1 _____
2 _____
3 _____

Daily to-do checklist of chores, homework and activities to be done today! (list the three most important ones below - do these first and do more if you can)

1 _____
2 _____
3 _____

Book(s) to read and finish this week (you should read at least one book per week) List how many pages you will read from your book(s) today and check off when completed.

1 _____   2 _____

What did I discover about myself today? (what worked and why):
_____
_____
_____
_____
_____

Who Are You? by JERALD SIMON

Today is YOUR Day!
                                   —————
                                   Date

A **Personal Improvement Outline** for YOU.

Redefine your expectations of yourself and of others.

DAILY FOCUS (main goal for the day) _____

DAILY VIRTUE (choose a virtue from the list of virtues on pg. 51) _____

DAILY BIOGRAPHY (Who did you learn about today and how has their life influenced you?)
_____

3 MICRO GOALS TO BE ACCOMPLISHED TODAY (list 3 steps, actions, or projects you can complete today toward one of the macro goals listed on pages 30 and 31)

1. _____
2. _____
3. _____

Daily to-do checklist of chores, homework and activities to be done today! (list the three most important ones below - do these first and do more if you can)

1. _____
2. _____
3. _____

Book(s) to read and finish this week (you should read at least one book per week) List how many pages you will read from your book(s) today and check off when completed.

1 _____ 2 _____

What did I discover about myself today? (what worked and why):
_____
_____
_____
_____
_____

Who Are You? by JERALD SIMON

Today is **YOUR** Day!
Date

A **Personal Improvement Outline** for YOU.

Learn everything about Self-Reliance today.

DAILY FOCUS (main goal for the day) _____
DAILY VIRTUE (choose a virtue from the list of virtues on pg. 51) _____
DAILY BIOGRAPHY (Who did you learn about today and how has their life influenced you?)
_____

3 MICRO GOALS TO BE ACCOMPLISHED TODAY (list 3 steps, actions, or projects you can complete today toward one of the macro goals listed on pages 30 and 31)

1 _____
2 _____
3 _____

Daily to-do checklist of chores, homework and activities to be done today! (list the three most important ones below - do these first and do more if you can)

1 _____
2 _____
3 _____

Book(s) to read and finish this week (you should read at least one book per week) List how many pages you will read from your book(s) today and check off when completed.

1 _____ 2 _____

What did I discover about myself today? (what worked and why):
_____
_____
_____
_____
_____

Who Are You? by Jerald Simon

Today is YOUR Day!   Date _____
A **Personal Improvement Outline** for YOU.

Who is Ibrahim Muteferrika?

DAILY FOCUS (main goal for the day) _____
DAILY VIRTUE (choose a virtue from the list of virtues on pg. 51) _____
DAILY BIOGRAPHY (Who did you learn about today and how has their life influenced you?)
_____

3 MICRO GOALS TO BE ACCOMPLISHED TODAY (list 3 steps, actions, or projects you can complete today toward one of the macro goals listed on pages 30 and 31)

1 _____
2 _____
3 _____

Daily to-do checklist of chores, homework and activities to be done today! (list the three most important ones below - do these first and do more if you can)

1 _____
2 _____
3 _____

Book(s) to read and finish this week (you should read at least one book per week) List how many pages you will read from your book(s) today and check off when completed.

1 _____   2 _____

What did I discover about myself today? (what worked and why):
_____
_____
_____
_____
_____

Who Are You? by Jerald Simon

<u>   Date   </u>   Today is **YOUR** Day!
A **Personal Improvement Outline** for YOU.

Can you list some of the contributions made by Plato?

DAILY FOCUS (main goal for the day) _____

DAILY VIRTUE (choose a virtue from the list of virtues on pg. 51) _____

DAILY BIOGRAPHY (Who did you learn about today and how has their life influenced you?)
_____

3 MICRO GOALS TO BE ACCOMPLISHED TODAY (list 3 steps, actions, or projects you can complete today toward one of the macro goals listed on pages 30 and 31)

1 _____
2 _____
3 _____

Daily to-do checklist of chores, homework and activities to be done today! (list the three most important ones below - do these first and do more if you can)

1 _____
2 _____
3 _____

Book(s) to read and finish this week (you should read at least one book per week) List how many pages you will read from your book(s) today and check off when completed.

1 _____ 2 _____

What did I discover about myself today? (what worked and why):
_____
_____
_____
_____
_____

Who Are You? by Jerald Simon

Today is YOUR Day! —— Date ——
A **Personal Improvement Outline** for YOU.

Learn how to repair one household item today.

DAILY FOCUS (main goal for the day) _____

DAILY VIRTUE (choose a virtue from the list of virtues on pg. 51) _____

DAILY BIOGRAPHY (Who did you learn about today and how has their life influenced you?)
_____

3 MICRO GOALS TO BE ACCOMPLISHED TODAY (list 3 steps, actions, or projects you can complete today toward one of the macro goals listed on pages 30 and 31)

1. _____
2. _____
3. _____

Daily to-do checklist of chores, homework and activities to be done today! (list the three most important ones below - do these first and do more if you can)

1. _____
2. _____
3. _____

Book(s) to read and finish this week (you should read at least one book per week) List how many pages you will read from your book(s) today and check off when completed.

1. _____ 2. _____

What did I discover about myself today? (what worked and why):
_____
_____
_____
_____
_____

Who Are You? by JERALD SIMON

___Date___ **Today is YOUR Day!**
A **Personal Improvement Outline** for YOU.

Who is Constantine the Great?

DAILY FOCUS (main goal for the day) _____
DAILY VIRTUE (choose a virtue from the list of virtues on pg. 51) _____
DAILY BIOGRAPHY (Who did you learn about today and how has their life influenced you?)
_____

3 MICRO GOALS TO BE ACCOMPLISHED TODAY (list 3 steps, actions, or projects you can complete today toward one of the macro goals listed on pages 30 and 31)

1 _____
2 _____
3 _____

Daily to-do checklist of chores, homework and activities to be done today! (list the three most important ones below - do these first and do more if you can)

1 _____
2 _____
3 _____

Book(s) to read and finish this week (you should read at least one book per week) List how many pages you will read from your book(s) today and check off when completed.

1 _____ 2 _____

What did I discover about myself today? (what worked and why):

_____
_____
_____
_____

Who Are You? by JERALD SIMON

Today is YOUR Day!
Date _____

A **Personal Improvement Outline** for YOU.

Who is Charles the Great or Charlemagne?

DAILY FOCUS (main goal for the day) _____

DAILY VIRTUE (choose a virtue from the list of virtues on pg. 51) _____

DAILY BIOGRAPHY (Who did you learn about today and how has their life influenced you?)
_____

3 MICRO GOALS TO BE ACCOMPLISHED TODAY (list 3 steps, actions, or projects you can complete today toward one of the macro goals listed on pages 30 and 31)

1. _____
2. _____
3. _____

Daily to-do checklist of chores, homework and activities to be done today! (list the three most important ones below - do these first and do more if you can)

1. _____
2. _____
3. _____

Book(s) to read and finish this week (you should read at least one book per week) List how many pages you will read from your book(s) today and check off when completed.

1. _____   2. _____

What did I discover about myself today? (what worked and why):
_____
_____
_____
_____

Who Are You? by Jerald Simon

___Date___ # Today is **YOUR** Day!
A **Personal Improvement Outline** for YOU.

What contributions did Jean-Jacques Rousseau make?

DAILY FOCUS (main goal for the day) _____
DAILY VIRTUE (choose a virtue from the list of virtues on pg. 51) _____
DAILY BIOGRAPHY (Who did you learn about today and how has their life influenced you?)
_____

3 MICRO GOALS TO BE ACCOMPLISHED TODAY (list 3 steps, actions, or projects you can complete today toward one of the macro goals listed on pages 30 and 31)

1. _____
2. _____
3. _____

Daily to-do checklist of chores, homework and activities to be done today! (list the three most important ones below - do these first and do more if you can)

1. _____
2. _____
3. _____

Book(s) to read and finish this week (you should read at least one book per week) List how many pages you will read from your book(s) today and check off when completed.

1. _____ 2. _____

What did I discover about myself today? (what worked and why):

_____
_____
_____
_____
_____

Who Are You? by JERALD SIMON

Today is **YOUR** Day!
Date
A **Personal Improvement Outline** for YOU.

Learn everything you can about Johann Wolfgang von Goethe.

DAILY FOCUS (main goal for the day) _____
DAILY VIRTUE (choose a virtue from the list of virtues on pg. 51) _____
DAILY BIOGRAPHY (Who did you learn about today and how has their life influenced you?)
_____

3 MICRO GOALS TO BE ACCOMPLISHED TODAY (list 3 steps, actions, or projects you can complete today toward one of the macro goals listed on pages 30 and 31)

1 _____
2 _____
3 _____

Daily to-do checklist of chores, homework and activities to be done today! (list the three most important ones below - do these first and do more if you can)

1 _____
2 _____
3 _____

Book(s) to read and finish this week (you should read at least one book per week) List how many pages you will read from your book(s) today and check off when completed.

1 _____ 2 _____

What did I discover about myself today? (what worked and why):
_____
_____
_____
_____
_____

Who Are You? by Jerald Simon

Date _____

Today is **YOUR** Day!
A **Personal Improvement Outline** for YOU.

Be at peace with the mistakes you have made in the past.

DAILY FOCUS (main goal for the day) _____

DAILY VIRTUE (choose a virtue from the list of virtues on pg. 51) _____

DAILY BIOGRAPHY (Who did you learn about today and how has their life influenced you?)
_____

3 MICRO GOALS TO BE ACCOMPLISHED TODAY (list 3 steps, actions, or projects you can complete today toward one of the macro goals listed on pages 30 and 31)

1. _____
2. _____
3. _____

Daily to-do checklist of chores, homework and activities to be done today! (list the three most important ones below - do these first and do more if you can)

1. _____
2. _____
3. _____

Book(s) to read and finish this week (you should read at least one book per week) List how many pages you will read from your book(s) today and check off when completed.

1. _____ 2. _____

What did I discover about myself today? (what worked and why):
_____
_____
_____
_____
_____

Who Are You? by JERALD SIMON

Today is YOUR Day!
Date
A **Personal Improvement Outline** for YOU.

What is Zen?

DAILY FOCUS (main goal for the day) _____

DAILY VIRTUE (choose a virtue from the list of virtues on pg. 51) _____

DAILY BIOGRAPHY (Who did you learn about today and how has their life influenced you?)
_____

3 MICRO GOALS TO BE ACCOMPLISHED TODAY (list 3 steps, actions, or projects you can complete today toward one of the macro goals listed on pages 30 and 31)

1 _____
2 _____
3 _____

Daily to-do checklist of chores, homework and activities to be done today!
(list the three most important ones below - do these first and do more if you can)

1 _____
2 _____
3 _____

Book(s) to read and finish this week (you should read at least one book per week) List how many pages you will read from your book(s) today and check off when completed.

1 _____ 2 _____

What did I discover about myself today? (what worked and why):

_____
_____
_____
_____
_____

Who Are You? by Jerald Simon

Today is **YOUR** Day!
Date

A Personal Improvement Outline for YOU.

Be happy with who you are and who you are becoming!

DAILY FOCUS (main goal for the day) _____

DAILY VIRTUE (choose a virtue from the list of virtues on pg. 51) _____

DAILY BIOGRAPHY (Who did you learn about today and how has their life influenced you?)
_____

3 MICRO GOALS TO BE ACCOMPLISHED TODAY (list 3 steps, actions, or projects you can complete today toward one of the macro goals listed on pages 30 and 31)

1 _____
2 _____
3 _____

Daily to-do checklist of chores, homework and activities to be done today! (list the three most important ones below - do these first and do more if you can)

1 _____
2 _____
3 _____

Book(s) to read and finish this week (you should read at least one book per week) List how many pages you will read from your book(s) today and check off when completed.

1 _____ 2 _____

What did I discover about myself today? (what worked and why):
_____
_____
_____
_____

Who Are You? by Jerald Simon

Today is YOUR Day! ⎯⎯ Date

A **Personal Improvement Outline** for YOU.

Learn how to buy and sell something on the internet.

DAILY FOCUS (main goal for the day) _____

DAILY VIRTUE (choose a virtue from the list of virtues on pg. 51) _____

DAILY BIOGRAPHY (Who did you learn about today and how has their life influenced you?)
_____

3 MICRO GOALS TO BE ACCOMPLISHED TODAY (list 3 steps, actions, or projects you can complete today toward one of the macro goals listed on pages 30 and 31)

1 _____
2 _____
3 _____

Daily to-do checklist of chores, homework and activities to be done today! (list the three most important ones below - do these first and do more if you can)

1 _____
2 _____
3 _____

Book(s) to read and finish this week (you should read at least one book per week) List how many pages you will read from your book(s) today and check off when completed.

1 _____ 2 _____

What did I discover about myself today? (what worked and why):
_____
_____
_____
_____
_____

Who Are You? by Jerald Simon

Date _____

Today is YOUR Day!
A **Personal Improvement Outline** for YOU.

Take a bus from your city to another city.

DAILY FOCUS (main goal for the day) _____
DAILY VIRTUE (choose a virtue from the list of virtues on pg. 51) _____
DAILY BIOGRAPHY (Who did you learn about today and how has their life influenced you?)
_____

3 MICRO GOALS TO BE ACCOMPLISHED TODAY (list 3 steps, actions, or projects you can complete today toward one of the macro goals listed on pages 30 and 31)

1. _____
2. _____
3. _____

Daily to-do checklist of chores, homework and activities to be done today! (list the three most important ones below - do these first and do more if you can)

1. _____
2. _____
3. _____

Book(s) to read and finish this week (you should read at least one book per week) List how many pages you will read from your book(s) today and check off when completed.

1. _____   2. _____

What did I discover about myself today? (what worked and why):
_____
_____
_____
_____
_____

Who Are You? by JERALD SIMON

Today is YOUR Day!
Date

A **Personal Improvement Outline** for YOU.

Study about personal defense today. Can you protect yourself?

DAILY FOCUS (main goal for the day) _____
DAILY VIRTUE (choose a virtue from the list of virtues on pg. 51) _____
DAILY BIOGRAPHY (Who did you learn about today and how has their life influenced you?)
_____

3 MICRO GOALS TO BE ACCOMPLISHED TODAY (list 3 steps, actions, or projects you can complete today toward one of the macro goals listed on pages 30 and 31)

1 _____
2 _____
3 _____

Daily to-do checklist of chores, homework and activities to be done today! (list the three most important ones below - do these first and do more if you can)

1 _____
2 _____
3 _____

Book(s) to read and finish this week (you should read at least one book per week) List how many pages you will read from your book(s) today and check off when completed.

1 _____ 2 _____

What did I discover about myself today? (what worked and why):
_____
_____
_____
_____
_____

Who Are You? by Jerald Simon

___Date___ ## Today is **YOUR** Day!
A **Personal Improvement Outline** for YOU.

Take a photography class (you can take online classes for free).

DAILY FOCUS (main goal for the day) _____
DAILY VIRTUE (choose a virtue from the list of virtues on pg. 51) _____
DAILY BIOGRAPHY (Who did you learn about today and how has their life influenced you?)
_____

3 MICRO GOALS TO BE ACCOMPLISHED TODAY (list 3 steps, actions, or projects you can complete today toward one of the macro goals listed on pages 30 and 31)

1 _____
2 _____
3 _____

Daily to-do checklist of chores, homework and activities to be done today! (list the three most important ones below - do these first and do more if you can)

1 _____
2 _____
3 _____

Book(s) to read and finish this week (you should read at least one book per week) List how many pages you will read from your book(s) today and check off when completed.

1 _____ 2 _____

What did I discover about myself today? (what worked and why):

_____
_____
_____
_____

Who Are You? by Jerald Simon

Today is YOUR Day!

_____ Date

A **Personal Improvement Outline** for YOU.

Learn how to change a tire today.

DAILY FOCUS (main goal for the day) _____
DAILY VIRTUE (choose a virtue from the list of virtues on pg. 51) _____
DAILY BIOGRAPHY (Who did you learn about today and how has their life influenced you?)
_____

3 MICRO GOALS TO BE ACCOMPLISHED TODAY (list 3 steps, actions, or projects you can complete today toward one of the macro goals listed on pages 30 and 31)

1 _____
2 _____
3 _____

Daily to-do checklist of chores, homework and activities to be done today! (list the three most important ones below - do these first and do more if you can)

1 _____
2 _____
3 _____

Book(s) to read and finish this week (you should read at least one book per week) List how many pages you will read from your book(s) today and check off when completed.

1 _____ 2 _____

What did I discover about myself today? (what worked and why):
_____
_____
_____
_____
_____

Who Are You? by JERALD SIMON

___Date___ **Today is YOUR Day!**
A **Personal Improvement Outline** for YOU.

Learn about sales and companies that teach how to sell.

DAILY FOCUS (main goal for the day) _____

DAILY VIRTUE (choose a virtue from the list of virtues on pg. 51) _____

DAILY BIOGRAPHY (Who did you learn about today and how has their life influenced you?)
_____

3 MICRO GOALS TO BE ACCOMPLISHED TODAY (list 3 steps, actions, or projects you can complete today toward one of the macro goals listed on pages 30 and 31)

1 _____
2 _____
3 _____

Daily to-do checklist of chores, homework and activities to be done today! (list the three most important ones below - do these first and do more if you can)

1 _____
2 _____
3 _____

Book(s) to read and finish this week (you should read at least one book per week) List how many pages you will read from your book(s) today and check off when completed.

1 _____ 2 _____

What did I discover about myself today? (what worked and why):
_____
_____
_____
_____
_____

Who Are You? by JERALD SIMON

Today is YOUR Day!

Date _____

A **Personal Improvement Outline** for YOU.

Clean out the garage today. Donate what you don't use.

DAILY FOCUS (main goal for the day) _____

DAILY VIRTUE (choose a virtue from the list of virtues on pg. 51) _____

DAILY BIOGRAPHY (Who did you learn about today and how has their life influenced you?)
_____

3 MICRO GOALS TO BE ACCOMPLISHED TODAY (list 3 steps, actions, or projects you can complete today toward one of the macro goals listed on pages 30 and 31)

1. _____
2. _____
3. _____

Daily to-do checklist of chores, homework and activities to be done today! (list the three most important ones below - do these first and do more if you can)

1. _____
2. _____
3. _____

Book(s) to read and finish this week (you should read at least one book per week) List how many pages you will read from your book(s) today and check off when completed.

1. _____ 2. _____

What did I discover about myself today? (what worked and why):
_____
_____
_____
_____
_____

Who Are You? by JERALD SIMON

___Date___ ## Today is **YOUR** Day!
A **Personal Improvement Outline** for YOU.

Study your own religion and learn about 10 other religions.

DAILY FOCUS (main goal for the day) _____
DAILY VIRTUE (choose a virtue from the list of virtues on pg. 51) _____
DAILY BIOGRAPHY (Who did you learn about today and how has their life influenced you?)
_____

3 MICRO GOALS TO BE ACCOMPLISHED TODAY (list 3 steps, actions, or projects you can complete today toward one of the macro goals listed on pages 30 and 31)

1 _____
2 _____
3 _____

Daily to-do checklist of chores, homework and activities to be done today! (list the three most important ones below - do these first and do more if you can)

1 _____
2 _____
3 _____

Book(s) to read and finish this week (you should read at least one book per week) List how many pages you will read from your book(s) today and check off when completed.

1 _____ 2 _____

What did I discover about myself today? (what worked and why):
_____
_____
_____
_____
_____

Who Are You? by Jerald Simon

Today is YOUR Day!   _____
                                                                                  Date

A **Personal Improvement Outline** for YOU.

Learn 5 conversational phrases in Spanish today.

DAILY FOCUS (main goal for the day) _____

DAILY VIRTUE (choose a virtue from the list of virtues on pg. 51) _____

DAILY BIOGRAPHY (Who did you learn about today and how has their life influenced you?)
_____

3 MICRO GOALS TO BE ACCOMPLISHED TODAY (list 3 steps, actions, or projects you can complete today toward one of the macro goals listed on pages 30 and 31)

1 _____
2 _____
3 _____

Daily to-do checklist of chores, homework and activities to be done today! (list the three most important ones below - do these first and do more if you can)

1 _____
2 _____
3 _____

Book(s) to read and finish this week (you should read at least one book per week) List how many pages you will read from your book(s) today and check off when completed.

1 _____   2 _____

What did I discover about myself today? (what worked and why):
_____
_____
_____
_____
_____

Who Are You? by Jerald Simon

Today is **YOUR** Day!
Date

A **Personal Improvement Outline** for YOU.

Learn about the basics of food storage today.

DAILY FOCUS (main goal for the day) _____
DAILY VIRTUE (choose a virtue from the list of virtues on pg. 51) _____
DAILY BIOGRAPHY (Who did you learn about today and how has their life influenced you?)
_____

3 MICRO GOALS TO BE ACCOMPLISHED TODAY (list 3 steps, actions, or projects you can complete today toward one of the macro goals listed on pages 30 and 31)

1 _____
2 _____
3 _____

Daily to-do checklist of chores, homework and activities to be done today! (list the three most important ones below - do these first and do more if you can)

1 _____
2 _____
3 _____

Book(s) to read and finish this week (you should read at least one book per week) List how many pages you will read from your book(s) today and check off when completed.

1 _____ 2 _____

What did I discover about myself today? (what worked and why):
_____
_____
_____
_____
_____

Who Are You? by JERALD SIMON

Today is YOUR Day!
Date
A **Personal Improvement Outline** for YOU.

Learn what to do in an earthquake, a flood, or a hurricane.

DAILY FOCUS (main goal for the day) _____
DAILY VIRTUE (choose a virtue from the list of virtues on pg. 51) _____
DAILY BIOGRAPHY (Who did you learn about today and how has their life influenced you?)
_____

3 MICRO GOALS TO BE ACCOMPLISHED TODAY (list 3 steps, actions, or projects you can complete today toward one of the macro goals listed on pages 30 and 31)

1 _____
2 _____
3 _____

Daily to-do checklist of chores, homework and activities to be done today! (list the three most important ones below - do these first and do more if you can)

1 _____
2 _____
3 _____

Book(s) to read and finish this week (you should read at least one book per week) List how many pages you will read from your book(s) today and check off when completed.

1 _____ 2 _____

What did I discover about myself today? (what worked and why):
_____
_____
_____
_____
_____

Who Are You? by JERALD SIMON

---Date---

Today is YOUR Day!
A **Personal Improvement Outline** for YOU.

Who is Cleopatra? How is she connected to Marc Antony?

DAILY FOCUS (main goal for the day) _____

DAILY VIRTUE (choose a virtue from the list of virtues on pg. 51) _____

DAILY BIOGRAPHY (Who did you learn about today and how has their life influenced you?)
_____

3 MICRO GOALS TO BE ACCOMPLISHED TODAY (list 3 steps, actions, or projects you can complete today toward one of the macro goals listed on pages 30 and 31)

1 _____
2 _____
3 _____

Daily to-do checklist of chores, homework and activities to be done today! (list the three most important ones below - do these first and do more if you can)

1 _____
2 _____
3 _____

Book(s) to read and finish this week (you should read at least one book per week) List how many pages you will read from your book(s) today and check off when completed.

1 _____ 2 _____

What did I discover about myself today? (what worked and why):

_____
_____
_____
_____
_____

Who Are You? by Jerald Simon

Today is YOUR Day! —— Date ——
A **Personal Improvement Outline** for YOU.

Who is Julius Caesar? What did he do? Did he know Cleopatra?

DAILY FOCUS (main goal for the day) _____

DAILY VIRTUE (choose a virtue from the list of virtues on pg. 51) _____

DAILY BIOGRAPHY (Who did you learn about today and how has their life influenced you?)
_____

3 MICRO GOALS TO BE ACCOMPLISHED TODAY (list 3 steps, actions, or projects you can complete today toward one of the macro goals listed on pages 30 and 31)

1 _____
2 _____
3 _____

Daily to-do checklist of chores, homework and activities to be done today! (list the three most important ones below - do these first and do more if you can)

1 _____
2 _____
3 _____

Book(s) to read and finish this week (you should read at least one book per week) List how many pages you will read from your book(s) today and check off when completed.

1 _____ 2 _____

What did I discover about myself today? (what worked and why):

_____
_____
_____
_____
_____

Who Are You? by Jerald Simon

---Date---   **Today is YOUR Day!**
A **Personal Improvement Outline** for YOU.

Learn as much as you can today about impressionism.

DAILY FOCUS (main goal for the day) _____
DAILY VIRTUE (choose a virtue from the list of virtues on pg. 51) _____
DAILY BIOGRAPHY (Who did you learn about today and how has their life influenced you?)
_____

3 MICRO GOALS TO BE ACCOMPLISHED TODAY (list 3 steps, actions, or projects you can complete today toward one of the macro goals listed on pages 30 and 31)

1 _____
2 _____
3 _____

Daily to-do checklist of chores, homework and activities to be done today! (list the three most important ones below - do these first and do more if you can)

1 _____
2 _____
3 _____

Book(s) to read and finish this week (you should read at least one book per week) List how many pages you will read from your book(s) today and check off when completed.

1 _____ 2 _____

What did I discover about myself today? (what worked and why):
_____
_____
_____
_____

Who Are You? by JERALD SIMON

Today is YOUR Day! ⎯⎯ Date
A **Personal Improvement Outline** for YOU.

Listen to music by Robert Schumann today. Who was Clara?

DAILY FOCUS (main goal for the day) _____

DAILY VIRTUE (choose a virtue from the list of virtues on pg. 51) _____

DAILY BIOGRAPHY (Who did you learn about today and how has their life influenced you?)
_____

3 MICRO GOALS TO BE ACCOMPLISHED TODAY (list 3 steps, actions, or projects you can complete today toward one of the macro goals listed on pages 30 and 31)

1 _____
2 _____
3 _____

Daily to-do checklist of chores, homework and activities to be done today! (list the three most important ones below - do these first and do more if you can)

1 _____
2 _____
3 _____

Book(s) to read and finish this week (you should read at least one book per week) List how many pages you will read from your book(s) today and check off when completed.

1 _____ 2 _____

What did I discover about myself today? (what worked and why):
_____
_____
_____
_____
_____

Who Are You? by Jerald Simon

<u>_____Date_____</u> # Today is YOUR Day!
A **Personal Improvement Outline** for YOU.

What are atoms? Molecules? Electrons? Ions? The Nucleus?

DAILY FOCUS (main goal for the day) _____
DAILY VIRTUE (choose a virtue from the list of virtues on pg. 51) _____
DAILY BIOGRAPHY (Who did you learn about today and how has their life influenced you?)
_____

3 MICRO GOALS TO BE ACCOMPLISHED TODAY (list 3 steps, actions, or projects you can complete today toward one of the macro goals listed on pages 30 and 31)

1 _____
2 _____
3 _____

Daily to-do checklist of chores, homework and activities to be done today! (list the three most important ones below - do these first and do more if you can)

1 _____
2 _____
3 _____

Book(s) to read and finish this week (you should read at least one book per week) List how many pages you will read from your book(s) today and check off when completed.

1 _____ 2 _____

What did I discover about myself today? (what worked and why):
_____
_____
_____
_____
_____

Who Are You? by Jerald Simon

Today is YOUR Day! ___Date___
A **Personal Improvement Outline** for YOU.

What is the electromagnetic spectrum?

DAILY FOCUS (main goal for the day) _____

DAILY VIRTUE (choose a virtue from the list of virtues on pg. 51) _____

DAILY BIOGRAPHY (Who did you learn about today and how has their life influenced you?)
_____

3 MICRO GOALS TO BE ACCOMPLISHED TODAY (list 3 steps, actions, or projects you can complete today toward one of the macro goals listed on pages 30 and 31)

1 _____
2 _____
3 _____

Daily to-do checklist of chores, homework and activities to be done today! (list the three most important ones below - do these first and do more if you can)

1 _____
2 _____
3 _____

Book(s) to read and finish this week (you should read at least one book per week) List how many pages you will read from your book(s) today and check off when completed.

1 _____ 2 _____

What did I discover about myself today? (what worked and why):
_____
_____
_____
_____
_____

Who Are You? by JERALD SIMON

___Date___ # Today is **YOUR** Day!
A **Personal Improvement Outline** for YOU.

Don't talk very much today, if at all. Just listen.

DAILY FOCUS (main goal for the day) _____
DAILY VIRTUE (choose a virtue from the list of virtues on pg. 51) _____
DAILY BIOGRAPHY (Who did you learn about today and how has their life influenced you?)
_____

3 MICRO GOALS TO BE ACCOMPLISHED TODAY (list 3 steps, actions, or projects you can complete today toward one of the macro goals listed on pages 30 and 31)

1 _____
2 _____
3 _____

Daily to-do checklist of chores, homework and activities to be done today! (list the three most important ones below - do these first and do more if you can)

1 _____
2 _____
3 _____

Book(s) to read and finish this week (you should read at least one book per week) List how many pages you will read from your book(s) today and check off when completed.

1 _____ 2 _____

What did I discover about myself today? (what worked and why):
_____
_____
_____
_____
_____

Who Are You? by JERALD SIMON

Today is YOUR Day!
Date

A **Personal Improvement Outline** for YOU.

Chase a sunset today. Get in your car and follow the light.

DAILY FOCUS (main goal for the day) _____

DAILY VIRTUE (choose a virtue from the list of virtues on pg. 51) _____

DAILY BIOGRAPHY (Who did you learn about today and how has their life influenced you?)
_____

3 MICRO GOALS TO BE ACCOMPLISHED TODAY (list 3 steps, actions, or projects you can complete today toward one of the macro goals listed on pages 30 and 31)

1 _____
2 _____
3 _____

Daily to-do checklist of chores, homework and activities to be done today! (list the three most important ones below - do these first and do more if you can)

1 _____
2 _____
3 _____

Book(s) to read and finish this week (you should read at least one book per week) List how many pages you will read from your book(s) today and check off when completed.

1 _____ 2 _____

What did I discover about myself today? (what worked and why):
_____
_____
_____
_____
_____

Who Are You? by JERALD SIMON

<u>   </u>   Today is **YOUR** Day!
    Date

A **Personal Improvement Outline** for YOU.

What is lightning? What makes lightning flash?

DAILY FOCUS (main goal for the day) _____

DAILY VIRTUE (choose a virtue from the list of virtues on pg. 51) _____

DAILY BIOGRAPHY (Who did you learn about today and how has their life influenced you?)
_____

3 MICRO GOALS TO BE ACCOMPLISHED TODAY (list 3 steps, actions, or projects you can complete today toward one of the macro goals listed on pages 30 and 31)

1 _____
2 _____
3 _____

Daily to-do checklist of chores, homework and activities to be done today! (list the three most important ones below - do these first and do more if you can)

1 _____
2 _____
3 _____

Book(s) to read and finish this week (you should read at least one book per week) List how many pages you will read from your book(s) today and check off when completed.

1 _____ 2 _____

What did I discover about myself today? (what worked and why):
_____
_____
_____
_____
_____

Who Are You? by Jerald Simon

Today is YOUR Day!
Date

A **Personal Improvement Outline** for YOU.

Listen to music by Gustav Mahler today.

DAILY FOCUS (main goal for the day) _____

DAILY VIRTUE (choose a virtue from the list of virtues on pg. 51) _____

DAILY BIOGRAPHY (Who did you learn about today and how has their life influenced you?)
_____

3 MICRO GOALS TO BE ACCOMPLISHED TODAY (list 3 steps, actions, or projects you can complete today toward one of the macro goals listed on pages 30 and 31)

1 _____
2 _____
3 _____

Daily to-do checklist of chores, homework and activities to be done today! (list the three most important ones below - do these first and do more if you can)

1 _____
2 _____
3 _____

Book(s) to read and finish this week (you should read at least one book per week) List how many pages you will read from your book(s) today and check off when completed.

1 _____ 2 _____

What did I discover about myself today? (what worked and why):
_____
_____
_____
_____
_____

Who Are You? by Jerald Simon

___Date___ ## Today is **YOUR** Day!
A **Personal Improvement Outline** for YOU.

Be content with what you have and where you are.

DAILY FOCUS (main goal for the day) _____
DAILY VIRTUE (choose a virtue from the list of virtues on pg. 51) _____
DAILY BIOGRAPHY (Who did you learn about today and how has their life influenced you?)
_____

3 MICRO GOALS TO BE ACCOMPLISHED TODAY (list 3 steps, actions, or projects you can complete today toward one of the macro goals listed on pages 30 and 31)

1 _____
2 _____
3 _____

Daily to-do checklist of chores, homework and activities to be done today! (list the three most important ones below - do these first and do more if you can)

1 _____
2 _____
3 _____

Book(s) to read and finish this week (you should read at least one book per week) List how many pages you will read from your book(s) today and check off when completed.

1 _____ 2 _____

What did I discover about myself today? (what worked and why):
_____
_____
_____
_____
_____

Who Are You? by JERALD SIMON

Today is YOUR Day!   _____
Date
A **Personal Improvement Outline** for YOU.

Draw a picture today using a pencil.

DAILY FOCUS (main goal for the day) _____
DAILY VIRTUE (choose a virtue from the list of virtues on pg. 51) _____
DAILY BIOGRAPHY (Who did you learn about today and how has their life influenced you?)
_____

3 MICRO GOALS TO BE ACCOMPLISHED TODAY (list 3 steps, actions, or projects you can complete today toward one of the macro goals listed on pages 30 and 31)

1 _____
2 _____
3 _____

Daily to-do checklist of chores, homework and activities to be done today! (list the three most important ones below - do these first and do more if you can)

1 _____
2 _____
3 _____

Book(s) to read and finish this week (you should read at least one book per week) List how many pages you will read from your book(s) today and check off when completed.

1 _____ 2 _____

What did I discover about myself today? (what worked and why):
_____
_____
_____
_____
_____

Who Are You? by Jerald Simon

Date _____

Today is **YOUR** Day!
A **Personal Improvement Outline** for YOU.

Who is Confucius?

DAILY FOCUS (main goal for the day) _____

DAILY VIRTUE (choose a virtue from the list of virtues on pg. 51) _____

DAILY BIOGRAPHY (Who did you learn about today and how has their life influenced you?)
_____

3 MICRO GOALS TO BE ACCOMPLISHED TODAY (list 3 steps, actions, or projects you can complete today toward one of the macro goals listed on pages 30 and 31)

1. _____
2. _____
3. _____

Daily to-do checklist of chores, homework and activities to be done today! (list the three most important ones below - do these first and do more if you can)

1. _____
2. _____
3. _____

Book(s) to read and finish this week (you should read at least one book per week) List how many pages you will read from your book(s) today and check off when completed.

1. _____ 2. _____

What did I discover about myself today? (what worked and why):

_____
_____
_____
_____

Who Are You? by JERALD SIMON

Today is YOUR Day!
Date

A **Personal Improvement Outline** for YOU.

What are elements? What is the periodic table?

DAILY FOCUS (main goal for the day) _____

DAILY VIRTUE (choose a virtue from the list of virtues on pg. 51) _____

DAILY BIOGRAPHY (Who did you learn about today and how has their life influenced you?)
_____

3 MICRO GOALS TO BE ACCOMPLISHED TODAY (list 3 steps, actions, or projects you can complete today toward one of the macro goals listed on pages 30 and 31)

1 _____
2 _____
3 _____

Daily to-do checklist of chores, homework and activities to be done today! (list the three most important ones below - do these first and do more if you can)

1 _____
2 _____
3 _____

Book(s) to read and finish this week (you should read at least one book per week) List how many pages you will read from your book(s) today and check off when completed.

1 _____ 2 _____

What did I discover about myself today? (what worked and why):
_____
_____
_____
_____
_____

Who Are You? by Jerald Simon

___Date___ ## Today is **YOUR** Day!
A **Personal Improvement Outline** for YOU.

Learn everything you can about Ralph Waldo Emerson.

DAILY FOCUS (main goal for the day) _____
DAILY VIRTUE (choose a virtue from the list of virtues on pg. 51) _____
DAILY BIOGRAPHY (Who did you learn about today and how has their life influenced you?)
_____

3 MICRO GOALS TO BE ACCOMPLISHED TODAY (list 3 steps, actions, or projects you can complete today toward one of the macro goals listed on pages 30 and 31)

1 _____
2 _____
3 _____

Daily to-do checklist of chores, homework and activities to be done today! (list the three most important ones below - do these first and do more if you can)

1 _____
2 _____
3 _____

Book(s) to read and finish this week (you should read at least one book per week) List how many pages you will read from your book(s) today and check off when completed.

1 _____ 2 _____

What did I discover about myself today? (what worked and why):
_____
_____
_____
_____
_____

Who Are You? by Jerald Simon

Today is YOUR Day! ———
Date
A **Personal Improvement Outline** for YOU.

What are you grateful for today?

DAILY FOCUS (main goal for the day) _____

DAILY VIRTUE (choose a virtue from the list of virtues on pg. 51) _____

DAILY BIOGRAPHY (Who did you learn about today and how has their life influenced you?)
_____

3 MICRO GOALS TO BE ACCOMPLISHED TODAY (list 3 steps, actions, or projects you can complete today toward one of the macro goals listed on pages 30 and 31)

1 _____
2 _____
3 _____

Daily to-do checklist of chores, homework and activities to be done today! (list the three most important ones below - do these first and do more if you can)

1 _____
2 _____
3 _____

Book(s) to read and finish this week (you should read at least one book per week) List how many pages you will read from your book(s) today and check off when completed.

1 _____ 2 _____

What did I discover about myself today? (what worked and why):
_____
_____
_____
_____
_____

Who Are You? by Jerald Simon

___Date___ ## Today is **YOUR** Day!
A **Personal Improvement Outline** for YOU.

What weakness will you overcome today?

DAILY FOCUS (main goal for the day) _____
DAILY VIRTUE (choose a virtue from the list of virtues on pg. 51) _____
DAILY BIOGRAPHY (Who did you learn about today and how has their life influenced you?)
_____

3 MICRO GOALS TO BE ACCOMPLISHED TODAY (list 3 steps, actions, or projects you can complete today toward one of the macro goals listed on pages 30 and 31)

1. _____
2. _____
3. _____

Daily to-do checklist of chores, homework and activities to be done today! (list the three most important ones below - do these first and do more if you can)

1. _____
2. _____
3. _____

Book(s) to read and finish this week (you should read at least one book per week) List how many pages you will read from your book(s) today and check off when completed.

1. _____ 2. _____

What did I discover about myself today? (what worked and why):
_____
_____
_____
_____
_____

Who Are You? by Jerald Simon

Today is YOUR Day! ———— Date

A **Personal Improvement Outline** for YOU.

Who are you going to be 10 years from now?

DAILY FOCUS (main goal for the day) _____

DAILY VIRTUE (choose a virtue from the list of virtues on pg. 51) _____

DAILY BIOGRAPHY (Who did you learn about today and how has their life influenced you?)
_____

3 MICRO GOALS TO BE ACCOMPLISHED TODAY (list 3 steps, actions, or projects you can complete today toward one of the macro goals listed on pages 30 and 31)

1 _____
2 _____
3 _____

Daily to-do checklist of chores, homework and activities to be done today! (list the three most important ones below - do these first and do more if you can)

1 _____
2 _____
3 _____

Book(s) to read and finish this week (you should read at least one book per week) List how many pages you will read from your book(s) today and check off when completed.

1 _____ 2 _____

What did I discover about myself today? (what worked and why):
_____
_____
_____
_____
_____

Who Are You? by JERALD SIMON

---Date--- **Today is YOUR Day!**
A Personal Improvement Outline for YOU.

Learn everything you can about the Amazon rainforest.

DAILY FOCUS (main goal for the day) _____
DAILY VIRTUE (choose a virtue from the list of virtues on pg. 51) _____
DAILY BIOGRAPHY (Who did you learn about today and how has their life influenced you?)
_____

3 MICRO GOALS TO BE ACCOMPLISHED TODAY (list 3 steps, actions, or projects you can complete today toward one of the macro goals listed on pages 30 and 31)

1 _____
2 _____
3 _____

Daily to-do checklist of chores, homework and activities to be done today! (list the three most important ones below - do these first and do more if you can)

1 _____
2 _____
3 _____

Book(s) to read and finish this week (you should read at least one book per week) List how many pages you will read from your book(s) today and check off when completed.

1 _____ 2 _____

What did I discover about myself today? (what worked and why):
_____
_____
_____
_____

Who Are You? by JERALD SIMON

Today is YOUR Day!
_____ Date

A **Personal Improvement Outline** for YOU.

Start reading through a dictionary. It can be a visual dictionary.

DAILY FOCUS (main goal for the day) _____
DAILY VIRTUE (choose a virtue from the list of virtues on pg. 51) _____
DAILY BIOGRAPHY (Who did you learn about today and how has their life influenced you?)
_____

3 MICRO GOALS TO BE ACCOMPLISHED TODAY (list 3 steps, actions, or projects you can complete today toward one of the macro goals listed on pages 30 and 31)

1 _____
2 _____
3 _____

Daily to-do checklist of chores, homework and activities to be done today! (list the three most important ones below - do these first and do more if you can)

1 _____
2 _____
3 _____

Book(s) to read and finish this week (you should read at least one book per week) List how many pages you will read from your book(s) today and check off when completed.

1 _____ 2 _____

What did I discover about myself today? (what worked and why):
_____
_____
_____
_____
_____

Who Are You? by JERALD SIMON

_____Date_____ ## Today is **YOUR** Day!
A **Personal Improvement Outline** for YOU.

How many push-ups can you do? Set a goal to do 40 in a minute.

DAILY FOCUS (main goal for the day) _____
DAILY VIRTUE (choose a virtue from the list of virtues on pg. 51) _____
DAILY BIOGRAPHY (Who did you learn about today and how has their life influenced you?)
_____

3 MICRO GOALS TO BE ACCOMPLISHED TODAY (list 3 steps, actions, or projects you can complete today toward one of the macro goals listed on pages 30 and 31)

1 _____
2 _____
3 _____

Daily to-do checklist of chores, homework and activities to be done today! (list the three most important ones below - do these first and do more if you can)

1 _____
2 _____
3 _____

Book(s) to read and finish this week (you should read at least one book per week) List how many pages you will read from your book(s) today and check off when completed.

1 _____ 2 _____

What did I discover about myself today? (what worked and why):
_____
_____
_____
_____

Who Are You? by JERALD SIMON

Today is YOUR Day!
Date

A **Personal Improvement Outline** for YOU.

Choose a profession that interests you and study about it.

DAILY FOCUS (main goal for the day) _____

DAILY VIRTUE (choose a virtue from the list of virtues on pg. 51) _____

DAILY BIOGRAPHY (Who did you learn about today and how has their life influenced you?)
_____

3 MICRO GOALS TO BE ACCOMPLISHED TODAY (list 3 steps, actions, or projects you can complete today toward one of the macro goals listed on pages 30 and 31)

1 _____
2 _____
3 _____

Daily to-do checklist of chores, homework and activities to be done today! (list the three most important ones below - do these first and do more if you can)

1 _____
2 _____
3 _____

Book(s) to read and finish this week (you should read at least one book per week) List how many pages you will read from your book(s) today and check off when completed.

1 _____ 2 _____

What did I discover about myself today? (what worked and why):
_____
_____
_____
_____
_____

Who Are You? by Jerald Simon

<u>   </u> Date

Today is **YOUR** Day!
A **Personal Improvement Outline** for YOU.

Who was Joan of Arc? What happened to her?

DAILY FOCUS (main goal for the day) _____

DAILY VIRTUE (choose a virtue from the list of virtues on pg. 51) _____

DAILY BIOGRAPHY (Who did you learn about today and how has their life influenced you?)
_____

3 MICRO GOALS TO BE ACCOMPLISHED TODAY (list 3 steps, actions, or projects you can complete today toward one of the macro goals listed on pages 30 and 31)

1 _____
2 _____
3 _____

Daily to-do checklist of chores, homework and activities to be done today! (list the three most important ones below - do these first and do more if you can)

1 _____
2 _____
3 _____

Book(s) to read and finish this week (you should read at least one book per week) List how many pages you will read from your book(s) today and check off when completed.

1 _____ 2 _____

What did I discover about myself today? (what worked and why):

_____
_____
_____
_____

Who Are You? by JERALD SIMON

Today is YOUR Day!
Date

A **Personal Improvement Outline** for YOU.

Study the artwork of Raphael today.

DAILY FOCUS (main goal for the day) _____

DAILY VIRTUE (choose a virtue from the list of virtues on pg. 51) _____

DAILY BIOGRAPHY (Who did you learn about today and how has their life influenced you?)
_____

3 MICRO GOALS TO BE ACCOMPLISHED TODAY (list 3 steps, actions, or projects you can complete today toward one of the macro goals listed on pages 30 and 31)

1 _____
2 _____
3 _____

Daily to-do checklist of chores, homework and activities to be done today! (list the three most important ones below - do these first and do more if you can)

1 _____
2 _____
3 _____

Book(s) to read and finish this week (you should read at least one book per week) List how many pages you will read from your book(s) today and check off when completed.

1 _____ 2 _____

What did I discover about myself today? (what worked and why):
_____
_____
_____
_____
_____

Who Are You? by Jerald Simon

___Date___ ## Today is **YOUR** Day!
A **Personal Improvement Outline** for YOU.

Listen to music by Franz Shubert today.

DAILY FOCUS (main goal for the day) _____
DAILY VIRTUE (choose a virtue from the list of virtues on pg. 51) _____
DAILY BIOGRAPHY (Who did you learn about today and how has their life influenced you?)
_____

3 MICRO GOALS TO BE ACCOMPLISHED TODAY (list 3 steps, actions, or projects you can complete today toward one of the macro goals listed on pages 30 and 31)

1 _____
2 _____
3 _____

Daily to-do checklist of chores, homework and activities to be done today! (list the three most important ones below - do these first and do more if you can)

1 _____
2 _____
3 _____

Book(s) to read and finish this week (you should read at least one book per week) List how many pages you will read from your book(s) today and check off when completed.

1 _____ 2 _____

What did I discover about myself today? (what worked and why):
_____
_____
_____
_____
_____

Who Are You? by JERALD SIMON

Today is YOUR Day!

Date

A **Personal Improvement Outline** for YOU.

Try to be an optimist. Never be a pessimist.

DAILY FOCUS (main goal for the day) _____
DAILY VIRTUE (choose a virtue from the list of virtues on pg. 51) _____
DAILY BIOGRAPHY (Who did you learn about today and how has their life influenced you?)
_____

3 MICRO GOALS TO BE ACCOMPLISHED TODAY (list 3 steps, actions, or projects you can complete today toward one of the macro goals listed on pages 30 and 31)

1 _____
2 _____
3 _____

Daily to-do checklist of chores, homework and activities to be done today! (list the three most important ones below - do these first and do more if you can)

1 _____
2 _____
3 _____

Book(s) to read and finish this week (you should read at least one book per week) List how many pages you will read from your book(s) today and check off when completed.

1 _____ 2 _____

What did I discover about myself today? (what worked and why):
_____
_____
_____
_____
_____

Who Are You? by JERALD SIMON

<u>　　　　　</u> Date # Today is **YOUR** Day!
A **Personal Improvement Outline** for YOU.

Become a student of life!

DAILY FOCUS (main goal for the day) _____
DAILY VIRTUE (choose a virtue from the list of virtues on pg. 51) _____
DAILY BIOGRAPHY (Who did you learn about today and how has their life influenced you?)
_____

3 MICRO GOALS TO BE ACCOMPLISHED TODAY (list 3 steps, actions, or projects you can complete today toward one of the macro goals listed on pages 30 and 31)

1 _____
2 _____
3 _____

Daily to-do checklist of chores, homework and activities to be done today! (list the three most important ones below - do these first and do more if you can)

1 _____
2 _____
3 _____

Book(s) to read and finish this week (you should read at least one book per week) List how many pages you will read from your book(s) today and check off when completed.

1 _____   2 _____

What did I discover about myself today? (what worked and why):
_____
_____
_____
_____

Who Are You? by JERALD SIMON

Today is YOUR Day!

Date

A **Personal Improvement Outline** for YOU.

Learn about the House of Medici and the House Sforza.

DAILY FOCUS (main goal for the day) _____

DAILY VIRTUE (choose a virtue from the list of virtues on pg. 51) _____

DAILY BIOGRAPHY (Who did you learn about today and how has their life influenced you?)
_____

3 MICRO GOALS TO BE ACCOMPLISHED TODAY (list 3 steps, actions, or projects you can complete today toward one of the macro goals listed on pages 30 and 31)

1 _____
2 _____
3 _____

Daily to-do checklist of chores, homework and activities to be done today! (list the three most important ones below - do these first and do more if you can)

1 _____
2 _____
3 _____

Book(s) to read and finish this week (you should read at least one book per week) List how many pages you will read from your book(s) today and check off when completed.

1 _____ 2 _____

What did I discover about myself today? (what worked and why):
_____
_____
_____
_____
_____

Who Are You? by JERALD SIMON

___Date___ # Today is YOUR Day!
A **Personal Improvement Outline** for YOU.

Who do you admire most? Why? What can they teach you?

DAILY FOCUS (main goal for the day) _____

DAILY VIRTUE (choose a virtue from the list of virtues on pg. 51) _____

DAILY BIOGRAPHY (Who did you learn about today and how has their life influenced you?)
_____

3 MICRO GOALS TO BE ACCOMPLISHED TODAY (list 3 steps, actions, or projects you can complete today toward one of the macro goals listed on pages 30 and 31)

1 _____
2 _____
3 _____

Daily to-do checklist of chores, homework and activities to be done today! (list the three most important ones below - do these first and do more if you can)

1 _____
2 _____
3 _____

Book(s) to read and finish this week (you should read at least one book per week) List how many pages you will read from your book(s) today and check off when completed.

1 _____ 2 _____

What did I discover about myself today? (what worked and why):
_____
_____
_____
_____

Who Are You? by JERALD SIMON

Today is YOUR Day!

Date

A **Personal Improvement Outline** for YOU.

Be an example to your family.

DAILY FOCUS (main goal for the day) _____

DAILY VIRTUE (choose a virtue from the list of virtues on pg. 51) _____

DAILY BIOGRAPHY (Who did you learn about today and how has their life influenced you?)
_____

3 MICRO GOALS TO BE ACCOMPLISHED TODAY (list 3 steps, actions, or projects you can complete today toward one of the macro goals listed on pages 30 and 31)

1 _____
2 _____
3 _____

Daily to-do checklist of chores, homework and activities to be done today! (list the three most important ones below - do these first and do more if you can)

1 _____
2 _____
3 _____

Book(s) to read and finish this week (you should read at least one book per week) List how many pages you will read from your book(s) today and check off when completed.

1 _____ 2 _____

What did I discover about myself today? (what worked and why):
_____
_____
_____
_____
_____

Who Are You? by Jerald Simon

Date _____

Today is YOUR Day!
A **Personal Improvement Outline** for YOU.

Who is St. Thomas Aquinas?

DAILY FOCUS (main goal for the day) _____
DAILY VIRTUE (choose a virtue from the list of virtues on pg. 51) _____
DAILY BIOGRAPHY (Who did you learn about today and how has their life influenced you?)
_____

3 MICRO GOALS TO BE ACCOMPLISHED TODAY (list 3 steps, actions, or projects you can complete today toward one of the macro goals listed on pages 30 and 31)

1 _____
2 _____
3 _____

Daily to-do checklist of chores, homework and activities to be done today! (list the three most important ones below - do these first and do more if you can)

1 _____
2 _____
3 _____

Book(s) to read and finish this week (you should read at least one book per week) List how many pages you will read from your book(s) today and check off when completed.

1 _____ 2 _____

What did I discover about myself today? (what worked and why):
_____
_____
_____
_____

Who Are You? by Jerald Simon

Today is YOUR Day!

_____ Date

A **Personal Improvement Outline** for YOU.

Study everything about the artwork and life of Jan Vermeer.

DAILY FOCUS (main goal for the day) _____

DAILY VIRTUE (choose a virtue from the list of virtues on pg. 51) _____

DAILY BIOGRAPHY (Who did you learn about today and how has their life influenced you?)
_____

3 MICRO GOALS TO BE ACCOMPLISHED TODAY (list 3 steps, actions, or projects you can complete today toward one of the macro goals listed on pages 30 and 31)

1 _____
2 _____
3 _____

Daily to-do checklist of chores, homework and activities to be done today! (list the three most important ones below - do these first and do more if you can)

1 _____
2 _____
3 _____

Book(s) to read and finish this week (you should read at least one book per week) List how many pages you will read from your book(s) today and check off when completed.

1 _____ 2 _____

What did I discover about myself today? (what worked and why):
_____
_____
_____
_____
_____

Who Are You? by Jerald Simon

Date _____

Today is **YOUR** Day!
A **Personal Improvement Outline** for YOU.

Listen to the music of Pyotr Ilyich Tchaikovsky today.

DAILY FOCUS (main goal for the day) _____
DAILY VIRTUE (choose a virtue from the list of virtues on pg. 51) _____
DAILY BIOGRAPHY (Who did you learn about today and how has their life influenced you?)
_____

3 MICRO GOALS TO BE ACCOMPLISHED TODAY (list 3 steps, actions, or projects you can complete today toward one of the macro goals listed on pages 30 and 31)

1 _____
2 _____
3 _____

Daily to-do checklist of chores, homework and activities to be done today! (list the three most important ones below - do these first and do more if you can)

1 _____
2 _____
3 _____

Book(s) to read and finish this week (you should read at least one book per week) List how many pages you will read from your book(s) today and check off when completed.

1 _____ 2 _____

What did I discover about myself today? (what worked and why):
_____
_____
_____
_____
_____

Who Are You? by JERALD SIMON

Today is YOUR Day!

Date

A **Personal Improvement Outline** for YOU.

Learn one new thing today and teach it to someone else.

DAILY FOCUS (main goal for the day) _____

DAILY VIRTUE (choose a virtue from the list of virtues on pg. 51) _____

DAILY BIOGRAPHY (Who did you learn about today and how has their life influenced you?)
_____

3 MICRO GOALS TO BE ACCOMPLISHED TODAY (list 3 steps, actions, or projects you can complete today toward one of the macro goals listed on pages 30 and 31)

1 _____
2 _____
3 _____

Daily to-do checklist of chores, homework and activities to be done today! (list the three most important ones below - do these first and do more if you can)

1 _____
2 _____
3 _____

Book(s) to read and finish this week (you should read at least one book per week) List how many pages you will read from your book(s) today and check off when completed.

1 _____   2 _____

What did I discover about myself today? (what worked and why):
_____
_____
_____
_____
_____

Who Are You? by Jerald Simon

___Date___ **Today is YOUR Day!**
A **Personal Improvement Outline** for YOU.

Learn everything you can about personal fitness.

DAILY FOCUS (main goal for the day) _____
DAILY VIRTUE (choose a virtue from the list of virtues on pg. 51) _____
DAILY BIOGRAPHY (Who did you learn about today and how has their life influenced you?)
_____

3 MICRO GOALS TO BE ACCOMPLISHED TODAY (list 3 steps, actions, or projects you can complete today toward one of the macro goals listed on pages 30 and 31)

1 _____
2 _____
3 _____

Daily to-do checklist of chores, homework and activities to be done today! (list the three most important ones below - do these first and do more if you can)

1 _____
2 _____
3 _____

Book(s) to read and finish this week (you should read at least one book per week) List how many pages you will read from your book(s) today and check off when completed.

1 _____ 2 _____

What did I discover about myself today? (what worked and why):
_____
_____
_____
_____

Who Are You? by JERALD SIMON

Today is **YOUR** Day!   ——Date——
A **Personal Improvement Outline** for YOU.

Give someone a hug today! Hugs heal troubled hearts!

DAILY FOCUS (main goal for the day) _____

DAILY VIRTUE (choose a virtue from the list of virtues on pg. 51) _____

DAILY BIOGRAPHY (Who did you learn about today and how has their life influenced you?)
_____

3 MICRO GOALS TO BE ACCOMPLISHED TODAY (list 3 steps, actions, or projects you can complete today toward one of the macro goals listed on pages 30 and 31)

1 _____
2 _____
3 _____

Daily to-do checklist of chores, homework and activities to be done today! (list the three most important ones below - do these first and do more if you can)

1 _____
2 _____
3 _____

Book(s) to read and finish this week (you should read at least one book per week) List how many pages you will read from your book(s) today and check off when completed.

1 _____ 2 _____

What did I discover about myself today? (what worked and why):
_____
_____
_____
_____
_____

Who Are You? by JERALD SIMON

<u>   Date   </u> # Today is **YOUR** Day!
A **Personal Improvement Outline** for YOU.

What are you most afraid of doing today? Why?

DAILY FOCUS (main goal for the day) _____

DAILY VIRTUE (choose a virtue from the list of virtues on pg. 51) _____

DAILY BIOGRAPHY (Who did you learn about today and how has their life influenced you?)

_____

3 MICRO GOALS TO BE ACCOMPLISHED TODAY (list 3 steps, actions, or projects you can complete today toward one of the macro goals listed on pages 30 and 31)

1 _____
2 _____
3 _____

Daily to-do checklist of chores, homework and activities to be done today! (list the three most important ones below - do these first and do more if you can)

1 _____
2 _____
3 _____

Book(s) to read and finish this week (you should read at least one book per week) List how many pages you will read from your book(s) today and check off when completed.

1 _____ 2 _____

What did I discover about myself today? (what worked and why):

_____
_____
_____
_____
_____

Who Are You? by JERALD SIMON

Today is YOUR Day!
Date

A **Personal Improvement Outline** for YOU.

Create a list of 100 influential men and women to study.

DAILY FOCUS (main goal for the day) _____

DAILY VIRTUE (choose a virtue from the list of virtues on pg. 51) _____

DAILY BIOGRAPHY (Who did you learn about today and how has their life influenced you?)
_____

3 MICRO GOALS TO BE ACCOMPLISHED TODAY (list 3 steps, actions, or projects you can complete today toward one of the macro goals listed on pages 30 and 31)

1 _____
2 _____
3 _____

Daily to-do checklist of chores, homework and activities to be done today! (list the three most important ones below - do these first and do more if you can)

1 _____
2 _____
3 _____

Book(s) to read and finish this week (you should read at least one book per week) List how many pages you will read from your book(s) today and check off when completed.

1 _____ 2 _____

What did I discover about myself today? (what worked and why):

_____
_____
_____
_____
_____

Who Are You? by Jerald Simon

___Date___ # Today is **YOUR** Day!
A **Personal Improvement Outline** for YOU.

What virtue will you be working on today? Why?

DAILY FOCUS (main goal for the day) _____
DAILY VIRTUE (choose a virtue from the list of virtues on pg. 51) _____
DAILY BIOGRAPHY (Who did you learn about today and how has their life influenced you?)
_____

3 MICRO GOALS TO BE ACCOMPLISHED TODAY (list 3 steps, actions, or projects you can complete today toward one of the macro goals listed on pages 30 and 31)

1 _____
2 _____
3 _____

Daily to-do checklist of chores, homework and activities to be done today! (list the three most important ones below - do these first and do more if you can)

1 _____
2 _____
3 _____

Book(s) to read and finish this week (you should read at least one book per week) List how many pages you will read from your book(s) today and check off when completed.

1 _____ 2 _____

What did I discover about myself today? (what worked and why):
_____
_____
_____
_____
_____

Who Are You? by Jerald Simon

Today is YOUR Day!   —— Date

A **Personal Improvement Outline** for YOU.

If you need to, saying your sorry is the best way to apologize.

DAILY FOCUS (main goal for the day) _____

DAILY VIRTUE (choose a virtue from the list of virtues on pg. 51) _____

DAILY BIOGRAPHY (Who did you learn about today and how has their life influenced you?)
_____

3 MICRO GOALS TO BE ACCOMPLISHED TODAY (list 3 steps, actions, or projects you can complete today toward one of the macro goals listed on pages 30 and 31)

1 _____
2 _____
3 _____

Daily to-do checklist of chores, homework and activities to be done today! (list the three most important ones below - do these first and do more if you can)

1 _____
2 _____
3 _____

Book(s) to read and finish this week (you should read at least one book per week) List how many pages you will read from your book(s) today and check off when completed.

1 _____ 2 _____

What did I discover about myself today? (what worked and why):
_____
_____
_____
_____
_____

Who Are You? by Jerald Simon

<u>   Date   </u>   Today is **YOUR** Day!
A **Personal Improvement Outline** for YOU.

Listen to the music of Giacomo Puccini today.

DAILY FOCUS (main goal for the day) _____

DAILY VIRTUE (choose a virtue from the list of virtues on pg. 51) _____

DAILY BIOGRAPHY (Who did you learn about today and how has their life influenced you?)
_____

3 MICRO GOALS TO BE ACCOMPLISHED TODAY (list 3 steps, actions, or projects you can complete today toward one of the macro goals listed on pages 30 and 31)

1. _____
2. _____
3. _____

Daily to-do checklist of chores, homework and activities to be done today! (list the three most important ones below - do these first and do more if you can)

1. _____
2. _____
3. _____

Book(s) to read and finish this week (you should read at least one book per week) List how many pages you will read from your book(s) today and check off when completed.

1. _____ 2. _____

What did I discover about myself today? (what worked and why):
_____
_____
_____
_____
_____

Who Are You? by JERALD SIMON

Today is YOUR Day! ___Date___
A **Personal Improvement Outline** for YOU.

Study everything you can about Van Gogh today.

DAILY FOCUS (main goal for the day) _____
DAILY VIRTUE (choose a virtue from the list of virtues on pg. 51) _____
DAILY BIOGRAPHY (Who did you learn about today and how has their life influenced you?)
_____

3 MICRO GOALS TO BE ACCOMPLISHED TODAY (list 3 steps, actions, or projects you can complete today toward one of the macro goals listed on pages 30 and 31)

1 _____
2 _____
3 _____

Daily to-do checklist of chores, homework and activities to be done today! (list the three most important ones below - do these first and do more if you can)

1 _____
2 _____
3 _____

Book(s) to read and finish this week (you should read at least one book per week) List how many pages you will read from your book(s) today and check off when completed.

1 _____ 2 _____

What did I discover about myself today? (what worked and why):
_____
_____
_____
_____
_____

Who Are You? by Jerald Simon

___Date___ ## Today is **YOUR** Day!
A **Personal Improvement Outline** for YOU.

We must control ourselves, our thoughts, our speech, and habits.

DAILY FOCUS (main goal for the day) _____
DAILY VIRTUE (choose a virtue from the list of virtues on pg. 51) _____
DAILY BIOGRAPHY (Who did you learn about today and how has their life influenced you?)
_____

3 MICRO GOALS TO BE ACCOMPLISHED TODAY (list 3 steps, actions, or projects you can complete today toward one of the macro goals listed on pages 30 and 31)

1 _____
2 _____
3 _____

Daily to-do checklist of chores, homework and activities to be done today! (list the three most important ones below - do these first and do more if you can)

1 _____
2 _____
3 _____

Book(s) to read and finish this week (you should read at least one book per week) List how many pages you will read from your book(s) today and check off when completed.

1 _____ 2 _____

What did I discover about myself today? (what worked and why):
_____
_____
_____
_____

Who Are You? by JERALD SIMON

Today is YOUR Day!

Date

A **Personal Improvement Outline** for YOU.

Make a difference in someone's life today.

DAILY FOCUS (main goal for the day) _____
DAILY VIRTUE (choose a virtue from the list of virtues on pg. 51) _____
DAILY BIOGRAPHY (Who did you learn about today and how has their life influenced you?)
_____

3 MICRO GOALS TO BE ACCOMPLISHED TODAY (list 3 steps, actions, or projects you can complete today toward one of the macro goals listed on pages 30 and 31)

1 _____
2 _____
3 _____

Daily to-do checklist of chores, homework and activities to be done today! (list the three most important ones below - do these first and do more if you can)

1 _____
2 _____
3 _____

Book(s) to read and finish this week (you should read at least one book per week) List how many pages you will read from your book(s) today and check off when completed.

1 _____ 2 _____

What did I discover about myself today? (what worked and why):
_____
_____
_____
_____
_____

Who Are You? by JERALD SIMON

<u>　　Date　　</u> ## Today is **YOUR** Day!
A **Personal Improvement Outline** for YOU.

Learn everything you can about Science today.

DAILY FOCUS (main goal for the day) _____
DAILY VIRTUE (choose a virtue from the list of virtues on pg. 51) _____
DAILY BIOGRAPHY (Who did you learn about today and how has their life influenced you?)
_____

3 MICRO GOALS TO BE ACCOMPLISHED TODAY (list 3 steps, actions, or projects you can complete today toward one of the macro goals listed on pages 30 and 31)

1 _____
2 _____
3 _____

Daily to-do checklist of chores, homework and activities to be done today! (list the three most important ones below - do these first and do more if you can)

1 _____
2 _____
3 _____

Book(s) to read and finish this week (you should read at least one book per week) List how many pages you will read from your book(s) today and check off when completed.

1 _____ 2 _____

What did I discover about myself today? (what worked and why):
_____
_____
_____
_____

Who Are You? by JERALD SIMON

Today is YOUR Day!   Date _____
A **Personal Improvement Outline** for YOU.

What do you know about the Industrial Revolution?

DAILY FOCUS (main goal for the day) _____
DAILY VIRTUE (choose a virtue from the list of virtues on pg. 51) _____
DAILY BIOGRAPHY (Who did you learn about today and how has their life influenced you?)
_____

3 MICRO GOALS TO BE ACCOMPLISHED TODAY (list 3 steps, actions, or projects you can complete today toward one of the macro goals listed on pages 30 and 31)

1 _____
2 _____
3 _____

Daily to-do checklist of chores, homework and activities to be done today! (list the three most important ones below - do these first and do more if you can)

1 _____
2 _____
3 _____

Book(s) to read and finish this week (you should read at least one book per week) List how many pages you will read from your book(s) today and check off when completed.

1 _____   2 _____

What did I discover about myself today? (what worked and why):
_____
_____
_____
_____
_____

Who Are You? by Jerald Simon

Today is YOUR Day!
A Personal Improvement Outline for YOU.

Date _____

Who was Napoleon Bonaparte? What did he do?

DAILY FOCUS (main goal for the day) _____

DAILY VIRTUE (choose a virtue from the list of virtues on pg. 51) _____

DAILY BIOGRAPHY (Who did you learn about today and how has their life influenced you?)
_____

3 MICRO GOALS TO BE ACCOMPLISHED TODAY (list 3 steps, actions, or projects you can complete today toward one of the macro goals listed on pages 30 and 31)

1 _____
2 _____
3 _____

Daily to-do checklist of chores, homework and activities to be done today! (list the three most important ones below - do these first and do more if you can)

1 _____
2 _____
3 _____

Book(s) to read and finish this week (you should read at least one book per week) List how many pages you will read from your book(s) today and check off when completed.

1 _____ 2 _____

What did I discover about myself today? (what worked and why):
_____
_____
_____
_____

Who Are You? by JERALD SIMON

Today is YOUR Day!   Date _____
A **Personal Improvement Outline** for YOU.

Who is Amerigo Vespucci? What did he do?

DAILY FOCUS (main goal for the day) _____

DAILY VIRTUE (choose a virtue from the list of virtues on pg. 51) _____

DAILY BIOGRAPHY (Who did you learn about today and how has their life influenced you?)
_____

3 MICRO GOALS TO BE ACCOMPLISHED TODAY (list 3 steps, actions, or projects you can complete today toward one of the macro goals listed on pages 30 and 31)

1. _____
2. _____
3. _____

Daily to-do checklist of chores, homework and activities to be done today! (list the three most important ones below - do these first and do more if you can)

1. _____
2. _____
3. _____

Book(s) to read and finish this week (you should read at least one book per week) List how many pages you will read from your book(s) today and check off when completed.

1. _____ 2. _____

What did I discover about myself today? (what worked and why):
_____
_____
_____
_____
_____

Who Are You? by Jerald Simon

___Date___   **Today is YOUR Day!**
A Personal Improvement Outline for YOU.

Do you know the origins of Longitude and Latitude?

DAILY FOCUS (main goal for the day) _____
DAILY VIRTUE (choose a virtue from the list of virtues on pg. 51) _____
DAILY BIOGRAPHY (Who did you learn about today and how has their life influenced you?)
_____

3 MICRO GOALS TO BE ACCOMPLISHED TODAY (list 3 steps, actions, or projects you can complete today toward one of the macro goals listed on pages 30 and 31)

1 _____
2 _____
3 _____

Daily to-do checklist of chores, homework and activities to be done today! (list the three most important ones below - do these first and do more if you can)

1 _____
2 _____
3 _____

Book(s) to read and finish this week (you should read at least one book per week) List how many pages you will read from your book(s) today and check off when completed.

1 _____ 2 _____

What did I discover about myself today? (what worked and why):

_____
_____
_____
_____

Who Are You? by JERALD SIMON

Today is **YOUR** Day!
        Date

A **Personal Improvement Outline** for YOU.

What do you think you will be known for 100 years from now?

DAILY FOCUS (main goal for the day) _____
DAILY VIRTUE (choose a virtue from the list of virtues on pg. 51) _____
DAILY BIOGRAPHY (Who did you learn about today and how has their life influenced you?)

---

3 MICRO GOALS TO BE ACCOMPLISHED TODAY (list 3 steps, actions, or projects you can complete today toward one of the macro goals listed on pages 30 and 31)

1. _____
2. _____
3. _____

Daily to-do checklist of chores, homework and activities to be done today! (list the three most important ones below - do these first and do more if you can)

1. _____
2. _____
3. _____

Book(s) to read and finish this week (you should read at least one book per week) List how many pages you will read from your book(s) today and check off when completed.

1. _____ 2. _____

What did I discover about myself today? (what worked and why):

_____
_____
_____
_____
_____

Who Are You? by Jerald Simon

<u> Date </u> ## Today is **YOUR** Day!
A Personal Improvement Outline for YOU.

Create a "DREAM BOARD" with pictures to inspire you.

DAILY FOCUS (main goal for the day) _____

DAILY VIRTUE (choose a virtue from the list of virtues on pg. 51) _____

DAILY BIOGRAPHY (Who did you learn about today and how has their life influenced you?)
_____

3 MICRO GOALS TO BE ACCOMPLISHED TODAY (list 3 steps, actions, or projects you can complete today toward one of the macro goals listed on pages 30 and 31)

1 _____
2 _____
3 _____

Daily to-do checklist of chores, homework and activities to be done today! (list the three most important ones below - do these first and do more if you can)

1 _____
2 _____
3 _____

Book(s) to read and finish this week (you should read at least one book per week) List how many pages you will read from your book(s) today and check off when completed.

1 _____ 2 _____

What did I discover about myself today? (what worked and why):

_____
_____
_____
_____

Who Are You? by JERALD SIMON

Today is YOUR Day!   ──Date──
A **Personal Improvement Outline** for YOU.

Who is Sir Isaac Newton and what did he do?

DAILY FOCUS (main goal for the day) _____

DAILY VIRTUE (choose a virtue from the list of virtues on pg. 51) _____

DAILY BIOGRAPHY (Who did you learn about today and how has their life influenced you?)

---

3 MICRO GOALS TO BE ACCOMPLISHED TODAY (list 3 steps, actions, or projects you can complete today toward one of the macro goals listed on pages 30 and 31)

1 _____
2 _____
3 _____

Daily to-do checklist of chores, homework and activities to be done today! (list the three most important ones below - do these first and do more if you can)

1 _____
2 _____
3 _____

Book(s) to read and finish this week (you should read at least one book per week) List how many pages you will read from your book(s) today and check off when completed.

1 _____ 2 _____

What did I discover about myself today? (what worked and why):

_____
_____
_____
_____
_____

Who Are You? by Jerald Simon

<u>　　Date　　</u> ## Today is YOUR Day!
A **Personal Improvement Outline** for YOU.

Listen to the music of Wilhelm Richard Wagner today.

DAILY FOCUS (main goal for the day) _____

DAILY VIRTUE (choose a virtue from the list of virtues on pg. 51) _____

DAILY BIOGRAPHY (Who did you learn about today and how has their life influenced you?)
_____

3 MICRO GOALS TO BE ACCOMPLISHED TODAY (list 3 steps, actions, or projects you can complete today toward one of the macro goals listed on pages 30 and 31)

1 _____
2 _____
3 _____

Daily to-do checklist of chores, homework and activities to be done today! (list the three most important ones below - do these first and do more if you can)

1 _____
2 _____
3 _____

Book(s) to read and finish this week (you should read at least one book per week) List how many pages you will read from your book(s) today and check off when completed.

1 _____　　2 _____

What did I discover about myself today? (what worked and why):
_____
_____
_____
_____

Who Are You? by Jerald Simon

Today is YOUR Day!
Date: _____

A **Personal Improvement Outline** for YOU.

What are your goals for next year?

DAILY FOCUS (main goal for the day) _____
DAILY VIRTUE (choose a virtue from the list of virtues on pg. 51) _____
DAILY BIOGRAPHY (Who did you learn about today and how has their life influenced you?)
_____

3 MICRO GOALS TO BE ACCOMPLISHED TODAY (list 3 steps, actions, or projects you can complete today toward one of the macro goals listed on pages 30 and 31)

1 _____
2 _____
3 _____

Daily to-do checklist of chores, homework and activities to be done today!
(list the three most important ones below - do these first and do more if you can)

1 _____
2 _____
3 _____

Book(s) to read and finish this week
(you should read at least one book per week) List how many pages you will read from your book(s) today and check off when completed.

1 _____ 2 _____

What did I discover about myself today? (what worked and why):
_____
_____
_____
_____
_____

Who Are You? by Jerald Simon

SUMMARIZE YOUR YEAR

If you have made it this far in the book, you have made it through your first year on your journey of self discovery. Congratulations! I am sure you have had life changing successes along the way. I know you probably had a few failures and setbacks that were difficult and trying. That, unfortunately, is a part of life that everyone must live with. But even with the bad times, you have learned how good the good times can be.

The next two pages are blank for you to write a summary about your journey this year. What did you learn? What did you accomplish? How have you grown? What goals did you set and achieve? What goals were close to being finished but not entirely accomplished? Where did you succeed? Where did you fail? Take some time and review everything that has happened over this past year. Look back through this book and see the books you read, the goals you set, and the biographies you read or watched. It's important to review what did and did not work the way you thought it might. This is your time to reflect, ponder, review, and put down in writing what this year has meant to you. Be satisfied with your success. You've come a long way!

_____
_____
_____
_____
_____
_____
_____
_____

Who Are You? by Jerald Simon

Your summary of this past year (continued)

Who Are You? by Jerald Simon

Your summary of this past year (continued)

What's next for your future goals? The next step to take is to begin working on next year's goals. You can, as before, select 10 Macro Goals and three accompanying Micro Goals for each Macro Goal. You can purchase this goal book again, **"Who Are You?" (Your Personal Success Goal Book)** by Jerald Simon, from my personal website, **musicmotivation.com**, or from Amazon, Barnes and Noble, or any of the other major book retailers as well. The wonderful part of having this book is that you can keep it on your desk, next to your bed, or anywhere close by throughout the year as you focus on your daily goals. As you finish one of these "Who Are You?" goal books and begin the next one, you will begin to accumulate your own personal library of your life. This is a great way to periodically look over the goals you have made and completed from previous years and know that you are improving and progressing. It is a personal improvement journal that becomes an heirloom for your posterity.

Each day that comes your way can be viewed as a new milestone of personal accomplishment as you continue to progress on your personal journey through life. Continually work on the FORMULA FOR SUCCESS: **1. DREAM, 2. PLAN AND PREPARE, and 3. GO TO WORK!** After performing these steps, you can continue to learn and develop *SKILLS*, understand and follow *PRINCIPLES*, and define and live your life by your *VALUES*.

Setting and achieving any goal in life, whether big or small, is simply a matter of understanding and following this simple formula for success and then *living your life.* Today is *your* day. Make it great!

Book Jerald as a Presenter/Performer for your next event:

Contact: Suzanne
jeraldsimon@musicmotivation.com

Below is a list of some of the speaking and performing events Jerald has done and is willing to do.

We can customize to your specific needs.

Speaking and Performing (singing and playing the piano) at Events:

Workshops, Seminars, Music Camps, and Concerts (i.e. Concerts/Mini Concerts, Corporate Events/Parties/Dinners, Schools, Youth Groups, Recitals, MTNA Conventions and Conferences, MTNA Chapter Meetings, other Music Organizations, Schools, Groups, etc., Workshops, Summer Camps, Devotionals and Firesides, and any of the following:

Anniversaries, Awards Nights, Banquets, Birthday Parties, Children's Birthday Parties, Celebrations, Christmas Parties, Church Services, Clubs, Community Events, Conventions, Corporate Functions, Country Clubs, Cruise Ships, Dinner Dances, Festivals, Fund Raisers, Funerals, Graduation Parties, Grand Openings, Hotels, Jingles, Movie Sound tracks, Picnic, Private Parties, Proms, Resorts, Restaurants, Reunions, Showers, Studio Session, TV Sound tracks, Weddings, and customizable performances to meet your personal needs).

Book Jerald as the next Speaker/Entertainer for your next event! Motivate those who attend the event with Music Motivation®! Music Motivation® Workshops, Seminars, and Music Camps are focused on Theory Therapy, Innovative Improvisation, and Creative Composition with a Music Mentor. The emphasis is on teaching music students with "Music that excites, entertains, and educates". If you are interested in becoming a Music Motivation® Mentor, please email Music Motivation® at musicmentor@musicmotivation.com . If you would like to book Jerald Simon as the Music Mentor presenter or motivational speaker for your next event (i.e. recital, MTNA chapter meetings, workshops, summer camps, devotionals and firesides, corporate events, etc.) Please email Music Motivation®.

Booking Jerald is subject to his availability and waiting list.

Music Motivation®
http://musicmotivation.com

"Cool music that excites, entertains, and educates."
"Let music motivate you!"

The Music Motivation® website was created as a resource for music teachers (primarily piano teachers), music students (primarily piano students) and parents. The focus is on making music fun, exciting, entertaining, and educational. We noticed a problem:

PROBLEM: "How do we keep piano students excited and motivated to continue with their piano lessons - especially during their teenage years?"

SOLUTION: MOTIVATE PIANO STUDENTS TO PLAY THE PIANO WITH COOL MUSIC Composed by JERALD SIMON - The Cool Songs for Cool Kids Series (pre-primer, primer, books 1, 2, & 3) and Cool Songs that ROCK books 1 and 2 - Learn music theory the fun through Piano FUNdamentals!

visit the Music Motivation® website to learn more**:**
http://musicmotivation.com/coolsongs

Subscribe to Jerald's YouTube Channel:
http://youtube.com/jeraldsimon for weekly piano videos on learning and playing the piano: Fun to Play! Videos (piano lessons with Jerald) and Theory Tip Tuesday Tutorials.

Be sure to **subscribe to The Music Motivation® newsletter on our website.**
(We will not sell or share your information)

The three main areas of focus for Music Motivation® are: Theory Therapy, Innovative Improvisation, and Creative Composition.

The theme for Music Motivation® is: "Let music motivate you!"

Music Motivation® Goal: Make music lessons (primarily piano lessons) cool, exciting, entertaining, and educational.

Music Motivation® Goal (for music educators): One of our primary goals at Music Motivation® is to help prepare the next generation of composers, arrangers, musicians, music teachers, and musicologists to use their music and their love of music to make a difference in their own lives, their community, and the world.

Learn more about Music Motivation® at musicmotivation.com

I have several CDs of original music I have composed that I would love to have you listen to. You can listen to my music on Spotify, Pandora, etc., or purchase my music on i Tunes, Amazon, and all on-line music stores. I compose several different styles from hymn arrangements to meditation music, new age piano solos to pop, tech-no-pop, rock, and even scary Halloween music. Let me know what you think of my music!

Every month I produce and release a new **"Cool Song"** available for all piano students and piano teachers on my website (musicmotivation.com). Each new "Cool Song" is emailed to Music Motivation® mentees (piano teachers and piano students) according to their preferred subscription. See which subscription is the best fit for you and for your piano students (if you are a piano teacher) by visiting: http://musicmotivation.com/annualsubscription. I also comes out with **Theory Tip Tuesday** videos.

I have also created 21 music books of original piano solos - most with music backing tracks of other instruments and sounds. In total there are over 250 fun piano solos between the 21 books from pre-primer to advanced level pieces that have been composed primarily to motivate teenage boys to play the piano! Visit **musicmotivation.com/shop** to learn more.

Check out these best sellers by Jerald Simon

visit *musicmotivation.com* to purchase, or visit your local music store - Chesbro music is the national distributor for all Music Motivation® books. Contact Chesbro Music Co. if you are a store (1.800.243.7276)

All of my books are available from Amazon, Barnes and Noble, and all online and traditional book stores.

CHECK OUT JERALD'S MOTIVATIONAL BOOKS

MOTIVATION IN A MINUTE
$18.95

FULL COLOR PICTURES
AND MOTIVATIONAL MESSAGES

Purchase books as Paperback, e Books, or Audio Books

PERCEPTIONS,
PARABLES,
AND
POINTERS
$19.95

216 PAGES

A SELF-HELP
MOTIVATION
MANUAL

THE "AS IF"
PRINCIPLE
(MOTIVATIONAL
POETRY)
$16.95

154 PAGES

222 INSPIRATIONAL
AND MOTIVATIONAL
POEMS WRITTEN
BY JERALD

Other poetry books by **Jerald Simon**:
* Motivational Poetry * Poetry Smoetry * Season of Life

Make the most of each minute!

This is the last page of this book, but it is the beginning of a new day for you and for me. Every day that comes our way is pure, free from mistakes, perfect. It only becomes imperfect if we allow ourselves to get in the way and mess things up. We can make the most of each minute we have by focusing on doing our best right now. Don't worry about what is on the horizon. Take it into consideration as how you can prepare right now for what is to come, but stay in the moment and enjoy everything right now.

Life is too short to get tangled up in the tragedies of tomorrow. Be happy this hour. It's a new day for change, growth, improvement, happiness, love, laughter, and giving. Every second should be sacred because they add up to more than minutes - they add up to memories. Make the most of each moment and make good memories. Make great memories. Life should be about learning and growing, but in addition to being meaningful, it should and must be memorable.

If you slip up and get down on yourself, as we all do, it's okay. Start over every second with a clean slate and a glad attitude. You can refer to it as your gladitude.

Look in the mirror and tell yourself you love yourself. Be honest and sincere and mean it. It's more than learning to like yourself, which you must do, it's about loving your strengths, accepting your weaknesses and being willing to work on them, and letting go of any unrealistic expectations of yourself. Your future is bright and beautiful, and wonderful.

I'm excited for your future and I'm excited for mine. We are both on a wonderful journey of self discovery, personal growth, some heartache and pain here and there, but overall we will triumph! We are stronger than our sorrows. We are working together on being the very best we can be because we believe in each other. We hope for the best that is in each other. We pray for each other and know that together we can do great things in life because we can bring out the best in each other.

Love life! Live it to the fullest and be actively engaged in helping others as you help yourself. I know God will bless you and help you through the good times and the bad times of life. Have faith. Have hope. Have an outlook of optimism in all that you do and you will continually be happy because you see the happiness around you and strive to help others be happy as well!

Be Happy! Smile all the while and be your best!

- JERALD

www.ingramcontent.com/pod-product-compliance
Lightning Source LLC
Chambersburg PA
CBHW071644090426
42738CB00009B/1424